WAN Survival Guide

Strategies for VPNs and Multiservice Networks

Howard Berkowitz

Wiley Computer Publishing

John Wiley & Sons, Inc.

NEW YORK · CHICHESTER · WEINHEIM · BRISBANE · SINGAPORE · TORONTO

01-3382

Publisher: Robert Ipsen
Editor: Carol Long
Associate Editor: Margaret Hendrey
Managing Editor: John Atkins
Text Design & Composition: Benchmark Productions, Inc.

Designations used by companies to distinguish their products are often claimed as trademarks. In all instances where John Wiley & Sons, Inc., is aware of a claim, the product names appear in initial capital or ALL CAPITAL LETTERS. Readers, however, should contact the appropriate companies for more complete information regarding trademarks and registration.

This book is printed on acid-free paper. ∞

Published by John Wiley & Sons, Inc.

Published simultaneously in Canada.

This publication is designed to provide accurate and authoritative information in regard to the subject matter covered. It is sold with the understanding that the publisher is not engaged in professional services. If professional advice or other expert assistance is required, the services of a competent professional person should be sought.

Library of Congress Cataloging-in-Publication Data:
Berkowitz, Howard.
    WAN survival guide : strategies for VPNs and multiservice networks / Howard Berkowitz.
        p. cm. — (Wiley Networking Council series)
    Includes bibliographical references and index.
    ISBN 0-471-38428-3 (pbk. : alk. paper)
    1. Extranets (Computer networks) 2. Integrated services digital networks. I. Title. II. Series.
TK5105.875.E87 B47 2000
004.67—dc21   00-060033

Printed in the United States of America.

10 9 8 7 6 5 4 3 2 1

CONTENTS

The Networking Council Series was created in 1998 within Wiley's Computer Publishing group to fill an important gap in networking literature. Many current technical books are long on details but short on understanding. They do not give the reader a sense of where, in the universe of practical and theoretical knowledge, the technology might be useful in a particular organization. The Networking Council Series is concerned more with how to think clearly about networking issues than with promoting the virtues of a particular technology—how to relate new information to the rest of what the reader knows and needs, so the reader can develop a customized strategy for vendor and product selection, outsourcing, and design.

In *WAN Survival Guide: Strategies for VPNs and Multiservice Networks* by Howard Berkowitz, you'll see the hallmarks of Networking Council books—examination of the advantages and disadvantages, strengths and weaknesses of market-ready technology, useful ways to think about options pragmatically, and direct links to business practices and needs. Disclosure of pertinent background issues needed to understand who supports a technology and how it was developed is another goal of all Networking Council books.

The Networking Council Series is aimed at satisfying the need for perspective in an evolving data and telecommunications world filled with hyperbole, speculation, and unearned optimism. In *WAN Survival Guide: Strategies for VPNs and Multiservice Networks*, you'll get clear information from experienced practitioners.

We hope you enjoy the read. Let us know what you think. Feel free to visit the Networking Council web site at www.wiley.com/networkingcouncil.

Scott Bradner
Technical Consultant, Harvard University

Vinton Cerf
Senior Vice President, MCIWorldCom

Lyman Chapin
Chief Scientist, BBN/GTE

Wiley Networking Council Series

Series Editors:

Scott Bradner
Technical Consultant, Harvard University

Vinton Cerf
Senior Vice President, MCIWorldCom

Lyman Chapin
Chief Scientist, BBN/GTE

Books in series:

Many have contributed to my growth in learning to build networks. It's hard to count the number of colleagues in the North American Network Operations Group who have helped me understand issues and with whom I brainstormed issues. Thanks to Sean Donelan, Susan Harris, Sue Hares, and from various other Sides of the Force, Yakov Rekhter, Paul Ferguson, John Stewart, and Jeff Doyle.

My new employer, Nortel Networks, has encouraged an environment in which I can be creative and in which I can share my ideas. Let me thank colleagues including Francis Ovenden, Gerald deGrace, Dan Joyal, Jim Booth, Elaine deLoach, and Colleen Macdonnell.

Other employers and contract managers also helped give me the freedom to write, especially Curt Freemyer of Gett Communications and Gary Rubin of Information Innovations Incorporated.

My home life stayed sane through a third book largely though the skill of my housekeeper and assistant, Mariatu Kamara, and my distinguished feline editorial assistant, Clifford.

Carol Long of Wiley has been incredibly supportive in this project.

CHAPTER 1

What Is the Problem You Are Trying to Solve?

What hath God wrought?

SAMUEL F. B. MORSE

Come here, Mr. Watson. I want you.

ALEXANDER GRAHAM BELL

*The difference between a turnkey and a turkey installation is "N."
N is often interpreted as the spending on the system, but it is more
often a reflection of the clue level of both buyer and seller.*

HOWARD C. BERKOWITZ

This book deals with wide area networks (WAN). More specifically, it focuses on defining problems that WANs can solve and evaluating solutions to these problems.

Among the first issues in looking at a WAN problem is understanding precisely how a WAN differs from other sorts of networks. With the advent of newer technologies, WANs have become harder to define. They are not simply networks with greater range than local area networks (LAN).

While we usually think of networking in technological terms, the key strategy in making useful distinctions between modern WANs and LANs is *administrative*, not *technological*. WAN implementations involve a service provider and a service consumer, which are different organizations. LANs are operated by the same organization that uses their services (see Figure 1.1).

Defining WANs in terms of administrative models solves some otherwise awkward definitions based on technology. *Asynchronous transfer mode (ATM)* is a modern high-speed networking technology with the capability of transcontinental range. Yet ATM is also a viable technology for metropolitan area and campus networks.

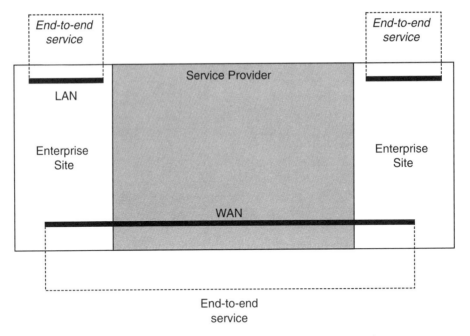

Figure 1.1 WANs divide responsibility between consumer and provider.

The administrative versus technological distinction has been with us for well over a hundred years, but only recently has become blurred.

History: Basis for WAN Regulation and Competition

Wide area networks (WAN) are not new in human history, even when physical relay networks such as the Pony Express are excluded. In the Napoleonic period, Captain Horatio Hornblower acted decisively to cripple Napoleon's critical wide area network: the French semaphore system. The French telegraph system began with optical networking in 1793, although the optical transmitters were flags and lanterns, and the receivers were human eyes. This system used a series of line-of-sight relays at which operators wrote down messages sent by the position of movable arms at other stations, and then signaled the message using their semaphore to the next station.

In 1844, Samuel F. B. Morse demonstrated the first practical electrical wide area network: the telegraph. As with the semaphore, users of the system gave messages to operators for transmission. Using Morse code, these operators relayed the message from station to station until it was transcribed onto paper for delivery to the recipient. Government regulation entered the embryonic telecommunications industry with the Post Roads Act of 1866, setting rates for government telegrams. An 1878 judicial interpretation of the Commerce Clause of the Constitution specifically established telegraphs as part of the commerce that fell under Federal jurisdiction.

Morse telegraphs used a single physical medium for each session of telegraphy, a method that will not scale to huge size. Other inventors sought ways of carrying multiple sessions over a single physical medium. One such inventor attempted to develop a *harmonic telegraph*, which would encode telegraph sessions into different tones, and impose these tones onto a wire. Today, we would call this technique *frequency division multiplexing*; like Charles Babbage's computers, the technique was beyond its time, since it needed true electronics to be practical. Who was this experimenter, frustrated with the harmonic telegraph? He was a teacher of the deaf, named Alexander Graham Bell.

In 1876, Bell further enhanced electrical communication with the telephone. Again, the model of this service differentiated between end users who actually spoke and listened, and a service provider. The service provider maintained the wires and the switching system, which originally was the manual switchboard.

At the time of Bell's invention, the Western Union Telegraph Company, established in 1856, was the dominant telecommunications provider. Bell offered to license his patents to them, but they refused the offer on the basis there was little business case for the ability for people to talk over wires. In fairness to Western Union, there were alternate patents by Elisha Gray to which Western Union had access. Bell's technology, rather than Gray's, predominated to become what our industry calls *plain old telephone service* (POTS). The *public switched telephone network* (PSTN) often is used as a synonym for POTS; PSTN is really the more correct term.

Bell formed his own company, which became American Telephone and Telegraph (AT&T). Ironically, AT&T subsequently acquired Western Union, but, after regulators became concerned that AT&T was monopolizing communications, relatively cheerfully divested itself of Western Union as part of the 1913 Kingsbury Commitment. AT&T, however, did not rename itself AT.

Soon after Bell's invention, telephone companies, each with its own local wiring between the subscriber and the switchboard in the central office, proliferated. Pictures from the turn of the twentieth century show desks littered with telephones from different companies, a painful but practical necessity unless one wished to be limited to calling other subscribers on the Bell System, the Home System, etc. The idea of a telephone on every desk, or in every home, came later.

Even during times when telecommunications were largely under monopoly control, there were still opportunities for optimizing the communications of a particular enterprise. Since enterprises often had many internal calls, they introduced *private branch exchanges* (PBX) or private switchboards to connect internal users to one another, then to shared external trunks. At first, PBXs were manual plugboards, but as the automation of telephone switching progressed, PBXs began to use electromechanical and then electronic switching. The term *private automatic branch exchange* (PABX) attempted to capture the essence of technological advances in the PBX, but the term PABX never won wide acceptance.

Let us pause the historical discussion for a moment, and review some terminology associated with PBX operation. In Figure 1.2, the PBX connects to external switches over *trunks*, also called *trunk lines*. *Tie trunks* connect PBX sites within the enterprise.

Central office (CO) trunks connect the PBX to a telephone service provider. Such a provider is usually assumed to be the LEC, but there may also be *bypass* trunks that connect to IXCs.

CO trunks, whether to the LEC or the IXC, can be two-way, incoming-only, or outgoing-only with respect to the PBX. Other than the very smallest sites will need multiple trunks, which, from the perspective of the PSTN, are called *trunk groups*. A trunk group contains multiple voice channels, which can be physical analog pairs; but for larger and more modern installations, they are likely to be digital carrier facilities or Integrated Services Digital Network (ISDN) physical links.

A special case of a CO trunk is a *foreign exchange* (FX) trunk that connects logically to an alternate central office, so that the telephone number associated with the trunk appears to be in the serving area of the remote CO. FX trunks fill a function much like Wide Area Telephone Service (WATS) lines, but FX tends to provide service inside the LEC,

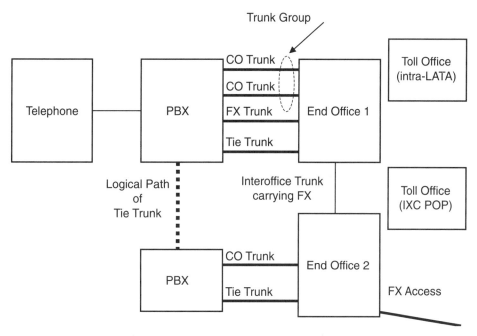

Figure 1.2   Telco telephone terminology.

while WATS services tend to be provided by IXCs. Their real function is similar: Do not make the calling party pay long-distance charges.

Another special case of CO trunk is *Direct Inward Dialing* (DID), in which the central office allows individual extensions of the enterprise to be dialed from the outside. DID has signaling that tells the PBX which extension needs to be rung. There are fewer physical DID trunks than there are extensions, because the PBX is intelligent.

A variant is Centrex service, in which the intelligence is in the central office switch, not at the enterprise. In Centrex service, there must be the same number of Centrex trunks as there are enterprise extensions. While Centrex trunking is more expensive than DID to an intelligent PBX, it offers the advantage that the telephone company, not the enterprise, does the detailed management of service. Centrex, in many respects, is the direct ancestor of what we call *virtual private networks* (VPN) today. VPNs most commonly are data-oriented, but they offer the ability to outsource the detailed management of that network, especially in the WAN.

Automatic Switching

With its use of manual switching, with human operators, early telephony was too labor-intensive to grow to its present size. Automated switching was as major an advance as the basic speech-over-wires technology. Even in today's environment, you must always be aware that any connectivity that is not preprogrammed into your switch requires expensive manual intervention. Related challenges, still not completely solved, are the broad issues of *provisioning* and *mobility*.

Provisioning involves the issues of telling the switching system about the existence of subscriber equipment or connections to other carriers, so the switching system can recognize them. Traditionally, provisioning has required manual input to start the process. Large providers have invested huge amounts in automating the process once begun.

Mobility, however, involves some degree of automation in starting the process. Cellular telephony is an everyday model of a mobility-based service in which the telephone operates in many locations within the territory of the cellular service provider. *Roaming* services, in which the telephone continues to operate in other providers' geographic coverage area, is more of a challenge. Roaming for data connectivity is a less-developed commercial idea. See Chapter 8 for a further discussion of roaming, which is intimately associated with security measures for verifying that the roaming user is indeed entitled to use facilities in the other provider's area, and to reach the home provider.

The Bell System concentrated on urban markets, and, even after it gained a practical monopoly there, there were certainly competitors, especially in rural areas. One such company was formed in 1899 in Abilene, Kansas, by Jacob and C.L. Brown. Their first long-distance connection was operational in 1900, and they formalized their existence as the Brown Telephone Company in 1902. The Brown Telephone Company was an example of what is called an independent telephone company, to distinguish it from Bell/AT&T. We shall see more of the Browns and their descendants as we follow telecommunications history.

Universal Service

A radical *organizational*, not technological, advance came from Theodore Vail, CEO of the new AT&T. In 1907, Vail introduced the

Could Color Blindness Start World War III?

Government offices, especially at the highest levels, have been some of the last strongholds of multiple telephones on the same desk. Any self-respecting novel or movie of the Cold War period made references to the Red Phone. In reality, what Hollywood often thought was the Red Phone—the Presidential alerting phone—was actually the Gold Phone; the Red Phone was a Strategic Air Command operational service. Gray phones usually, but not always, were for the early AUTOSEVOCOM military secure voice network, while beige phones were for AUTOVON, the unsecure voice network. Green phones were on the CIA network, and black phones provided POTS. There were white and blue phones in some facilities, and I don't remember what they connected to. Given the importance of courage to the military, I could understand why there were no Yellow Phones.

I remember attending an unclassified meeting in a military facility, and needing to call my office at the Library of Congress. Asking to use a phone, my host pointed to the corner of his office. This phone, however, was not black, but green. I turned to my host and inquired, "is this a green phone because it's a Green Phone, or is this a green phone because it's colored green?" As I reflected that I had had one of those life experiences where one asks oneself, "did I really say that?" my host assured me it would work for my call rescheduling lunch.

concept of *universal service*, although his usage of the term differs somewhat from current practice. Vail intended it to mean that every telephone should be able to establish connectivity with every other telephone, not that everyone should *have* a telephone. His usage was closer to the current concept of interoperability. Even given this policy, it took regulatory intervention, in 1913, to force AT&T to accept connections from independent telephone companies.

The 1913 Kingsbury Commitment established the differing roles of what would, much later, be formalized as *local exchange carriers* (LEC) and *interexchange carriers* (IXC). Real-world telephony over long distances required the cooperation of multiple service providers (Figure 1.3). To have such multivendor connectivity, there needed to be agreement on interconnection standards, so the telephony industry had a tradition of standardization long before computers, much less a computer industry.

Originally, the scope of competition was limited to non-Bell firms in the LEC role. The idea of multiple LEC firms in the same geographical area seemed, until quite recently, to be a natural, technical monopoly.

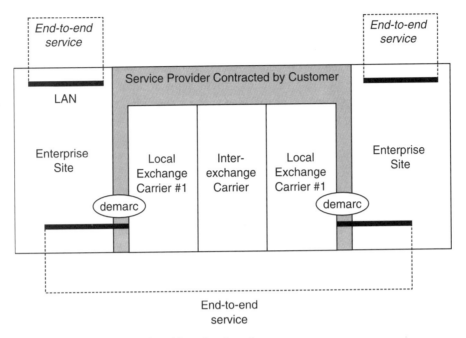

Figure 1.3 Dividing local and long-haul services.

It seemed undesirable to have different LECs running masses of copper wire over and under city streets. Alternatives have emerged, and today we speak of *incumbent LECs* (ILEC) as the first LEC in a given area (i.e., the one that owns the predominant copper), and *competitive LECs* (CLEC). We will discuss the details of ILECs and CLECs later on, as well as the evolution of the IXC, but the important thing to realize now is that the idea of separate organizations, of separate technologies, at the edge and core of a common network is not new.

Today's usage of universal service refers more to a social policy of entitlement. It is no accident that basic telephone service often is called *lifeline* service. A new debate in social policy considers whether universal Internet access is a desirable goal, preventing non-Internet connected people to be information have-nots. This debate overlooks some realities of the use of these media: What is the set of skills needed for basic telephone access, versus those needed for effective Internet use?

Widespread use of telephony initially was a North American phenomenon. Social customs in the United Kingdom, for example, at the time of the invention of the telephone, militated against private telephone use. The sense that only the "right people" should be allowed into one's home made the idea that a random person could telephone a rather unpleasant one. French traditions of centralized governmental guidance, if not control, of key resources also discouraged decentralized communications systems.

The Brown Telephone Company was not the only independent that grew as AT&T increased its dominance. By 1896, Ohio-based independent companies formed an association, followed by a Kansas association in 1903, which, by 1911, joined the Brown Telephone Company to form United Telephone Company. In 1925, this became United Telephone and Electric, which was a holding company, although much smaller than AT&T.

In the beginnings of telephony in the United States, there was a practical need for centralized technical control of the telephone network.

A Perspective on Universality

While I tend to detest the coining of "isms," a term used by historians, "presentism," is one I've found rather useful. The term refers to analysts who judge actions in the past by the standards of the present, rather than those that applied at the time.

Do not assume that the first business telephones were on every desk in an enterprise. While some executives had them, they started as a resource used by designated people, and became ubiquitous over time.

Most telecommunications technologies go through such an evolution. When I started working, people would occasionally ask, "do you have a facsimile machine?" As time went by, people would assume the company had one, and ask for its number. The technology was assumed to be present, but it was not common enough to put on business cards. The next generation of facsimile universality came when fax numbers routinely went onto business cards. Home faxes became yet a next generation, although those that suggest car faxes as a plausible next generation are people I tend to suspect become very hairy during the full moon.

Every communications technology goes through a similar evolution. At a given point in the lifecycle of any technology, you must ask yourself if it is truly reasonable to make every technology available to everyone. Will it improve their productivity, or be a toy? Is the technology in a sufficient state of flux that giving it to everyone, early in the lifecycle, may leave you with large amounts of obsolete equipment?

You may, indeed, find that early adoption will give you a strategic business advantage. Handheld communications devices for package delivery services, or for retail inventory, have had major positive results. I would have little use today, however, for my first pager, which only beeped loudly to signal I needed to call my message operator.

The slogan "One Policy, One System, Universal Service," translated to a technical monopoly for AT&T, one that lasted until the 1980s.

While many speak of the AT&T monopoly as an extreme case of capitalism, an overlooked reality is that flexible telephone switching systems that could permit competitive connectivity probably were impractical until digital electronics and computer-controlled switching were widespread. The feasibility of the eventual breakup of AT&T came as much from new technological realities as it did from legal and regulatory theory.

Those that think of the Star Trek universe's Borg as science fiction should first look at the telecommunications industry, where large providers constantly assimilate others. Perhaps the Borg is not the only science fiction model that applies, for other corporate behavior is reminiscent of some of the "blob" movies of the 1960s, in which fragments of a shattered monster would ooze back together unless totally destroyed.

This universal connectivity model grew worldwide, and many countries kept their telecommunications service a part of their government, usually in their Ministry of Post, Telegraph and Telephone, or PTT. PTTs became the most influential bodies in formal telecommunications standards organizations such as the CCITT. Private companies in countries that allowed competition were somewhat condescendingly known as Registered Private Operating Agencies (RPOA).

Universal service became more formalized in the United States by the Communications Act of 1934, with its purpose cited as to:

> . . . regulate interstate and foreign commerce in communication by wire and radio so as to make available, so far as possible, to all the people of the United States a rapid, efficient, Nation-wide, and worldwide wire and radio communication service with adequate facilities at reasonable charges, for the purpose of the national defense, [and] for the purpose of promoting safety of life and property through the use of wire and radio communications.

AT&T's role was affirmed with the 1956 Consent Decree, which put AT&T in the role of a technical monopoly for long-distance services—with powers otherwise banned by antitrust legislation, but under closer scrutiny by regulators. Again, you must look at this decision not in terms of pure economic and competitive theory, but under technological constraints. This decision was made at a time when computers were in their infancy, computer-controlled telephone switches were a dream, and digital transmission systems were, at best, in research laboratories.

In 1960, AT&T carried out field trials of an early electronic switch that used tone dialing—TouchTone, or dual-tone multifrequency (DTMF)—rather than dialing. This was an application of electronic switching (not even digital) in a signaling function at the network edge, not in the true switching function. Electronic Switching System 1 (1ESS) was introduced by AT&T Bell Labs in 1965 (see Figure 1.4). The control function of 1ESS would barely qualify as a computer in modern terms—it was more of an electronically programmable configuration memory. Subsequent ESS products used true computers, which were slower than general-purpose computers of the time but were optimized for high availability.

While the first AT&T electronic switches did run on specialized operating systems, switches in the 1970s used UNIX variants with high availability features, such as multiprocessing with failover. The need for availability has long differentiated telecommunications equipment from general-purpose computers. See Chapter 6, "Carrier Infrastructure and Optical Networking," for even more details of high-availability

Figure 1.4 1ESS.
Source: Lucent Technologies

approaches in the carrier environment. One of the impediments to deployment of IP-based telephony in the enterprise has been that many early IP-based PBX replacements run on Windows rather than UNIX. While clustering and other mechanisms are making Windows NT more fault-tolerant, that operating system does not have the high-reliability history of UNIX. See Chapter 7, "Fault Tolerance," for a discussion of the networking aspects, and the excellent book by Marcus and Stern, *Blueprints for High Availability: Designing Resilient Distributed Systems* dealing with host reliability. A technology that had as much regulatory as technical impact was the migration of long-distance transmission from wire-based systems to microwave radio. While electronic multiplexing methods, reminiscent of Bell's harmonic telegraph, greatly improved the capacity of wire to carry multiple calls, wire-based systems still were labor intensive to install.

Radio Services Disrupt the Monopoly Model

Microwave technologies developed in World War II secrecy, as the basis of many radar systems. After the war, they entered commercial use for radio, cooking, and radar. In 1951, AT&T began operations of the first transcontinental microwave radio system. Radio systems do not have as stringent a requirement for rights of way as do buried cables or telephone poles for wired systems. While there remained a need for coordination of radio frequency use to ensure noninterference among radio systems, there was much less argument to justify monopolies among microwave-based providers. Use of radio-based services in WANs has been cyclical: Microwaves provided a strong alternative to wired long-haul carriers, but optical fiber provides so much more bandwidth than microwave that it was able to displace microwave services. Other radio technologies, however, have become competitive with fiber. These technologies include mobile and fixed cellular, satellite, and niche wireless systems for remote areas.

As competitive services became more reasonable as a business proposition, alternative carriers began to appear in the United States, initially in specialized niches. Electrical, gas, and railroad companies that had physical rights-of-way between cities began installing their own communications paths, initially for internal use. One such company was the Southern Pacific Railroad. There are various urban legends about what their service was called, but one version of folklore explains it as Southern Pacific Railroad Internal Network Technology

(SPRINT). The firm that ran that internal network technology spun off from the railroad and went through a series of acquisitions. Another company, which was an early alternative carrier, was Datran, which was bankrupt by 1977 and was absorbed into another company that could better withstand the competitive rigors.

The surviving company had begun in 1962, called Microwave Communications. It obtained an FCC ruling that it could offer private microwave services, not connected to the POTS network. Initially, this small firm installed and operated microwave services along the existing rights-of-way of its customers, which included railroads and pipeline companies. Microwave Communications and other *specialized common carriers* pressured to increase their markets during the 1960s, but the regulatory environment initially ruled against them, continuing the primary monopoly of AT&T.

The Rise of Competitive Services

An early break in the technical monopoly on end equipment came with the 1968 Carterphone Decision. One of the results of this decision was a need to define interfaces between customer and carrier equipment, interfaces that protected the telephone network. Initial deployment of interface devices—Data Access Arrangements—put a good deal of protective electronics between the two worlds. As interconnection became more routine, interface microelectronics and connectors became much more standardized, and separate protective devices became more trusting. The familiar modular jacks—RJ11, RJ12, RJ45—are direct products of requirements to standardize the customer-provider interface.

There is a valid need for a well-defined interface point, or *demarcation point* (demarc) between the customer and the carrier. Having such an interface makes troubleshooting much more straightforward. In simple situations such as the Network Interconnection (NI) used between local telephone companies and residential telephones, the principle is that if the telephones are disconnected from the NI and there is still a problem with dial tone or connectivity, the responsibility is that of the local carrier. If the carrier can demonstrate normal operation but the problem occurs when customer equipment is reconnected at the NI, the problem, in principle, is the responsibility of the customer.

Data service units (DSU) and channel service units (CSU), which are demarcation devices used for data applications, may contain a loopback function or other diagnostics that can be remotely commanded by the carrier.

Another competitive breakthrough came in 1972, when Microwave Communications, Inc., better known today as MCI, petitioned the FCC to permit it to offer interstate POTS through its microwave network. While its entry into the market was considered experimental, its market share grew considerably. In fairness to AT&T's arguments for a monopoly, MCI's initial services only aimed at high-volume, highly profitable business-to-business service in selected geographic areas. AT&T's network serviced the entire nation.

In the United States, Vail's original model of regulated universal service ended with the 1975 Modified Final Judgment issued by Judge Harold Greene. The MFJ divested the original AT&T into seven "Baby Bells" or Regional Bell Operating Companies (RBOC), along with unregulated subsidiaries for long-distance services and equipment manufacturing. Divestiture in the United States anticipated privatization of national telecommunications organizations (PTTs) throughout the world.

MCI was now a major competitive player. Another important player came from a combination of United Telephone (descendant of the Brown Telephone Company) and Southern Pacific telecommunications assets: Sprint.

Yet another firm whose initial carrier systems ran along pipelines was Wiltel. Most Wiltel fiber migrated to Qwest. Some industry observers note that it is obvious that some fiber providers' rights-of-way run along now-disused natural gas pipelines because the signs warning construction crews of buried high-pressure gas lines have not been removed by the fiber provider. Backhoe operators sometimes are more concerned by the imminent threat of personal cremation than they are by mere service disruption!

Competitive long-distance services offered what would be generally called physical layer services. Other commercial services operated at higher layers, forwarding packets.

Do not assume, however, that these service offerings strictly followed OSI layering. Especially, do not assume that these service offerings followed the simple seven-layer model usually presented as OSI, rather than various extensions to the OSI model from ISO and other standards bodies.

Architecture and Regulatory Models

Technical standards for WANs, developed both by the International Telecommunications Union (ITU, formerly the CCITT) and national bodies such as the American National Standards Institute (ANSI), often reflect the regulatory split. These "formal" standards tend to deal with traditional services and transmission systems (see Chapter 4, "Basic Services"). Formal standardization tends to be slow, and various industry groups such as the ATM and Frame Relay Forums have evolved to develop accelerated interim standards. The Internet Engineering Task Force (IETF) develops consensus standards much faster than the formal standards bodies.

The OSI Reference Model was spawned in the formal standards arena, and was initially focused on connection-oriented WAN services for data. After the OSI work was started in the late 1970s, CCITT/ITU began the Integrated Services Digital Network (ISDN) effort in 1980.

ISDN, which included both narrowband and broadband (B-ISDN) services, was intended as an advanced service interface to the public carrier network. The ISDN effort broke new ground in architectural specification, building on the OSI experience (see the next section, "B-ISDN and ISDN Architecture").

For effective deployment, ISDN required two key components to be present inside carrier networks: digital transmission and internal control using Signaling System 7 (SS7). Both of these components were valuable for the carriers, whether or not ISDN existed. See Chapter 6 for a discussion of the use of these components by carriers.

When approaching WAN services, readers with a pure data, especially a pure LAN, background need to take care not to fall into one trap that interferes with understanding. The trap is trying to force the specifics of the OSI Reference Model onto WAN technologies that were not designed with strict adherence to that model. While the basic idea of reference models and the principle of layering are universal with respect to modern protocols, the specific seven layers of the original OSI model simply do not apply to many technologies. It can be frustrating and futile to try to force a given ATM, SONET, ISDN, etc., WAN technology into a specific OSI layer.

Classic telecommunications technical standards are architected to allow distinctions between *bearer services* and *value-added services*, between *customer premises equipment* (CPE) and provider equipment, and between local carrier and interexchange carrier responsibility.

B-ISDN and ISDN Architecture

ISDN followed the regulatory model of the time, with the bearer versus value-added services distinction inherent in ISDN protocols. Bearer services, in the context of traditional telephony, offer "dial tone" connectivity. Historically, these more advanced services, such as voicemail, are value-added and technically must be offered competitively.

A model developed for broadband ISDN (see Figure 1.5) is excellent for describing a great many WAN relationships. Think of the process of making a telephone call. The first step is not speaking, but is picking up the phone (releasing the hookswitch), waiting for a dial tone, dialing, and waiting for the network or dialed telephone to respond. Network responses include the "fast busy" or *reorder* tone, while dialed telephone responses include answering, ring/no answer, or busy.

Sensing the hookswitch position, dialing, and ringing are all *control plane* (C-plane) functions between the customer equipment and the

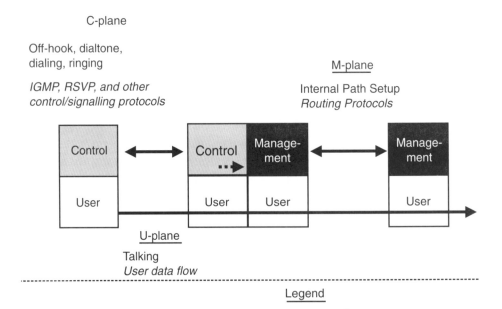

Figure 1.5 B-ISDN model for protocol functions.

entry point into the telephone network. These are not end-to-end functions and are not seen, in their original form, by internal switching resources in the network. C-plane protocols often are fairly complex, or *heavyweight*. Complexity in call setup often allows a simple *lightweight* mechanism to be used for the actual user data transfer.

C-plane functions are present in LAN communications as well. Indeed, LAN C-plane functions such as the Address Resolution Protocol (ARP) often form the basis of exhausting discussions of "what layer does protocol X belong to," when the protocol's role becomes much clearer using the U/C/M protocol model.

Internal network resources attempt to create the requested end-to-end path using *management plane* (M-plane) functions. In telephony networks, this is the role of Signaling System 7 (SS7). In private ATM networks, the M-plane call setup function is the role of the *private network to network interface* (PNNI) or *interim interswitch signaling protocol* (IISP). In routing networks, the M-plane function of determining reachability is the function of routing protocols such as *open shortest path first* (OSPF), *routing information protocol* (RIP), *enhanced interior gateway routing protocol* (EIGRP), *intermediate system to intermediate system* (IS-IS), or the *border gateway protocol* (BGP).

Only after a successful answer can the human conversation begin. Information flow between the end users is a *user plane* (U-plane) function. If a lightweight transfer protocol is used, it typically will include a small, transient *connection identifier* as efficient shorthand for the long endpoint identifiers that were used by C-plane protocols. Figure 1.6 presents these additional planes in a more general way then the traditional OSI two-dimensional drawing. The key thing to realize is that the U, C, and M planes operate in parallel at each layer. OSI often suggests there is only a single protocol function at each layer.

Semaphore, telegraph, and telephone systems are all wide area networks (WAN). Their critical difference from local area networks (LAN) lies in their administrative model. In each one of these technologies, there is a service user (e.g., the person who uses a quill pen to write the message to be given to the telegrapher) and a service provider (the operators and maintainers of the telegraph system). There is a C-plane interaction between the service user and the first point in the carrier network.

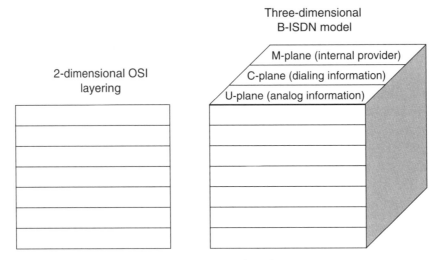

Figure 1.6 Traditional and B-ISDN protocol stacks.

Figure 1.7 shows internal provider and interprovider demarcations of responsibility, using terminology from circuit switching and X.25.

Figure 1.8, the ISDN model of *functional groups* and *reference points* formalizes many of these relationships. The C-plane interaction between consumer and provider is between the *network termination* (NT). Contrast these functions with the traditional telephone model in Figure 1.2.

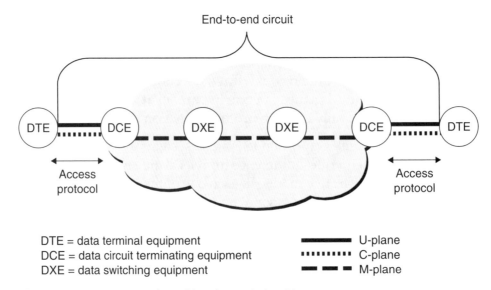

Figure 1.7 Customer and provider plane relationships.

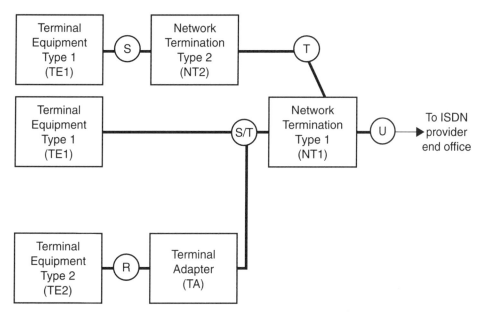

Figure 1.8   ISDN functional groups and reference points.

Semaphore, telegraph, and telephone systems also distinguish between responsibility for the content of a message and the means of its transmission. The transmission service offers a bearer service and is not responsible for such things as the human language used to send the message.

NOTE

Separation of the responsibilities for content and transmission is a well-established operational model, even though there are periodic attempts to make the carrier responsible for content. Beyond the constant battle between sender privacy and what some define as "decency," there are practical operational aspects—can the carrier economically monitor all traffic? Law enforcement and national intelligence interests complicate these issues even more.

Using administrative models solves some otherwise awkward definitions based on technology. Asynchronous transfer mode (ATM) is a modern high-speed networking technology with the capability of transcontinental range. Yet ATM is also a viable technology for metropolitan area and campus networks.

Technological models often are used, inadequately, for categorizing ATM. Some technological models of WAN versus LAN claim "WANs are slower than LANs." However, a 622 Mbps ATM OC-12 facility is far faster than a 10 Mbps Ethernet; speed alone no longer works as a differentiator. In fact, 10 Gigabit Ethernet and ATM/SONET OC-192 use exactly the same physical signaling. Pure distance capability also fails as a differentiator, given ATM might be perfectly usable when limited to a campus or building.

The administrative model of WANs especially fits today's business environment, with its emphasis on outsourcing. In this model, the service user defines the functionality of the service desired, and contracts with a service provider to implement it. To succeed with WANs, the customer must be able to define the services required and to monitor the provider's contractual compliance. Well-developed definition and monitoring skills are valuable for enterprises whose core competence is other than running networks. These skills are applicable to transcontinental networks, but they also are useful in outsourcing network operation within a building complex.

Technological models do have their roles, and Figure 1.9 shows a good one: edge versus core. At a high level, the edge contains end users and their access to provider networks. The core contains provider devices optimized to support large numbers of users and large volumes of traffic.

A further refinement of the edge will distinguish between internal LAN devices and the devices that interconnect LANs. Another valid distinction is the user access technology for users and small sites using dial-up or other low-volume technologies, into the concentration or distribution points of the WAN service provider.

Distinguishing between the edge and the core is a perfectly valid carrier model as well. ILECs and CLECs have an edge function, in contrast to IXCs at the core of the public network.

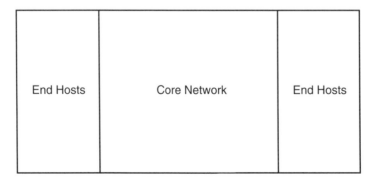

Figure 1.9   Core versus edge.

AT&T began deployment of the first T1 digital carriers in 1961–1962, although these were intended for improving voice and early video applications, not for data transmission. T1 was intended as an edge technology, complementing microwave and long-distance analog coaxial cable (L carrier). T carrier was a replacement for an analog edge/short-haul multiplexing system called N carrier. The choice of bandwidths in T carrier was selected, in part, to maximize interoperability with the analog multiplexing systems of the time. T3, for example, can carry up to 672 voice channels, but it was initially used simply as a central office interconnection technology between T carrier and 600-channel L carrier blocks called *mastergroups.*

Alternatives for the Last Mile

T1 systems originally were intended for interconnecting urban telephone central offices. Another internal carrier application soon emerged: *pair gain* or *subscriber carrier* multiplexing, not between central offices, but between end central offices and large concentrations of telephone users, such as office and apartment buildings. Two copper pairs running T1 could replace 24 copper pairs in an existing cable of good quality, avoiding the need for labor-intensive new cable installations.

Subscriber carrier systems were economically attractive to carriers, and continued to evolve. Optical transmission was introduced to give longer range and noise immunity. Subscriber carrier, however, often interfered with high-speed modem operation by more tightly limiting analog bandwidth than did central office equipment. Increased use of subscriber carrier technologies, and the limitation they imposed on high-speed data transmission, have led in part to a new family of technologies often called *residential broadband*, although they are as applicable to small offices as they are to home users.

One important residential broadband alternative is data transmission over cable television (CATV) systems, which introduces yet another set of regulatory challenges. Cable carriers generally received local monopolies when they were purely in the business of distributing television broadcasts. When cable providers began to offer data transmission, ILECs cried out in protest, but at nowhere the volume of the howls of protest the ILECs emitted when IP-based telephony gave the cable companies the technical capability of offering dial tone to the home and small business. ILECs had been prohibited from offering CATV services. This situation is still being resolved.

There is competitive pressure on cable firms both from ILECs and from ISPs. Many CATV providers that offer data services insist that subscribers use the cable company's ISP for Internet access. There is an argument that if CATV providers wish to become CLECs and compete for telephone service, it is only fair that they act as regulated providers of local loops and offer connectivity to any willing ISP. Court tests of these theories are underway.

Another wired last-mile alternative is xDSL, or the family of *digital subscriber loop* (DSL) technologies. DSL technologies carry signals over existing telephone pairs, coexisting on the same pair as existing analog telephony in many members of the DSL family. Typically, DSL services are provided by ILECs and CLECs, and compete with CATV-based residential broadband. To complicate things even further, the higher bandwidth DSL alternatives are fast enough to support video on demand. While ILECs were barred from offering CATV service, fast DSL services let them compete with CATV providers for pay-per-view services.

Complicating the situation further is the potential impact of high-definition television (HDTV). The increased bandwidth requirements of HDTV, if more than one or two channels are available, will obsolete existing coaxial cable CATV systems. To support large numbers of HDTV channels, residential fiber connectivity will be needed.

Wired local loops are not the only alternative for connectivity to WAN providers. Ironically, while many long-haul carriers are scrapping their microwave towers, appropriately placed towers are being spared from the death penalty, rehabilitated into cellular radio service. While cellular radio is most often associated with mobile telephony, there are distinct applications for fixed-location radio. Remote areas tend to use point-to-point radio technology. Cellular radio is more useful in built-up areas with many users.

Remember that one of the basic principles of cellular radio is consciously limiting its power and range, so that a limited radio frequency space can be reused in small geographic cells. Mobile telephony requires a handoff from cell to cell. Fixed cellular access, however, defines single cells containing the user and the WAN access point. While cellular hardware may be more expensive than the hardware used with copper pairs, not needing to dig up streets to run those copper pairs can result in enormous cost savings. Fixed wireless systems have been especially attractive in developing countries where no copper plant or underground duct exists.

What Are You Trying to Connect?

Among the first steps in defining your WAN requirements is defining the endpoints to which service is to be delivered, characterizing the workload generated at those endpoints, and quantifying the quality of service and availability required at those endpoints.

Return to the core versus edge model and begin to place users and servers into the edge (see Figure 1.10). Don't overly structure things at this point, but concentrate on the identification of users and services. I recommend using flip charts or whiteboards and simply writing the names of user types and services. Encourage managers to call off names as quickly as possible, and do not try to refine the names in the early stages.

Once you identify users and services, decide which users need access to which services. Each set of users and the services they use forms a *community of interest* (see Figure 1.11). These sets are joined by a network, that at this point should simply be considered magical; its details beyond the scope of the current discussion. Draw the COIs as connections among the edge devices.

You may want to distinguish among sets that contain the same users and services, but have different requirements for availability, performance, and security. The present discussion deals with discovering facts about requirements, while Chapter 2, "Policies and Workloads," will guide you in formalizing what you have discovered. On a practical

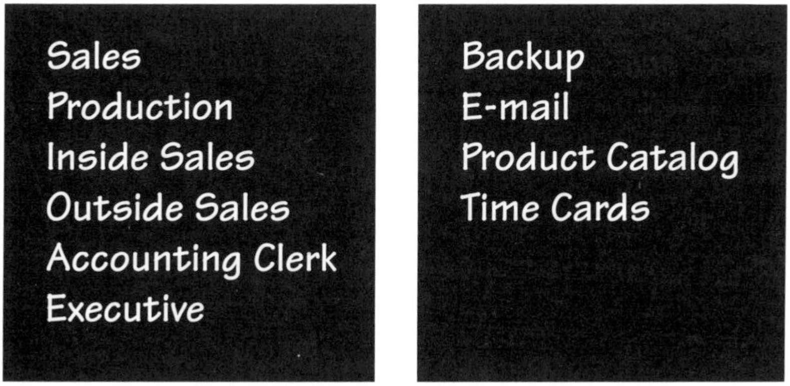

Sales
Production
Inside Sales
Outside Sales
Accounting Clerk
Executive

Backup
E-mail
Product Catalog
Time Cards

Figure 1.10   Taking inventory at the edge.

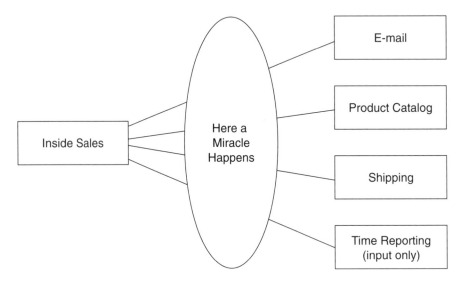

Figure 1.11 Creating communities of interest.

basis, you will often begin defining the endpoints in discussions with upper management, and then defining traffic and performance characteristics with information technology staff.

Very early in your requirements analysis, you will need to define your security policy. As with the services to be provided, top management input is necessary for defining a workable security *policy*. Defining security *mechanisms*, however, is more a matter for discussions with information technologists. See Chapter 2 for guidance on formalizing your security policy. Again, the approach here is to discover requirements, not yet to formalize them.

By defining communities of interest, you have taken a solid first step to defining your security policy. Think of the basic requisites of security as:

- Ensuring your legitimate users have reliable access to the resources they need to do their jobs.
- Preventing unauthorized users from diverting resources from the legitimate users of those resources.

While there is an assumption of universal service in POTS and the Internet, there are also lots of nasty people about who emphatically do not belong in your intranet or extranet.

If you are doing business on the Internet, you want your server name to be visible to the worldwide Internet, just as you want your public telephone number to be visible on the worldwide public switched telephone network (PSTN). Like a telephone number, a server name is a virtual identifier. While it may map to a single server address, it may actually map to the "outside" address of a device that spreads load across a cluster of local servers, or even servers at different locations with non-Internet WAN connectivity among them. When you are "on the Internet," you want outsiders restricted to being able to access the virtual server names, not your internal infrastructure.

The first commercial WAN services imposed data onto voice circuits, either dedicated or dial. As telecommunications carriers converted their internal networks to digital, new methods emerged, but the reader needs to understand he or she may be putting their network saddle on a beast over a century old. This is not to say that is wrong—there are still many uses for horses and mules—but today's effective designer needs to look at the beast, the sons and daughters of the beast, and several generations of great-grandchildren.

In the first steps, designers must focus on the capabilities of these beasts, not their diet, diseases, or demeanor. Requirements analysis must always precede technology selection.

The Relevance of the Beast

There are those who criticize the speed of the formal standards process and its tendency to develop specifications that are overloaded with features added to gain votes, as the source of the elephant. It has been suggested that an elephant is a mouse that was implemented in conformance with formal international standards.

Formal international standards bodies, such as ISO and ITU, go through a systematic voting process. In contrast, the rule of thumb of the IETF is "rough consensus and running code." Implementation forums, such as the ATM and Frame Relay forums, also have an accelerated process.

A new paradigm for WAN services is evolving, in which the user requirements are abstracted into a virtual network, which is then mapped onto appropriate transmission systems. The first chapters of this book deal with obtaining requirements and creating the virtual service model. The virtual network can map onto different transmission technologies, and the enterprise designer will need to compare the costs and benefits of each plausible mapping.

After WAN charges, the largest lifecycle cost component in most enterprises is moves, adds, and changes. Again, investments that reduce these operational costs have substantial payoffs. A special benefit of the new virtualized technologies comes when integrating voice services with the data network. In many enterprises, it can take days to relocate a telephone extension, where voice over IP can provide dynamic relocation.

Network designers will need external input to understand the specific financial model of a given enterprise. It is much easier to quantify the effects of a network design on cost reduction (e.g., reducing or consolidating bandwidth requirements) than it is to quantify how the network improves productivity.

Financial benefits of new network-based business products, paradoxically, can be easier to quantify than productivity improvements, if the new products would not exist without network services. The marketing plan for such products should contain revenue estimates. There should be financial analyses that show the benefit of new internal processes, such as the inventory (and cost of inventory) reduction from just-in-time supply models.

Workforce Distribution

Let's begin to look at requirements that will affect the technologies chosen at the edge. Sites with multiple users will almost certainly need a LAN. The function of the LAN varies with the particular network, even if the main servers are remote from the site. Even with remote servers, there will usually be local support servers such as printers and network management devices.

Depending on your application architecture, it also may be extremely useful to have application-level caches at sites remote from the main servers. Appropriate caches can significantly reduce WAN bandwidth requirements. Caches are most appropriate when multiple users will make use of the same piece of information retrieved from a remote server, whether that information is the corporate telephone directory, a stock quote history, or the current day's Dilbert page.

A large site may be a single building or blur into a *campus network* linked by private transmission facilities. Occasionally, it may be useful to think of campus networks as interconnected by specialized facilities leased from local providers (e.g., "dark fiber" or "dry" copper pairs). In a campus network built with leased facilities, the end enterprise takes a greater operational role than the typical WAN provider model. The owner of the physical medium is not responsible for the data quality, only for correcting physical disruption.

Small and home offices are at fixed locations. It may be useful to split them into the satellite office category, which interconnects multiple users with a small LAN, and telecommuters, who are single users at fixed sites.

In contrast to telecommuters, *road warriors* are single users who conduct business from a variety of sites, such as hotels and client premises. While the road warrior conducts a communication session, the road warrior's location does not change. Most commonly, road warriors connect by dialing through POTS facilities to a network access point. This access point can be a local service provider with roaming capability, or a toll-free number at a central point.

Truly mobile users do change their location during communications sessions. Until there is a truly revolutionary breakthrough in the elasticity and flexibility of extension cords, this means that mobile users must connect through some type of wireless service.

A variety of business initiatives will work only if there is greater use of WANs. There is great demand for skilled workers, and enterprises are more attractive to workers when they offer flexible working environments using telecommuting, part-time and job-sharing arrangements that may need to be network-enabled, etc. Regional anti-pollution initiatives also encourage telecommuting.

"Virtual corporations" may not put their staffs into traditional offices, but may link full-time staff, contractors/consultants, and part-time staff using networks. In my own case, my manager's office is in Massachusetts, my principal office is in my home in Virginia, and the developers with whom I work frequently are in Ontario.

When applications become mission-critical, flexible WANs also facilitate disaster recovery planning. The potential exists for users not to notice a failure of one site, if the WAN can reroute them to an alternate facility.

Why such transparency to failures is "potential" rather than a given is more a matter of application and transport layer architecture rather than that of the network layer. The most basic requirement is that the alternate site has the same data as the primary site. Traditional batch backups, in which files are saved in the wee hours, will not keep real-time databases in synchronization. To keep databases closely (but not necessarily exactly) synchronized, your network will need to copy database updates and send them, with minimal delay, among sites. Full synchronization involves even more bandwidth, due to additional commit protocol traffic. The commit protocols signal that updates have actually occurred; the originator will wait for its peers to be updated before it continues.

Another issue of transparency to failures comes at the transport layer. If the application runs over a connection-oriented transport such as the *transmission control protocol* (TCP), how do sequence numbers stay synchronized over multiple sites? It may be more practical not to try to keep the TCP level synchronized, but simply to rely on it for reliable transmission, and accept that an individual application message in transit may need to be reconnected. Alternatively, explicit session layer protocols such as the *remote procedure call* (RPC) may provide transaction-level reliability.

Cryptographic services present yet another level of complexity. To keep a cryptographic session synchronized among multiple points, every site must track the state of the cryptographic association, have the same dynamically calculated cryptographic association keys, etc. Again, it may be most reasonable to allow the higher layers to keep the application traffic synchronize, accept a short cryptographic resynchronization delay during failover, and concentrate on making resynchronization as fast as possible.

Application Distribution

Increasingly, applications use multiple servers to service a transaction, even though the user perceives a single virtual server. Chapters 5 and 7 deal extensively with virtualization methods. WAN designers will need to understand the traffic patterns between pairs of clients and servers, as well as the relationship between the user and final servers. The application designer may be unaware of the multiple servers involved.

Domain name service (DNS) is a basic and pervasive example of application distribution. A highly distributed database system, it makes extensive use of caches to reduce total bandwidth requirements.

DNS is relatively passive. In the course of a DNS lookup (as distinct from a zone transfer), only cached information may change. In contrast, a complex distributed database such as those found in travel reservations involves synchronization with commit protocols.

Not all distributed, fault-tolerant databases need the lockstep synchronization of commit protocols. The industry, unfortunately, has not settled on a precise definition of related terms such as "mirrored," "replicated," etc. In planning your WAN, however, you must understand how "fault tolerance" and "load sharing" are interpreted by your applications. Not understanding these application aspects means that you will be unable to estimate the volumes of traffic that flow not from end user client to server, but that flow among servers to maintain backups and synchronization.

The fundamental issue of database fault tolerance is based on Murphy's Law: What can go wrong, will. Sooner or later, any given disk drive will fail. There are ways to increase the reliability of local mass storage, such as RAID arrays and clusters of servers over which load is distributed. If the nature of the enterprise is such that information technology is concentrated at a single site and a backup site is illogical or impractical, then improving reliability at a site is very reasonable.

Other applications are inherently more distributed, and can benefit from an assortment of backup site techniques. The backup site can be *cold standby*, in which the application and database must be loaded onto a new server and that server brought into operation, possibly needing system software to be set up. Cold standby means a restoral time, at best, of hours. It will be accurate up to the last physical backup taken.

Hot standby sites have communication links to the primary site and are updated in near real-time. There are several strategies for hot standby, of increasing cost but also that will result in decreasing outage time in the event of a failure:

Remote transaction logging. The incremental log file of the primary site is recorded (or copied) at the remote site. In the event of a primary site failure, this file will be closed and used to update the database.

Mirrored but not synchronized. As the primary database records each transaction, it generates a message containing the contents of the transaction and sends this message to the backup system. Beyond the TCP or other transport-level error control, the primary system does not know whether the secondary system actually has updated with the change. When this method works well, there may be only one record difference between the two in the event of a failure. Congestion or other errors can leave more records in an ambiguous state.

Mirrored and transaction-synchronized. As the primary prepares to record a transaction, it sends a copy to the backup and waits for a confirmation before it commits the change to its own database. If no confirmation is received, the change is "rolled back" and retried, or treated as an error depending on site policy. An additional safeguard may include waiting for the remote database to confirm that the primary database has been changed. This method has the highest overhead, but also the best protection for database integrity.

The Business Case

Where would your network fit if it lived in the age of the dinosaurs? Would it be a giant herbivore superbly adapted to the swamps in which it lived, cushioned by the water and readily finding the resources it needs close to home? Would it be an early mammal, surviving through intelligence, stealth, and picking its fights appropriately? Would it be a tyrannosaur taking what it wants, not terribly concerned with taste (remember that the tyrannosaur in *Jurassic Park* ate a lawyer)?

Herbivore networks are optimized for bulk data transfers among well-defined, comfortable sites. At the smaller end of the herbivore spectrum are enterprises with data centers at several major campuses, with the majority of their traffic flowing between data centers. At the higher end of the scale come carrier networks that interconnect large number of customer access points, or, at the highest end, interconnect other carriers.

Small mammal networks emphasize flexibility and low cost over pure transmission efficiency. Solutions for mammalian networks today tend to include significant use of virtualization of customer networks onto shared infrastructures such as the PSTN or Internet.

Carnivorous networks face a different challenge. A modern corporate carnivore eats smaller companies, including their resources in the larger, stronger beast. Integrating the networks of the prey can be a significant technical challenge, because the smaller networks were not designed to interwork efficiently with those of the carnivore.

An even more complex problem comes when it is time for networks to leave the nest. Established enterprises may have long used contiguous blocks of address space. When they spin off subsidiaries, does part of the larger organization's address space go with the new enterprise, leaving a "hole" in the larger enterprise aggregate generally known to the world?

To the best of our knowledge, dinosaurs were not terribly bright. Large herbivorous dinosaurs may have responded to threats with stampedes. Again, this sort of behavior may be replicated in the current corporate environment. During high-level design, the network architect also is likely to have to educate the enterprise that some things that "everyone knows" actually are serious misconceptions:

- Load sharing is practical on the public Internet.
- High availability servers require customer BGP connectivity.
- Using multiple carriers guarantees facility diversity.
- VPN over IP = VPN over Internet.
- "Whee! I can replace all my frame relay with twenty-dollar-a-month ISP connections!"
- VPN = "selling on the Net."
- Membership must be established before communication.
- "The VPN does all my security."
- "I can get controlled QoS over the Internet."

Cost Justification

While networks have a charm and beauty of their own, they rarely will exist unless there is some business need to fund them. The first requisite in effective LAN use is being sure that functional user requirements are met. If WAN services do not meet application requirements, it makes little difference how efficiently bandwidth is delivered to the wrong locations, or with unacceptable performance or availability.

WANs are often an enterprise-wide resource, so it can often be difficult to do a strict cost benefit model for changes to the WAN. Often, you will need to look at incremental changes to recurring costs.

Over the lifecycle of most enterprise networks, WAN line charges usually dominate total costs, often between 75 and 90 percent of total costs. Resources spent at the beginning of the enterprise lifecycle, when such spending reduces bandwidth requirements, usually are wise investments. This book will guide the reader in using the most cost-effective set of resources.

Many people have likened business to a more civilized form of warfare. There are lessons in world strategy that network planners would do well to consider. Many networking books speak of "building networks," as if most networks are built anew for every new application. Construction analogies can be useful, but, for many environments, the correct analogy is "remodeling" rather than "building."

To understand the cost of remodeling, you will need to understand the current cost of your network, and the incremental cost of remodeling it for new capabilities. The simplest cost analyses for remodeling come when the new capability is an addition to the current network, not displacing any existing capabilities.

Much more frequently, you will be both adding capabilities and modifying existing capabilities. Modification can take the form of replacing aging technologies with new ones, or replacing resources of a given capacity with new resources that exhibit greater economies of scale. A sane approach to changes usually has some period of parallel operation between old and new.

The core of WAN financial analysis centers on costs. If a particular WAN function directly generates revenue, the business analysis is easier than that of one that simply reduces costs.

Financial Factors

Some WANs, such as airline reservation systems, are intimately associated with generating revenue. The association is so strong that you can usefully model them as producing so many dollars per hour, perhaps even down to the level of dollars per user per hour.

Other WANs create new business capabilities, and, in the early phases of a new business relationship, it can be hard to calculate the direct revenue contribution. This is ironic, because new business partnerships may become incredibly lucrative.

Let's examine some ways in which the WAN generates revenue or avoids costs. Be sure to distinguish between two key forms of electronic commerce: using IP in an intranet or extranet, and "selling over the Internet." Both use the IP protocol suite, but there is a very fundamental difference with a crucial difference for security, availability, and quality of service.

What Kind of Net?

In this book, an *intranet* is an IP-based network under the control of a single enterprise. While there will be WAN service providers, there is a clear structure by which the single enterprise contracts for services.

An *extranet* is a collaborative effort among multiple enterprises, but the participants are known (not necessarily to the end-user level) before any bits flow.

The global *Internet* is the set of organizations interconnected with BGP-4 routing of registered IP address space. It includes Internet service providers (ISP) to which individuals can connect. The state and participants of the Internet are constantly changing.

Strategic Alliances and New Markets

Consider a small machining business that would like to sell to the automotive industry. Until recently, the need to have sales offices near major customer factories was a bar to entry into the automotive market. The automotive industry, however, initiated the Automotive Network Exchange (ANX). From the perspective of that industry, the ANX lowered costs. From a vendor perspective, it lowered the bar to entry and created new vendor revenue opportunities.

The previous section explored WAN motivations based on changing relationships with individual employees and contractors. In other words, these individual relationships are known prior to establishing communications, a prerequisite for the use of virtual private network technologies.

Direct Transactions with Customers

There are several kinds of transactions with consumers. Among the most basic distinctions are "selling on the Internet" and "servicing customers on networks."

Internet sales involve an initial relationship where the potential buyer (the client) and the potential seller (the server) do not initially have a configured, validated relationship. Servicing customers, either on the Internet or on private extranets, does require relationships to be known in advance.

In the case of Internet sales, the most common mechanism both for authenticating the user and obtaining payment is a credit card. While credit card use may seem simple, that is due to familiarity. Credit card transactions involve several client-server interactions, each of which consumes bandwidth.

Visa makes the important distinction between *card-present* and *card-not-present* applications, along with *back office* requirements. Back office requirements are those that are not involved with real-time transactions, such as reconciliation and credits for all the charges made to a merchant. Card-present applications are simpler than card-not-present, but still involve several client-server interactions.

Card-present point-of-sale applications generate direct revenue for merchants and service fees for the credit card servicing organizations and card-issuing banks. In this manner, card-present applications are very much like automatic teller machine applications, especially when the cash card holder is a customer of a bank different from the one that owns the teller machine.

Point-of-sale applications of the card-not-present variety form the bulk of direct sales on the Internet. Internet business is more general than point of sale. The only thing we can say about it in general is that it will involve WAN connectivity among customers, suppliers, and business partners.

Financial services industries such as banking and online trading must have clients and servers predefined. The Internet may be used for connectivity for these client and service interactions, but predefinition is necessary to establish trust relationships. Trust relationships are the business-level policies that guide the application of security mechanisms. Generalizing trust relationships into security policies is discussed in Chapter 2.

"Selling on the Internet," however, involves relationships between the enterprise and individuals who are not previously known to the enterprise. These are not typical applications for VPNs, but they have critical availability requirements for which a wide variety of WAN multihoming methods may be necessary.

There is an extremely wide range of evolving applications between enterprises, such as just-in-time purchasing, electronic funds transfer, real-time inventory control, etc. Again, all of these are likely to be WAN-enabled. Security considerations are strong here and may require isolation from the general Internet, typically using VPNs.

Cost Avoidance through Multiservice Networking

Pressure increases for enterprises to provide more services with budgets that increase very little. As a consequence, network managers need to use their resources more efficiently. In many enterprises, there are separately funded networks for voice and facsimile services. If the resources on these separate networks can be shared with data requirements, the limited dollars may go farther.

In addition to the voice, fax, and data requirements, there are many new applications for images and video. Applications also are emerging that integrate, for example, Web and voice services.

Integrating services to consolidate bandwidth is an obvious cost saving, as is reducing the need for usage-sensitive dial circuits. Enterprise networks commonly have tie lines for voice traffic between their campuses, and migrating tie lines into an integrated voice-data-video network is an excellent place to begin adding multimedia services. Tie lines can be fairly risk-free, since you can use a mixture of VoX and PSTN tie lines between sites.

A less obvious cost avoidance comes from avoiding idle staff who cannot work without telephones. In an organization that uses a conventional PBX, how long does it take to move voice service from one office to another? Contrast the usual period of days or sometimes weeks with the time it takes to relocate a PC, which can plug into a LAN, obtain a dynamic address and register it, and immediately be productive. The advent of IP telephony offers the potential for telephones to move as quickly, simply plugging into the LAN.

Downtime Cost Avoidance

While downtime hardly produces revenue, I have found it useful to consider the cost of downtime as more closely associated with revenue generation than the basic cost of providing service. Even if you know the revenue produced by a given WAN-based application, you may not know the full cost of downtime.

For example, assume that a consumer banking network produces $1,000 per hour in transaction fees, and these fees clearly are lost when the network is down. Further analysis might show, however, that the money not deposited loses the bank $10,000 per hour in "float" on the funds not in the bank.

Bankers are very aware that response time at automatic teller machines is quite critical for business. After response time exceeds a certain level, which is considered highly proprietary and sensitive by banks, users are apt to abandon the transaction and seek another ATM. In today's environment, where ATMs from many providers are available, the consumer has alternatives.

Bankers also have observed that occasional long delays lose transactions, but consistently long delays and downtime will cause consumers to seek other ATM providers or home banks. What is the real revenue loss to the bank if a potential 10-year, $1,000 per year customer becomes frustrated and changes her account to a competitor?

Patterns of network delays and outages that have a negative effect on shareholder value can lead to shareholder suits. In some industries, such as broadcasting and transportation, companies can be fined by regulators for having services that are not available. Medical networks that cannot meet critical objectives can cost lives, and failures in military networks can cost lives in wholesale lots.

But there are budgetary realities any designer needs to consider. The same shareholders who might sue because their value is lost due to failures also might sue because they believe management has invested an inappropriate amount of profits in network availability improvements.

The problem definition needs to come up with appropriate compromises between the cost and benefits of protection mechanisms. To come up with appropriate compromises, the network architect needs to consider the threats of both random failures and natural disasters, as well as of deliberate attacks on the network.

Developing the Requirement

When an enterprise requests a quote from a provider, the enterprise is looking for cost factors that can be balanced against revenue factors and internal cost avoidances. Before requesting the quote, you should have a clear idea of:

- The ability of your organization to present the requirement in a meaningful way
- The ability of your organization to understand and compare proposals
- The split of operational responsibilities desired between your organization and the provider

Shortfalls in skills within your organization can be by hiring short-term consultants, by using a system integrator to deal with WAN providers, or by carefully selecting providers with value-added design capabilities. Good network design skills can be a scarce and expensive commodity, but are often far cheaper than the effects of a badly designed, badly contracted network.

Assessing in-house expertise can become quite complex, when managers consider the other responsibilities that employees with the requisite knowledge may have, and the possible impact on morale and retention of deciding that in-house staff are "too busy" to work on interesting bleeding-edge problems.

Often, the implementation decision is not a simple build-it-all versus buy-a-turnkey-service. The main offering of many WAN providers has historically been raw bandwidth, rather than intelligent networks and understanding of applications. System integrators and resellers may be extremely useful in mapping between application requirements and WAN provider offerings. Some WAN providers do have the staff to do user-oriented analysis.

How Formal a Procurement?

The more centralized a point of contact an enterprise desires, and the more it wants to outsource day-to-day operations, the more formal a procurement document it is likely to need. This need is from the buying enterprise perspective, and may or may not be perceived as a need by vendors. Very few ISPs will go to the trouble of responding with a detailed proposal to an Internet connectivity requirement that will only yield tens or hundreds of dollars per month in revenue.

For more traditional bandwidth services, commercial and regulatory factors also will apply. If you are in a geographic area served only by one plausible provider, it doesn't need to respond competitively, but can simply point to its published specifications. If your geographic area is larger, there certainly may be competitive alternatives, but if your requirement is relatively small, the larger competitors do not need the business sufficiently to go to great expense in preparing their responses.

Using consultants and resellers may be a reasonable compromise for organizations with small requirements. For larger requirements and potential vendor revenue, however, providers may become a nuisance in the amount of information they are willing to provide!

Assuming you are trying to meet a requirement rather than simply buy technology, your Request for Proposal (RFP) should include:

- Identification of large sites to be connected
- Requirements for connection to other enterprises (i.e., extranets) and to the Internet
- Generic user connection requirements (small office, telecommuting, and mobile access)
- Availability and security policies with which the provider must comply
- Traffic estimates among the sites and user types
- Value-added features required for voice, data, image, video, facsimile, and other services
- A description of current networking resources and goals for transition. Specify which facilities will remain, which are to be replaced, and which must operate in parallel with new resources during a transition period.

Cost Analysis

Many, but not all, components of WAN charges are easily quantified. There are both one-time and recurring charges, and there are both direct (payments to suppliers) and indirect costs (staff time, etc.). One-time costs can be incurred for the enterprise as a whole, or for individual sites as they are added.

A Context for One-Time Charges

A note of caution applies to evaluating one-time charges. Such charges should not be considered simply as dollar figures, but as costs amortized over a period of time. Be especially sensitive to situations where you may be faced with repeated one-time costs over the lifecycle of a project, as well as termination charges.

For example, wireless telephones or LANs might have a greater acquisition cost than wired facilities. It might be false economy to use wired facilities, however, if your workers are in temporary leased space and need to move to new offices, which again need to be wired.

In real networks, more than one WAN technology is apt to be needed. Even for a single community of interest, different technologies are appropriate for small user access and server connectivity to the WAN.

A strategy for building your cost analyses includes considering costs that are associated with:

- The entire enterprise (e.g., staff training)
- Specific applications (e.g., software licenses)
- Specific sites (e.g., physical connectivity to sites, site licenses)
- Specific servers
- Communities of users and with specific users (e.g., user authentication certificates and administration)
- User access points (e.g., toll-free numbers on enterprise-operated access servers) and services (e.g., ISP roaming access)
- Usage-sensitive costs (connect time and amount of information transferred)

For any of the cost components listed, there may be both direct and indirect costs. You can link a direct cost to the cost of providing a particular application, while an indirect cost is that application's share of the overall network architecture.

Both direct and indirect costs can be one-time or recurring. There can be subtleties to one-time costs. In the telecommunications industry, it is common to have *terminal liability* for installed services, much like an unbreakable lease on an apartment. If you have a one-year terminal liability on a high-speed line, and discontinue its use because you move to new premises, you still owe a year's charges to the provider of that line.

Looking Ahead

The next chapter deals with turning business requirements into operational network policies.

Policies and Workloads

First Law of Plumbing: If it don't leak, don't fix it.

Second Law of Plumbing: Water runs downhill

TEACHINGS OF AN OLD MASTER PLUMBER

A budget is a statement of priorities, and there's no more political document.

EDWARD K. HAMILTON

To understand networking requirements, it's not a bad start to understand military history and plumbing. The military gave us the idea of policies, which, in a peaceful world, are guidance for imposing business objectives onto resources. Plumbing gives us a great many useful analogies for understanding data flow.

The concept of "policy" most likely originated in the Prussian General Staff in the 14th or 15th century. In the military tradition, policy is a form of guidance given to a subordinate, to guide the subordinate to act, in a given situation, as if he or she were the responsible commander who issued the policy.

Originally, policies were not synonyms for rules; they were intended for intelligent people who could make independent decisions. Please join me in a moment of raw hostility to the myriad of functionaries in modern life who deflect a pointed question with the meaningless incantation, "It's our policy." The most irritating of such functionaries tend to be encountered in medical institutions, when you are on a table, in a gown that hardly conveys Olympian dignity. At such times, I find it beneficial to describe myself not as a patient, but as an impatient, and point out to staff their misconception that I am somehow bound by their policies. Simply because something "is hospital policy" does not mean it is *my* policy.

In networking, however, policies need to be agreed to between customer and provider. Qualitative enterprise requirements need to be translated into quantitative business policies for WAN services, and the service policies of the provider need to match those business policies. This chapter deals with formalizing both kinds of policies, as well as more specific policies internal to the provider network.

> . . . with respect to networking, policy refers to the ability to administer, manage and control access to the network resources of network elements in order to provide a set of services to the "clients" of the network. "Clients" in this context refer to users as well as applications and services. *[IETF Policy Framework draft]*

Policies and Modern Networking

Having vented my spleen about misuse of the term *policy*, there are some valid uses for it in modern networking. I suggest that a networking policy is most usefully considered a user objective. For example, the applications staff of an enterprise might specify a quality of service policy for an interactive transaction processing application, which would define the maximum latency the application needs to provide its response-time goal.

The *information technology* (IT) staff of this enterprise would refine this user policy, determining the contributions of latency of the end hosts and the enterprise's local network, and then determining the maximum latency of WAN links used by the application. While the terms *quality of service policy* and *service level agreement* are often synonymous, a *service level agreement* (SLA) is most often a contract between the user of a service and the provider of a service. End-user organizations often write SLAs with their enterprise's IT staff, which, in turn, contracts with WAN providers for WAN SLAs that will work in the context of the broader SLA.

WAN service providers need to agree to SLAs that are achievable in the real world. Quality of service documents glibly speak of "best effort" versus "guaranteed service," and these terms will be discussed further in the next chapter. WAN providers offering "guaranteed service" still have to conform to reality, no matter how their sales departments plead.

Providers executing a service under SLA might be faced with a choice imposed by limited resources. Under resource constraints, the policy executor must prioritize certain traffic to achieve a performance objective. If internal network management traffic and application traffic are contending for the same limited bandwidth, an intelligent executor will prioritize the network management traffic. Not to do so is to jeopardize the continuing existence of the network. No service can be "guaranteed" on a broken network.

For providers and for their customers, policies must recognize the realities of budgets. Monetary cost for a service is an obvious aspect of budgeting in the network, but there are other things to budget. From a technical standpoint, any interface to a provider has a certain bandwidth. If the bandwidth budget is exceeded, something has to compensate. Some traffic may need to be delayed or dropped if it is sent beyond the budgeted capacity.

Time also needs to be considered in the budget. If it takes 16 weeks to have the latest, most expandable optical fiber connection to the provider installed, but multiple copper circuits are available in two weeks, is the value of long-term expandability worth 14 weeks of delay in starting your connectivity? Do interim, lower-capacity methods make sense?

Do not confuse policies and mechanisms! Policies are formal definitions of the problem you are trying to solve. Chapter 1, "What Is the Problem You Are Trying to Solve?" looked at ways of identifying the problem. Subsequent chapters will discuss mechanisms for enforcing policies.

Clausewitz defined *war* as the continuation of national policy by military means. In building a modern WAN, the customer needs first to know the rules for continuing business policy into the geographic distribution enabled by WAN service. Network architects need to help the customer clarify confused assumptions that go into policy formulation, and then to specify a set of means that carry out the policies.

Layers of Management TMN

Policy and management are closely related but different. A key concept in the ITU's *Telecommunications Management Network* (TMN) architecture is applying the well-known technique of layering to management. *Services* are visible to end users as a result of the behavior of *elements* internal to the network providing connectivity. Figure 2.1 illustrates this separation of service, network, and element management.

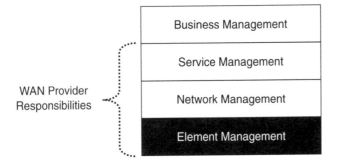

Figure 2.1 TMN model.

TMN was developed with traditional carrier models in mind, independently of IETF work. Its model fits telephony traditions.

The IETF view of policy management generally corresponds to what TMN calls network and element management. Policy specification is at the network level, while policy management is element-specific.

TMN breaks the management problem into four major layers:

Element management. The direct monitoring control of network components such as routers and switches. It includes device statistics collection, error detection, updating firmware, resetting devices, etc. While TMN describes element management as vendor-specific, it is reasonable to generalize element management to managing the abstract devices specified with MIBs.

Network management. The monitoring and control of functions that involve the interactions of multiple elements. From a monitoring standpoint, network management could involve viewing the network topology. Dynamic routing protocol exchange is a control function in TMN network management.

Service management. The control and management functions that are visible to the network's users. Such users could be enterprises or value-added carriers. End-to-end quality of service is associated with service management, as is network accounting and user administration. WAN providers will have their own set of policies for providing services. Typically, there will be a price associated with each policy.

Business management. Strategic and tactical business requirements.

From the user perspective, policy is created at the business management layer, and mapped to service definition. A practical problem definition states business objectives in a manner that can be mapped into service definitions achievable by carriers. It also includes requirements for services operated by the enterprise, such as campus networks.

TMN concentrates on the lower layers of management, while the IETF policy work, although not defined in strict TMN terms, starts at the upper layers.

Formal Policy: IETF Policy

The distribution of policy decisions to the network elements that enforce them is a manual process in most enterprises, but the ideas of policy definition front-ends, policy databases, and tools for detecting and resolving conflicts between policies and operational experience are beginning to be deployed in products. Vendor-specific tools to assist with policy formulation and distribution are entering the market, such as Nortel Preside and Cisco Policy Manager.

The IETF has chartered a Policy Working Group that is attempting to provide a multivendor framework for describing and storing policies that can be distributed to the management interfaces of policy enforcement elements of the network. This framework is quite different from a centralized network management system that directly controls network elements.

This difference is important. It separates the business-oriented service definition process from the technology-oriented network element management process. It frees application-oriented people to concentrate on the end-to-end behavior of the service.

Whether manual or automated, whether single-vendor or multivendor, it's useful to think of most networks as policy-based. You will go through the intellectual process of defining rules that specify your policies. According to the IETF Policy Framework, you will need to consider:

- The composition of Policy Rules.
- The characteristics of devices that are being controlled by Policy Rules.
- The relationships and interactions among the objects being managed.

In the formal model, format and organization of the policy rules are described in the Schema specification. Conditions for executing policies, and actions taken on conditions, are in the Model specification. Figure 2.2 shows the relationships among the major policy system elements.

The *policy management tool* interacts with humans, or perhaps with expert systems, to codify the desired policies. Early commercial products begin by presenting classes of end hosts. The person defining policies draws templates for flows among these classes, and attributes to the flows, such as desired security quality of service.

Once the policies are defined, they are stored in the *policy repository*. The policy repository is a database, and it is repository-to-repository interoperability that is one of the goals of the IETF effort. Repositories will most commonly run on general-purpose computers, such as the machines used for SNMP management stations.

Policy consumers are responsible for acquiring appropriate rules from the repository and deploying them to the managed policy targets, possibly translating to implementation-dependent commands for the targets. The consumer and target functions may be in the same or different platforms. Policy consumption might be on a *push* model, where the consumer decides when to change a target's behavior (e.g., at a given time of day). Policy consumers also might follow a *pull* model in which events in the targets cause requests for guidance to be sent to the consumer.

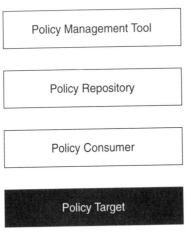

Figure 2.2 Policy system.

As of early 2000, quality of service policies were probably most advanced in the working group and were being used as the prototype. Perhaps the most important limitation of automated policy products in the marketplace is that they are network-oriented, and do not pay a great deal of attention to end host components of policy.

On a practical basis, policy needs to be implemented at:

- Selected/trusted client hosts, which generate traffic and may mark it.
- Network elements.
- Server farms and servers. It can be useful to separate network optimization from server optimization. The network can see a virtual server, with micro-level load distribution among the multiple real servers that make up the virtual server.

The TMN and IETF models are not mutually exclusive. I find Figure 2.3 to be useful in seeing how the two models complement one another.

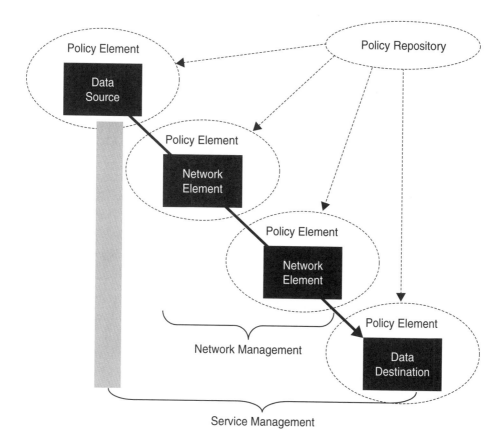

Figure 2.3 A fusion of TMN and IETF policy models.

TMN helps define the human framework in which policy formulation takes place. IETF provides a framework for the distribution of policy information.

Requirements and Workload

Policies are nice things to have, but they need to be implemented on real networks. In most cases, WAN providers can't respond honestly to a customer request for service that will comply with some policy unless:

- The provider knows what arbitrary users and servers are to be interconnected, and where they are located.
- The provider knows how much traffic will flow among those endpoints.

In other words, policies specify what to do with traffic, but until you define how much traffic flows among which points, you cannot make realistic use of policy. As an enterprise analyst, you need to begin by creating a basic traffic matrix.

When you work for a carrier, you need to verify that your connectivity to the user sites is sufficient to carry out the policies you agree to with your customer. At the same time, carrier staffs need to avoid providing too much capacity to sites, capacity that will go unused for the expected project lifetime. There is a delicate balance in providing facilities; however, it is extremely expensive to install new physical transmission paths of copper or optical fiber. It is considerably less expensive to install higher-capacity electronics at the ends of the path. The trend is to install upwardly compatible facilities, either fiber that will support a wide range of new optical technologies, or copper pairs that can support the higher-speed digital subscriber loop (DSL) technologies (see Chapter 6, "Carrier Infrastructure and Optical Networking").

The word *flow* is an intuitive term for describing streams of data, but it has a specific and useful meaning in networking. Flows are unidirectional relationships between either a data source and a single destination, or a data source and multiple destinations. At the simplest level, the source and destination are defined in terms of IP addresses. Quite commonly, they are further defined in terms of source and destination port numbers for TCP or UDP.

Projecting Traffic from LAN Observations

Many applications start as prototypes on LANs, and then are distributed onto an enterprise-wide WAN. Assuming the application is client-server, all user traffic will eventually enter and leave the servers. Connecting the server to the ports of LAN switches with good per-port monitoring can be an excellent starting point.

Before migrating a LAN-based application to the WAN, it is wise to review the protocol stacks it uses. Broadcast-intensive stacks, such as NetBEUI or NetWare 3.x, create appreciable overhead that may not be significant on a LAN, but will present a problem in a bandwidth-limited WAN.

While connecting servers through LAN switches usually helps performance, be careful when first connecting heavily utilized servers to a switch. If those servers previously were connected through a shared-medium hub, contention on the shared medium may have limited the rate at which transactions could reach the server. Servers have been known to crash when first connected to an efficient switch, because the increased bandwidth allows enough additional workload to consume a critical amount of resources.

If you do have a heavily loaded shared-medium network, it may be safer to connect a passive protocol analyzer to appropriate hub ports. In the long term, however, you cannot ignore overloaded servers. All too frequently, perceived problems with network performance really are associated either with the bandwidth of the LAN interface on a server, or with the processing capacity of the server itself.

Classifying traffic as belonging to a particular flow tends to be computationally intensive, and is best distributed to the edge of the network. Tracking single flows (i.e., specific source-destination pairs) is not very scalable. It is more likely that you will want to track flows in which one or both ends is a wild card. For example, it is reasonable to track any source address to destination port 80, the TCP port number for HTTP to give an aggregate amount of Web requests.

Per-flow tracking sometimes can be useful for accounting, for associating demand with specific users. Even in such cases, it may be just as practical to measure per-user resource use over a period of time rather than for a specific flow lifetime.

In centrally managed corporate networks, you may be able to trust end hosts to classify their traffic. Alternatively, you may decide that you can provision enough bandwidth on campuses that fine-grained bandwidth management is only needed on traffic leaving the campus, so you might only classify traffic on outgoing WAN interfaces. See Chapter 3, "Quality of Service," for these and other detailed alternatives in marking, or *coloring*, data.

In the general Internet, if there were no economic penalties to marking traffic at the highest priority, some users would mark all their traffic as high priority. Economists call this the "tragedy of the commons," where, in a sufficiently large population, some people will always take an unfair share of a shared resource, eventually destroying the resource.

You can even consider flows as running through hosts, and create end-to-end response time models for interactive services, as shown in Figure 2.4.

Communities of Interest (COI)

When designing networks, I find that the idea of communities of interest can be made clear to nontechnical people and, at the same time, is an excellent start on defining quantitative requirements.

The set of users of a set of services forms a *community of interest* (COI), shown graphically in Figure 2.5 and as a matrix in Table 2.1. COI may further be broken down if certain users of the same set of servers have different availability, security or performance requirements than other users. At this stage of the discussion, assume all users within a class have the same requirements.

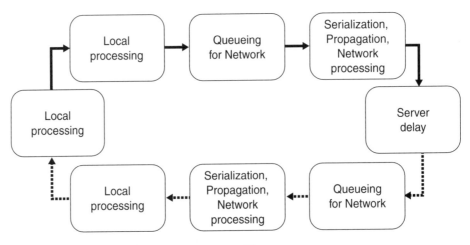

Figure 2.4 Response time as a sequence of flows.

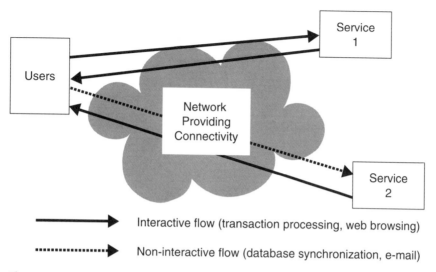

Interactive flow (transaction processing, web browsing)

Non-interactive flow (database synchronization, e-mail)

Figure 2.5   Communities of interest.

COI matrices are excellent ways to formalize the requirements of many business policies. Tables 2.1 through 2.4 capture the workloads over which policies are defined.

Table 2.5 captures a security policy. When a given class of users is not trusted to use a resource, the corresponding cell of the matrix should be blank. When a class of users is trusted, fill in the desired degree of protection in the cell representing the combination of user and protected resource.

Data Applications

Start with your data, rather than multimedia, applications. Begin by listing the classes of users, and see if there are important subclasses, such as "inside sales" versus "outside sales." Once you have the list of users, draw the matrix, but be willing to revise it if review gives more insight into the business process.

When you initially fill the matrix, use business-specific metrics such as transactions or connect time. Actual byte counts will come later, after consideration of factors such as replication for fault tolerance, application caching, compression, etc.

Table 2.1 Initial Traffic Estimates for a Community of Interest

	EMAIL	CATALOG	SHIPPING	PAYROLL
Inside sales				
Outside sales				
Production				
Accounting				

A typical refinement of the model considers not only human users, but computer-to-computer interactions.

Table 2.2 Refining the Communities of Interest

	EMAIL	CATALOG	SHIPPING	PAYROLL	BACKUP
Inside sales					
Outside sales					
Production					
Accounting					
Backup					

Once you have a good sense of the communities of interest, you are ready to look at the geographic distribution of traffic.

Table 2.3 Geographic Workload Estimation

	SITE 1	SITE 2	SITE 3	SITE 4	SITE 5
Inside sales					
Outside sales					
Production					
Accounting					
Backup					

Another way to describe traffic and connectivity refers to *hoses and pipes* [Duffield 1998]. Pipes are the user view of a service, as shown in Figure 2.6. A pipe joins a user and a service. To calculate the requirements for pipes, the enterprise needs to know the traffic pattern and volume between endpoints. In the real world, enterprises do not always know these patterns.

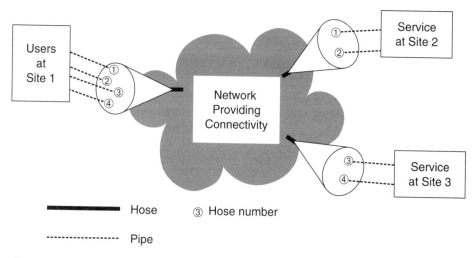

Figure 2.6   Hoses and pipes.

It's not unreasonable to observe that both flows and pipes are source-destination pairs. The difference is one of context. Pipes are flows that are visible to the WAN service provider, and for which the service provider gives a performance guarantee.

In contrast to the user-oriented pipe, the hose is the logical interface from the enterprise to the provider network at a given site. "Logical" means that the sum of the user flows can be greater than the physical interface bandwidth (i.e., oversubscription), equal to the physical interface bandwidth, or less than the physical bandwidth.

While hoses are coarser than pipes, they are also simpler to provision. An enterprise is safe, although it may be expensive, if it provisions a hose large enough to satisfy the bandwidths of all server interfaces at a site. Since providers commonly charge by the size of an access hose, costs are predictable. Provider service-level agreements usually are based on performance at entry to the hose, rather than host to host.

What is the difference between a hose and a simple access link? The hose implies a performance guarantee by the service provider. This guarantee holds as long as the customer does not exceed the bandwidth defined by contract. In other words, the customer may have a T1 physical pipe to the site, but only have contracted for 128 Kbps of bandwidth. Without contractual specifications for burst tolerance, there are no performance guarantees when the customer sends more than 128 Kbps.

Consider real-world constraints in using hoses to specify traffic. While you may not know the complete distribution of traffic, in a network with centralized servers, the capacity of the server farm limits the amount of traffic that can possibly be transmitted or received from any user site.

The Overhead of the Infrastructure

Network management and related infrastructure functions, such as directory services, may add surprising amounts of traffic. Peak loads tend to be at master directory servers, such as the DNS server accessed through the public Internet.

While a popular Internet site could have appreciable DNS traffic, some of the heaviest infrastructure loads can be inadvertent. Be very careful in using network management tools that proactively search for new hosts. Host autodiscovery, in which the management application systematically pings every possible address, probably should be limited to LANs.

An unforgettable telephone bill resulted when autodiscovery was enabled throughout one enterprise network, with the network management package polling both for new hosts and statistics every five minutes. Unfortunately, this particular U.S.-based enterprise had several dial-on-demand circuits to Japan, but did not have filters on these circuits to prevent their being triggered by network management. The package was enabled on the Friday before a long weekend, and thousands of intercontinental calls were billed before the problem was discovered.

Older routing protocols that do periodic updates, such as IP routing information protocol (RIP), interior gateway routing protocol (IGRP), and workgroup routing protocols such as Novell IPX RIP and Apple routing table maintenance protocol (RTMP) also can generate large amounts of traffic due to poor routing design. A customer of mine had a large campus network with several thousand routing and service announcements per minute. These caused noticeable degradation on 56 Kbps links to small branch offices. Ironically, the small WAN-linked offices could not do anything useful with the large routing updates, because they simply default-routed toward the network core.

Multimedia Applications

Multimedia applications include voice, facsimile, (nonmoving) images, and video. There are strong economic motivations to have combined networks for traditional voice and facsimile services, and more exotic image services are finding niches.

Projecting Traffic from LAN Observations

Traffic estimation for voice over IP, voice over ATM, or voice over Frame Relay involves different approaches than used for LAN-based traffic. These services, collectively called VOX, may puzzle data-oriented networking people unfamiliar with their traffic requirements. In most cases, however, a very detailed traffic analysis is available: It's called the telephone bill! See Chapter 3 for a discussion of the performance requirements for voice.

While the detailed characteristics of voice traffic will be discussed in the next chapter, some common misperceptions of voice should be considered now. Voice services do not take large amounts of bandwidth. With modern compression techniques, conversations with good voice quality can take less than 10 Kbps of bandwidth.

The critical issue about voice, however, is not that it needs a large amount of bandwidth, but that the bandwidth it receives cannot be delayed. Excessive latency has terrible effects on voice quality.

Latency is far more important to voice than is reliable delivery. Human hearing can compensate quite well for occasional voice drops. In contrast to data traffic, retransmission is neither practical nor desirable for voice and video traffic. Retransmission either would introduce excessive latency, or cause out-of-sequence conditions in the information stream. What is the effect of sequencing errors in voice transmission? Consider the observation of *Star Wars*, "If Yoda so strong in Force is, why words can he not in right order put?"

Another motivation for voice-over-IP specifically is the operational advantage of IP-based telephones and/or integrated voice/data workstations. Most traditional PBX systems need explicit programming to move telephone extensions from one location to another, often resulting in days or weeks of delay when people move. IP-based telephones, however, can plug into the LAN and autoconfigure using DHCP and DNS.

Many enterprises are amazed when they review the amount of facsimile traffic that flows among their sites. Adding delays of minutes to facsimile traffic rarely has a significant effect on its usability, but dynamic allocation, or withholding, of bandwidth for internal faxes can have dramatic effects on total enterprise WAN bandwidth requirements.

Table 2.4   Multimedia Workload Estimation

	INTERNAL VOICE	EXTERNAL VOICE	FACSIMILE	IMAGERY	VIDEO
Inside sales					
Outside sales					
Production					
Accounting					

Facsimile is by no means the only source of image traffic. Many organizations assume that since they have no exotic videoconferencing, they do not have significant image traffic. Consider, however, an insurance company that is attempting to build a paperless office. The digitized document retrieval system can transfer very large images.

Document retrieval systems may or may not have large WAN requirements. Often, the image store is LAN-attached, and is updated only by local devices. The image store can be populated by magnetic or optical media physically shipped to the site, or by overnight batch transfers on the WAN.

While many people associate video with videoconferencing, and assume videoconferencing competes with business travel, a far more common application is employee training. From the WAN perspective, many training applications do not need full real-time bandwidth, but can be sent to the user from a local cache or file store. See Chapter 5, "Virtualizing in Modern Networks," for further discussion of the role of application caches.

Membership and Trust

Your network potentially will be accessed by employees, contractors, business partners, network vendors, and the general public. After someone has gained access, it is too late to formulate policy about whether that person is trusted. The *membership policy* for a network has aspects both for administration and security. In an intranet, it may be reasonable not to impose extensive security controls, if the network and hosts are physically protected. Even there, however, it's wise to distinguish between end users and staff who have administrator authority.

As with the airlines, end users are first concerned that the network goes where their traffic needs to go. To use the previous analogy, users conceptualize traffic flow as a set of pipes. Membership in a network can be defined by:

- **Physical connectivity.** When a user is at the right site, the user has network access.

- **Dynamic joins through secure authentication.** The user must present credentials before joining the network.

There is an implicit *trust policy* in these requirements. Before you decide on security mechanisms, you need to decide the trust policy. For many organizations, the default policy is that any employee has access to any resource, but outside users only have access to public Web servers.

Table 2.5   Trust Policies

	USER SITE 1	USER SITE 2	SITE 3	DIAL-UP	ROAMING
Inside sales					
Outside sales					
Production					
Accounting					
Backup					

TIP

Security design should start from the Principle of Least Privilege, which states that users should be granted only those privileges essential to do their job. Reflecting this principle, begin your trust matrix from the perspective that no trust is given by default.

In the real world, the more secure a system, the more inconvenient its use often becomes. As a system designer, you need to make tradeoffs between security and operational convenience. For example, system administrators may need to access arbitrary resources. A good security compromise may be allowing administrator access by default, but also making sure that administrator access is logged in an auditable way, and that administrators cannot delete log files.

The knowledge level of the user really has little to do with whether administrative rights should be granted. I once worked at a network research center where we had 104 programmers. Approximately 80 knew how to use administrator commands, about 40 actually understood administration, and only one was actually the network administrator. Until the 79 "experts" were forbidden to use administrator commands, the network was in chaos.

The most basic members of an enterprise network will be the employees of the enterprise. Some employees will have special privileges, such as system administrators or those entitled to have access to designated sensitive data.

Contractors may be treated as employees, or have more limited access. In most organizations, the most important difference between employees and contractors is that the access of contractors is allowed only over a defined set of dates, while employees have access of undefined duration. This difference tends to be unimportant in real networks, because employees, in a network requiring any substantial degree of security, are issued credentials that have dates of activation and deletion.

Network membership becomes more complex when extranets are involved, in which the enterprise connects to other enterprises via bilateral or multilateral private arrangements. It is perfectly plausible that an organization might be a business partner in some roles, but a direct competitor in others (see Table 2.6).

Table 2.6 Trust Policies for Extranets

	SERVICE AB	SERVICE CD	SERVICE ACE	SERVICE DE	SERVICE A
Partner A	Permitted		Permitted		Permitted
Partner B	Permitted				
Partner C		Permitted	Permitted		
Partner D		Permitted		Permitted	
Partner E			Permitted	Permitted	

There are several nonexclusive ways in which an enterprise may need to make hosts on the public Internet part of its network, although such hosts are unlikely to have the same privileges as employees, contractors, or suppliers. The enterprise may do Internet commerce, which implies that arbitrary Internet-connected hosts need to access enterprise servers. Such access is usually limited to designated servers, but these servers do not exist in isolation to the rest of the enterprise. Support staff of the enterprise will need to access the servers for maintenance. Servers visible to the public may need to communicate with each other for load sharing and backup, and they may also need to communicate with nonpublic servers inside the enterprise, such as inventory and shipping hosts (see Table 2.7).

Table 2.7 Trust Policies for Internet Services

	SERVICE 1	SERVICE 2	SERVICE 3	SERVICE 4	SERVICE 5
Public					

Many enterprises, such as educational institutions, have users who need to access arbitrary hosts on the Internet. Whenever such access exists, those arbitrary hosts are to some extent part of the enterprise network (see Table 2.8).

Table 2.8 Trust Policies for Internet Use by Internal Users

	E-MAIL	SELECTED WEB	UNLIMITED WEB	FTP	TELNET
User type 1					
User type 2					
User type 3					
User type 4					
User type 5					

Once the membership is defined, you will then need to establish policy guidelines for operational responsibilities (see Table 2.9).

Service Provider Requirements

Not surprisingly, the internal information needs of the service provider are a mirror image of the enterprise. Where the enterprise is concerned with the end hosts, the provider is concerned with the traffic those end hosts inject into the WAN. The traffic model is that of the hose, not the pipe.

Table 2.9   Trust for Operational Control

	SERVICE 1	SERVICE 2	SERVICE 3	SERVICE 4	SERVICE 5
Shift operator					
Network admin					
Security officer					
Partner 1					
Partner 2					
Partner 3					
Partner 4					
Partner 5					

Since providers serve multiple customers, they must heed the words of Mr. Spock, "The good of the many outweighs the good of the few." Any decision made by a WAN provider must first be weighed against the viability of the provider network as a whole, rather than the requirements of any one customer. For example, provider network management traffic *must* get through. It is better to drop or delay some customer traffic than it is to lose control of the network infrastructure.

Many very practical WAN services do not guarantee bandwidth. It is a statistical reality that not all devices will transmit at once, so providers can realize great economies by oversubscribing at the edge of a packet-switched network.

As we will see in Chapter 6, new models for carrier provisioning may be emerging. Optical networking makes the cost of transmission media extremely low, so that carriers *may* begin to do less of a juggling act between backbone and user bandwidth. There remain bottle-necks, however, at the interconnection devices between huge-capacity optical media.

Providers that connect to the Internet or to the public network also must detect and protect against network abuse (see Table 2.10).

Availability, Security, and Quality of Service

All too often, the availability of a network-based application, its security mechanisms, and its quality of service are treated as separate func-

Table 2.10   Trust Policies for Service Providers

	SERVICE 1	SERVICE 2	SERVICE 3	SERVICE 4	SERVICE 5
User Type 1					
User Type 2					
User Type 3					
User Type 4					
User Type 5					

tions. Accounting services also tend to be treated separately, when all four of these functions are closely related.

End users tend to have a simple view of their networks: The network is usable, or it is not. The user really doesn't care if the network is unusable because a backhoe dug through the cable between the enterprise and the WAN end office, because an Evil Hacker smashed the router software, or because there is so much traffic on the line that response time is impossibly slow.

Failures can come from several sources:

- Deliberate attacks by crackers/malicious hackers/disgruntled employees (keep all employees as gruntled as possible)
- Errors of software, hardware, or administrators
- External disasters
- Congestion

Traditional security mechanisms deal with deliberate attacks that are intended to deny service—to create failures. Security mechanisms also deal with information compromise, a somewhat different problem. Nevertheless, you must first state your availability objectives against all threats, and then balance the cost of protective measures against the weighted risk of failures.

Availability Policy

How do I explain weighted risk? Storytelling helps. All too often, my consulting clients declare, "We want to be protected against everything." I respond to this by going to a nearby window and pointing to an arbitrary building on the horizon. "Well, you're going to have to buy up all the land from this building to that building I'm pointing to."

Typically, the customer responds, "WHAAAT?"

And I explain, "Well, to protect your data center against a 747 crashing into it, you have to put your antiaircraft guns a fair distance away, so the plane has room to crash before it hits you."

The customer will bluster back, "That's crazy! I don't need to protect against that!" At this point, I remind them that they started out saying they *did* have to protect against everything. When the customer accepts this, they begin to have wisdom about protection.

Weighted risk is the product of the cost of an adverse event (e.g., the 747 crashing into the data center) times the probability of that event happening. If the crash would cost 1 million dollars, and the probability of it occurring is one in 100 million, the weighted risk—the exposure—is one cent. If the protective measures were no more costly than one cent, they would be justified. In this case, it is far wiser not to protect against the specific physical threat, but to be sure that business insurance covers such catastrophes.

Each case is different. If the enterprise were a military command post during the Cold War, the threat of attack was much different. The North American Aerospace Defense Command operations center is buried in Cheyenne Mountain, Colorado. Even that site, however, was expected only to survive near misses with modern nuclear weapons.

Far more probable than nuclear attack is simpleminded cable cutting by construction crews, led by the dreaded backhoe. I often shake my head sadly at enterprises that insist on having multiple long-distance WAN providers, providers that have highly fault-tolerant optical backbones, but have a single cable from their building to the local telephone office that connects them to their long-distance providers. See Chapter 7, "Fault Tolerance," for discussions of multihoming for availability, both at the long-haul and local-loop levels.

So, look at your communities of interest and define availability policies for them (see Table 2.11).

Security Policy

Mark Twain called conscience "the still, small voice that tells you someone is watching." Security policy is the conscience of the membership and trust policy. The security policy specifies the rules that

Table 2.11   Trust Policies for Service Providers

	SERVICE 1	SERVICE 2	SERVICE 3	SERVICE 4	SERVICE 5
User Type 1	24x7 2 hour MTTR				
User Type 2	8x5				
User Type 3					
User Type 4					
User Type 5					

will be enforced. Do not confuse the security policy with the specific security design, which specifies the actual mechanisms of security enforcement. A good security policy is no more than two pages long, has the support of top management, is understandable to its users, and meets both technical and legal requirements.

Top management needs to know that ensuring security and availability are never-ending processes, and need to follow a process improvement model generally called the "security wheel." The results of auditing, for example, need to feed back to defining requirements. Audit results may show threats that had not been considered in the original design. They will show the actual availability, which needs to be compared to business objectives to see if more or less resources are appropriate.

Authentication is the first part of security. The most basic goals of "security" are ensuring users have the resources to do their jobs, and that unauthorized parties do not interfere with enterprise resources. These goals need to be written in a short, clear security and availability policy, and all technical solutions need to be reality-tested against this policy.

Once you identify threats, you can start to think of the services you need to protect against threat. Before planning a vague "security," you should establish the attributes of a secure communication for your various applications.

Attributes of a secure communication can include:

- **Identification**, **Authentication**, and **Credentialing**
    - *User authentication* Is the user who he or she purports to be?
    - *User credentialing* Once identity is confirmed, what does the user have the right to do? The assignment of credentials can change

Involving the User

In the early 1970s, I did a policy study on the U.S. security classification system for the Ripon Society, a moderate to liberal Republican research group. Today, I regard being a moderate Republican as the political equivalent of slight pregnancy, but the study was informative.

I interviewed a substantial number of security managers, including representatives of the Central Intelligence Agency (CIA) and National Security Agency (NSA). The CIA was exceptionally cooperative, and discussed, among other things, their philosophy for staff security education. If employees objected to some security regulation, the security office actively encouraged them to come and discuss it. True, the security office had the advantage of being able to have a classified discussion of the subject. This discussion, however, would normally review what threats the regulation was safeguarding against. The intention of discussing it was intended to get the user's buy-in that the practice had a real purpose. According to security officials, on several occasions, employees managed to convince the security office that a regulation was ill-advised, and it was changed.

At least internally, the CIA regarded security as a partnership. The director of physical security told me that he was most concerned about what people could take out in their heads, rather than what could be stolen by the apocryphal spy in trenchcoat and dark glasses.

At the NSA, however, the emphasis was on physical protection. In the 1970s, armed Marine guards, who had the reputation of shooting at least three times before crying "halt," guarded not just the fence, but were stationed in the main corridors. When I entered an office as a visitor without security clearance, my escort would push along a device which, in retrospect, I hope was the product of a sick sense of humor rather than a serious tool. The device, which seemed to be modified from a floor polisher, had a yellow rotating beacon, much like the light on a tow truck, that was the NSA's equivalent of a medieval leper bell, screaming "Uncleared! Uncleared!"

Looking around the NSA, I had the general sense that they were protecting against the threat of a Soviet airborne division landing on the roof, and the Marines were to buy time while the destruction plan was implemented.

Is there a lesson in this? According to open sources, the NSA has had far more security leaks than the CIA. Authoritarian security enforcement can be far less useful than cooperative practice.

with context, such as granting general Web browsing access only after normal business hours.

- *Server authentication* Is the user connecting to the true server? There have been impostors such as `m1cr0s0ft.com`.

- *Network and security device authentication*
- **Integrity Services**
    - *Unitary integrity* Have individual records been altered?
    - *Sequential integrity* Have correct records been added or deleted from a sequence (e.g., file)? Has the order of records been changed?
- **Nonrepudiation** Can the sender claim "the check is in the mail" without having proof of sending it? Can the receiver deny receiving a payment when the sender has a return receipt?
- **Confidentiality** Can unauthorized receivers read the communication? How long do they need to be protected?
- **Protection from Denial of Service** Can intruders crash the service?

In the broad sense, protecting against denial of service includes both "security" and "availability" protection methods. In other words, a backup link may be as important as a firewall (see Table 2.12).

Table 2.12 Security Requirements

	SERVICE 1	SERVICE 2	SERVICE 3	SERVICE 4	SERVICE 5
User Type 1					
User Type 2					
User Type 3					
User Type 4					
User Type 5					

Accounting

In the context of networking, accounting is not just what the financial bean-counters do, but the broader process of qualitatively and quantitatively tracking the interactions among users (authorized and unauthorized) and services.

There are several dimensions of accounting: by user, by service, and by site. Not all of these may be relevant in your environment, but you need to consider them (see Table 2.13).

Table 2.13 Accounting Requirements

	CONNECT TIME	CONNECT LOG	TRAFFIC	DETAILS OF TRAFFIC
User Type 1				
User Type 2				
User Type 3				
User Type 4				
User Type 5				

Documenting server access can be important depending on your security policy, but also can be extremely useful for server capacity planning. While the emphasis here is on network behavior, it is good practice to take snapshots of server loading in a manner that you can correlate with network traffic. Server loading includes processor utilization, available memory, and available scratch disk. Other measures such as disk fragmentation may be relevant.

Often, a perceived network congestion problem is really a problem of server capacity, or the speed of the local interface to the server (see Table 2.14).

Table 2.14 Accounting Requirements for Servers

	CONNECT TIME	CONNECT LOG	TRAFFIC	DETAILS OF TRAFFIC
User Type 1				
User Type 2				
User Type 3				
User Type 4				
User Type 5				

Site-level traffic fits the "hose" model of traffic engineering. Both the enterprise and the provider will want to know the traffic per site, to be sure that adequate capacity is provided. Depending on the physical means of access to the site, capacity may involve the number of dial-up ports, the speed of access lines, the capacity on multiplexed lines, etc. (see Table 2.15).

Table 2.15 Site-Oriented Accounting

	CONNECT TIME	CONNECT LOG	TRAFFIC	DETAILS OF TRAFFIC
Site 1				
Site 2				
Site 3				
Site 4				

The preceding discussions of capacity are based on ideal bandwidth delivery. Quality of service mechanisms either attempt to provide quantitatively guaranteed performance, or establish qualitative rules for prioritizing traffic when congestion is encountered.

Quality of Service Policy

While there are many possible metrics for quality of service, the most important are bandwidth, latency, and loss rate. You could agonize over setting precise numerical goals for these metrics, but things are simpler in the real world.

The industry press makes much play on fine-tuned service-level agreements, but the real world is simpler. Think about flying on an airplane. If you are a human, rather than a package, you really have only two or three ways to fly: first class, business class, and coach. Now, different airlines interpret these ways differently; seat pitch is not a constant! But as a frequent flyer, I tend to make a decision based on:

- Which airlines fly where I want to go? Do I have special frequent flyer status on any of them?
- Of the airlines that go to my destination, what is the best affordable class of service, when upgrades are considered? When I fly to the UK, I think highly of Virgin Atlantic's "Upper Class," which is presented as a business class, but really is first. The bulk of my frequent flyer miles are on Delta, an airline that I like very much, but which is now partnered with Air France, an airline I go to significant effort to avoid.
- If I am flying into a troubled part of the world, safety might become a differentiator. While its security requires a fair bit of inconvenience, El Al takes security to a different level than most commercial airlines.

There is, however, an extremely broad range of *prices*, even within the same airline, for the same service. Let me put it in these terms: On domestic flights, I like the first class service from both Delta and Continental. If I can upgrade most easily on Delta, I will take that flight. Not infrequently, I will give my business to Northwest or TWA, if I am flying on a full coach fare that these airlines will automatically upgrade to first. If I can't upgrade, Northwest is one of my least preferred airlines.

Much as there are a limited number of actual flight classes, there are a limited number of practical QoS requirements (see Tables 2.16 and 2.17). A reasonable first approximation splits workload into:

- Voice and interactive video
- One-way video
- Response-time critical transaction processing and real-time database synchronization
- Less critical interactive applications (e.g., Web browsing)
- Noninteractive file and message transfer

Table 2.16   QoS Requirements by COI

	SERVICE 1	SERVICE 2	SERVICE 3	SERVICE 4	SERVICE 5
User Type 1					
User Type 2					
User Type 3					
User Type 4					
User Type 5					

Table 2.17   QoS Requirements

	BUSINESS TRANSACTIONS	INTERNET	VOICE OVER IP	SERVICE 4	SERVICE 5
User Type 1					
User Type 2					
User Type 3					
User Type 4					
User Type 5					

Operational Responsibilities

To understand the thrust of this section, those readers who have seen the movie *Ghostbusters* should start humming the theme song: "Who ya gonna call?" An early part of network design is deciding exactly whom you do call for network changes and troubleshooting.

Given that WANs are administratively separate from servers and LANs, the operational problem becomes more complex. Some WAN providers will contract to provide operational support beyond simple connectivity. If your contractual relationship only specifies connectivity, then your users need to contact an internal help desk that will call the WAN service provider when needed.

Both real-time troubleshooting and LAN moves and changes often are separate from moves and changes that affect the WAN.

In developing your operational model, consider who will be responsible for the functions in Table 2.18. These responsibilities can involve an assortment of enterprise- and provider-operated help desks. Wherever possibly, try to have a single point of contact for your end users.

Table 2.18 Assigning Operational Responsibilities

SITE FUNCTION	ENTERPRISE ADMINISTRATOR	WAN SERVICE ADMINISTRATOR	PROVIDER	OTHER
Creating sites				
Defining services				
User accounts				
Customer workstations				
Customer local servers (e.g., printer)				
Customer main servers				
Customer LAN devices (cabling, hubs, switches)				
Customer WAN router				
ISP router at customer site				
Provider Point of Presence (POP)				
Interprovider connectivity				

Looking Ahead

In the next chapter, we will go more deeply into quality of service, both its specification and mechanisms for enforcing it. Having medium-independent criteria for describing quality of service capabilities will help compare actual transmission services in Chapter 4, "Basic Services."

Quality of Service

Come give us a taste of your quality.

WILLIAM SHAKESPEARE, *HAMLET*

Cease dependency on inspection to achieve quality

W. EDWARDS DEMING

He tried each art, reproved each dull delay,

Allured to brighter worlds, and led the way.

OLIVER GOLDSMITH

Quality of service (QoS) includes both valid technology and a great deal of marketing hype. In many situations, it is made far more complex than it needs to be. In other situations, QoS mechanisms are claimed to do things that are practically impossible. Let's try to put things into perspective, with due respect to the KISS (keep it simple, stupid) principle: While there are a great many QoS control mechanisms, the minimum adequate set should be used in any given configuration.

A classic television show about the Chicago mobs of the 1920s, *The Untouchables,* gives insight into priorities for QoS. Frank "The Enforcer" Nitti was a powerful figure, but it always was clear he reported to the Big Boss, Al Capone. So it is with QoS: Enforcement is useful, but it is far less important than QoS policy.

Adequate services for an enterprise may not include any enterprise-level QoS enforcement mechanisms. If an enterprise can define its requirements, it can contract with a provider to provide a service that meets these requirements. The enterprise, or its consultants, might audit the adequacy of service, but the actual control mechanisms would remain a provider responsibility. There certainly will be situations, in carrier or complex enterprise networks, where extensive QoS mechanisms are necessary.

Where do these mechanisms go? Figure 3.1 extends the B-ISDN reference model, informally, to show how end hosts *signal* their requirements to the network using C-plane protocols. This picture is conceptual, because the end host request often will be not be an actual protocol interaction, but rather a matter of provisioning. When the resource request is in real time, then M-plane mechanisms come into play if resource reservations need to be made.

Not all QoS mechanisms reserve resources. They may simply police the traffic at various interfaces, dropping or delaying traffic as needed to meet the particular QoS requirements.

Some QoS mechanisms are connection or quasi-connection oriented. In those cases, the C-plane interaction may deny connection establishes if the M-plane determines there are insufficient resources to service the request.

Certain realities apply to any network. Regardless of the priorities given to any application, routing updates and other network infrastructure traffic must receive the highest priority. The absolute business priority of a given application may not properly reflect its priority in the network.

Availability is another reality. There is no quality of service if there is no service. If the network provides perfect latency characteristics for

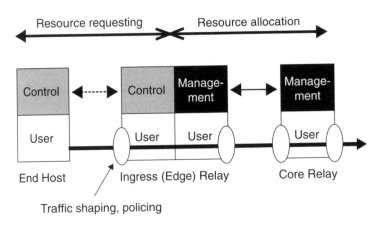

Figure 3.1 QoS mechanisms apply to control and flow.

one percent of the time, it will probably be useless in practical terms. The practical context of any network, of course, varies. I worked on Cold War command and control networks that had the basic requirement "work flawlessly for only 20 minutes, but you will never know when the 20 minutes will begin, and, during those 20 minutes, many of your network elements will receive nuclear input and become mushroom clouds. Mushroom clouds cannot retransmit."

Service-Level Agreements

The goal in a customer relationship with a service provider is to reach agreements about the traffic the customer will generate, and the QoS that will be provided to that amount of traffic. At this point, it is useful to describe, at a high level, the mechanisms for service description in the IETF and in the ATM Forum. This discussion is meant to be at a high level, with details later in the chapter.

In the IETF, the Integrated Services working group describes the traffic to be offered as a *Tspec* (traffic specification) and the QoS to be provided as a *Rspec* (reservation specification). Figure 3.2 shows the directions in which Tspecs and Rspecs flow, and also makes the point that each endpoint can negotiate a different service contract with the provider.

You will notice there are two sets of Tspecs and Rspecs in Figure 3.2. Tspecs and Rspecs apply to specific flows, and flows are one-directional.

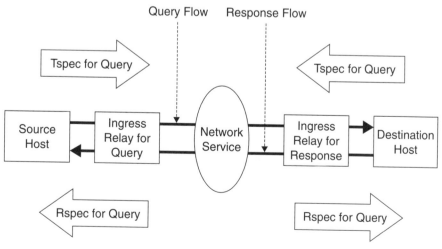

Figure 3.2   Tspecs and Rspecs.

This illustration shows a query-response model, which will use a flow in each direction. There can be different service contracts in each direction. For example, in most Web applications, there is a small query, the URL request, in one direction, which should have a small Tspec. The larger response would have a larger Tspec.

Service contracts, in both the IETF and ATM Forum, include two major categories, *guaranteed service* (GS) and *best effort* (BE). There are subcategories of each, and, even if you are not using the specific technology of the group that defined them, understanding the categories and subcategories will add to your general understanding of QoS.

Figure 3.3 shows the ATM structure and its rough relationships to the IETF structure. The GS branch of the ATM service tree includes the *constant bit rate* (CBR) service, which is used to provision *circuit emulation service* (CES). CES is intended as a way to provision a customer facility that appears to be a physical T1/E1 service, with all the characteristics of a dedicated line.

Variable bit rate (VBR) services are highly reliable, predictable services that have wider tolerance for delay than does CBR. Not shown in this figure are the subcategories of real-time and non-real-time VBR.

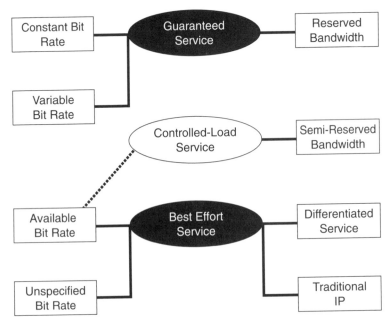

Figure 3.3 ATM classes.

When ATM was introduced and its evangelists claimed it was the answer to every question, and, above all, the answer to providing QoS and totally reliable service, I was always amused by *unspecified bit rate* (UBR). I don't think it's too cynical to say UBR is ATM's way to look like IP: a best-effort service in which delay and loss are not specified.

The additional category for *integrated services* (IntServ) is *controlled-load service*, which is roughly similar in application to the ATM VBR services. VBR does not require an absolutely constant bit rate, but still assumes a steady traffic stream with minimal bursting. VBR and CLS have greater tolerance for a low level of loss and delay variability than does CBR.

In the IP world, *differentiated services* (diffserv) complements IntServ. ATM does not have a direct equivalent to diffserv, which marks individual packets to denote their priority. While ATM does have some flags that affect priority, they deal with management versus generic user traffic. User traffic divides into GS and BE, but the detailed ATM contract is at connection establishment time. Diffserv is not inherently connection-oriented.

Performance Objectives

One basic way to think about QoS requirements is for common applications such as:

- Network management
- Delay-critical traffic (voice and interactive video)
- Limited tolerance (video stream)
- Transaction processing
- General interactive
- File transfer

You will find the basic requirements of applications covered by a relatively small number of basic parameters:

- Delay, often called latency
  - Constant delay
  - Variable delay, often called jitter
- Packet loss probability

Absolute Latency

First, the network needs to protect itself. Routing updates, keepalive messages, and critical network management information must get through. Routing protocol timeouts are one set of limits.

Real-time voice and video applications begin to suffer when the end-to-end delay exceeds 150 to 200 milliseconds. Poor-quality conversations, reminiscent of CB radio, are still possible within 400 milliseconds, and may be acceptable for some applications. A 200 to 400 millisecond delay will remove the nuances of emotion, but one rarely needs to give poetic directions to the warehouse on what part number to pull from the shelf.

People begin to notice delay at approximately 200 milliseconds. Fast typists of 120 words per minute press a key approximately every 400 milliseconds, so a delay of more than 600 milliseconds would lose the illusion of local typing.

Delay limits for transaction processing are far more subtle. Human factors studies on forms-oriented data entry showed that minimizing response time did not maximize productivity. For reasons not immediately apparent, clerks doing insurance data entry, with a forms-oriented mainframe application, were most productive when response time was between 1 and 3 seconds.

The reason for greater productivity over significant time, on the order of an hour, is that one- to three-second response time was noticeable without being extremely annoying. When the same operators had sub-second response times, they would type quickly and send their screens without pausing to look for typing errors, relying on the host for editing and validation.

Increasing the response time to 1 to 3 seconds was just noticeable enough that the operators would pause before entering the screen, and manually correct errors. With subsecond response time, the operator might reenter the screen several times until correct, decreasing the total number of correct screens entered per hour.

Jitter

Jitter is latency that varies from packet to packet, and can have critical impact on multimedia. As an example of the effect of jitter, compare the meaning of the two spoken phrases:

- "He is a very nice man."
- "He is a very [significant pause] nice [significant pause] man."

The ITU has defined objectives for jitter in multiservice networks as [ITU 1999] (see Table 3.1).

Loss Probability

While jitter is a major concern for multimedia, less so for interactive data applications, and has little effect on noninteractive traffic, packet loss is a quite different situation.

Up to this point, we have talked about delay as composed of serialization, propagation, and queueing components. Loss, however, introduces its own delays if the application expects reliable transmission and lost packets need to be retransmitted. Packets are not instantly retransmitted in classic TCP, but have to wait for a timer to expire.

Multimedia applications have paradoxical behavior with respect to loss. Human senses are wonderful things, and have the ability to interpolate content if part—not an excessive part—of a stream is missing. This is a Good Thing, because it is impractical to retransmit lost packets belonging to a stream.

A frequently quoted study by Jonathan Rosenberg, "Error Recovery for Internet Telephony," at the 1997 Voice over Networks conference, reported on experimental experience with human perceptions of packet loss in voice over Internet protocol (VoIP). These perceptions were measured by an established technique, *mean opinion score* (MOS), used to quantify telephone listeners' subjective experience (see Table 3.2).

Again, this is a subjective measurement. Telemarketers calling at dinnertime, even with a speech quality of 5, are very annoying and objectionable.

Table 3.1 Jitter Objectives

DEGRADATION CATEGORY	PEAK JITTER
Perfect	0 msec.
Good	75 msec.
Medium	125 msec.
Poor	225 msec.

Table 3.2 Speech Quality

MOS	SPEECH QUALITY	LEVEL OF DISTORTION
5	Excellent	Imperceptible. Toll quality
4	Good	Just perceptible, not annoying. Toll quality
3	Fair	Perceptible, slightly annoying
2	Poor	Annoying but not objectionable
1	Unsatisfactory	Very annoying, objectionable

SLAC interprets the unacceptable loss rate as corresponding to a total packet loss rate of 10–12 percent. Still, there is a suprisingly good tolerance for lost packets in voice, leading to the observation that it is more important not to delay or jitter voice packets than it is to drop them (see Table 3.3) [Cottrell 1999].

In Table 3.4, SLAC figures reflect a current environment that includes IP telephony and X/Windows. They interpret the loss rate for VoIP by assuming the VoIP packets are spaced 20 milliseconds apart, so 10 percent loss causes 2 consecutive frames to be lost approximately every 2 seconds, while 2.5 causes the same loss every 30 seconds.

VoIP runs over the *user datagram protocol* (UDP). Vern Paxson was quoted by Stanford Linear Accelerator Center (SLAC) as giving the conventional wisdom that 5-percent loss rates have a significant adverse effect on standard TCP. Effects become significant when loss rate exceeds 3 percent.

Table 3.3 Effect of Packet Loss on Voice

CUMULATIVE PACKETS LOST	MOS
1	4.2
2	3.2
3	2.4
4	2.1
5	1.7

Table 3.4 Loss Objectives

QUALITY	SLAC CURRENT	SLAC ORIGINAL	ITU	MCI TRAFFIC PAGE
Good	0-1	0-1	<3	<5
Usable	1-2.5	1-5	<15	<10
Poor	2.5-5	5-12	25	>10

What Interferes with Quality?

With the intense coverage of quality of service enforcement mechanisms, it's easy to lose track of the essentials of the problem. Quality of service first involves specifying certain performance objectives, and then involves mechanisms to be sure they are met. Sometimes, those objectives are not set realistically due to pure physical limitations. Let's begin by examining performance in a simple example, and then generalize to examine performance control in more complex examples. The two simple limitations on any service are the *serialization* and *propagation delays* of the medium. More complex issues arise from congestion, where more devices attempt to offer a greater load to the medium than the medium can handle. Congestion interacts with loss, because loss can be caused either by a transmission error or by the system having to drop the information because it is out of capacity. Congestion causes *queueing delay*.

A medium's capacity is expressed in bandwidth—the number of bits per second it can carry. Media are not perfect. Bits do not move instantaneously across media, and media may have transmission errors that cause some bits to be lost.

Often, the serialization delay in clocking bits onto the medium is the most significant, and most overlooked, part of total latency. Serialization delay is the reciprocal of bandwidth. Table 3.5 shows representative serial delays.

Once the bits are on the wire, they must move along the wire to the destination. This propagation delay is the product of the speed of light in the specific medium, and the length of the medium. For most terrestrial facilities, the propagation delay can be approximated as 6 microseconds per kilometer of airline distance between two reasonably distant points.

Table 3.5 WAN Serialization Delays (milliseconds)

FRAME LENGTH	BIT RATE				
	64,000	128,000	1,540,000	44,736,000	155,000,000
64	8.000	4.000	0.332	0.011	0.003
128	16.000	8.000	0.665	0.023	0.007
1,500	187.500	93.750	7.792	0.268	0.077

TIP

Within a metropolitan area (i.e., distances in blocks or a few miles), it's reasonable to assume the medium length is three times the line-of-sight distance between the endpoints. A multiplier of 3 is a fair approximation of the additional distance imposed by routing along streets, up and down poles, etc.

For short distances, serialization delay is far more important than propagation delay.

Figure 3.4 shows two hosts connected by a point-to-point WAN link with 64 Kbps of bandwidth. The goal is to send a 1,500-byte frame from source to destination. Host **cherry** is sending to host **grape**.

cherry cannot send data faster than the link speed. Converting bytes to bits, **cherry** will take (1500*8)/64000 seconds, or 188 milliseconds, to move the bits onto the wire.

Assume that **cherry** does not send continuously, but sends bursts to router **ginger**. **ginger**, as shown in Figure 3.5, sends traffic directly out the WAN interface when the WAN link is not busy; however, when the link is congested, **ginger** queues the data and schedules it for transmission when the link is again available.

To simplify this drawing, the router does not separate its input and output buffers, which would be characteristic of real-world devices.

Now, let's make the problem more realistic. In Figure 3.6, two hosts, **cherry** and **apple**, connect via a LAN to router **ginger**. Traffic to the outside will now go through two media, the LAN and the WAN. LAN

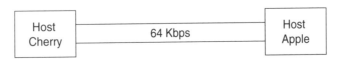

Figure 3.4 Basic quality of service.

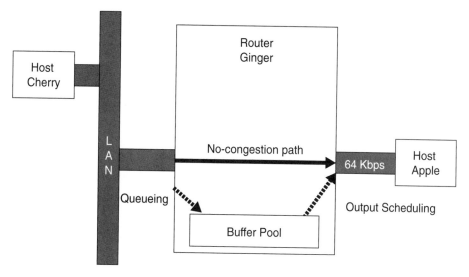

Figure 3.5   Basic router buffering.

delay usually will be far less than that of the WAN, but it is not zero. Serialization delay for a 1,500-byte Ethernet frame is 1.2 milliseconds (1,200 microseconds).

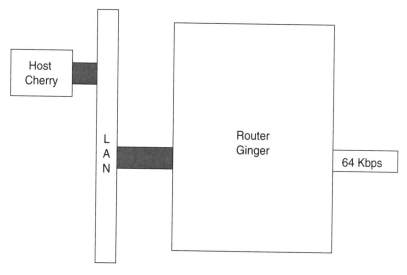

Figure 3.6   Opportunities for congestion.

The 64 Kbps dedicated link runs from **ginger** directly to the destination host. There are several ways to look at the performance characteristics of this situation.

NOTE

Assuming the router is doing no protocol conversion or other processor-intensive functions, in the absence of congestion, typical purpose-built routers have port-to-port transfer times of approximately 50–100 microseconds. Internal transfer times are rarely the major limiting factor in moderate-speed enterprise networks, since serialization delay is typically much larger than transfer delay.

Some router configurations may pause in their forwarding when they are processing routing updates. As speed increases, it becomes increasingly important to separate router processing into at least two tracks: *path determination* is the process determines maintains that updates the main routing table, the *routing information base* (RIB). The RIB is usually organized for speed of updating rather than speed of lookup.

The process of *packet forwarding* uses a *forwarding information base* (FIB), which is optimized for speed of lookup and is derived from the RIB. Path determination tends to use a general purpose RISC or CISC processor chip, while packet forwarding is more likely to use an application-specific integrated circuit (ASIC).

The FIB may have an entry for every entry in the RIB, or a subset of the RIB. If there is not one-for-one correspondence between the RIB and the FIB, forwarding may be delayed on some packets due to the need to retrieve a RIB entry and install it in the FIB.

There isn't one right way to use caching. In an enterprise with a single server site, there may not be that many routes. A 500-entry cache in the router at the major site may be quite sufficient to handle plausible sets of remote device. A 500-entry cache would be grossly inadequate for an internet core router.

A basic way to look at this situation is to divide the available bandwidth over the number of users. Dividing 64 Kbps by 2 gives 32 Kbps. When the line is busy sending a frame from **cherry**, **apple** encounters queueing delay waiting for the line to become available, assuming that **ginger** can hold **apple**'s transmission in a temporary buffer, shown in Figure 3.7.

Relays—routers or switches—can buffer either on input (i.e., before the routing decision is made) or output. In this example, we will deal with output buffering that takes place when the output WAN interface is busy (i.e., the associated medium is congested).

Buffering, or queueing, mechanisms have two parts. First, a queueing algorithm defines when traffic is placed in a queue rather than being sent to the original resource (e.g., the output interface). A scheduling

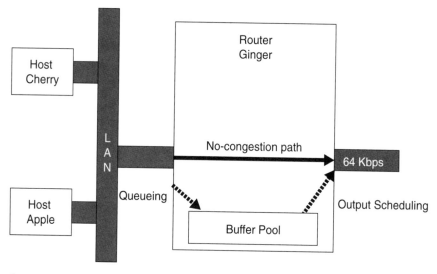

Figure 3.7 Buffering.

algorithm defines when to take traffic to be sent from a queue, and which queue to select if there is more than one.

Queueing Incoming Traffic

Early buffering implementations sent all traffic to the queues, until it was realized it seemed silly to delay traffic in queues if the output interface was available. Implementations then began putting traffic on a direct, not a queued, path when no congestion was present.

More recent implementations, however, add capabilities of *rate limiting* and *traffic shaping*, in which the fastest possible delivery is not the principal goal. The goal is that traffic comply with a Tspec, and, if it is arriving faster than the Tspec, it needs to be slowed.

In any case, queueing does not magically create bandwidth. In the absence of rate limiting requirements, if the bandwidth is lightly used (e.g., below 50 percent), it is quite likely that no link-level congestion will occur and packets would never queue.

Even in lightly loaded networks, queueing may be necessary to prioritize traffic, such as allowing voice packets to go ahead of data packets.

Scheduling Outgoing Traffic

Assuming that **ginger** has an infinite supply of buffers, **apple** and **cherry** will share the line. The line can be considered congested. Congestion occurs whenever the offered load is greater than the capacity of the resource that services the load.

In a pure world, there are only three ways to deal with congestion:

1. Decrease the offered load
2. Increase the resource capacity
3. Pray for divine intervention. St. Jude, the patron saint of lost and hopeless causes, is a good choice.

In the real world, a certain amount of congestion may be perfectly acceptable. Alternatively, much as airlines offer first class and coach, some traffic may receive different treatment when congestion exists. If **apple** is considered first class while **cherry** is in coach, the router might follow a strategy of always preferring **apple**'s traffic. With such a strategy, **apple** would be delayed at most by one of **cherry**'s frames.

Is this a realistic model? Refer to the general rule of networking design: it depends.

If both source hosts send constantly, the approximation of 32 Kbps is reasonable. Interactive applications, however, rarely send constantly. They are *bursty*. There is human "think time" between queries and responses. As the pauses between the transmissions of **cherry** and **apple** grow longer, the higher the probability that any given transmission will not have to wait for another transmission ahead of it.

Burst Traffic

With typical interactive traffic loads, it can be perfectly reasonable to have a potential load greater than the capacity of the outgoing link, a condition called *oversubscription*.

When the offered load exceeds the link capacity, but it is possible to buffer the entire load, we can say the offered load is within the *burst tolerance* of the relay-to-link system.

One of the effects of bursting is to cause *jitter*, or *variable delay*. A given workstation will transmit at random intervals. In Figure 3.8, the top case involves a stream of equal-length packets from one source. While the destination will encounter serialization and queueing delay, that delay should be constant.

In the next case, equal-length packets from two different sources are mixed in the buffer. The destination will see variable delay with respect to a single source. Queueing delay experienced by **apple's** destination depends on how much traffic was produced by **apple** and **cherry**. Introducing more local hosts will cause more variability, and scaling to large routing systems with tens of router hops and thousands or millions of hosts will certainly not make the delay less variable.

The next two cases in Figure 3.8 show how variable-length packets can make the delivery even more variable.

We'll deal shortly with the effects of jitter on real-time applications, and means for coping with it. Non-real-time applications are not as affected by jitter as real-time applications, although absolute delay can have an effect on the performance of non-real-time applications.

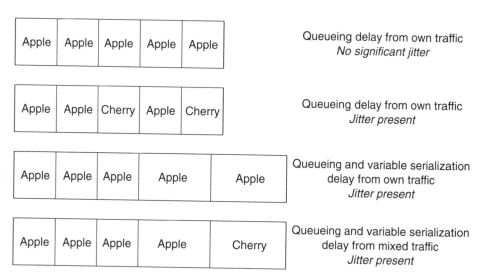

Figure 3.8 Jitter.

A More Complex Problem

Real-world networks are far more complex than the single-router example of the preceding problem. A packet will travel through many relays (i.e., layer 2 switches or layer 3 routers) along its path. The QoS implementation needs to influence the *per-hop behavior* (PHB) of each router or switch along the path. That doesn't mean, and generally should not mean, that every relay should be aware of the detailed *service level agreement* (SLA) for a given customer.

In complex networks, classification and marking should be done on the ingress devices. It is generally impractical to classify traffic in a high-speed path. Core relays are optimized to be big and fast, but not necessarily extremely intelligent. Returning to our dinosaur analogy in Chapter 1,"What Is the Problem You Are Trying to Solve?" they are tyrannosaurs, with edge devices in the role of the small mammals that depend on cunning and numbers for survival.

At each hop in the path, traffic can be buffered or dropped. Buffering can simply be intended to manage bursts, or it can use complex scheduling schemes to prioritize certain traffic, and to stabilize the rates of other traffic types.

Multiple Traffic Types

Now, assume that each host runs multiple applications: Voice over IP, internal web browsing, and electronic mail. Regardless of the machine that generated it, Voice over IP always must go out first. Internal web browsing has the next priority, and electronic mail the lowest priority.

Figure 3.9 shows some basic principles of dealing with multiple traffic types. With multiple traffic types, intelligence applies both to classification and scheduling. No more is it simply putting all the traffic into a single queue and scheduling transmission on a first-in-first-out (FIFO) basis. In general, it will service individual queues on a FIFO basis, but it may limit the amount of service given to a given queue at a given instant. See "Reactive Congestion Response" later in this chapter.

There are two parts to handling such traffic. First, traffic needs to be classified into categories for handling. Classification may actually mark the traffic, assign it to a specific queue, or both. Another action can be rate-limiting or shaping the traffic on input.

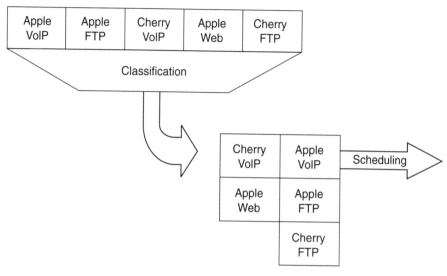

Figure 3.9 Multiple queues.

Second, the outgoing interface needs to schedule packets for transmission. In real implementations, if the outgoing interface is not busy and a single packet arrives, it is sent out without queueing.

Jitter, Fragmentation, and Dejittering

As mentioned previously, jitter is a serious impairment for multimedia applications. There are several potential causes for jitter, congestion being a basic one. Another source of jitter comes from variable serialization delay of packets that have different lengths.

In the real world, hosts tend not to send individual packets, but rather trains of packets. If the maximum packet payload is 1,500 bytes, but you are viewing a Web image file of 150 Kbytes, that download will form a train of 100 packets. Have you ever been driving, late to an appointment, get to a railroad crossing and have to wait for 100 train cars to pass?

These trains are actually an extreme case for Web applications themselves, which will usually adjust the TCP size so huge trains do not form. Still, bulk transfer applications such as FTP will try to use all the bandwidth they can. The problem may be less that HTTP itself forms long trains as that other protocol traffic creates trains that interfere with HTTP.

Depending on the scheduling algorithm, the router may try to send that entire packet train, or, to optimize throughput if a sliding-window transport protocol is used, send at least a full window. TCP windows are 64 Kbytes, so approximately 44 packets are needed to send the window. At 64 Kbps (see Table 3.5), it will take slightly more than eight seconds to send the window.

Tying up the interface for eight seconds is not necessarily a bad thing. If you are doing downloads, it will minimize overhead. If, however, you are doing anything interactive, there will be at least an eight-second pause in your interaction whenever a download window is being transferred. It would be one thing if such a pause, like a television commercial, were long enough and predictable enough to be used for bathroom breaks, but eight-second delays are simply frustrating.

Some scheduling mechanisms, such as *class based queueing* (CBQ), *weighted fair queueing* (WFQ), and *deficit round robin* (DRR), all discussed later in this chapter, limit the number of bytes sent from any one flow, in order to better share the medium among multiple flows. This is good when some of the traffic is interactive, but it is not particularly helpful for bulk data transfer.

Another approach is to reduce the MTU, encouraging fragmentation and limiting the number of packets sent by any flow—or by any retransmission. Reducing MTU is an extreme remedy that can be useful in tuning the retransmission performance of very slow, high-error rate, or long-delay paths. For a case using X.25, see "Reapplying Traditional Rules" in Chapter 4, "Basic Services."

At the other end of the speed range from typical X.25, ATM is an extreme case of fragmenting information to optimize interleaving among multiple flows, with its small fixed payload of 48 bytes. The purpose of cell fragmentation is to minimize latency and maximize interleaving, not to tune retransmission performance.

Medium congestion, packet training, different frame lengths, and transmission failures all affect jitter. Audio and video streams can be deferred in delivery, less so for interactive communications and more so for downloads. Once these streams are presented to the user, however, jitter must be minimized, or a graceful ballet dancer will transform into a lurching Frankenstein monster.

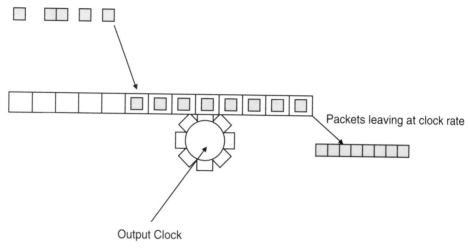

Figure 3.10   Dejittering.

A common approach to dejittering is shown in Figure 3.10. At the destination, traffic flows into a fairly large buffer at the actual, variable,
transmission rate. Think of this buffer as a conveyor belt. Packets are
clocked out of the buffer at a constant rate, producing a smooth stream.

Implementers are exploring different methods for dejittering. Traditionally, the basic mechanism was *leaky bucket*, or the constant-rate
clocking of bytes out of a buffer. Leaky bucket requires there to be a
sufficient backlog of delivered packets to allow a constant-speed output stream to run continuously. When using a video stream application such as RealPlayer, and the video display pauses with the
message "buffering," the application is pausing to get enough video
packets to be able to sustain a display stream of reasonable length.

Token bucket schemes are gaining popularity at the ingress and the
core, because they avoid the delay caused by buffering at intermediate
points. Leaky bucket is moving to destination nodes.

Statelessness, Soft State, and Hard State

The amount of information that a relay must store to manage QoS
varies with the mechanisms involved. There are high-level rules
derived from policies, and there may be additional information kept
on flows or aggregates of flows (see Table 3.6).

Table 3.6   Protocols and Degrees of Statefulness

	LAYER 3 AND "2.5"	LAYER 2
Stateless	IP precedence	IEEE 802.1p
Soft state	RSVP	
Hard state		ATM QoS Frame relay with QoS

Stateless mechanisms have no memory of prior packets. They assign each packet to queues, for example, based on information in the incoming packet.

Hard state mechanisms have a distinct connection phase in which resources are committed and a disconnection phase in which resources are released.

Soft state mechanisms establish relationships based on hearing a request, and require requests to be heard periodically for the relationship to continue. If no more requests are received in a certain interval, the relationship times out and resources are released. Some soft state protocols, such as the *resource reservation protocol* (RSVP) (discussed later in the chapter) and *Internet group management protocol version 2* (IGMPv2), do have optional explicit release mechanisms.

In dealing with congestion, the broad problem is congestion control. A subset of congestion control is flow control, which assumes a connection-oriented model in which the receiver has a known reverse channel by which it can restrain the source.

Flow control can be explicit or implicit. Explicit control, generally used in older protocols such as SDLC, X.25, and LAP-B, send *receiver not ready* (RNR) acknowledgements that indicate that the receiver properly received data, but desires that no further data be sent until the receiver sends *receiver ready* (RR). Typically, the receiver sends RNR because it detects an internal buffer shortage, either for inbound or outbound packets.

Implicit flow control, used by TCP, is based on the principle that death is nature's way of telling you to slow down. Classic TCP implementations assume that all packet loss is due to congestion. When a packet sent by a transmitter is not acknowledged, the transmitter assumes it was lost due to congestion, and slows the rate at which it sends [RFC2581].

TCP also will slow the rate at which it transmits when it detects a significant slowdown in the round-trip time for acknowledgments.

Merging

In an ideal world, the transport network would provide a precisely tuned path for every individual flow. In a real world, there is too much overhead associated with tracking flows to make large-scale per-flow handling a scalable solution.

Realistically, flows can be aggregated into service classes that have similar characteristics. Another way to look at grouping of flows that go to one exit point, such as the WAN connection of an enterprise site, is that they belong to the same *forwarding equivalence class* (FEC). FEC is the key idea of multiprotocol label switching (MPLS), further discussed in Chapter 4.

The differentiated services (diffserv) architecture defines *behavior aggregates* as "a collection of packets with the same codepoint crossing a link in a particular direction." [RFC2474]. See "Marking" later in this chapter for more detailed discussion of codepoints.

Multicasting inherently merges flows, so it is straightforward for a bandwidth reservation mechanism to reserve capacity in a multicast system.

Originally, the *resource reservation protocol* (RSVP) was developed to do bandwidth reservations for multicast flows; point-to-point RSVP support was a later addition. RSVP uses merging to avoid multiply committing identical bandwidth.

In Figure 3.11, the first receiver, **cinnamon**, to enter the multicast tree must reserve bandwidth on a path from itself back to the source, **ginger.** That path goes through **sesame.** When a second receiver, **garlic**, joins the multicast group, it only has to reserve the incremental bandwidth between itself and **sesame**, the merge point. **garlic** will use the bandwidth already reserved by **cinnamon**.

Source Behavior

Some QoS mechanisms make assumptions about the behavior of hosts, and you should consider both the protocol stack your hosts use and specific implementation behavior. Also, host-based measurement of QoS may measure host performance as much as network performance.

Urban Legends about Multicasts

"Broadcasts are huge consumers of bandwidth" is a rather common, and incorrect, statement throughout our industry. A broadcast or multicast packet takes up exactly as much bandwidth as a unicast packet of the same number of bytes.

It is true that broadcast storms consume significant bandwidth. Even in broadcast storms, the negative effect is as likely to be due to the host processing load in handling many broadcasts as it actually is to bandwidth starvation (assuming the hosts are connected to a fast LAN).

It is also true that some obsolete protocols, such as NetBEUI and NetWare 3.x, send frequent broadcasts as part of their resource location mechanism. Such broadcasts are acceptable with typical medium speeds of small LANs, the environment for which these mechanisms were developed. The bandwidth load is not inherently high simply because it consists of broadcast or multicast packets. Rather, the large load is due to the higher-level resource location protocol periodically sending information that is not needed.

Appropriately used, broadcasts and multicasts actually save bandwidth, when they are used as an alternative to sending multiple unicasts to a group of sources.

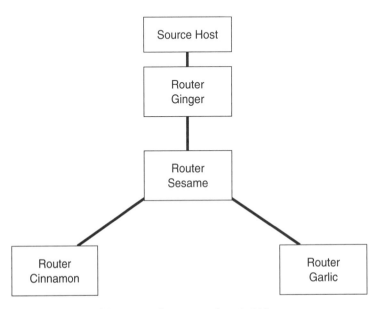

Figure 3.11 Multicast merging reuses bandwidth.

A nontrivial question to ask is, "Which host are you measuring?" Increased use of load distribution mechanisms are discussed in Chapter 5, "Virtualizing in Modern Networks," and Chapter 7, "Fault Tolerance."

A very basic distinction comes between TCP- and UDP-based stacks. UDP does not claim to have any intelligent response to congestion. As such, it is called *uncooperative* or *nonresponsive*, as are some improper TCP implementations. Correct TCP implementations are *responsive* to congestion.

TCP and Talking Camels

It is well known that TCP retransmits when packets are dropped, but it is less well known that TCP assumes packet loss is always due to congestion. In the absence of congestion, TCP will increase its transmission rate, in a manner reminiscent of the talking camel.

And so it is with TCP, which uses a *slow start algorithm* that starts with a minimal transmission rate, and increases that rate until it senses apparent congestion.

Simplifying its algorithm to make a point, TCP monitors the round-trip delay of acknowledgments. When this delay increases more than would be expected simply because more data is sent, the sender assumes mild congestion and slows the rate at which it transmits. When packets are lost, the sender resets its rate to zero, and then begins again to test the limits, much as did the camel.

The first issue to be aware of with TCP is that while TCP is intended to respond intelligently to congestion, individual implementations have been known to deliberately violate the congestion-response rules, in order to show "better throughput" than competing implementations. Such violation of implementation guidelines for commercial benefit is rather reminiscent of the real-world personalities of camels.

Second, TCP implementations may get into trouble at high speeds. The throughput of TCP is limited by the product of the bandwidth and the delay of the path [RFC 1323].

There is an assortment of experimental methods to improve the performance of basic TCP, such as selective acknowledgment. Rate control mechanisms, discussed under "Traffic Shaping Proxies," manipulate the TCP window size or delays ACKs rather than relying on end hosts.

Once Upon a Time

Once upon a time, a camel put his head into the camel driver's tent, and said, "Oh, kind and wise master. I want so much to help you, and obey you. Oh, I tried to obey you today, but failed. I realized the reason just now.

"It gets very cold in the desert at night, and I have large ears. When I tried to hear your honeyed words of wisdom today, my ears were cold from the previous night, and I could not hear you clearly.

"So tonight, oh kind and wise master, may I put my head in the tent and keep my ears warm?" The camel driver consented.

During the next day, however, the camel driver noted no difference in the camel's obedience. That night, however, the camel again put his head into the tent. "Oh, kind and wise master, who was so kind to me last night. I want so much to help you, and obey you. Oh, I tried to obey you today, but failed. I realized the reason just now.

"It gets very cold in the desert at night, and I have a long neck. When I tried to hear your honeyed words of wisdom today, my ears were warm from the previous night, but my neck was stiff and cold, and I could not twist it to hear you clearly.

"So tonight, oh kind and wise master, may I put my neck in the tent and keep it warm?" The camel driver consented.

During the next day, however, the camel driver noted no difference in the camel's obedience. That night, however, the camel again put his head into the tent. "Oh, kind and wise master. I want so much to help you, and obey you. Oh, I tried to obey you today, but failed. I realized the reason just now."

The camel began to wail, "It gets very cold in the desert at night, and I have a..." But the camel driver took that moment to kick the camel out of his tent, because he knew that if he continued to listen to the camel, it soon would be sleeping in his bed.

Non-Point-to-Point

When I first encountered QoS-critical applications such as streaming audio and video, I wondered why they ran over congestion-insensitive UDP. When I learned the answer, I was reminded of a professor who, on a Tuesday class, was merrily writing equations on the board, and commented about some obscure point, "It is obvious."

A student called out, "Professor, is that, in fact, obvious?"

The professor looked at the board, paused, and called "Class dismissed."

On Thursday, the class returned to find a haggard professor at the board, who certainly had not changed clothing and might not have slept at all. Turning to the class with a demented expression, the esteemed educator croaked out, "Yes! It is obvious!"

I have found that some things may be obvious once someone else points them out. It was not intuitively obvious to me that the applications in question had to run over UDP, because the application topology was point-to-multipoint, but TCP only supports point-to-point connectivity.

RFC 1889 specifies the real-time transport protocol (RTP), which imposes order on point-to-multipoint, QoS-sensitive traffic running over UDP. It does not guarantee QoS, but contributes to a QoS-supportive environment. This RFC defines another support protocol, Real Time Control Protocol, with the somewhat unfortunate acronym RTCP. RTCP is *not* a variant of TCP.

RTP packet headers contain timing and synchronization information that helps the receiver resequence or drop packets. At the receiver, packets will be queued in a dejittering buffer, and then replayed at a constant rate that reflects the sampling interval used to create the stream. The sampling rate is not in the fixed RTP header, but in a payload profile type identifier.

RTCP provides several functions that can be likened to the feedback of the acknowledgment process in traditional TCP. Feedback here does not mean retransmission, but more along the lines of TCP's rate adjustment based on round-trip time. First, RTCP verifies the data are indeed being distributed to the appropriate set of recipients. Second, it provides a name for source(s), so a receiver can link several related data streams, such as audio and video.

The RTCP packets are not simply sent to the source, but to all other participants in the group. This mechanism allows the participants to be aware of other participants. RTCP can also serve as a minimal communication among participants, such as conveying the identity of participants.

Traffic-Shaping Proxies

The previous section showed that TCP responds to congestion. A router-based mechanism described later, weighted fair queueing, uses selective discarding of TCP packets to implicitly flow-control the sending host. By causing the hosts to reduce the rate at which they send, congestion can be proactively avoided.

More sophisticated control of TCP performance can be provided with traffic-shaping devices such as the PacketShaper from Packeteer, Inc. *[Packeteer 1999]*. These devices manipulate TCP sessions in ways more subtle than selective discarding. They are installed between end hosts and an ingress router.

For example, selectively delaying acknowledgments will increase their round-trip time, eventually causing the TCP sender to slow its transmitting rate. Alternatively, the shaping device may simply try to equalize the acknowledgment times, to smooth out the transfer rate for a flow.

Connection admission control for TCP sessions becomes possible. The traffic-shaping device may reject a TCP connection request at the source if it knows there is congestion in the network or at the destination.

Yet another strategy is to have the packet shaper recognize when the network is not congested, and send an immediate ACK to the source to force it to send data in its buffers. In this scenario, if the transmitter waited until its window were full, it might then try to send a larger volume into a now-congested network.

Source and Destination Load Distribution

An apparent QoS failure may actually not be due to the network, but to host delays at the destination. Host delays can be true processing delays, or bottlenecks caused by the speed of the local interface into the server.

Packet shapers can look inside data streams and redirect traffic based on detailed flow characteristics, URL, etc. Packet shapers, however, may be too expensive for small sites. They also cannot look into encrypted packets. More distributed load sharing methods may be appropriate, such as intelligent DNS that directs a client to the least loaded and/or lowest routing cost server, or redirection in HTTP, FTP, or NFS. See Chapters 5 and 7.

Signaling QoS Requirements

Enterprises have a range of choices about QoS-enabled networking. They may take responsibility for end-to-end QoS, or they may contract with WAN service providers to support an agreed-to QoS at the WAN interface. There are three parts to defining a strategy:

- Developing the performance parameters of the service agreement.

- Deciding if all enterprise traffic is to be treated the same way, or if the enterprise needs to dynamically signal which traffic is to receive preferential treatment, by reserving resources or by marking packets.

- Enforcing the service agreement by limiting connections, buffering traffic, or dropping packets.

Whether the enterprise or the carrier is responsible for detailed QoS, the two must agree on how to recognize traffic that needs prioritized handling, and how to recognize traffic eligible to be deferred or dropped in the event of congestion.

Service agreements either need to be manually configured by the service provider, or need to be signaled by the enterprise to the provider. There are two basic approaches to signaling: setting up virtual circuits or other mechanisms to reserve resources, and marking individual packets.

Virtual circuits may be explicit, as in ATM, or soft state, as defined by the Resource Reservation Protocol. RSVP is independent of the underlying transmission system. QoS signaling is part of the ATM call setup mechanism.

Ingress relays can mark packets. The marking may be explicit, using the IP header's precedence field at layer 3. Cisco routers implemented pattern matching rules (i.e., access lists) that can set the precedence bits.

The IETF diffserv architecture redefines the Type of Service byte, dividing it into a 6-bit codepoint (DSCP) and 2 reserved bits. At layer 2, the IEEE 802.1p standard defines a 3-bit priority field similar to the IP precedence field. ATM LAN emulation version 2 (LANEv2) uses 802.1p conventions for virtual circuits.

Before delving into the mechanisms that send QoS requests, a philosophy of first asking, "what is the problem to be solved?" suggests that it is wise to look first at the QoS parameters that can be signaled, or how prioritized traffic can be identified.

Any protocol that allows preferences to be set needs an economic enforcement mechanism. If there are no consequences to requesting the highest priority, users are apt to do so. Inside enterprises, this enforcement mechanism can simply be imposed by top IP management. In the general Internet, there needs to be some mechanism for charging for preferred service, just as first-class airline tickets cost more.

QoS specification need not be quantitative. The Differentiated Service architecture provides a relative prioritization mechanism at layer 3, and 802.1P (now part of 802.1D) provides a layer 2 equivalent.

Whether or not you use ATM in your network, the ATM QoS parameters are a well-defined base for comparison. The IP Integrated Services parameters are used by RSVP.

Qualitative Marking

Historically, the Type of Service field in the IPv4 header was split into two parts: a 4-bit part indicating the optimization to be done in routing, and a 3-bit precedence field. Potential optimizations were defined as:

- Minimize delay
- Maximize reliability
- Minimize monetary cost
- Maximize throughput

These optimizations, however, proved to be a nice concept, but not terribly useful in reality. The 3-bit precedence field was intended for military applications.

The IEEE 802.1P LAN priority work defines a 3-bit field that goes into an appropriate protocol header. Each interface in the path can make shaping or dropping decisions based on this field.

It is far less processing intensive to make on-the-fly decisions on a small field than it is to make quantitative decisions. The general industry trend is to use DS or 802.1P in the core of a network, be it LAN or WAN. Quantitative session-oriented service is more an edge approach, with flows aggregated into categories that can be marked.

Codepoint(s) map to a "description of the externally observable forwarding treatment applied at a differentiated services-compliant node to a behavior aggregate."

Quantitative Description in ATM

ATM has always emphasized QoS, and its architecture provides a structure for QoS that is useful with other media as well. This structure divides service contracts into guaranteed service (GS) and best effort (BE). Service is "guaranteed" to the extent that animals are "equal" in Orwell's *Animal Farm*: "All animals are equal, but some are more equal than others." Guaranteed services cannot be guaranteed in the presence of severe carrier network disruptions. What is true about guaranteed services is that they always will be given preference to best-effort traffic.

Guaranteed services further divide into constant bit rate (CBR) and variable bit rate (VBR) services. Constant bit rate most commonly is used in the circuit emulation service (CES). CES provides a mechanism to aggregate individual DS1 and DS3, or E1 and E3, channels into an ATM network, but with end equipment still assuming it has a dedicated channel. Since the time slots of the virtual circuit are nailed, there should be little chance of congestion-induced jitter, Like a dedicated facility, CES provides a fixed sustained bit rate, and does not have additional burst capacity.

Use a Hammer when It's the Right Tool

When looking at requirements that need constant bit rates, do keep things in perspective. I had a client who insisted he needed ATM for a relatively small network. Perhaps making myself unpopular, I asked the sometimes embarrassing question, "Why?"

He responded that he needed constant bit rate service. When I asked how much bandwidth, he said "twenty four 64 Kbps channels". He responded with shock when I inquired, "Then why don't you just order a T1?" ATM may give the precision and power of a surgeon's scalpel, but sometimes a hammer is sufficiently precise—and much cheaper.

Always remember that ATM and SONET were developed as carrier, not user, technologies. For small organizations, if what you want can be met with a basic carrier offering, it may be far more cost effective for the carrier to do much of the provisioning. In larger organizations, there may be economies of scale in moving ATM and SONET into the enterprise.

BE services divide into *available bit rate* (ABR) and unspecified bit rate (UBR). UBR service truly is best effort; there is no QoS enforcement. ABR uses connection admission control.

Quantitative Description with Integrated Service

RSVP, discussed later, is actually a signaling mechanism that carries QoS requests. RSVP itself does not understand QoS values. Specification of the QoS parameters it carries is the task of a different IETF Working Group, Integrated Services.

Integrated Services defines two types of information: the traffic specification (Tspec) that indicates what traffic a network endpoint will generate, and the service request specification (Rspec) that defines the service being requested by the endpoint. The endpoint asks the network for a contract that meets the Rspec, and that the network need not honor if the endpoint violates the Tspec. If the endpoint subsequently sends more traffic than the contract covered, the network may police the traffic by delaying or dropping some of it.

Guaranteed Service

When a service is guaranteed, the provider is promising that packets will be delivered with an end-to-end delay less than or equal to the maximum latency defined in the Rspec. The provider also promises that packets will not be discarded because of congestion, as long as the rate of packets sent does not exceed the rate defined in the Tspec.

Guaranteed service is most appropriate for user services such as voice and video, where either the delays are significant, or where packets are useless if they arrive after some time interval or some event, such as the delivery of other packets. Guaranteed service minimizes jitter.

Late delivery of packets can be likened to a criminal confession being obtained just after the jury finds the defendant not guilty. Late delivery includes misordering packets. Video and voice are inherently streams—ordered sequences—and out-of-sequence packets change the meaning of streams.

A proper specification contains user-specified values, or implementation defaults, for the following parameters:

- **r** A floating-point rate measured in bytes per second, with an accuracy of at least 0.1 percent.

- **b** A floating-point bucket size.

- **n** A floating-point peak rate measured in bytes per second. It is the maximum rate at which the source, and any traffic shaping relays along the Path, can inject into the network. p must be greater than or equal to r.

- **m** An integer minimum policed unit (i.e., packet size).

- **M** An integer maximum policed unit.

By themselves, these parameters do not define the total end-to-end delay that will be experienced by a packet. They deal with queueing delays in network elements, not speed-of-light propagation delay between relays.

And You Thought You Had a Guarantee?

In Guaranteed Service, the maximum delay in the Rspec is no more and no less than what it is called. It is a maximum, not a mean or minimum. In real networks, the delay will usually be less than the maximum, and certainly will vary with traffic conditions.

When delay varies, jitter increases. Having GS does not free applications from the need for having dejittering buffers. Jitter can be cumulative through multiple router hops, so having dejittering—traffic shaping—on each router or switch in the path is preferred.

Pay attention to these parameters being described as maximums; they truly are. Many packets will arrive in less time than the maximum, potentially causing jitter unless they are buffered. The goal of buffering typically is to delay packets so they correspond to the maximum, trading speed against predictability.

Rspecs for guaranteed service contain:

- **R** A rate that must be greater than or equal to the Tspec rate r. The rate is represented as a bucket and a peak rate.

- **S** A slack term measured in microseconds, which is the difference between the desired delay and the delay obtainable with a reservation of rate R.

Sometimes the Whole Is Not Equal to the Sum of Its Parts

Because policing operates on packets of a specific size range, $\underline{m}$ to $\underline{M}$, IP fragmentation along the path could throw off policing assumptions. To avoid fragmentation, use dynamic MTU path discovery, or define an MTU that will not be fragmented, and have that value returned with DHCP responses.

Remember that tunneling along the path can add overhead bytes, leading to fragmentation on maximum-length packets. For example, if you only considered the MTU of the host, but the path included an IPsec gateway, the MTU must be further decreased to consider the additional header overhead of IPsec.

Best-Effort Services

IP was developed as a best-effort (BE) service, in which the protocol does not guarantee delivery or QoS. In the original architecture, if reliable delivery was needed, appropriate retransmission needed to be done at the transport layer (e.g., TCP) or higher layers (e.g., RPC).

Best effort simply means that bandwidth has not been reserved for the traffic. Within best effort, there certainly can be different classes of service. Regardless of the class, packets will reach their destination if the medium is error free and has adequate bandwidth.

I cannot make the point strongly enough: QoS enforcement does not create bandwidth when none exists. QoS enforcement can resolve conflict for bandwidth by giving preference to some classes and degrading the performance of other classes.

If the performance of a network is monitored closely, and additional bandwidth is provisioned before links become significantly congested, best effort can indeed be a very high quality. Best effort in the context of the public Internet, however, is not likely to be of high quality, because there is no one organization responsible for assuring adequate bandwidth between arbitrary endpoints.

BE services can be mixed with reserved-bandwidth services. Consider, for example, Cisco's implementation of RSVP. Many people accept the idea that this implementation defaults to committing 75 percent of the bandwidth on an interface to RSVP GS traffic. They have more difficulty realizing that default means that 25 percent of the bandwidth will be committed to BE. See Figure 3.12.

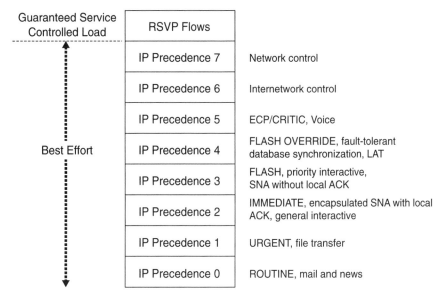

Figure 3.12 Highest priority BE gets bandwidth.

Some BE traffic, therefore, will always go through. You can use qualitative QoS enforcement to prioritize critical traffic—network management and real-time voice/video—so that traffic will always get through.

Do be aware of the specific vendor defaults when mixing GS and BE. In the Bay RS enterprise router operating system, Nortel, for example, defaults to 100 percent of the bandwidth being assigned to RSVP, but that percentage can be decreased. Cisco IOS defaults to 75 percent.

Controlled-Load Service

Controlled-load service, defined in RFC 2211, is intended to support adaptive real-time applications. It is an alternative to GS, which remains appropriate for intolerant real-time applications. Roughly speaking, controlled load is intended for the class of applications for which ATM VBR would be appropriate, while GS would be the layer 3 equivalent of ATM CBR.

Ferguson and Huston [Ferguson 1998] call it "better-than-best-effort" delivery, or, effectively, the behavior of a BE service in an unloaded network. The service will have low latency and packet loss, but will have more jitter than GS. It will use less resources than GS.

In controlled-load service, as long as the originating host complies with the Tspec, the probability of losing packets due congestion should be negligible. Also, most packets will not encounter queueing delay. The delay encountered should be comparable to transmission and propagation of the media comprising the path, plus the internal delays of routers along that path.

If the Tspec is exceeded, service may degrade dramatically.

QoS Setup

Once you have defined what you want, you need to establish service contracts for the specific traffic. This may simply be an administrative agreement between customer and provider, or it may involve mechanisms to indicate which subsets of the customer traffic should be handled in a given manner.

Best current practices for networks recognize that scalable design involves different techniques at the edge and the core. Different policies will be needed in the edge and core, and appropriate QoS enforcement mechanisms selected.

The most important mechanism at the edge is packet classification: recognizing the type of information so appropriate PHB can be enforced on each relay in the path. Hosts can also mark traffic they originate, but must be trusted to do so.

When ingress relays classify traffic, they most commonly do so by matching some protocol fields of the incoming information. Other methods of classification depend on traffic volumes exceeding some predefined threshold.

Be careful in reserving bandwidth for data applications, because end-to-end flow control may suffice to avoid congestion. Typically, the applications most appropriate for reserved bandwidth are multimedia: voice and video. Application-level server synchronization is a data application that might well justify reserved bandwidth. Only the most critical user data traffic should receive reserved bandwidth. It is generally much better to assign critical user data to a high best-effort priority than it is to guarantee service.

Once traffic is classified, it can be marked to tell the network how to handle it. *Coloring* is another widely used term equivalent to marking.

Marking Mechanisms

Marking is usually thought to involve setting bits in a protocol header, but a logical equivalent to marking each unit of data is assigning it to a virtual circuit that has been established with the appropriate quality of service (see Table 3.7). For example, the differentiated services architecture sets the IP precedence bits in the IP header. Flow-based reservations in IPv6 set a flow identifier field.

Virtual circuits may be used for aggregates of flows, or for individual flows. If a virtual circuit will be created for each new flow, another QoS control mechanism can come into play. An end host or ingress router can request that a virtual circuit can be created, but if there are insufficient resources in the core to provide the desired service, the network can deny the connection request. Limiting VC establishment to those that can be created without exceeding resources is called *connection admission control* (CAC).

Explicit Marking in Differentiated Services

The diffserv architecture developed by the IETF is based on marking using the 3-bit precedence field in the header of IP packets. In practice, the highest priorities are reserved for network management and for reserved-bandwidth flows, allowing traffic to be classified into five categories.

Routers can shape or drop traffic based on the diffserv field.

Simply setting high priority does not mean that it will be honored in the general Internet. Today's reality is that differentiated services in the WAN can be provided by contract with service providers that take end-to-end responsibility. When such providers do not have geographic presence along the desired path, they must contract for differentiated service with other appropriate providers.

Table 3.7 Marking Mechanisms

	LAYER 3 AND "2.5"	LAYER 2
Explicit	IP precedence RSVP ID IPv6 flow	IEEE 802.1p
Implicit	MPLS	ATM QoS Frame Relay with QoS

In an intranet or extranet with WAN connections, diffserv can be deployed today. Do remember that diffserv is not a substitute for adequate bandwidth. If, for example, you have voice and Web services, and voice is prioritized over Web traffic, Web traffic will be delayed. The more voice, the more delay.

Explicit Marking in VLAN

A common format, originally defined by IEEE 802.1p, defines marking for both IEEE LANs and ATM LANEv2 ELAN setup. The actual signaling of this mechanism uses Tagged Frames as defined in IEEE 802.1q. The tag contains a 3-bit priority field and a VLAN identifier.

Tags are used both internally in bridges, and on media that support multiple priority levels. When used internally, the priority value of a tag can be used to define output queueing priorities.

It is far easier to respond to tag values than it is to set them appropriately. There are two basic alternatives: having the host set 802.1p bits, and setting them on an ingress switch.

To set them on a host, the host must have software drivers that are aware of 802.1p and are able to set priority bits. Drivers alone do not solve the software problem; applications must be QoS aware to pass the appropriate requests to the driver, or the driver needs to be able to distinguish among applications and set the priority. When the host has the appropriate software, it also must be trusted to request appropriate priorities.

To set them on an ingress switch, the switch needs criteria for appropriate marking. A simplistic approach of setting priority on a per-physical-port basis might work in some specific cases, such as prioritizing IP telephony ports over general workstation ports. If the same port, however, has different kinds of application traffic, the problem becomes more difficult.

Regardless of where these bits are set, how is the priority knowledge used in the WAN? An ingress router with appropriate software can transfer them to the IP diffserv field, or use them to select an output interface.

Remember that a basic switch has layer 2 awareness. If the desired server is on the same subnet, the switch can set priorities based on destination MAC address. If the server is on a different subnet, however, the switch only knows the MAC address of the first-hop router, and cannot consider the final destination.

Of course, if the "switch" has awareness of higher layers, it can consider final destination or even ports. Repeat after me: A switch that has layer 3 awareness is a router, regardless of what marketing image it has. If the "switch" has this level of intelligence, it can reasonably be asked whether 802.1p makes sense at all, when more flexible mechanisms such as RSVP and diffserv presumably are available.

A stronger case can be made for using ATM QoS, especially with *multiprotocol over ATM* (MPOA), because there is awareness of the final destination. On the other hand, ATM is more expensive than Ethernet.

Implicit Marking in LANE v2 QoS and MPLS

Where 802.1p clearly is a campus technology, the underlying ATM will run in the WAN. One of the enhancements in Version 2 of ATM LAN Emulation (LANEv2) is multiple classes of service. Up to eight classes of service can be defined, marked in a 3-bit field using 802.1p conventions. Separate ATM virtual circuits between LAN Emulation Clients are associated with different priorities.

The VCs leading from the LEC use regular ATM service classes and parameters, such as CBR and ABR, SCR and CDV. The precise method by which packets are given priorities is implementation-specific.

Like any other technology, QoS-enabled LANEv2 has scaling limits. One consideration is that real ATM devices, such as the LEC, can handle finite numbers of VCs, and adding QoS multiplies the number of VCs required by the topology by the number of service classes.

Resource Reservations: Requirements, Realities, and the Future

Using the RSVP [RFC2208], ingress routers and trusted end hosts can request bandwidth reservations. RSVP allocates bandwidth in one direction, so IP over voice, for example, would need to do RSVP requests in each direction. The internals of RSVP also require that the path over which bandwidth is requested must be the same path, when reversed, over which the bandwidth is granted.

RSVP can set up its own allocations among routers, which will classify traffic by flow identifier. RSVP also can be used as a signaling protocol for setting up MPLS label-switched paths.

RSVP gives finer granularity than diffserv, but is not as scalable, for that very reason. The more reservations on which a router must keep state, the more workload on the router's processor. The IETF applicability statement for RSVP [RFC2208] suggests it is more appropriate to use RSVP at the edges of networks, and aggregate the RSVP flows into a form that imposes less overhead on high-capacity backbone devices. In practice, that aggregation means either to mark RSVP traffic as associated with a diffserv category, to create MPLS paths, or to map it to ATM virtual circuits with appropriate service contracts.

Its capability for fine granularity makes RSVP a natural approach for hosts, although it can be initiated between routers. RSVP is unidirectional, so setting up interactive two-way sessions requires separate reservations in both directions. Setting up multicast distribution with RSVP needs reservations for each participant. Multicast flows can be merged, as discussed later in the chapter.

While RSVP is a client/server protocol, the roles of clients and servers within it can be somewhat confusing. RSVP senders send **PATH** messages in the direction of potential receivers, indicating that the sender is offering a particular flow. No resources are reserved in this process, although the sender does maintain awareness of the source host's Tspec.

When a receiver wants to receive a flow, it sends a **RESV** message to the sender. This message follows the reverse path back to the source, reserving capacity at each hop, or discovering that capacity does not exist. Readers familiar with the explorer process in source route bridging will see a certain similarity. Be aware that RSVP has an implicit assumption that routing is symmetrical: If a path exists between a sender and a receiver, RSVP assumes that the reverse of that path, from receiver to sender, has the same latency characteristics.

Be careful not to assume RSVP does more than it actually does. People often complicate it by assuming that RSVP contains functions actually performed by other protocols, or that they are functions within Integrated Services. RSVP does not understand the semantics of the parameters it passes.

RSVP does not create formal connections. It uses a soft state model, in which the **RESV** messages must periodically be retransmitted by the receiver to maintain the resource reservation. When no longer interested in a flow, the receiver can simply let the reservation time out, or send an explicit teardown.

RSVP is not a routing protocol, but it will be able to cooperate with QoS-aware routing protocols under development. See [Durham 1999] for a much more detailed discussion of RSVP.

Issues in Marking Traffic on Hosts

Before implementing host marking, think through the issues of how the hosts will mark. It will probably be more difficult for LAN-connected hosts to obtain end-to-end QoS if they rely on layer 2 mechanisms for marking. The issue here is that the layer 2 information may not transfer to the WAN access devices. Marking traffic at layer 3, however, avoids the layer 2 issues.

Trust policy applies to host marking. Within an enterprise, letting the hosts set these parameters often is reasonable, because a central administrator can enforce policies. In a public environment, or in a less-controlled enterprise such as a university, the ingress relay should either check to see if host-set parameters are allowed, or simply override them with its own settings.

Host marking is not a simple matter of having appropriate layer 2 or layer 3 support in the interface drivers. Applications on the hosts need to be aware that they can request QoS. If the applications are not QoS aware, it will generally be easier to mark traffic on an ingress switch or router.

Recent releases of most end host operating systems support RSVP requests, but a lesser number of applications are QoS aware. With Microsoft systems, NetMeeting is one RSVP-aware application that can be used for testing.

Issues in Marking Traffic on Ingress Relays

Marking traffic by ingress switches and routers is often more flexible than marking it on end hosts. Traffic-marking functions are more widely implemented on routers than on hosts, although Windows 2000 adds marking, With router-based marking, the problem of applications not knowing how to request the QoS features in their hosts disappears.

Ingress relays can aggregate similar traffic into virtual circuits, reducing the total number needed. Remember that while ATM, for example, provides a large VC identifier space, real interfaces have finite table sizes for VC identifiers.

Enforcing QoS

Once traffic is classified, there are several broad mechanisms for enforcing QoS:

Connection admission control (CAC). Preventing sessions from being created if there are insufficient network resources to give the needed quality. CAC implies some type of stateful mechanism that controls connection establishment, such as hard state (e.g., ATM) or soft state (e.g., RSVP).

Dropping or policing. Discarding within a traffic stream in accordance with the state of a corresponding meter enforcing a traffic profile.

Shaping. Delaying packets that arrive at a rate faster than specified by the traffic profile. Perfect shaping assumes infinite buffers, and a flow that constantly exceeds the traffic profile will eventually begin to have its packets dropped.

The intention of this discussion is to give you sufficient information to select mechanisms that can carry out your QoS policy, at the speeds you will use. Detailed discussion of the algorithms is beyond the scope of this book; they will be described only to the extent needed to understand their capabilities. See Ferguson & Huston [1998 #348] and the technology-specific RFCs and Internet Drafts.

The techniques just discussed are appropriate for the edge of the network. Other techniques, which are less processor intensive, are useful both at the edge and in the core.

Not all mechanisms are appropriate for the multimedia traffic becoming increasingly more important on modern networks [Cisco 1999a]. Other mechanisms can provide the prioritized handling needed for multimedia traffic, but only at low speeds.

Reactive Congestion Response

There are two fundamental approaches for dealing with congestion on relays. Reactive methods prioritize outgoing traffic in the presence of congestion. Proactive methods either limit transmission rates within a well-designed traffic engineering model, so critical network elements cannot be congested, or impose implicit flow control on TCP transmitters.

As the industry moves to gigabit speeds, certain congestion-handling strategies are inherently too slow. Methods first developed in the 1980s reflected the routers of their time: Path determination, packet forwarding, and traffic management all took place in a general-purpose processor. To operate at gigabit rates, it is necessary to select algorithms that can operate in ASICs or at least specialized processor modules.

FIFO

First-in-first-out queueing does not prioritize traffic. It may be appropriate when all traffic has the same priority, is bursty, and the concern is avoiding packet loss. Latency, of course, will increase when bursts of traffic are buffered.

Preemptive Queueing

When some traffic absolutely, positively, must go through, preemptive queueing can be a straightforward solution. Both Nortel and Cisco call this method priority queueing.

Preemptive queueing is a relatively old technique, developed when router forwarding was done in the main processor. It does not scale well to gigabit-rate hardware routing.

The basic policy of preemptive queueing is to establish three or four queues ranging from high priority to low priority. In the presence of congestion, incoming packets are placed in one of the queues, according to predefined filters. Typical filtering rules include destination address and TCP/UDP port number. If a given queue is full, the packet is dropped.

Priorities assigned are implicit in the assignment to a queue. Preemptive queueing does not set IP precedence bits.

When the scheduler transmits a packet, it looks for the next packet to send. Assume, for this example, there are three queues: high, medium, and low. If one or more packets are in the high-priority queue, the first-in will be sent by the scheduler. After sending the packet, the scheduler will again check the high-priority queue. As long as packets are in this queue, the overall policy will simplify to FIFO for the high-priority queue only.

Regardless of priority, queues have finite capacity. If the high-priority queue has 20 slots, and a 21st packet arrives, that packet will be dropped under the principles of tail drop. Even if there were slots in lower-priority queues, it would do no good to put the 21st packet into the medium-priority queue. If there is enough traffic to overfill the high-priority queue, it is a safe assumption that medium and low priorities are not being serviced at all.

Even if the medium and low priorities were being serviced, putting traffic of the same priority into different queues is likely to result in out-of-order packet delivery. While some transport protocols can reorder packets, order should be preserved whenever possible.

Preemptive queueing is a Darwinian survival of the fittest, fitness defined as the priority set by packets. It can solve political as well as technical problems, although in a coarse manner. Think of an enterprise that is merging its IP intranet with its previously separate IBM SNA network. SNA is intolerant of delay, and of variability in general. SNA was architected for an environment where it controlled all resources.

Class-Based Queueing

Class-based queueing is intended to share a channel fairly, guaranteeing a minimum bandwidth to each class of traffic. It is the opposite of traffic shaping, discussed later, which guarantees maximum bandwidth.

Nortel calls it *bandwidth queueing*, and Cisco calls it *custom queueing*. In common implementations, the major limitation is that you need to have a good knowledge of packet length statistics to configure CBQ properly.

The *enqueueing algorithm* uses filters to categorize traffic as belonging to a class. An implementation establishes a set of queues, one per class, each of which is assigned a fraction of the available bandwidth. This fraction represents a guaranteed minimum bandwidth for the class when there is traffic for that class. Nortel specifies this fraction as a percentage of the bandwidth, while Cisco specifies it as a byte count.

The appropriate number of queues is controversial. Greater numbers of queues gives finer granularity and the ability to fine-tune allocations, but increasing the number of queues also increases the delay before any given queue is serviced. In enterprise-oriented routers, which do not do classification in hardware, Cisco currently supports up to 16 user classes, while Nortel has three standard classes. When hardware assistance becomes involved, Cisco reduces the number of classes to four or eight, while Nortel carrier routers have eight classes.

The scheduling algorithm begins by checking the high-priority queue for packets. If packets are present, it transmits packets until the bandwidth allocation is exhausted.

Deficit Spending

As long as the allocation has a positive value, packets are transmitted. This can lead to unfair use of bandwidth. Assume, for example, that a given queue has a 1,000-byte allocation. The packets in the class are 400 bytes long.

When the first packet is sent, the remaining allocation is 600. Sending the second packet reduces the allocation to 200. Since there still is a positive allocation, the third packet is scheduled and sent.

It would be silly to stop sending in the middle of the third packet, since that certainly would preclude useful transmission. Nevertheless, that the third packet entered the queue and overfilled the allocation means that this queue received, in this cycle through the queues, a 1,200-byte allocation.

Different policies are possible when a queue goes into negative or *deficit* allocation. The implementation can ignore the deficit and restore the allocation on the next cycle, which will give more bandwidth to the queue than was intended.

Alternatively, the implementation can remember the negative value and add the next allocation to it, limiting the number of bytes sent for that class in the next cycle. Doing this will make the traffic more bursty, as it oscillates between deficit and restrained cycles.

After the highest-priority class is serviced, the scheduler checks the next priority class. If there is traffic in that queue, it is transmitted until its allocation is exhausted. If there is no traffic in queue, the queue is skipped and its bandwidth effectively spread among the nonempty queues.

The algorithm continues to move down the list of queues, servicing each until empty or their allocation is used up. After the lowest-priority queue is serviced, the algorithm returns to the highest-priority queue and starts a new cycle.

Weighted Fair Queueing

Weighted fair queueing (WFQ) is actually a method that is achievable theoretically but not practically. The actual methods used include self-clocked weighted fair queueing and other variants, but WFQ is the term used for simplicity.

Basic WFQ operates on a simple yet surprisingly accurate assumption. Interactive applications tend to involve small volumes of traffic, while noninteractive traffic tends to involve large volumes. WFQ tracks flows and calculates their volume, and, when the output interface is congested, sorts the packets into two queues.

The high-priority queue holds low-volume flows that presumably are interactive traffic, while the low-priority queue holds high-volume flows. When the output scheduler sends a packet, it checks the high-priority queue and sends the next packet. The high-priority queue will be serviced as long as there are any packets in it.

Only after the high-priority queue is empty is the low-priority queue checked. After sending a low-priority packet, the scheduler again checks the high-priority queue and services it until it is empty. When the high-priority queue is empty, the next flow in the low-priority queue is serviced, and the high-priority queue checked again.

The technology is still emerging. Cisco, for example, introduced WFQ in IOS Version 11.0, using the basic two-category model discussed earlier. In IOS Version 11.2, WFQ became IP-precedence aware, with a larger number of queues. Cisco deemphasized WFQ to some extent when it introduced IP RTP Priority in IOS 12.0(5)T, which allows a strict high priority to be set by voice, and then prioritize other traffic in *class-based WFQ* (CBWFQ).

By combining IP RTP prioritization and CBWFQ, you can have WFQ for nonvoice/video flows while maintaining a separate, high-priority queue for delay-intolerant flows.

Round-Robin Algorithms

Round-robin algorithms lend themselves to high-speed hardware processing, and have the potential of operating at gigabit rates. The major versions used in WAN applications are deficit round robin (DRR) and modified deficit round robin (MDRR).

DRR is, in many respects, an improvement on CBQ, both in delivering smoother packet streams and in being hardware-assisted. It defines a set of queues, each with a *service quantum* similar to the byte counts of CBQ [Shreehar 1995]. The service quantum, indeed, is specified in bytes.

Traffic is usually placed in queues based on the value of the IP precedence field after the packets are marked on edge devices.

Unlike CBQ, the DRR algorithm knows the packet lengths before they are serviced, and will not service a packet if its length exceeds the remaining credit available.

Basic DRR is fair, and, as such, may not give the appropriate priority to multimedia traffic. A variant called modified deficit round robin (MDRR) establishes a high-priority queue separate from the queues serviced in round-robin order. When there are packets in the high-priority queue, that queue is serviced until empty. The round-robin queues wait on the high-priority traffic.

MDRR queues also can have WRED applied to them. See the section "Random Early Detect."

It may also be appropriate to rate-limit the high-priority queue so it does not starve the round-robin queues. Another variation of MDRR, called *fair priority*, alternates between servicing the high-priority queue and the set of round-robin queues. This variation gives the potential for every other packet to be a high priority, but the remaining packets will come from the diffserv queues.

The algorithm begins by enqueueing packets based on IP precedence, into a set of eight queues. Each queue starts with a *deficit counter* value of zero, to which the service quantum is added.

Much as in CBQ, the queues are serviced in round-robin order. DRR does allow a packet to be sent as long as the deficit counter is nonzero, but always adds the negative deficit to the service quantum on the next cycle.

Proactive Congestion Management

Football analysts say that the greatest athletic ability is needed on defense, not offense, because defensive players have to react and make on-the-fly decisions. Reactive congestion management is defensive, only starting after there is a problem.

Proactive methods try to keep congestion from occurring. Some, such as overprovisioning, involve brute force. Other mechanisms, such as Random Early Detect, are almost fiendishly subtle.

Overprovisioning

A Navy adage says "If it doesn't fit, get a hammer. If it still doesn't fit, get a bigger hammer." At a time when the costs of bandwidth continue to drop, the appropriate hammer may simply be to provide much more potential bandwidth than seems necessary, keep utilization low, and thus avoid congestion.

While this approach is simple, it is intuitively repellent to financial people. General George Patton once suggested that his supply people would only have been happy if the European campaign had ended with the last resisting enemy soldier being shot with the last bullet in the inventory. Financial people tend to want expensive resources to be utilized fully. They need to see the potential cost savings of simplified operation and better customer satisfaction, not only the loss of revenue from overprovisioning.

Overprovisioning is not a panacea. It does not actually guarantee bandwidth, and needs continued monitoring to be sure that adequate bandwidth is available as user demand increases.

Selective Overprovisioning at the Edge

Overprovisioning makes the most sense in campus networks, where the incremental cost of adding fiber is minimal. To avoid repetitive labor cost, a good rule is to install three times the number of fibers needed for the current requirement.

It is not unreasonable, however, to overprovision from the enterprise edge to the WAN POP, and then traffic engineer from the POP into the core. Reason must enter into such a strategy.

Realities of the physical layer become involved very early. With traditional T1 and E1 technology, once the edge bandwidth requirement is greater than 64 Kbps, it becomes necessary to install a physical T1/E1 even if only a fraction of it is used. In like manner, there is an incremental point, which varies with local conditions, at which it stops being cost effective to add T1s for substantial bandwidth, and begins to make sense to install a T3.

Selective Overprovisioning in the Core

Economies of scale do enter the provisioning paradigm at the core tier. Once fiber is in the ground, it offers a tremendous upgrade path by fork-lift upgrades of optoelectronic equipment at the ends. SONET, for example, moved from OC-3, to OC-12, OC-48, and now OC-192. DWDM allows multiple OC-192s to be multiplexed onto single fiber, with aggregate bandwidth over a terabit (Tbps, 10^{12}) and continuing to grow, so advanced planning documents are even talking about petabit (Pbps, 10^{15}).

Getting fiber into the ground, and keeping it from being cut by new construction, is not trivial in effort or investment. The bottleneck, however, seems less in the capacity of the medium, but of the capacity of optical cross-connects and routers in major carrier switching centers.

Connection Admission Control

Think of driving in rush hour. You are approaching a busy intersection, and the driver in front of you, whom we will henceforth refer to as "that idiot," insists on entering the intersection during a yellow light. Of course, the light changes and gridlock ensues. The idiot would explain his actions by saying "well, the yellow light was advisory."

Now, think of a freeway on-ramp that has a "one car per green" light that controls the rate at which individual cars can enter the shared freeway. Such lights are controlled by traffic monitors that apply queueing theory to measurements of the capacity of the road.

Connection admission control is like the freeway ramp rather than the less controlled intersection. It enforces a policy that it is better to deny access to some users than to give poor service to all.

ATM supports CAC for some, but not all, service classes, using hard connections. Real-world implementations depend on the combination of Q.2931 setup and private network-network interconnection (PNNI) QoS-aware routing to see if a given call should be admitted.

RSVP also performs CAC, although using a soft state model. In its soft state model, reservation requests are issued periodically. If resources are not available, the request is denied.

Traffic Policing and Shaping

CAC operates at a macro level, only allowing connections to be established if there are sufficient resources. When there is no CAC, or when there is a need for enforcement after a connection is made, traffic policing and shaping comes into play.

The most common way of specifying criteria for policing and shaping is to state a sustained data rate and a peak rate, and then define what to do when either of these levels is exceeded.

One basic technique, *single leaky bucket*, is used when there is a policy that individual flows can arrive at the input interface at varying rates, but will be clocked out at a steady rate. The usual assumption is that a FIFO discipline will be used. Conceptually, the bucket overflows when the sum of flows fills it, but the leaky bucket can be taken down to the level of granularity of specific flows. Bursts are handled by the capacity of the bucket. If the bucket overflows, traffic will be dropped (see Figure 3.13).

A more complex technique, called *double leaky bucket* or *token bucket*, gives greater control. Like single leaky bucket, flows enter the first

Characteristically
Varying Flows

Leaky Bucket

FIFO
Queue

Fixed Transmit
Rate

Smoothed Traffic
Flows

Figure 3.13 Single leaky buckets smooth flow and discard excess.

Source: P. Ferguson and G. Huston. (1998) *Quality of Service.* New York: John Wiley & Sons.

bucket at variable rates. The "leaks" at the bottom of this bucket correspond to the sustained data rate (see Figure 3.14).

Traffic over the sustained limit, but below the burst limit, can be sent only when the bucket receives tokens from the second bucket. Think of the bottom of the bucket as having faucets rather than holes. These faucets are spring-loaded so they constantly let water data flow at the sustained rate. Tokens open the faucets wider, and, when there are no more tokens available, the faucet snaps back to the sustained-flow position.

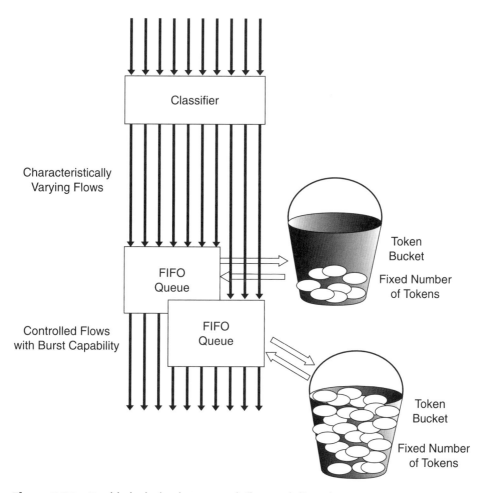

Figure 3.14 Double leaky buckets smooth flow and discard excess.

Source: P. Ferguson and G. Huston. (1998) *Quality of Service.* New York: John Wiley & Sons.

In both single and double leaky bucket schemes, the bucket has finite capacity. Traffic beyond the burst rate overflows the bucket and is discarded.

Random Early Detect

Have you ever seen one of the classic "lifeboat" movies, in which there are too many shipwrecked survivors for the capacity of the lifeboat, and a steely-eyed hero must make the decision of who lives or dies? Random Early Detect and its variants have distinct similarities to lifeboat movies, except that they have happy endings.

To understand the basic technology, assume a single lifeboat...er...queue. RED monitors the number of packets in this queue, as a fraction of its total capacity. It is aware which packets belong to which flows.

There is a low limit of total capacity at which RED takes no action: The lifeboat has enough space for all. There is a high limit at which RED drops all incoming packets: The lifeboat capsizes. Between those lifeboats, the boat officer, Captain Red, takes action.

Captain Red takes out a large revolver, and loads it with a single cartridge. He spins the cylinder, places the revolver at the head of the first survivor, and pulls the trigger. *click*

He goes to the next survivor and spins again. Another *click*. Going to a third survivor and spinning again, the result is BANG. Tragedy? Well, these are packets, not real people. With TCP, death is simply nature's way of telling one to slow down.

Since the packet that was shot...discarded...will never reach its destination, no acknowledgment will be generated for it. When the TCP acknowledgment timer at the sender expires, the sender will reduce its transmission rate. Captain Red will make his lethal rounds more or less frequently depending on the fullness of the RED queue. Eventually, if enough sources slow their transmission rates, the network should not be congested.

The happy ending comes because the sender will eventually retransmit the discarded packet, which should arrive in the less-congested network.

RED, of course, will be most effective on TCP flows. In the absence of higher-level flow control mechanisms (e.g., RTCP), UDP will not slow down in the event of loss. It may be very reasonable to establish a RED-monitored queue for UDP traffic, and begin dropping there, simply as a disincentive to UDP-based applications.

Separating TCP from UDP breaks the basic RED assumption of fairness. Life and networks, however, inherently are unfair. *Weighted RED* (WRED) sorts TCP flows into queues based on IP precedence, and then begins the random discard process at the lowest priority, moving up the priority levels only when the trend to congestion persists.

In Cisco's implementation, RSVP flows are exempt from WRED.

Looking Ahead

In the next chapter, we will examine specific WAN technologies, including their inherent QoS capabilities.

Basic Services

*If I have seen farther than other men, it is because I have
stood on the shoulders of giants.*

SIR ISAAC NEWTON

The line must terminate
Yet my heart rises, I know I've gladdened a lifetime
knotting, undoing a fishnet of tarred rope
the net will hang on the wall when the fish are eaten

ROBERT LOWELL

Once there was an elephant
Who tried to use the telephant
No! No! I mean an elephone
Who tried to use the telephone

LAURA ELIZABETH RICHARDS

Ignoring telegraphy, WAN services, as we know them, began with voice service. More specifically, in the beginning, there was analog voice over analog transport facilities.

WAN services began with dial and dedicated analog services. When telephone companies began using digital services internally in the early 1960s, customer use followed slowly until regulatory changes opened the market in the early to mid 1970s. The view of integrated services started in the 1980s, but has been slow to deploy.

Integrated services means a common network for carrying data, voice, and multimedia traffic. Another aspect of service integration, however, is the operational model. Significant numbers of enterprises make a point, even a fetish, of outsourcing functions that are not part of their "core competency." Network services are not part of the core competency of most enterprises. The outsourcing trend, in many cases, removes the enterprise from the details of WAN connectivity. They may be concerned only with access to a carrier public or private network, or even contract for the management of their LANs.

Remember that the purpose of this book is to help you make choices, rather than go into the details of protocols. How these services map into protocol stacks is relevant to decision making, since you have choices. You do not have choices about the internal operation of the protocols. When a protocol detail is mentioned here, the usual purpose is to identify a "gotcha" in ordering the service.

The basic services discussed in this chapter are just that: basic. A few are more of historic than current interest, but the remaining services have been proven to work. New services constantly are being introduced to the industry, but the decision to replace a working existing service should be made more conservatively than selecting a new service for a new application. Last-mile technologies such as xDSL and cable TV services will be discussed in the context of carrier provisioning, and are deferred to Chapter 6, "Carrier Infrastructure and Optical Networking." Virtual private networks are a software-defined overlay onto basic services, and are detailed in Chapter 7, "Fault Tolerance."

When you consider any WAN service, remember that its true cost will include more than the cost of the WAN link alone. There will be costs associated with the end equipment, and the costs of people and equipment to operate the service (see Table 4.1).

The cheapest end equipment, such as WAN routers, usually cannot be upgraded easily if the requirements change significantly. At a minimum, they will have a LAN interface and a WAN interface. As needs for WAN bandwidth increase, the original WAN interface may not be sufficient.

Several alternatives face the network designer. They depend in part on the particular router in use. The least expensive routers have a fixed hardware configuration. Their interfaces can be changed only with *forklift upgrades*, in which the router chassis is completely replaced with another chassis with more appropriate interfaces.

Fixed configuration routers are cheaper than the alternative, modular routers whose interfaces can be changed in the field. Admittedly, changing interface cards does require basic hardware skills, so both forklift upgrades and card changes may require site visits by technicians.

Approaches available include changing the original interface type, using multiple interfaces in parallel (i.e., inverse multiplexing), or beginning with a physical interface on which the medium speed can grow. No one answer fits all situations.

Table 4.1 Cost Components in WAN Equipment

COMPONENT	INITIAL	RECURRING
Fixed router	Common equipment Number and type of interfaces Remote maintainability Dial/ISDN backup	Maintenance
Modular router	Common equipment Remote maintainability Line cards	Maintenance
Line card	Number and type of interfaces	Maintenance
DCE	Number and type of interfaces Remote maintainability Backup capabilities	Maintenance
Line	Bandwidth Distance Quality of service requirements High availability requirements	Maintenance
Traffic	Contractual	Contractual

Even in apparently simple PSTN dial-up. Are your telecommuting and mobile users local to one calling area, or are they distributed every-where? If the bulk of communications are in the local area, it is often reasonable to run your own dial-in servers. The major reason not to do so is that you do not want to be concerned with the detailed adminis-tration of the dial pool.

In such cases, you can outsource to a local or national ISP. There are carriers that specialize in *dial wholesaling*, which operate very large modem pools and route the dialed data to the enterprise data center. When you outsource dial access, you are creating an access virtual private network (VPN). VPNs are discussed in Chapter 8, "VPNs, Security, and Roaming."

A stronger reason to outsource dial pools is that your users are widely distributed, and a substantial number would need to make long dis-tance calls to reach your servers. Things are never absolute. Large firms may run local access pools in areas with high densities of employees (to be distinguished from pools of dense employees), and outsource national and international access.

Some enterprises find it quite cost effective to run a central 800 dial pool. These are typically large firms with extensive telecommunications contracts, and excellent volume discounts from their carriers.

Beginnings for Data Services

The first analog services put one telephone channel on each physical medium, which simply did not scale. Multiplexing soon entered the analog world as a means of scaling the physical plant.

Data services began as a digital overlay onto analog services, with modems over voice channels. These first services used dedicated lines; dial-up data came later.

Traditional WAN services are based on services that were first designed for telephony, onto which data services were mapped. This ancestry means that they are connection-oriented, and follow a strict subscriber-provider model. Their basic migration began with copper wires intended to carry individual conversations to switching centers, which, in turn, had analog and the digital connection facilities between the centers.

The original services were dial-up and dedicated links. While the first data services were highly experimental and segregated onto dedicated links, the evolution of basic services makes more sense if one deals first with dial services, and looks next at dedicated lines as a special case of dial-up. First, one must understand multiplexing.

Dedicated Lines

The first thing to realize in dealing with dedicated lines is that you are not leasing a physical facility, but an amount of bandwidth. This is equally true on analog and digital facilities.

Voicegrade Services

The first *voicegrade* dedicated lines used carrier-supplied modems with analog private lines. Initial speeds were at that of mechanical teleprinters, but point-to-point lines gained in speed. Certain lines were optimized for data, or *conditioned*. The original conditioning grades of C1 through C4 could get transmission rates as high as 4,800 bps, although

2,000–2,400 bps was more common. D conditioning allowed reliable 9,600 bps communications.

When you have a dedicated line between Washington and San Francisco, pulling on the cable in Washington will not cause the end in San Francisco to move, regardless of the perception of Dilbert-style management.

We've all picked up phones that do not require dialing, to call a cab or to answer the ubiquitous White Courtesy Phone at airports. I always wonder if there are White Discourtesy Phones used to summon classical New York cabdrivers, but the answers to some questions are things humanity should not know.

In telephony-speak, such telephones are called *ringdown* or *off-hook* services. Many of today's ringdown phones are really regular telephones with no external dial, but with a single number to dial programmed inside them. More classical ringdown phones, however, may go through a process much like permanent dialing, as defined by the telco.

Wideband Services

As mentioned in Chapter 1, "What Is the Problem You Are Trying to Solve?" multiplexing first came to voice networking. Individual 4 kHz telephone channels were usually multiplexed into *groups* of 12 channels or *digroups* of 24 channels. The digroup is the ancestor of T1/DS1's 24 channels. Higher levels in the hierarchy included 600-channel *mastergroups*, for which T3/DS3 was meant to be the interconnection speed.

Wideband services used more than one voice channel. The early 50 and 56 Kbps services used in military and ARPANET applications used specialized modems interconnected with a full analog group.

Multidrop and Modem Multiplexing

Old enterprise networks often used dedicated lines strung among a set of stations or *drops*. All remote stations listened passively to frames from the central site. The central device, a mainframe or communications processor, would periodically invite remote stations to transmit. The process of invitation is called *polling*, and can be thought of as a token-passing medium access control, in which the token is under the control of the central device.

Multiplex or Moo?

One of my favorite analog multiplexing comes from before World War II, when telephone companies were experimenting with ways to service farms especially distant from the telephone office. Simple copper pairs with loading coils did not reach far enough to push analog signals, so some sort of RF carrier system was needed. This system could analog multiplex three calls onto one physical facility.

One of the nonobvious but expensive parts of servicing a remote telephone location is the cost of telephone poles to get there. It is not true that this particular carrier system was intended to run over barbed wire. It was, however, intended to be run over fenceposts supporting the telephone wire, and not need telephone poles.

As a consequence, the physical media was a pair of uninsulated wires, with conductive copper plated over a steel strength core. The two open wires were separated a few inches, and were supported by insulators when they ran over the pole.

Unfortunately, the engineers involved did not have detailed familiarity with cattle ranching. Cows are herd animals. A sick cow will try to follow the herd out to the pasture, even though the farmer wants to keep a close eye on it. As a consequence, the farmer might chain the cow to something near the barn or farmhouse.

Grass around the barn would get depleted, so the farmers liked to chain the sick cows in a fresh area. Unfortunately, it didn't work for the chain to be clipped to barbed wire on a fence, because the chain would get caught on the barbs.

Aha! But now . . . there were pairs of smooth wires attached to the fenceposts! Just the thing, it seemed, for attaching the chain.

OK. The cow is now chained to the telephone wire. Eventually, the cow would notice some interesting grass right next to the fence, and wander over to it. As the cow approached the fence, the chain would sag. Eventually, the metal chain sagged across both open wires and shorted the carrier system.

Telephones went out. The farmer might drive to a neighbor and report the problem. A responding crew would drive up the farmer's path to check the line.

As the strange truck drew near the fence where the sick cow was tethered, the cow would become afraid of the truck and move away from the fence. Of course, this tightened the chain and removed the short.

Was it any wonder that these systems were hard to troubleshoot?

Before multiplexed technologies such as frame relay, multidrop organization offered cost advantages over hub-and-spoke dedicated lines (see Figure 4.1).

Frame relay has become the preferred alternative for the topologies once supported by analog multidrop. Modern dial or packet over ISDN D-channel are attractive for low-speed applications such as

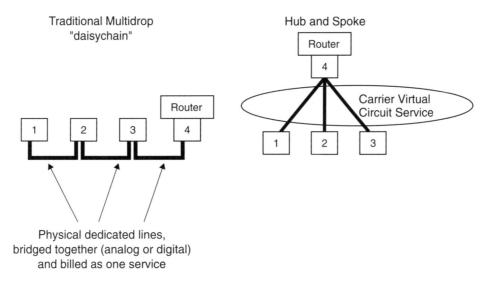

Traditional Multidrop "daisychain"

Hub and Spoke

Router

Router

Physical dedicated lines, bridged together (analog or digital) and billed as one service

Carrier Virtual Circuit Service

Figure 4.1 When dedicated lines come only in one speed, hub and spoke can be expensive.

automatic teller machines (the *other* kind of ATM) and credit card authorization.

Connection-Oriented Services

One can complain all one wishes about stodgy, traditional, telephone service. Unless you are in the far north, at sea, or in rural areas of developing countries, telephone wires accompany mankind. Even in these remote locations, there are well-understood radio techniques for connecting to the PSTN or to public packet-switched networks.

ISDN and X.25 were developed by technologists from a telephony culture. Table 4.2 compares the major low-speed connection-oriented data services.

The PSTN has a variety of charging options. The first question is, "who pays?" In general practice, the calling party pays for the call.

Alternatively, as in 800 service, the called party may pay. Reverse charging is the normal convention for public X.25 networks and is available for ISDN connections. X.25 services also add charges for traffic volume as well as call duration.

Table 4.2 Summary of Connection-Oriented Services

FEATURE	ANALOG	ISDN	X.25
Availability	Universal	Fixed sites	Universal if dial access; otherwise, fixed site
Connection establishment time	Seconds	Milliseconds	Usually < 1 second
Speed	53 Kbps maximum single connection; 28–40 more typical	64 or 128 Kbps	Typically 9.6 or 56 Kbps access speed. Throughput depends on amount of sharing
Inverse Multiplexing Capability	Yes	Yes	Restricted

The second question is, "how much?" U.S. local residential calls usually are charged at a fixed rate for unlimited outgoing calls, while business calls may be charged on a fixed rate per outgoing call or on call duration. When making calls outside the local calling area, higher time-sensitive rates come into effect.

Enterprises of substantial size can negotiate volume discounts. They may, for example, be able to obtain discounted 800 service that makes long-distance dial-up reasonably priced as a backup or low-volume solution. They may also be able to get discounted internal networks that permit internal long distance calls at low price.

Digital Dedicated Line Services

In parallel with the introduction of data services, digital transports such as the T1 system were introduced. Originally, these digital services were intended as new, efficient ways to carry analog services. Analog telephony would be converted into digital streams at the network edge.

In North America today, the most common dedicated line rates are DS1 (1.544 Mbps) and DS3 (44.736 Mbps). Common European speeds are E1 (2.032 Mbps) and E3 (34.368 Mbps). Not all this bandwidth is available, as there is some overhead component.

When traffic requirements are close to the T1 or T3 speed, using a dedicated line to provide the service can be simple and straightforward, minimizing the cost of extra equipment. If the bandwidth requirement were a small fraction of the standard speeds, other services may make more economic sense.

Dedicated lines are priced at a flat monthly rate based on speed and distance. There usually are installation charges, and there may be a *terminal liability*. Terminal liability is the telephone equivalent of the charge for breaking a lease.

T1/E1

Originally intended as a short-haul digital telephony carrier for inter-connecting central offices in a metropolitan area, T1/E1 technology is the most common digital technology. The original system, and most current installations, impose a DS1 (see "Provisioning Gotchas") signal onto copper twisted pairs. Copper wire has a maximum distance of 6,000 feet, but repeaters can be installed at the 6,000-foot (or shorter) interval to increase the range.

CSUs and DSUs

Channel service units (CSU) and *data service units* (DSU) provide demarcation points between the customer and the carrier. They may be intelligent, in that they have an IP address and are SNMP-manageable. An intelligent CSU/DSU most commonly has a dial-up modem port for remote access.

There will often be a physical facility between the customer premises and the telco end office, but even this may be shared (i.e., multiplexed). It may be *inverse multiplexed*, in which two or more physical links are combined into one faster link. See the more detailed discussion of multiplexing in Chapter 5, "Virtualizing in Modern Networks."

Provisioning Gotchas

While it is not the intention of this book to go into detailed protocol discussions, several aspects of the low-level protocols involved in digital dedicated lines can cause significant confusion in ordering the facilities. Even the apparent physical layer protocol has several sublayers, as shown in Figure 4.2.

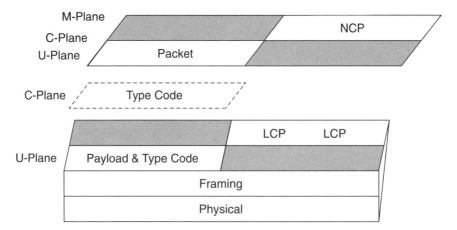

Figure 4.2 Several sublayers are involved even in "simple" dedicated lines.

There are different physical signals. Most use a bipolar encoded electrical signal, but there are variants for optical fiber.

The most basic constraint on the signal is that it have its one bits as bipolar signals. There are several schemes for enforcing the bit stream: *alternate mark inversion* (AMI), *binary 8 zero suppression* (B8ZS) and HDB3. B8ZS is the most common method in North America, although there still is widespread use of ATM. HDB3 is primarily used in Europe.

It is not the point here to pick a "best" encoding, but simply to remind you that you must know the expected encoding when provisioning a DSx interface. For connections to carriers, the carrier must tell you what encoding they expect. If the connections are through your own private facilities, you need to pick an encoding accepted by both ends.

Bit encoding deals with the sequence of bits. Digital facilities have a higher-level sequencing of channels inside frames. "Frame" here does not refer to a data link protocol, but to an agreement between multiplexers. As shown in Figure 4.2, the eventual user data link protocol will run on top of the channel output from multiplexer framing.

Two framing conventions are in common use: *superframe* (SF) and *extended superframe* (ESF). The mechanics of these are not important, but you must know which one you are getting in order to configure your equipment.

On general T1 lines that carry voice traffic, yet another option must be configured: the convention used to carry voice signaling information, such as on- and off-hook conditions. The basic options here are *channel associated signaling* (CAS) and *common channel signaling* (CCS).

Fractional T1

While a physical T1 facility runs at a fixed 1.544 Mbps, only part of its bandwidth may be made available to the customer. The cost of the physical T1 between the customer premises and the end office is identical, whether all or part is used. If only part of the bandwidth runs beyond the end office, it is reasonable to reduce the charges. The customer for a fractional T1 service is not consuming as much backbone resources as does a full T1 customer.

Fractional T1 services are provisioned in multiples of 64 Kbps, the DS-0 rate. Depending on the carrier, there may be one or more user channels on the physical facility. For example, 384 Kbps is a popular speed for videoconferencing—384 Kbps requires six 64 Kbps time slots, so four 384 Kbps channels can run over a single T1.

Each bandwidth bundle on a fractional service will run its own layer 2 protocol. If that layer 2 protocol supports link layer multiplexing, you may very well have multiple virtual circuits within each of the multiple bundles on a single physical fractional T1 interface.

At the customer premises, the DSU/CSU may have one or more interfaces, one for each channel. A multiport DSU/CSU may be cheaper than a router, but is less flexible. Especially when the goal is lowering network costs for legacy equipment unlikely to change in the near term, giving up flexibility may be a reasonable tradeoff.

Just to complicate your life, the tradeoff between a multiport DSU/CSU and a router with separate DSU/CSU is not the only one you face. Yet another alternative may be a router with an internal DSU/CSU. Internal interfaces are almost always cheaper than separate equivalents.

T3/E3 and Fractional T3

As bandwidth requirements grow, at some point, it often becomes more economical to install a DS3 than to keep incurring the installation costs of DS1 links. While the specific costs vary with location, the crossover point is often six or seven DS1s, even though a DS3 has the bandwidth of 28 DS1s.

The potential cost advantage of using T3, rather than multiple DS1s, is more than simple installation cost. With multiple DS1s, unless an external inverse multiplexer (with its own costs) is used, you will require an additional router interface for each one. Most commercial fixed-configuration routers only take one or two DS1 interfaces. To get additional density, modular routers offer multiple serial interface cards. Unfortunately, these routers also need the modularity to support Fast Ethernet and even faster media, so the card needs high-speed circuitry.

If for no other reason than physical geometry, a limited number of serial interfaces can go on a single card. Typically, the size of physical connectors may limit the card to eight interfaces. Even with an ideal processor on the card, this is 12 Mbps on a card that has to carry the expense of high-speed connectivity to the shared bus.

You do not need to buy the full DS3 of bandwidth. Much as there are fractional T1 services, there are fractional T3 services. These can provide the physical connectivity for frame relay services (discussed later in the chapter), and are not limited to a single channel per card.

DS3 ATM has a lower throughput, but still may offer advantages over multiple DS1 serial links. PPP over (fast) Ethernet is yet another emerging alternative.

First Steps to Shared Data Networks

In the 1970s, several factors combined to produce new commercial services. The most important factor was a growing need for bandwidth, at a time where core network bandwidth was much more expensive than it is in today's optical environment. To have reasonable pricing, it was highly desirable to have different users sharing the infrastructure.

True, two users cannot use the same resource, for different purposes, at the same time. If traffic is bursty, however, packets can share the same transmission medium. If traffic is continuous for limited periods, such as telephone calls, resources from a shared pool can be committed only for the period needed. The first approach is the key one in packet switching, while the second is the key to circuit-switched services using either real or virtual circuits. You can contrast them as models, respectively, of promiscuity versus serial monogamy.

X.25

X.25 is a virtual circuit technology principally developed in the traditional telephony standards process. It is optimized for an environment when the Telephone Company Is In Charge.

It has been observed that there are three kinds of people in this world: those who count well, and those who do not. It can also be observed that there are two kinds of people in networking: those who insist on forcing every protocol into a specific one of the seven OSI layers, and those who look at protocols realistically.

CCITT, the predecessor of ISO, issued its first X.25 standard in 1972. The OSI Reference Model was not formalized until 1984. OSI standards originally did assume that an X.25 subset would be the Connection-Oriented Network Protocol, but the reverse is not true. X.25 has its own layering structure which, depending on the application, can map to different OSI layers. Figure 4.3 shows the use of X.25 both as a virtual medium and as a full network layer.

While some people call X.25 an obsolete technology, it remains appropriate for some environments. In certain geographic areas, it may be the only service available.

Reapplying Traditional Rules

X.25 was designed with the assumption that transmission media had error rates of 1 in 10^5, which was typical of early analog lines. It is easy

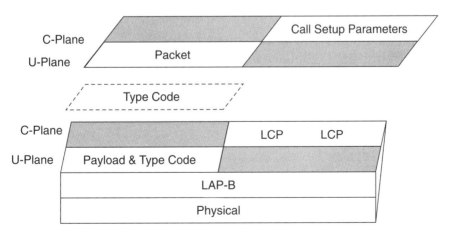

Figure 4.3   There are multiple relationships between X.25 and OSI.

to dismiss such requirements, but the reality is that such error rates are very real in selected environments, such as developing countries or links from shipboard high-frequency radios.

Especially when used with the optional modulus of 128 to minimize acknowledgment overhead, it can be efficient on long-delay paths, such as those running through one or more geosynchronous satellites.

In some applications, it may be adequate simply to use the frame level of the X.25. This level uses the LAP-B protocol, and actually does the retransmissions. While there is a retransmission capability at the packet level, use of this feature is deprecated; packet-level retransmissions take place only due to circuit resets.

X.25 defaults to a small MTU of 128 bytes and a window size of 2. These values do not begin to maximize throughput on modern media, but they are valid values for certain applications and still definitely have their place. They are values that optimize throughput on slow links (e.g., 9.6 Kbps or less) with high error rates (e.g., 1 in 10^5).

You will find such performance in developing countries and on high-frequency (HF) radio links from ships and other specialized platforms.

New Applications for an Old Protocol

A recent but growing application for X.25 is the replacement of analog multidrop to low-speed financial terminals. The D channel of ISDN can carry either Q.931 call management (which definitely has X.25 origins), or shared packet data in X.25 packet-level packets. By packet level, the packets are encapsulated in LAP-D, not LAP-B.

There are a great many Automated Teller Machines that have been on multidrop analog links using IBM and other proprietary protocols (Burroughs and Uniscope, for example). Many of these connections are being replaced with 0B+D ISDN connections, which provide only a 16 Kbps D channel over which application data is sent in X.25 packets.

Enter the Internet

As a user, and then provider, of X.25 services, I must confess that I was on the losing side in the early days. Given that background, I still see selected applications for X.25, but the direction of the industry is connectionless packet routing. There are some exceptions and a more connection-oriented model in very-high-speed backbone applications.

Wernher von Braun is said to have described research as "what you do when you don't know what you are doing, but know that." So it was with early packet-switching networks, and the development of IP.

These networks had several motivations, the most basic being shared resource use. Resources in question included both transmission facilities and hosts, for the ARPANET was a research and education network.

There certainly was military interest in packet switching as an approach to building networks that were survivable in nuclear war. This point is often overstated as an operational goal. During the Cold War, the majority of nuclear command and control networks were not packet switched.

Nevertheless, the focus of early connectionless public packet-switching networks was on research and education. These networks did not assume a hostile security environment, and were not designed to be "commercial strength" against attack.

IP and Transmission Services

One of the early goals for IP was that it is medium independent. As we will see later in this chapter, IP is independent of dedicated lines and LANs, but nonbroadcast multiaccess (NBMA) and on-demand media pose special challenges. Table 4.3 gives an overview of the various relationships between IP and specific transmission media.

Cost of IP Services

Nevertheless, the focus of early connectionless public packet-switching networks was on research and education. These networks did not assume a hostile security environment, and were not designed to be "commercial strength" against attack.

A reality is that mission-critical packet switching cannot coexist with uncontrolled public Internet services. Carriers, however, create infrastructures on which both public and private networks can be mapped, the traffic in each network type staying isolated.

The original research networks were fully subsidized. As time went on, and commercial organizations connected to them, the commercial

Table 4.3 Mappings between Logical and Transmission Levels

LOGICAL	IP							
Mapping	ARP	IPCP, static	IPCP, static	Static	Inverse ARP, static	Inverse ARP, static	ARP, static	ARP, static
Technology	LAN	Dial	ISDN	X.25	Frame	ATM AAL	SMDS	LANE
Protocol type ID	LLC, SNAP or Ether-type	PPP IPCP	PPP IPCP	RFC 1355	RFC 2427	RFC 2684, RFC 2225	LLC, SNAP or Ether-type	LLC, SNAP or Ether-type
Persistent endpoint identifier	MAC	E.163	E.164	X.121	DLCI	NSAP	MAC	MAC
Transient connection identifier	[1]	[2]	TEI	LCN		VPI & VCI	N/A	[3]
Next Lower Layer	LAN PHY	Analog	ISDN PHY	serial	serial	SONET, etc.	DS1, DS3, ATM	ATM

[1] Connectionless

[2] There is no specific identifier, because analog lines do not carry any complex signaling. There is effectively a connection identifier, but it tends to be physical. Think of a multibutton key telephone, on which a button blinks for incoming calls, and stays on when a line is in use. That button is the connection identifier.

[3] The ATM VC identifier does not specifically point to the MAC address. Instead, it points to the LAN Emulation Client to which the MAC address is connected.

organization typically paid for its access line and equipment, but had no transit charges. Counterbalancing this subsidy were *acceptable use policies* (AUP) that limited the content of traffic to nonprofit research and education.

Eventually, the *commercial internet exchange* (CIX) entered the picture as a member-supported exchange point for commercial traffic. While the CIX still exists, demand to interconnect commercial networks soon outstripped its capacity.

Intercarrier links, discussed in Chapter 6 are often bilateral private links between carriers of roughly equal size. Alternatively, the carriers may interchange data at neutral *exchange points*, often called *metropolitan area exchanges* (MAE). MAE is a somewhat unfortunate term, as the interconnections at a major exchange point are often anything but local. The first major exchange points are listed in Table 4.4; many more have been introduced since these pioneers.

Table 4.4 Initial Exchange Points

EXCHANGE	GENERAL LOCATION	INTRODUCED
MAE-East	Vienna, VA	Part of original NSFNET
Ameritech Advanced Data Services NAP	Chicago, IL	Part of original NSFNET
Sprint NAP (suburban New York)	Pennsauken, NJ	Part of original NSFNET
PacBell NAP	San Francisco, CA	Part of original NSFNET
Federal Internet Exchange East	College Park, MD	
Federal Internet Exchange West	NASA Ames Research Center, CA	
Commercial Internet Exchange	Palo Alto, CA	
MAE-West	San Jose, CA	

True metropolitan exchanges often link local ISPs and major content providers in their local areas. One of the first, if not the first, such exchange was the Tucson, Arizona, NAP.

There is a growing number of sites that combine the connectivity of an exchange point with the additional business of server hosting. The Palo Alto Network Exchange (PAIX) was one of the earliest successful major hosting sites.

Current practice is for enterprises to buy general Internet access from ISPs. Pricing is based on bandwidth, which may divide into a cost for bandwidth once traffic reaches the ISP, plus the installation-specific cost of dedicated access links.

The Internet offers no QoS guarantees. ISPs may offer premium services using virtual private network (VPN) technology, which is detailed in Chapter 7.

ISDN

"Innovations subscribers don't need." "I sense dollars now." These are only a few of the less complimentary explanations of the acronym ISDN, which, in reality, stands for *integrated services digital network.*

ISDN had a slow start, but is now a dependable service. As a service, however, it is beset by boa constrictors. Other services are constricting the scope of ISDN. At the low-cost end are modems much higher in speed than when ISDN was introduced. V.90 analog modems offer access wherever there is a telephone, and wireless modems provide even greater access. See Chapter 6 for additional information on the economics of ISDN.

Since ISDN needs a specific local loop, it is restricted to fixed locations. xDSL technologies offer far higher data rates over comparable media. Cable is another alternative for fixed location, and broadband wireless services are developing rapidly.

ISDN does offer native voice integration, but this capability is being pressured by the python of voice over IP.

At the physical layer, ISDN is provisioned with *basic rate interfaces* (BRI) and *primary rate interfaces* (PRI). BRI can carry up to two 64 Kbps user B channels and a 16 Kbps D control channel. When both B channels are available to the end user, the combination is called 2B+D. Some carriers may offer a service that allows the user to use only one B channel, in a configuration called 1B+D.

Each B channel has its own telephone number, which will be drawn from the E.164 address space. One of the configuration "gotchas" is that there also may need to be a *service provider identifier* (SPID) associated with the ISDN equipment. Be sure to find out the specific requirements of your ISDN provider. Not all carriers require SPIDs, and the format will vary from carrier to carrier. It usually is in the format of a telephone number.

Variants of the BRI are the S/T reference point and the U reference point.

S/T reference point, which usually is physically on an RJ45 modular connector. The data stream consists of the two B channels, a D channel, and 48 KBPS of physical overhead. S/T interfaces are either point-to-point or point-to-multipoint, and may have subaddressing for the individual user devices on the shared bus.

U reference point, using a two-wire electrical interface on an RJ11 modular connector, and including 16 KBPS of overhead.

PRI channels have either 23 or 30 B channels plus a 64 Kbps D channel. B channels can be inverse multiplexed into faster aggregates. Using multilink PPP (MLPPP) to create 128 Kbps channels from two B channels is quite common and flexible. Indeed, often a 64 Kbps flow is established, and when utilization reaches a predefined level, the second B channel is brought up dynamically to provide *bandwidth on demand*.

Another common rate created by inverse multiplexing six B channels is the 384 Kbps speed, designated H0 and intended for videoconferencing.

ISDN, as shown in Figure 4.4, is more than a single physical layer protocol. LAP-D, also called Q.921, runs over the D channel. It is a fairly complex protocol, because it has several functions. It can assign transient endpoint identifiers (TEI) to devices sharing the S/T bus, each with its own subinterface. A telephone, a facsimile machine, and a router could share the S/T bus. Alternatively, multiple telephones could share a bus and be conferenced together.

While the D channel is always used for control and for interacting with V.120 protocol translators, a lesser known but growing capability is to use it for low-speed shared data. User information is encapsulated in X.25 packets. Financial applications such as credit authorization and automatic teller machines increasingly are moving to 0B+D as a cost-effective alternative to multidrop analog local loops.

So what control information does LAP-D carry? ISDN end hosts, called *terminal equipment* (TE), request calls to be set up with the Q.931 signaling protocol. LAP-D carries Q.931 information between the host and the network.

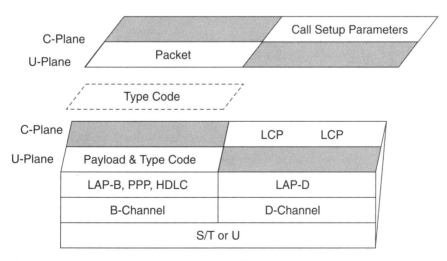

Figure 4.4 ISDN stack. ISDN does not precisely map to OSI layering.

When the Q.931 control messages arrive at the ISDN exchange, they are validated, and, if valid, cause call setup requests to be sent in the Signaling System 7 (SS7) management protocol, which is discussed in more detail in Chapter 6. SS7 determines if the call can be set up, and causes the called destination to be rung using analog or ISDN local loop control. If the called destination accepts the call, the TE now can exchange user information over B channel(s).

Transitional Services

In the 1980s, ISDN and ATM initiatives took a serious look at the integration of voice and data services, with the assumption that all services would run over a digital transmission services. Digital transmission, especially optically based, offered incredibly low error rates in comparison with analog transports.

Like FR and X.25, ATM is connection-oriented. Unlike these protocols, it was intended for the core, not the customer. FR was to be the low-speed access, while a *broadband ISDN* (B-ISDN) was to provide high speed. The industry, however, adapted ATM to high-speed customer sites, using a native ATM rather than a B-ISDN interface.

ATM, as opposed to the variable-length frames carried by FR and X.25, switches fixed-length *cells*. There are several arguments for using cells. Fixed-length formats lend themselves to doing switching in hardware. Short cells also reduce the latency for real-time applications.

FR, conceived as an afterthought to ATM, has far more enterprise market share than ATM. An 1999 study put the revenue from ATM and FR at $9.3 billion, of which 88 percent was FR.

Issues Common to Virtual Circuit Services

IP is usually described as medium independent, but the original idea of its medium independence really meant that it could run over dedicated lines and broadcast multiaccess LANs. IP and other protocol families often become confused by partial mesh nonbroadcast multiaccess (NBMA) and by demand (e.g., dial-up) media. As in so many other awkward cases in networking, the answer to these problems tends to be based on Schwarzenegger's Second Law.

Schwarzenegger's Laws of Networking

It seems all too little known that action star and bodybuilding champion Arnold Schwarzenegger is a very intelligent man with a wicked sense of humor. It should be obvious that any Republican who marries into the Kennedy clan *has* to have a sense of humor. He has a deep understanding of human psychology, which a few insightful critics realize is expressed in his sensitive, introspective movies intended for the intellectual audience, such as *Commando*.

Early in *Commando*, Arnold is captured by The Bad Guys, and put into one of those Classic Situations from which He Cannot Possibly Escape. One of the Bad Guys mocks Arnold, who calmly replies, "You know, Solly, you are a very funny man. I like you. Just for that, I will kill you last."

Of course, Arnold escapes within minutes. After the traditional car chase, he captures his first Bad Guy, who turns out to be none other than Solly.

Arnold uses modern psychotherapeutic techniques, based on rational emotive therapy, to interrogate Solly. He puts Solly in the proper environment for his counseling, which, in this case, means that he holds Solly by his foot over a thousand-foot drop. In response to Solly's defiant refusal to tell Arnold what he wishes to know, insisting what Arnold wants is not important, Arnold sagely responds, "No. Only one thing is important to you now.

"What's that?"

"Gravity."

Arnold has used a fine therapeutic technique with Solly, helping him see the rational consequences of his initial emotional response. With that help, Solly tells Arnold everything he wants. Solly then realizes he is still hanging by one foot over a thousand-foot drop, and cheerfully reminds Arnold, "Remember? You were going to kill me last?"

Arnold calmly opens his hand, saying "I lied."

And that is Schwarzenegger's Second Law of Networking: *lie*. If an upper layer has certain expectations of a lower layer, and the lower layer does not provide a service matching them, insert a shim layer between the two. This shim layer will tell the upper layer what it wants to hear.

In the same movie scene, Arnold also demonstrated his Third Law. Returning to his car, Rae Dawn Chong asked, "What happened to Solly?"

Arnold replied, "I let him go." And that is the Third Law: Do not retain resources when they are no longer needed.

ATM and frame relay share some common issues: how to handle protocols that need broadcasts or multicasts, how to map logical addresses to transmission system addresses, when and how to optimize with cut-through methods, and how they interact with dynamic routing.

Broadcasting and Multicasting

Routing protocols tend to understand point-to-point and broadcast media, but do not really understand NBMA. A common, but often expensive, workaround is pseudobroadcasting, in which a set of virtual circuits or other destination identifiers is manually configured. When a router sends a data unit with a broadcast destination address, the router copies it to the set of destination paths.

A single-node broadcasting to all others is not uncommon in frame relay and X.25, but subjects the router to a significant processing load in copying the protocol data units. This copying overhead would be even more severe at ATM speeds. Some ATM switches support a point-to-multipoint organization where the switch does the packet replication at the cell level, in specialized hardware

Address Resolution in Partial Meshes

A given FR DLCI tells you how to deliver traffic to a given administratively defined destination. By itself, the DLCI does not tell you what DLCI to use to reach what IP address. The frame relay provider will tell you what DLCI maps to which destination, but gives no information about the higher-layer addressing.

You have three choices to map between DLCIs and logical addresses: static definition, inverse ARP, and setting up /30 subnets for point-to-point VCs. Static definition is not necessarily a bad thing. Yes, it is labor-intensive if the network administrator must manually configure every mapping statement. If, however, you generate the mapping statements from the database you use to assign addresses, and use remote configuration to load them into routers, the workload becomes much more reasonable.

Inverse ARP has problems in partial mesh topologies. In Figure 4.5, how does router **chervil** obtain a layer 2 response from router **anise**? **chervil** has a layer 2 connection to **basil**, but not to **chervil.**

If the hub interface on **basil** can be configured to rebroadcast every broadcast frame it receives, inverse ARP can work. Pseudobroadcasting, however, can put a heavy processing load onto the hub router.

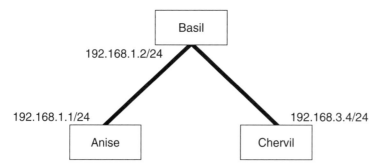

Figure 4.5 Inverse ARP in partial mesh.

Cut-Through

Schwarzenegger's First Law does enter into the cut-through problem. Cut-through is an extension to routing when the underlying layer 2 transport has the capability of establishing connections to the destination. Such connections can be physical, such as modem dial-ups, or virtual, such as ATM, FR, and X.25 VCs. Assuming that the overhead is less if one can have a connection directly to the destination, rather than going through multiple layer 3 routed hops, creating such a virtual circuit offers the potential of better performance.

What causes the cut-through to be created? There are two general strategies, *control-driven* and *data-driven*. Control-driven strategies rely on a specific command request to create the connection. Such commands would come from an end device, such as a host or ingress router. Data-driven strategies are triggered by an ingress or intermediate switch or router, when some previously established traffic level to the destination is detected.

What if a connection already exists to the destination? This is the key question related to Schwarzenegger's Third Law. Should the sender multiplex communications onto that VC, or open a new one? First, the connection has to support multiplexing. For example, ATM supports multiple sources over the same VC if and only if AAL3/4, discussed later, is used. AAL3/4 imposes more overhead than AAL5.

The Schwarzenegger Third Law problem and the question of data-driven versus control-driven connection establishment complement one another. A more formal way to look at the Third Law problem is to consider it as *liberal connection retention* or *conservative connection retention*.

Liberal connection retention keeps the connection as long as possible, under the assumption that once the connection is up, it is likely to be used. Conservative retention makes the opposite assumption. Borrowing from multiprotocol label switching (MPLS) terminology discussed in Chapter 5, you can think of a connection having a *holding priority* and/or a *holding* (i.e., inactivity) *timer*, and a *setup priority*. Holding timers specify how long an existing connection is retained when there is no demand for it. Setup priorities indicate whether new requests have the ability to "bump" new connections. When a new request does have bumping (i.e., preemption) rights, the connection with the lowest holding priority will be bumped. Depending on system design, even a cut-through currently in use could be bumped by a higher-priority requirement (see Table 4.5).

A second point associated with the Third Law, what if the user request that triggered the creation of the connection completes, but the second request still needs servicing?

Cut-through, like so many other networking techniques, is not a panacea, regardless of the exhortations of evangelists of the technology. It also can be an excellent solution for the right problem. One of the major tradeoffs in using it is that it takes time to create a connection, which adds to the delay before the first data unit can be sent. If the connection stays up, this delay can be avoided.

Keeping the connection is not free. Real-world layer 2 devices, such as ATM switches, have limits to the number of concurrent virtual circuits they can support per physical interface and per chassis.

If there are charges based on connection time, as with dial-up modems, leaving the call connected will result in additional monetary cost. You are betting the idle time will be less than the setup time for a new connection.

Table 4.5 Tradeoffs in Cut-Through

| SETUP | RETENTION | |
	LIBERAL	CONSERVATIVE
Data	Intelligent relays, bandwidth cheap.	Relatively intelligent relays with limited storage for tracking connections (e.g., ATM switches).
Control	Intelligent edge devices, bandwidth use must be justified. If it is justified, it should be highly available.	Bandwidth is costly and needs to be considered globally.

What Happened to Schwarzenegger's First Law?

The First Law is less important in modern LANs, which rarely use coaxial cable. The Law reminds us that 10Base2 or 10Base5 segments are physically composed of a cable and two terminators, T1 and T2. If a terminator is removed, the cabling support person Will Be Back. See " Never Underestimate the Power of Human Stupidity" in Chapter 7, "Fault Tolerance," for more discussion of the role of terminators.

Interactions with Dynamic Routing

Dynamic routing protocols, both IP and non-IP, again were developed with the assumption they would run either over dedicated or LAN media. Partial mesh NBMA and demand connectivity both present problems for many dynamic routing protocols.

Let us begin with the class of distance vector protocols:

- **IP.** RIP versions 1 and 2, *interior gateway routing protocol* (IGRP) and *enhanced IGRP* (EIGRP)
- **Novell IPX.** IPX RIP and EIGRP
- **AppleTalk.** *Routing table maintenance protocol* (RTMP) and EIGRP
- **DECnet.** Phase IV routing

First- and second-generation distance vector protocols (i.e., all except EIGRP) use the *split horizon* technique to avoid loops. In the first routing protocol implementations, based completely on hop count, loops could form. They were detected by a *count to infinity* mechanism, shown in Figure 4.6. When everything is working properly, the two routers know about all three networks.

Figure 4.6 Count to infinity.
Source: NA-IPRO-ctinf

Now, assume network 3.0.0.0 fails. Since **basil**'s route to this network came from direct hardware connection information, **basil** immediately knows the network is unreachable and removes it from its routing table.

Just after **basil** removes the entry, it receives a copy of **garlic**'s routing table. This table, of course, has **garlic**'s old entry that says that **garlic** can reach destination 3.0.0.0. **basil** assumes that any fellow router can be trusted, and adds the route to its own routing table. The new route in **basil** says that 3.0.0.0 can be reached by sending to **garlic**. **basil** adds 1 to the hop count for 3.0.0.0, to add the cost to reach **garlic**.

A little later, **basil** sends its routing table to **garlic,** which updates its own table with the route to 3.0.0.0. Since **garlic** only knows how to reach 3.0.0.0 by sending to **basil**, **garlic** adds 1 to the hop count in its own table.

Can you see that a loop has formed, as **basil** and **garlic** happily bounce the route between one another, the metric increasing by 1 on each iteration?

The count to infinity mechanism was the first to detect infinite loops, and is used in protocols that use metric as their hop count. These protocols have a maximum metric value, such as 15 for IP RIP. The next value above that metric is the "infinity" limit. When a RIP update is incremented so that its metric is 16, RIP assumes the packet is looping and deletes the route.

It would be better, however, to avoid the loop forming in the first place. Split horizon prevents count-to-infinity loops. Both RIP and IGRP use split horizon, which is very useful on point-to-point and LAN media (see Figure 4.7).

The split horizon mechanism does limit propagation. Think of it as what a good human manager does, or more precisely does not do. Good managers do not override the judgment of people who are dealing directly with the problem and have better information than the manager. Dilbert's bosses do not support split horizon.

In the split horizon mechanism used in RIP and IGRP, the router remembers the interface on which it first heard about a given destination. When that router sends out updates, it really doesn't send its entire routing table on any particular interface. On any given interface, it will send out only information on destinations it did not first learn about through that interface.

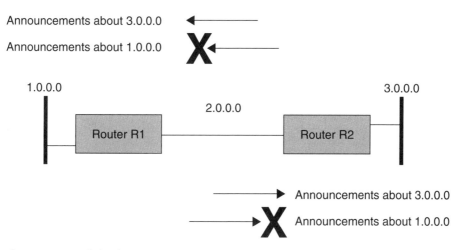

Figure 4.7 Split horizon.

Split horizon does several things for you. Obviously, it reduces traffic by reducing the update from the size of the routing table to a subset of the routing table. The more important motivation for split horizon, however, is preventing loops.

What about link state routing protocols? These protocols have loop avoidance mechanisms that obviate the need for split horizon. Life is never simple, and link state protocols have their own sets of problems.

In OSPF, for example, one issue is that various physical interface types may default to different values of the hello and dead timers. If the hello and dead timers do not match exactly between two interfaces, an adjacency cannot form.

A more basic problem is designated router election on NBMA media. You cannot let the router election occur at random. The hub router must become the designated router. Spoke routers must have their interface priority set to zero, which prevents them from becoming DR.

If you have a dual hub configuration, as shown in Figure 4.8, there must be a PVC between the hubs, the primary router should have the highest priority for DR election, and the backup router should have the next higher priority.

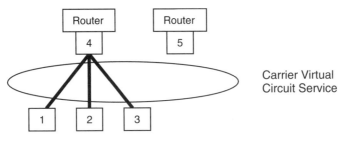

Figure 4.8 Dual hub NBMA.

ATM and B-ISDN

A T-shirt seen at the IETF reads "ATM. A Technological Miracle, solving today's problems...tomorrow." While I enjoy the T-shirt, it does overstate the situation. ATM does solve useful problems today, but it is not regarded as the general solution that it once was.

ATM and SS7 are core mechanisms for telcos, as discussed in Chapter 6, as are the SONET/SDH optical networking technologies that underlie them. All of these mechanisms should remain as the core that supports the PSTN, even with the growth of VoX in enterprises.

ATM Stacks

Unfortunately, the cell size chosen was not optimal either for voice or data. For voice and other real-time applications, small cells minimize latency. For data applications, larger cells maximize throughput. Voice-oriented representatives to the ATM standards committees wanted a cell payload length no longer than 32 bytes, while the data representatives wanted a cell payload length no shorter than 64 bytes.

King Solomon showed his wisdom by proposing a solution that divided a baby in half. The Solomonic solution to ATM was slightly more complex: The cell lengths preferred by each group were added together and *then* divided by two, resulting in a compromise length of 48 bytes. There is a 5-byte fixed header for each cell, resulting in a 53-byte total cell length.

ATM has a complex stack that includes U, C, and M plane protocols. While ATM stacks were not designed for precise compatibility with the OSI model, the top of the ATM stack corresponds generally to the top of the data link layer (see Figure 4.9).

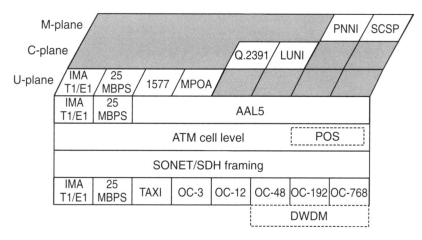

Figure 4.9 Protocols used in ATM, which again do not follow OSI.

Be very clear that higher layer functions do not deal directly with the ATM cell level, but see ATM through the filter of the *ATM adaptation layer* (AAL). Most data services use AAL type 5.

I find it quite useful to distinguish between the AT *protocols* and the *service* it provides to the layers above it. I consider ATM as providing a data link layer service. Some ATM specialists claim that ATM provides the service of a network layer, especially because it has end-to-end significant endpoint identifiers. To me, this argument is more religious than practical, since MPLS, discussed in Chapter 5, is unifying the IP and ATM worlds, reducing conflict.

Data services still need a means of identifying the payload the AAL frames carry. RFC 2225 describes the "classical," IP-specific means of identification. The more general multiprotocol over ATM (MPOA), currently defined in RFC2684, specifies using IEEE 802.2 Logical Link Control/Subnetwork Access Control (LLC/SNAP) to indicate the payload type.

The ATM Forum uses the term *MPOA* to include a broader specification, which involves a combination of layer 2 and layer 3 routing (see Table 4.6).

It is relevant, however, to consider the interactions of ATM services with mechanisms that unquestionably are part of the network layer, such as IP. One basic requirement is to be able to associate each VC with one or more network addresses at the distant end of the virtual circuit.

Table 4.6 Higher-Layer Protocols and ATM

TECHNOLOGY	PROTOCOLS	MAPPING	L2/L3 FEATURES	OTHER REDUNDANCY
RFC2684 MPOA	Layer 2 & 3	Manual		None
ATM Forum MPOA	Layer 2 & 3		Cut-through routing	NHRP & MARS
RFC2225 Classical IP	IP	Dynamic ARP	Interoperability over multiple LIS; multicasting as defined with RFC2022	Proprietary only
LANEv1	Layer 2	Manual	SVC setup	Proprietary only
LANEv2	Layer 2	Manual	QoS support, selective multicast	SCSP

ARP requires multicasting. The multicast address resolution server (MARS) [RFC 2022] provides a multicast server that replicates the multicast it hears, and sends them onto all other VCs in the subnet. MARS is a part of the MPOA architecture

When there is a single device, be it a MARS server or the BUS server in LAN emulation, that copies multicast frames, the device must operate on complete cells, not frames. The problem is that cells arrive at the replication node not necessarily in the order they belong in frames, but in fairly random order.

While the multicast server has a point-to-multipoint virtual circuit to the devices receiving the multicasts, cells can be arriving simultaneously on different interfaces. Let's say the multicast replication device is receiving a sequence of 32 cells on interface 1 and on interface 2, and will transmit the multicast cells on a point-to-multipoint VC from interface 3.

The multicasting device cannot simply accept an incoming cell and switch it to the point-to-multipoint VC. To do so would be to risk interspersing cells belonging to the stream being received on interface 1 with the stream arriving on interface 2. AAL5, the most bandwidth-efficient form of AAL for data applications, assumes cells on a VC are in order, from first cell of frame to last frame of cell.

To be able to mix cells from different frames, you would have to use AAL3/4, which imposes much more overhead. So, a real-world multicasting engine reassembles the cells on each VC into frames in its internal memory, and only after it knows it has a complete frame does it segment it back into cells that are copied onto the point-to-multipoint VC. The two steps of segmentation and reassembly introduce delay.

AAL and the Cell Tax

ATM's cell layer imposes 5 bytes of overhead for every cell. This is called the *cell tax*. Not all ATM cells carry user data. The Payload Type field allows certain cells to be identified as operation, administration, and maintenance (OAM). OAM cells are used for diagnostics and similar functions; the amount of OAM overhead is implementation-specific.

Just as there may be local as well as state sales taxes, there may also be an additional tax imposed by AAL. Depending on the AAL type, a cell may have 48 (AAL5), 47 (AAL1), or 44 (AAL3/4) bytes of payload (see Table 4.7).

If even one byte of a frame needs to be sent, a complete cell is needed to send it, so the number of cells needed to send a specific frame has to be rounded up. Table 4.8 shows the total number of bytes needed to transmit a 1,500-byte frame, and compares it to the overhead of the PPP over SONET alternative.

A single cell header prepended to the Ethernet frame would require 1,523 bytes, but you need more than a single header. The frame must be segmented into the payload fields of cells and reassembled at the destination.

Dividing 1,518 by 48 bytes, the payload available in an AAL5 cell, you get 31.625 cells. If you truncated this to 31 full cells, you would get 1,488 bytes of payload, which clearly is not enough to send all 1,518

Table 4.7 Cell Tax Part 1: Per-Cell AAL Overhead

AAL TYPE	AAL OVERHEAD BYTES PER CELL	PAYLOAD BYTES PER CELL	PER-CELL OVERHEAD OF COMBINED CELL HEADER AND AAL
AAL1	1	47	12%
AAL3/4	4	44	17%
AAL5	0	48	9%

Table 4.8   Cell Tax Part 2: Per-Frame Overhead

TRANSMISSION	TOTAL BYTES TO SEND 1,500 DATA BYTES	OVERHEAD BYTES	OVERHEAD
AAL1	1,696	196	12%
AAL3/4	1,855	355	19%
AAL5	1,696	196	12%
POS	1,507	7	Well under 1%

bytes. The payload, of course, is not all of an ATM cell. The true number of bytes in 31 cells is (5+48)*31, or 1,643 bytes.

To have enough payload space for the full frame, you must have 32 cells. The last cell will have some wasted padding space, but there is no way to avoid that loss with a fixed cell length. ATM has a fundamental assumption that the greater hardware efficiency possible with fixed cells makes up for any cell usage inefficiencies. The real requirement, therefore, is (5+48)*32, or 1,696 bytes.

ATM Virtual Circuit Setup

While call setup uses Q.2931, Q.2931 itself does not run over raw cells. Between Q.2931 and AAL5 is the service specific convergence protocol (SSCOP), a LAP-B variant designed for even higher availability.

SSCOP, for fault tolerance, can use two redundant links. Neither link should ever be loaded more than 50 percent. With two active SSCOP links, the same frame will be sent over both links. If the frame is received in error on one link, the other link is checked to see if the same frame has been received without error. If an error-free frame is available on the other link, there is no need to retransmit. If a redundant link fails, or if there is only one physical link, then all traffic runs over the single link and conventional retransmission is used.

Standard M-plane protocols are the interim inter-switch protocol (IISP) and the private network-to-network interface (PNNI) routing protocol.

Q.2931 sets up *switched virtual circuits* (SVC). ATM *permanent virtual circuits* (PVC) are configured manually, at each switch hop. To reduce manual administration, there is also the concept of a *soft PVC*. Soft

PVCs are created as if they were SVCs, using dynamic setup. The soft PVCs, however, are never torn down once established.

In some environments, nonreal-time software may generate PVC routes and install them automatically. Simply because a route is static does not mean it needs detailed human intervention to be provisioned.

ATM's Physical Layer and PPP over SONET

ATM primarily runs over SONET. SONET itself is a layered protocol, the layers of which are discussed in Chapter 6. The SONET speeds commonly used with ATM are OC-3 (155 Mbps) and OC-12 (622 Mbps), with OC-48 (2 Gbps) and OC-192 (10 Gbps) beginning to enter service.

When looking at these speeds, remember they are not the full speed available to the ATM service user; they are the optical transmission rates. SONET overhead and ATM overhead will both subtract usable bandwidth.

In most applications, this overhead is a very small part of the total, and may not really be noticeable for enterprises. The full bandwidth, in any case, may not be usable because some router interfaces can connect to OC-3, but cannot forward at the full line rate.

Large ISPs, however, need enough bandwidth that the ATM "cell tax" becomes significant. Their growing bandwidth requirements recall the words of former U.S. Senator William Proxmire: "A billion here, a billion there, and pretty soon you're talking about real money." They have gone to the alternative of PPP over SONET, using the SONET physical mechanism but eliminating ATM. In doing so, they lose the virtual circuit and multiplexing capabilities of ATM, but they are using it in point-to-point applications between internal concentration points or to exchange data between major carriers.

SONET is not the only alternative, especially at lower speeds. A 25 Mbps ATM physical layer, which is based on the IBM Token Ring chip set, is starting to gain popularity, especially for last-mile applications.

Another physical layer alternative is to use multiple conventional T1 links, and run cells over the inverse multiplexed bundle [IMA]. Such connectivity makes ATM available in areas that do not support its specific physical layers.

If enterprises manage their own ATM switching, routing comes into play. This is not the level 3 routing of IP, but ATM's own mechanism. Ignoring some interim solutions, the current ATM routing protocol is the private network to network interface (PNNI).

PNNI establishes the topology and knows the amount of bandwidth available. In response to call requests, PNNI finds paths through the system of ATM switches.

Provisioning, Pricing, and Gotchas

When you price an ATM service, you will need to consider both one-time and recurring costs for end equipment, the access link, and bandwidth in the ATM service (see Table 4.9).

VoATM

ATM, of course, was originally developed for voice. Of the three types of VoX, VoIP, VoFR, and VoATM, sending voice over ATM is the most conservative and reliable approach.

Table 4.9 ATM Costing

COMPONENT	NOTES	USUAL PRICING
Access link	Most commonly DS-3 or OC-3. OC-12, OC-48, and OC-192 entering service. Possible ATM inverse multiplex.	Installation plus distance and bandwidth-based monthly charges.
Router interface	Separate cost on modular routers.	Purchase or lease, monthly maintenance.
Router common	Total cost of fixed-configuration routers, or amortized cost of common equipment to which interface is inserted.	Purchase or lease, monthly maintenance.
Per-virtual circuit	Based on service class (CBR, VBR, UBR, ABR) and performance parameters within class.	Monthly rate.
Backup resources	Optional.	Depends on mechanism (analog dial, ISDN, etc.). Can be initiated from router or DSU/CSU.

There can be very practical reasons to use ATM. If an enterprise has a large PBX that it does not want to replace in the near term, that PBX is likely to have T1/T3 or ATM interfaces. The PBX is far less likely to understand VoFR or VoIP.

Remember that not all ATM provides guaranteed service. ATM constant bit rate (CBR) providing the circuit emulation service (CES), does provide a reasonable guarantee of service. It is also the most bandwidth-inefficient and thus expensive service variant.

Using ATM variable bit bate (VBR), available bit rate (ABR), or unspecified bit rate (UBR) makes ATM susceptible to the congestion variations that can be seen with VoIP or VoFR.

ATM in the Campus and Extended Campus

In campus networks, ATM has generally been replaced by Fast Ethernet and Gigabit Ethernet. Distance limitations were largely eliminated with Ethernet over fiber.

For point-to-point links between ISPs, PPP directly over SONET offered more efficiency than ATM. See Chapter 6 for a discussion of SONET. ATM still has a major presence for voice and some video applications.

The strength of ATM is its ability to provide intelligent multiplexing with controlled quality of service. Telephone carriers have immense investments in ATM, and it is a proven technology for carrying voice and video. While voice over IP may be the technology of the future, it does not offer enough incentives to replace existing facilities. New enterprises and new carrier services can consider alternatives, and traditional telcos may add such alternatives without discarding their existing services.

ATM and Integrated Services Today

One of my consulting clients, a government organization, provided an extremely critical service. It had a main operations facility and a backup, and it made its critical data available to customers and the public through servers at a redundant pair of Web hosting centers. The original plan (see Figure 4.10) was to interconnect the four sites with a partial mesh of DS3 links. Database updates and replication were known to need about 15 Mbps of bandwidth, so, with other data traffic, there was enough bandwidth that multiple DS1s made no sense. As is unfortunately common, my client showed me the Figure 4.10 design, which proposed a solution without truly identifying a problem.

My original discussions with the client focused on data flow among the four sites, frame relay to service other sites in the metropolitan area, and the LAN within the main site. On examining the physical installation plan, I discovered orders for about 40 DS1 facilities in addition to the DS3. Investigating, I found these were for voice and videoconferencing applications, including backup connectivity through a government voice network as well as through the PSTN. Figure 4.11 shows the actual requirements, independent of the solution, but for which a solution could be developed.

The entire project was on short deadlines, and could only use well-proven equipment. Nevertheless, going to ATM connectivity offered the opportunity to reduce system cost by 20 percent, while adding reliability through full meshing. Cost reduction came from economies of scale, in that a given amount of bandwidth costs less on a higher-speed facility. The cost of DS1s for voice and video had not been considered as part of the main plan.

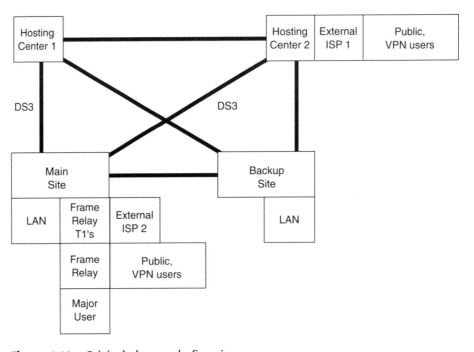

Figure 4.10 Original plan: ready, fire, aim.

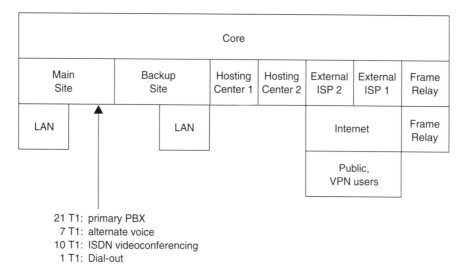

Figure 4.11 Requirements.

With equipment readily available, routers alone could not split off, with guaranteed bandwidth, the voice and video facilities. Figure 4.12 shows the revised design approach, which inserted an ATM switch between the two carrier points of presence and the routers. This switch was "carrier-class" (see Chapter 6) and internally fully redundant.

The ATM switch accepted two 155 Mbps OC-3 ATM links from the carriers. It split off DS1 circuits with Constant Bit Rate, which connected to the voice and video equipment.

From the switch, an OC-3 link ran to each of the two redundant routers. This link carried the 15 Mbps streams to the data centers and the backup site, tens of frame relay virtual circuits, and links to the two ISP points of presence. Having OC-3 interfaces as both input and output to the switch gave us maximum flexibility in reallocating bandwidth.

The plan had been to use the switch for connectivity to the PSTN, which certainly is technically feasible. Carriers commonly interconnect to other carriers with ATM links. Unfortunately, the two carriers providing service to my client did not have the administrative infrastructure to provide PSTN connectivity through ATM. In the final design, shown in Figure 4.13, it was necessary to provide some direct DS1s for PSTN connectivity, but we were able to connect to the government voice network via ATM.

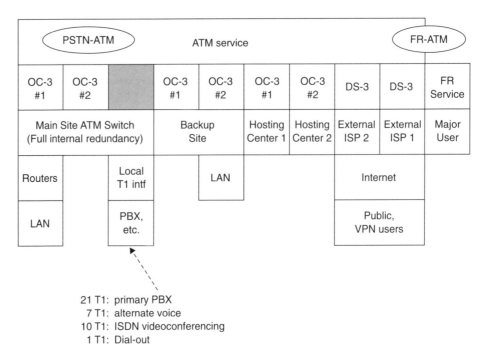

Figure 4.12   Revised plan.

Frame Relay

Frame relay started as part of the B-ISDN architecture, as a low- to medium-speed dedicated access technology. In the early 1990s, it soon overshadowed the developing B-ISDN work. To accelerate the effort, an industry consortium, the Frame Relay Forum, was founded. Its initial members were called the Gang of Four: Cisco, Digital Equipment Corporation, Nortel, and Stratacom.

Whether over ATM or not, FR is intended to runs over high-quality links, so that retransmissions would be needed only rarely. As a consequence, the responsibility for retransmission, when reliable transmission is needed, can move to the endpoints. Not all applications require reliable delivery. Making the endpoints responsible for reliable delivery, when required, is a fundamental part of IP design. See the discussion of the end-to-end assumption in Chapter 5.

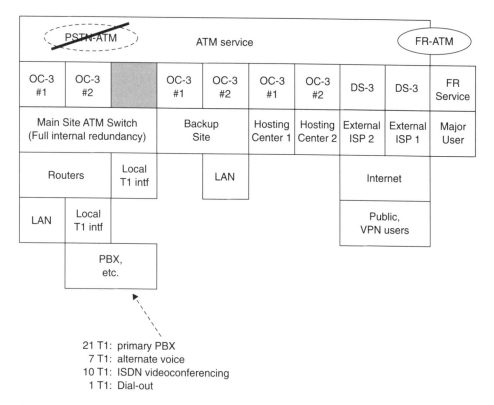

Figure 4.13 Phase 3 network.

The same bandwidth can be committed to a frame relay service and be priced lower than the same bandwidth on a dedicated line. Pricing is usually traffic-independent, but includes both bandwidth charges and physical connectivity charges.

You pay for the access link, which has a *local access rate*. This rate is the clock speed on the physical link.

For each virtual circuit, the service is defined by a *committed information rate* (CIR). The CIR is the rate at which the provider offers a high probability of delivery. There also may be an *excess burst rate* that the provider will attempt to deliver, but has a much higher probability of loss. Any frames beyond the excess burst rate will be dropped at the ingress switch.

When the sum of the CIRs exceeds the access rate, the interface is said to be *oversubscribed*. Oversubscription is a perfectly valid method to use when traffic is bursty, and you do not expect all VCs to be in use simultaneously.

Not all FR offerings have the same underlying assumptions. Some strictly police the CIR and allow minimal bursting. Such services approach dedicated line performance. At the other extreme, services have been offered that have a CIR of zero, and all traffic is best-effort.

When you price a frame relay service, you will need to consider the one-time and recurring costs of end equipment, access link(s), and bandwidth. FR requires a CSU/DSU function that is not required in ATM, although the CSU/DSU function is integrated into some routers (see Table 4.10).

Most people casually familiar with FR tend to think of it as a data link layer protocol, and leave it at that. Indeed, the LAP-F protocol is important. But to understand a FR service, you need to understand how protocols are identified in frames, how the status of individual VCs are known, and how logical addresses are learned.

Table 4.10 Frame Relay Access

COMPONENT	NOTES	USUAL PRICING
Access link	Most commonly 64 Kbps, T1,or T3. May be fractional. ISDN access common in Europe.	Installation plus distance and bandwidth-based monthly charges.
DSU/CSU	If not part of access link pricing.	Purchase or lease.
Router interface	Separate cost on modular routers.	Purchase or lease, monthly maintenance.
Router common	Total cost of fixed-configuration routers, or amortized cost of common equipment to which interface is inserted.	Purchase or lease, monthly maintenance.
Per-virtual circuit	Based on CIR and CBR.	Monthly rate.
Backup resources	Optional.	Depends on mechanism (analog dial, ISDN, etc.). Can be initiated from router or DSU/CSU.

The Network Layer and Frame Relay

It is useful to distinguish between the FR *protocol* and the FR *service*. The protocol indeed is of the OSI link layer. The overall service, however, has additional mechanisms that interact with the network layer.

One basic requirement is to be able to associate each DLCI with one or more network addresses at the distant end of the virtual circuit. This can be done either with static configuration or inverse ARP [RFC2390]. Another basic requirement is identifying the payload in a frame. As with ATM, this is done with an 802.2 LLC header [RFC2427].

The Link Layer and Congestion Management

Frame relay has one or more user data subchannels identified with *data link connection identifiers* (DLCI). Channel status can be monitored with the *local management interface* (LMI), which is on a reserved DLCI.

The FR protocol proper has several mechanisms associated with congestion management. As you will see, FR protocol features alone are an imperfect solution to congestion management.

Each frame, however, has congestion management flags. In the FR frame header are three bits:

- **Discard Eligibility (DE).** Set by the end host/router.
- **Forward Explicit Congestion Notification (FECN).** Set by switches internal to the FR service, in the direction of the source to destination.
- **Backward Explicit Congestion Notification (BECN).** Set by switches internal to the network, indicating that congestion was encountered in the source-to-destination path. BECN, however, is sent in the direction of the source.

Many commercial routers, certainly as their default, have no intelligent response to FR congestion flags, and may or may not set DE. This confusion is an artifact of the original assumption that FR went directly between end hosts, as opposed to current practice where most hosts are LAN attached. Today's FR circuits connect to routers, to which the host LANs connect.

It is the end host, not the router, that is generating the traffic that is contributing to congestion. Unfortunately, the end host does not see the FR congestion information because it does not see the FR frame.

Instead, it sees the LAN frame, which does not contain the BECN, FECN, and DE information.

There are several imperfect ways to deal with this problem. First, the end hosts may be trusted to deal with the problem at the transport layer. Second, the service provider may be trusted to have adequate capacity if the traffic contract is not exceeded, and the ingress router is trusted to police traffic to stay within the contract. Third, the service provider may have intermittent congestion, and the ingress router will police traffic down to "congestion" levels when the router sees BECN or FECN.

While the basic FR specifications indicate broadly what FECN and BECN do, the exact behavior that causes them to be issued varies among FR service providers. In the long run, it is probably much better to rely on transport layer mechanisms to manage control. After all, the difference between X.25 and FR was to move retransmission to the transport layer. Having the end hosts manage congestion is consistent with the FR architectural assumptions.

In the shorter run, there are features such as the frame relay adaptive-shaping option on Cisco routers. When this feature is enabled, the interface will respond to BECN, or to the proprietary equivalent in Cisco/Stratacom devices. While the router is in the congestion response condition, it will apply a special set of CIR and CBR limits to all traffic on the interface.

End hosts and routers connect to the FR *user-to-network interface* (UNI). There is a *network-to-network interface* (NNI) that interconnects FR carriers, which has an indirect effect on the user-perceived service. Figure 4.14 shows a real-world configuration, in which the FR service is ordered from a national carrier, but is actually provisioned by several local carriers and an interexchange carrier.

FR's Physical Layer: Freds, FRADs, and Other Access Devices

When I started to work with FR, I did a slight doubletake when my mentor said that Fred connects sites to the FR provider. "Who's Fred?" I asked.

"No, not Fred. Frad," was the response I *thought* I heard.

I tried to clarify. "OK, so Frad spells his name strangely. I still want to know who he is and what he has to do with frame relay."

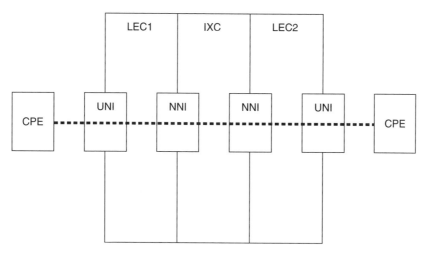

Figure 4.14 FR provisioning.

Eventually, I worked that Frad was not a person, but a FRAD: a *frame relay access device*. You can think of a FRAD as a DCE for FR service. As opposed to DCEs such as modems, DSUs, and CSUs, a FRAD is aware of the data link layer. A FRAD may contain an integrated DSU/CSU, or it may connect to an external DSU/CSU.

A simple FRAD has two serial interfaces: One connects to the FR network, while the other connects to the user equipment. A FRAD can be more intelligent with respect to the number and types of user interfaces it supports. The FRAD may offer more than one user interface, each of which is associated with a single virtual circuit. Some FRAD interfaces may encapsulate the user data link protocol, such as IBM SDLC, to frame relay encapsulation.

As the complexity of a FRAD increases, it looks more and more like a router. Cisco offers an interesting alternative for controlling costs, the CFRAD (Cisco FRAD). A CFRAD is actually a low-end router, such as the 2500 series, that has two serial interfaces and a LAN interface. The CFRAD executable has a lower price than full-featured code, but the CFRAD code does not enable the LAN interface.

The ideal CFRAD application is replacement of an existing IBM dumb terminal network, where it is eventually planned to replace the dumb terminals themselves with LAN-connected PCs. Costs of the network replacement are lowered by the difference between CFRAD and full software licenses. As sites replace their dumb terminals, the software can be upgraded to support the LAN.

The physical layer has become more complex. In many installations, there is a single physical interface using a common standard such as RS-232, V.35, etc. Recently, however, inverse multiplexing has come to FR with the *multilink FR* (MFR) specification defined by FRF XXX. The FR interface, either UNI or NNI, can be bundled into a single virtual interface that has greater bandwidth than any available real physical interface.

What problems does MFR solve? First, it can add fault tolerance. A failure of one link in a bundle will not bring the entire virtual interface down, although throughput will decrease. The more diverse the physical routing of the links inside the bundle, the more unlikely it is that a single failure will interrupt all of them.

MFR does not solve all availability problems. By definition, there is a single FR interface to the entire bundle, and this interface can fail. If diversely routed bundle links go through paths of significantly different length, latency can vary as frames go through paths of different delays.

Another problem that MFR solves is avoiding impact on an existing FR network when higher-speed physical interfaces, such as T3, are not available in the particular geographic area (see Figure 4.15).

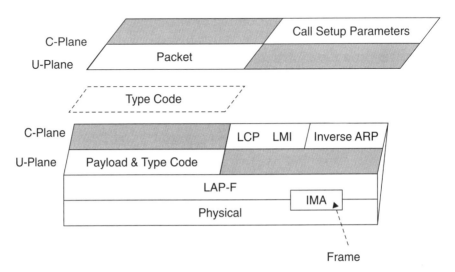

Figure 4.15   Even FR may be sublayered.

Recovering from FR Failures

Think about a physical interface that has several virtual circuits multiplexed onto it. There will be hardware indications if the access link proper goes down, but how does end equipment know if an individual virtual circuit has gone down?

If the individual virtual circuit has a backup mechanism (e.g., dial-up), there must be awareness that the FR VC has gone down and it is time to bring up the backup. The "school solution" is that the LMI will provide status information on each DLCI.

The problem becomes complicated, however, if any interprovider interface in the path does not use NNI. In Figure 4.16, VC 2 is tunneled from the IXC to LEC 3. If the local loop at LEC 3 fails, there is no way for LEC 3 to signal the IXC that a failure has occurred. The IXC, in turn, cannot send to LEC 1 an indication it did not receive from LEC3. There is no way, at layer 2, for the site 1 router to know that backup needs to be initiated.

Most commonly, the solution to lack of end-to-end NNI is to run a dynamic routing protocol that issues hellos, and to declare a failure when an FR-connected site becomes unreachable because its router's hellos are not heard. The router that detects unreachability will have a preconfigured static route that is less preferred than the route reached

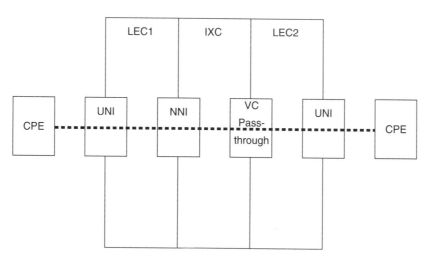

Figure 4.16 FR without NNI.

through dynamic routing. This static route will bring up the backup facility.

Provisioning Gotchas

There are three specifications for the Local Management Interface on FR: Annex A, Annex D, and "Gang of Four." The enterprise rarely has a choice, and the differences among the three versions are minor. The customer equipment, however, must use the right specification. This usually means that the enterprise must be told which specification is used by the carrier's switch, although some customer equipment can autodetect the LMI specification in use.

Just as the local telephone company must tell you the phone number associated with your dial line, the carrier must tell you the DLCI they have assigned to a given destination. Since the DLCI is locally significant, there will be two DLCIs associated with any virtual circuit. By Murphy's Law, it is not at all unheard of that the carrier reverses the DLCIs they tell the customer, or the customer swaps them during configuration.

VoFR

Voice over frame relay, defined in FRF.11, can be a good choice for enterprises with FR networks in place. This is not a magical technology.

One of the enhancements that help VoFR is fragmentation, as described in FRF.12. But what does fragmentation do? It splits the frame into smaller pieces to minimize latency. Have we heard this before, perhaps as an argument for small ATM cells?

VoIP can run over FR as well. What are the tradeoffs between VoIP running over FR connectivity and native VoFR (see Table 4.11)?

Table 4.11   Voice Tradeoffs

	VOFR	VOIP
Overhead	Lower	Higher
WAN topologies supported	Less flexible	More flexible
Perceived maturity	More	Less
Flexibility	Less	More

VoIP offers the flexibility of dynamic address assignment. This is a significant advantage in moves and changes.

SMDS

Switched Multimegabit Data Service (SMDS), while offered by a few carriers, is generally another service that has been bypassed by time. SMDS is a particular Bellcore/Telecordia-defined subset of the IEEE 802.6 metropolitan area network (MAN) standard. 802.6 originally offered multisite support for both multimedia and data traffic, but the SMDS implementation focuses on data flow from a single site to a carrier POP.

SMDS was really intended as a transitional method on the journey to B-ISDN. It offered customers a common interface before carriers had ATM in their internal networks, with the ability to segment traffic into cells and put them on DS1 or DS3 media feeding the carrier and inside the carrier (see Figure 4.17).

With the widespread introduction of ATM user-to-network interfaces (UNI), the need for user broadband interfaces decreased. In principle, B-ISDN is to the ATM carrier network as ISDN is to the SS7 network. SMDS is a transitional technology between dedicated lines and B-ISDN.

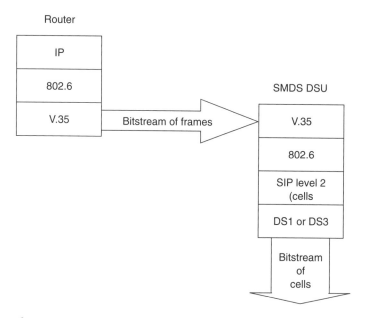

Figure 4.17 SMDS layers do not correspond to OSI layers.

If your local carrier offers SMDS at an attractive price, you may want to consider it for specific applications. In general, however, if you need high speed in the WAN, consider a more widely used technology.

Looking Ahead

You have seen the features and tradeoffs of basic services. Notwithstanding the fervor of new technology marketers, the basic services are proven, and indeed may be the best approach for many situations.

Emerging last-mile technologies such as xDSL and cable TV services will be discussed in the context of carrier provisioning, and are deferred to Chapter 6. Virtual private networks are a software-defined overlay onto basic services, and are detailed in Chapter 7.

VPNs often need security features, another focus of Chapter 8. Both basic and new services may require fault tolerance, the carrier aspects of which are in Chapter 6, but the enterprise multihoming strategies are the main content of Chapter 7.

CHAPTER 5

Virtualizing in Modern Networks

*When you have eliminated the impossible, whatever remains,
however improbable, must be the truth.*

SIR ARTHUR CONAN DOYLE

What is real? Would you like to play Global Thermonuclear War?

WOPR COMPUTER IN THE MOVIE *WAR GAMES*

*There is no problem in computer science that is not amenable
to a sufficient level of indirection.*

BUTLER LAMPSON

All too many users have an intuitive belief that if they were to pull on the London end of a London to New York circuit, wires would wiggle in Manhattan. The reality, of course, is that any network of complexity beyond a very simple LAN involves one or more layers of virtualization onto real media. At the OSI lower layers, virtualization usually involves multiplexing, but various name and address mapping functions provide virtual structure as one moves up the protocol stack.

Previously, you developed your network business case and the end-to-end policy goals for it. In Chapter 4, "Basic Services," you saw how basic WAN services fit, or did not fit, these goals. In this chapter, you will begin to learn means of virtualizing goal-oriented views onto basic services. Different virtualization methods allow you to extend into the WAN in ways close to what your applications expect, but sometimes with substantial overhead. Overhead, however, is part of the cost of doing business, as long as you can do what you need to do.

There are a great many issues and incompatibilities among tunnels, NAT, firewall proxies, and tunnels including IPsec. This chapter will explore these issues, discussing how the Internet is moving away from its original architectural assumption that IP addresses have end-to-end significance. Some of the practical matters to be discussed include when to pass tunnels through firewalls (or to bypass them), and the roles of authenticated firewall traversal and transport layer security.

In basic data communications, you probably recited mantras of protocol encapsulation, moving from the top to the bottom of a protocol stack: application messages in transport segments, transport segments in packets, and packets in frames. Tunneling is an extension of encapsulation. Tunnels add recursion at the same layer: a transport *protocol data unit* (PDU) encapsulated in another transport PDU, or a packet inside a packet.

Looking at one mechanism, such as multiplexing, will give insights into another, such as tunneling. The logic at one layer tends to bleed into the logic at the next layer. Load-sharing NAT, for example, has similarities to multilink PPP over L2TP, and to higher-layer tunneling.

Architectural Challenges

Some say the journey is its own reward, while others focus on the destination. Personally, I find myself all too distracted by roadkill on the Information Highway. Network designers need to ask questions about both aspects: What part of the problem definition centers on the journey—the route to the destination—and what part centers on the destination itself—the host?

If the problem is being defined in respect to the function of a host, several questions immediately come up:

- Is the application processing actually done on more than one host?
- Will the machine originally requesting the service be aware of the actual machine(s) that performs the service?
- If multiple machines are involved in serving the request, is the flow among them controlled by the requesting hosts, by some kind of directing engine, or by negotiation among the servers?
- Is the destination identified by a registered IP address? Such an address need not be visible to the client if the client locates the host through DNS, but it is still relevant what address DNS returns.

The End-to-End Model

The *end-to-end model* is considered the basis of the Internet protocols, but actually contains several subassumptions. Classic telephony uses the opposite of the end-to-end model: End devices are not intelligent, and the network makes all routing and load distribution decisions. The original timesharing computers used a similar model, using "dumb terminals" with just enough intelligence to handle frame-level communications for display and keyboard input.

The fundamental assumption of the end-to-end model (i.e., the fundamental assumption of the fundamental Internet assumption) really has two parts:

- Network elements—routers—specialize in forwarding packets efficiently.
- End hosts are intelligent and do everything the routers do not.

When a data network has to maintain state on all end hosts, as do telephony networks, its network elements are more complex yet slower than devices like routers and LAN switches. On the other hand, the end devices, such as telephones, historically are much cheaper than intelligent end hosts.

A second subassumption is that some functions can only be done thoroughly by end hosts, not the network. End-to-end reliable delivery through retransmission is one such function, as is end-to-end security [RFC1958]. Increasingly critical functions are active participation in quality of service and congestion management. A host that participates in these functions is neither pure end-to-end nor network-controlled.

Another major subassumption is that addresses of an originating and receiving host are consistent and globally unique throughout the lifetime of their interaction. IP addresses, originally intended only as routing destination identifiers, have been overloaded with a wide range of functions.

In particular, they have become endpoint identifiers, much like traditional telephone numbers in the public switched telephone network (PSTN). Unlike the PSTN, however, IP addresses were never meant to be persistent identifiers that would not change with operational requirements. Even in the PSTN, this assumption has been changing.

Toll-free numbers, for example, are only aliases for real telephone numbers, and need to be translated to the real numbers. Portable telephone numbers also need to be translated.

A variety of new developments challenge this assumption, yet provide useful services. Figure 5.1 shows the traditional end-to-end model and the more recent nontransparent model.

Where all addresses were once both unique and globally routable, there are now private addresses that are unique and routable only within the scope of a single address authority: an addressing realm. There also are addresses that are unique but have been designated as not routable in the public Internet. Such addresses would be routable only within the realms of certain extranets, such as closed military or financial networks.

Information commonly is virtualized from one realm to another. There are three basic strategies for such virtualization (see Figure 5.2):

Tunneling. Preserves original protocol headers. Think of this as a telephone conversation involving your strange relatives, in which you are actually speaking to Uncle Bill, who is constantly repeating the yelling in the background with the preface, "Aunt Shirley says..."

Translation. Removes protocol header and transfers payload, creating a new header at the destination. Think of a political press secretary saying "What the President really meant to say..."

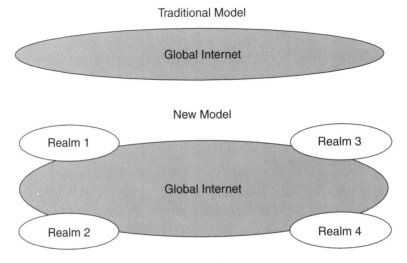

Figure 5.1 Evolving views of address significance.

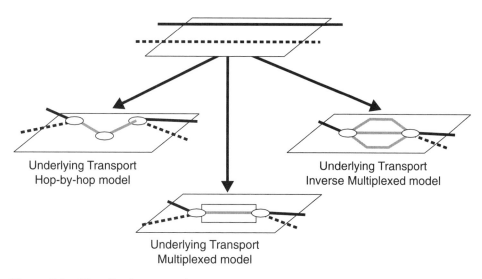

Underlying Transport
Hop-by-hop model

Underlying Transport
Inverse Multiplexed model

Underlying Transport
Multiplexed model

Figure 5.2 Virtualization strategies.

Multiplexing. Sending information over a channel that is identified by context outside the channel. Think of this in the context that once your Significant Other has answered your call, you do not need to keep identifying yourself during the call. (If you do, you have a *big* problem.)

In some respects, multiple realms connected by NAT have the potential of greater scaling for the Internet as a whole, since addressing can be reused. Along with this better scalability, however, comes much more complex troubleshooting. Troubleshooting is complex because traditional tools like ping and traceroute do not work properly in situations where the end-to-end model does not hold. In addition, NAT may break some higher-layer protocols.

Lear [2000] observed that transparency "demands that devices between two endpoints not modify information within the packet above layer 2, except under very specific well-defined circumstances (i.e., decrement the TTL or record route). Changing of IP addresses is not viewed as acceptable, nor is any change to layer 4 and above." He proposes a model of "illumination," in which hosts can discover they are routing through useful devices that violate the end-to-end model, and adjust their communications to compensate for the violation (see Figure 5.3). Examples of such illumination including a voice host recognizing when

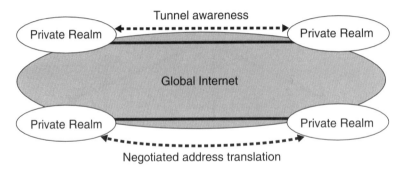

Figure 5.3 Illumination.

the current network performance is so bad as to be unusable, and returning a busy signal rather than bad service. Another example is recognizing there is a NAT in the path that will break IPsec, and substituting an end-to-end security protocol such as SSH.

With illumination, we move increasingly to a model that has the benefits, but not the liabilities, of a connectionless network. In the sense that there is a setup phase for connectionless communications, involving control plane protocols, resources need not be committed in the core network as they are in telephony networks.

The Local versus Remote Model

Another model challenged by newer virtual circuit technologies is local versus remote (see Figure 5.4). Many readers are confused with the best way to implement partial mesh networks, particularly with frame relay.

Sometimes, end-user organizations have a mental model that "nothing should change" when moving to a new WAN service. This is not always a productive assumption.

Point-to-multipoint subnets often are done not because they are inherently a good thing, but because they work around some limitations. Routing usually becomes much simpler in hub-and-spoke topologies when multiple point-to-point subnets replace a point-to-multipoint partial mesh (see Figure 5.5).

One motivation for keeping point-to-multipoint subnets is that the routing protocol in use does not understand arbitrary IP prefix lengths, so there is only one subnet size in the routing domain. If that

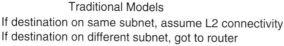

Traditional Models
If destination on same subnet, assume L2 connectivity
If destination on different subnet, got to router

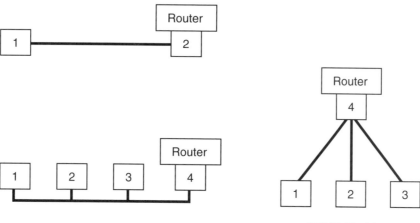

NBMA Model
If destination on same subnet,???
  Special arrangement to send to node,
  which pseudobroadcasts?
If destination on different subnet,
go to router

Figure 5.4   Local versus remote.

subnet size has to be large enough for a LAN segment, it will waste address space when space-efficient /30 prefixes cannot be used for point-to-point links. Classless routing protocols remove the technical objection here, although frequently there is human resistance to move

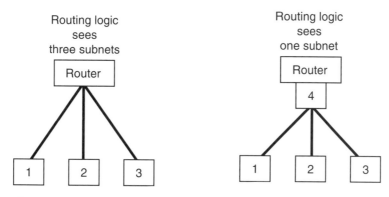

Figure 5.5   Many point-to-point versus point-to-multipoint.

away from familiar classful problems. Vendors that continue to insist on introducing beginners to IP addressing using the obsolete classful model aggravate this situation.

Another reason for using point-to-multipoint is a workaround to implementation restriction in major router implementations such as Cisco and Nortel. These operating systems have a finite and fairly small maximum number of software-defined and real interfaces. When a hub router has many point-to-point connections, it easily can run out of software-defined subchannel/virtual circuit interfaces.

There are perfectly reasonable applications for point-to-multipoint. It is a natural topology for multicast applications, where the hub originates most traffic.

Multiple point-to-multipoint links also are a means of implementing interactive and conferencing application, in which each participant has a point-to-multipoint connection to other members of its group.

Making Bigger Virtualizations Out of Little Ones

One of the keys to network scalability, both in performance and in reliability, comes under many names. Under whatever name, it is the concept of hierarchy. Theorists of human management long have known about the limits of span of control: the numbers of direct subordinates that a manager effectively can control. In networking, there is also a difference between the number of distinct information streams of which a router or switch can be aware, and the number of streams it can manage well. Introducing hierarchy is the only way we know how to build Really Big Networks.

The problems solved by acceptable Really Big Networks are reliability, performance, and maintainability.

Trunks are the basic facilities that link the aggregate, high-speed interfaces of multiplexers. They are fast physical facilities that contain multiple slower information streams. The trunk, however, can be switched as a unit without worrying about its constituent parts, as long as they remain associated, as a block, with the trunk. Unfortunately, multiprotocol label switching has adopted the term *traffic trunk* to refer to a group of end-to-end flows. Traffic trunks are not the same idea as multiplexed trunks.

Inverse multiplexing has the related concept of a *bundle*, in which multiple slow physical streams form a single higher-speed virtualized channel. When inverse multiplexing is used, the individual physical links can be moved, but care is needed to avoid accidentally dropping a link from the bundle during network changes.

It is common to bundle multiple IP addresses into an aggregate variously called a *supernet* or a *summary route*. Aggregation generally improves network stability and decreases workload on network elements, but it can lead to suboptimal routing. If some router along the path to a destination might have better routing for part of the aggregate, the information is not present for that router to *deaggregate* the supernet into more-specific pieces. For Internet routing, there often is a compromise: An enterprise sends more-specific routes to its provider(s), the providers optimize their routing for the enterprise, but aggregate the enterprise address space into aggregates before telling the rest of the Internet about it. This practice is most common with multiple points of connection to the same ISP, and is discussed further in Chapter 7, "Fault Tolerance."

ATM and MPLS have some useful terminology for aggregation. At a *merge point*, multiple streams and paths merge into a single common path. The common path is called an *aggregate stream*. Aggregate streams are the rough equivalent of trunks in multiplexing. Unfortunately, MPLS uses "trunk" in a different way, discussed later in the chapter.

In ATM *VP merging*, if a virtual path identifier (VPI) uniquely identifies the group of streams, and the virtual circuit identifiers (VCI) for each stream is unique with respect to the VPI, the individual streams can be deaggregated. Alternatively, ATM *VC merging* causes the individual streams to lose their identity. Such loss of identity is not a problem as long as the individual data units, such as IP packets with addresses, can be identified.

The MPLS equivalent of a virtual path could be thought of as a stack of labels. The topmost, current label would be equivalent to a VC, and the one below it equivalent to a VP.

Load Distribution

A fundamental concern in designing robust networks is load sharing, which appears early in the specification of networks with multiple

WAN paths and multiple servers. Once that concern is recognized, the next concerns are "What is load?" "What is sharing?"

Assume, for a moment, that loads and sharing are adequately defined. The application designer needs to look at client-to-server interaction at the application level, without becoming ensnared in the details of the network.

The problems that load sharing solves are to free the application designer from worrying about the exact location of local and remote servers, to provide application-level scalability by adding servers, and to prevent total application failure due to the death or disability of an individual server.

In Xanadu Did Kubla Khan Load Sharing Decree

Consulting to a carrier, I dealt with a large bank that said they had three server farms, and they wanted to make sure that one of their customers, dialing in to a provider POP anywhere in the world, would be routed to the server that had the least load, and, if multiple lightly loaded servers, that they would be routed to the server to which the path was least loaded.

Their assumption was that somehow, magically, BGP would solve their problem. They missed a key concept in what they were saying: They were referring to hosts, not subnets.

When we tried to explain the realities to them, one Dilbertian manager responded, "clearly you aren't worth the consulting money we pay you. Would you be so good as to give us the telephone number of the Person Who Is In Charge of the Internet?"

More seriously, one of the real problems in Internet operations is getting across to enterprise-oriented managers that they simply do not have end-to-end control.

While "rules of thumb" are always suspect as general solutions, a general guideline from queueing analysis of data link protocols is that latency begins to increase rapidly when utilization exceeds 50 percent. Load distribution is a way to avoid such latency. In particular, if the load distribution decision is made at the time of link establishment, rather than imposing overhead on each packet, the overhead can be amortized over each packet and have a minimal impact.

It can be useful to divide load sharing into local and distributed techniques, which complement one another. Local approaches distribute load across servers at a single site. Local load distribution is not visible to the WAN.

Distributed load distribution considers network costs as part of reaching a particular server. Link cost is not the only factor. Distributed load sharing also tries to equalize traffic across sites.

What controls load distribution? Nonintrusive methods are completely inside the load-sharing device, while intrusive methods either receive server feedback or send dummy transactions to servers.

Another question about load distribution is whether the mechanism is indirect or direct. Indirect mechanisms become involved during the setup phase of a transaction, such as its DNS lookup or the use of Portmapper for RPC/NFS. These mechanisms tell the client which server to use.

Direct and indirect load sharing takes place in devices generally considered part of the network rather than the application. In contrast, *redirection*, as seen in HTTP, FTP, and many other protocols, the original server passes the request to some other server.

Indirect methods give alternate addresses at session establishment. Direct mechanisms are "in-band," and affect the data stream. For example, they may change addresses in protocol headers of every packet of a session. Indirect and direct methods can complement one another. For example, a load-aware DNS server could send the session to a site with multiple servers, at which a direct load-sharing device distributes traffic among those servers.

Local Load Distribution

What assumptions can be made about the load? Are all servers of equal power, and all transactions have identical resource requirements? If so, a simple round-robin algorithm will be quite adequate. Do not confuse round robins with Norwegian Blue Parrots. Round robins simply start at the beginning of a sequence, go server by server to the end, and then return to the beginning.

Simple round robin can be inefficient when the execution time for a transaction varies. Some servers may be left idle when transactions complete earlier than others. [Srisuresh & Egevang] describe the *least load first* algorithm as an incremental improvement over simple round

No, No, It's Resting, Look!

Devotees of Monty Python, among whom I proudly count myself, consider the Pet Shop sketch, centering on the Norwegian Blue Parrot, one of their greatest skits [Python1989a]. Devotees of Monty Python who also are network architects, however, see a similarity between this bird of lovely plumage and one of the technical challenges of load distribution.

In the skit, John Cleese returns, irate, to a pet store where he bought a parrot. In response to the shopkeeper's (Michael Palin) question about the problem, Cleese says "I'll tell you what's wrong with it. It's dead, that's what's wrong with it." Palin insists it is merely resting, or perhaps pining, until Cleese thunders, "It's not pining, it's passed on. This parrot is no more. It has ceased to be. It's expired and gone to meet its maker. This is a late parrot. It's a stiff. Bereft of life, it rests in peace. If you hadn't nailed it to the perch, it would be pushing up the daisies. It's rung up the curtain and joined the choir invisible.

"It is an ex-parrot."

Load distribution mechanisms try to send transactions to the least utilized servers. Such mechanisms, however, must distinguish between servers that are lightly loaded because they are just resting, and not loaded at all because they are dead. Load distribution devices should periodically poll their servers for signs of life, removing them as candidates for work if they do not appear to be alive.

robin. The load distribution device for least load first keeps track of the number of sessions on each server, and distributes each new transaction to the server with the least number of active sessions.

Least load first assumes that transactions are of equal size. If the workload is fairly well approximated by the traffic volume sent by a given requester, the *least weighted load first* algorithm further refines load sharing.

When servers are of unequal capacity, *least weighted load* will give better server utilization than the previous method. This algorithm uses some estimate of workload, such as traffic type and volume (see Table 5.1). You can think of the goal of this approach as drawn from Karl Marx: From each according to his ability, to each according to his weighted load.

It may be useful to use a moving average for utilization, since transactions may complete while the load is being distributed.

Predictive methods may not be the most accurate. Actual load measurements are more accurate, but also more complex and more intrusive.

Table 5.1   An Extensible Distribution Algorithm

ServerCapacity(i):	Capacity of server i.
SessionCount (i,j)	Number of sessions of type j on server i.
LoadingUnit (j)	The unit of workload estimation. If the basic unit is a session, the LoadingUnit is 1. If workload is estimated by traffic, it is a number of bytes.
LoadingFactor (n)	Estimate of resource loading for 1 LoadingUnit of traffic type n. A factor of 1.0 means that a session of type n consumes all resources on the server'

```
Foreach server (i),
   serverUsage(i) = 0
   foreach session on server(i),
         serverUsage(i) = serverUsage +
                     (LoadUnit(j) *
                     LoadingFactor (i,j))
   endfor
```

Assign the new session to the server(i) with the lowest serverUsage(i)/serverCapacity(i).

One obvious method is to monitor the service provided to some dummy transaction that is representative of load. One of the simplest ways of doing this is by sending pings to the device and distributing the next transaction to the server with the lowest ping response time.

Ping may be overly simplistic. When pinging a router, the ping response may be artificially inflated because ICMP echo reply is at the lowest internal priority of the router. Pings through a router are not affected. An excellent alternative is using SNMP to poll an application MIB.

Distributed Load Distribution

Loads can be distributed across facilities even when the network cost of reaching them is a significant part of the overall preference criteria. Designers will need to ask questions such as, "is it better to take a more heavily loaded network path to a lightly loaded server? Should I take the less heavily loaded path to a heavily loaded server?" etc.

The fundamental challenge is defining criteria that separately deliver network and server preferences, and then combine these with weighting rules or more complex heuristics. [RFC2391] identifies two basic strategies, *weighted least load first* and *weighted least traffic first*. As with the local algorithms, these estimate load, respectively, on session count and traffic volume.

There is no utterly ideal load distribution algorithm. Applications *and* networks will differ in their characteristics. Using the queueing theory rule of thumb that queueing latency begins to increase rapidly when utilization exceeds 50 percent, the network part of a distributed load distribution algorithm should be biased against links that are utilized above that level.

You need to consider the relative impact of network and server performance for a particular application. Consider an interactive application for which the ideal server processing time will be 800 milliseconds, and the ideal network delay will be 200 milliseconds. Server load is four times as important, in this scenario, than network delay. In the algorithm of Table 5.2, this would mean a NetworkCostWeight of 0.2 and a ServerCostWeight of 0.8.

Table 5.2 An Extensible Distribution Algorithm

ServerCapacity(k, j):	Capacity of server j at site k.
NetworkCapacity(k):	Application load capacity of path to site k.
SessionCount (k,j,n)	Number of sessions of type n on server (k,j).
ServerLoadingFactor (n)	Estimate of server loading for load type n. A factor of 1.0 means that a session of type n consumes all resources on the server.
NetLoadingFactor (n,k)	Estimate of network loading for traffic type n on the path to site k. A factor of 1.0 means that a session of type n consumes the entire bandwidth to site k. The reason that the NetLoadingFactor is site-specific as well as traffic-specific is that the paths to different sites can have different bandwidths.
NetLoadingUnit (n)	Quantum of network load for load type n. If session adequately projects workload, then the value is 1. Otherwise, the unit could be bytes or some multiple of bytes.
ServerLoadUnit (n)	Quantum of server load for load type n. If session adequately projects workload, then the value is 1. Otherwise, the unit could be bytes or some multiple of bytes.
PureNetCost(k)	Load-independent cost of reaching site k. This could be a routing metric, a ping response time, an SNMP variable, etc.

Table 5.2 (Continued)

	The intention of this value is assessing the network latency to the destination, considering propagation time, shared resource congestion, and other factors not directly associated with application loads. It is assumed that LAN cost to reach a specific server is negligible.
NetCostWeight	Weight to be given to the network cost in selecting a server. NetCostWeight + ServerCostWeight = 1.
ServerCostWeight	Weight to be given to the server cost in selecting a server. NetCostWeight + ServerCostWeight = 1.

```
Foreach site (k),
  serverUsage(k,i) = 0
  foreach session on server(k,i)
      serverUsage(k,i) =
        serverUsage(k,i) +
          (ServerLoadUnit(j)*ServerLoadingFactor (j))
  endfor
  combinedCost(k,i) =
      (serverUsage(k,i) * ServerCostWeight)
    + (((netLoadUnit(n) * netLoadingFactor (k,n))
      / netCapacity(k))
      + PureNetCost(k))
      * NetCostWeight)
endfor
```

Assign the new session to the server(i) at site(k) with the least CombinedCost(k,i).

Operational Challenges

End users really have simple expectations of networks: that they work. Admittedly, their definitions may become as subtle as Bill Clinton's definition of "is," but the fundamental question remains: Can the network reach the end devices? Again, the wit and wisdom of Monty Python applies. In *Monty Python and the Meaning of Life*, learned physicians answer the question "what is the most important machine in the hospital?" with "the machine that goes **ping**."

And so it is with networks. On a practical basis, the most basic meaning of "work" is the user can **ping** the destination, and the network operations staff can **ping** the user.

Being able to **ping** a destination, however, does not mean that a **traceroute** to that destination will be consistent. Even **traceroute** will not reveal the details of tunnels in the path.

Ping and Traceroute: Complementary Mechanisms

Your basic tools for active connectivity checking are **ping** and **traceroute**. Think of **ping** as an end-to-end test. It's not quite a transport layer test because it doesn't consider transport identifiers, but it is end to end as long as there are no tunnels, proxies, or address translators in the path.

traceroute is hop by hop at the network layer. It uses different protocol mechanisms than **ping**, and relies on the TTL mechanism. **traceroute** information complements that given to you by **ping**.

traceroute generates UDP datagrams and encapsulates them in IP packets. The UDP packets don't have a predefined port.

Microsoft **traceroute** does not send out UDP probes, but uses ICMP echo requests with an altered TTL. Technically, this should not work, because if an error, such as TTL exceeded, is associated with an arriving ICMP packet, the rules of ICMP say that no ICMP error packet should be generated. Many implementations ignore this restriction.

traceroute, in its first iteration, the TTL is set to 1, and the packet, as it should, triggers an ICMP TTL Exceeded message to be returned from routers one hop away.

On the second iteration, **traceroute** sets the TTL to 2, and routers two hops away generate the ICMP response. In successive iterations, the TTL continues to be incremented, until either the destination is reached or a hop count limit is reached.

traceroute may fail due to access lists rather than lack of connectivity. Access lists that cause it to fail include deny rules for high-numbered UDP ports. **ping** and **traceroute** both can fail because outbound ICMP is being denied. If inbound ICMP is denied, **ping** might fail but **traceroute** may work.

While **ping** has serious limitations for estimating quantitative performance, it is generally adequate for qualitatively checking if a host is up. Of course, if there is an intrusive mechanism between NAT and server for monitoring performance, timeouts in such mechanisms would also detect black-hole servers.

Physical and Data Link Layer Virtualizations

Carriers have long overlaid their routing models onto layer 2 connection-oriented switching systems. Certain enterprises also can make use of overlays, especially using ATM as a substitute for traditional time-division multiplexing.

In an overlay model, the user of the service sees IP subnets, which may actually map to an assortment of layer 2 constructs. The user stream may have one-to-one correspondence with a physical medium. In multiplexing, more than one subnet maps to a single physical medium. Inverse multiplexing reverses the relationship, in which multiple physical media support a single logical medium.

Such models can be operationally challenging, and visualization tools can be quite important for people to understand exactly what path traffic is taking,

Multiplexed Services

Both connection-oriented and connectionless services can use multiplexing, to virtualize a physical link onto a shared medium. The problem solved by multiplexing is to free the logical-level network designer from the bandwidth limits of specific media types (see Figure 5.6).

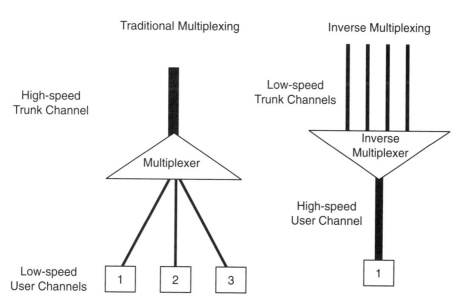

Figure 5.6   Multiplexing.

Virtual Circuit Services

In Chapter 4, you learned characteristics of virtual circuit services in common use: frame relay, ATM, and, in some niches, X.25. As their name suggests, they present the model of a connected circuit.

What virtualization do virtual circuit services provide? What problems do these solve?

One reason to look at such services is to get a better perspective on the worldwide environment. North Americans often assume the rest of the world uses flat-rate facilities, but connection time charges are common practice on most other continents. Virtual circuit services avoid connection charges when nothing is being sent. In Europe, ISDN is often a cost-effective way to access frame relay.

Virtual circuit services are limited in the topologies they support. ISDN and X.25 do not generally support point-to-multipoint, with the caveat that ISDN can do conference calls for voice. While ATM itself is point-to-point or NBMA, ATM LAN emulation (LANE) does support multicast and broadcast multiaccess topologies.

Virtual/Emulated LAN

In a book on WANs, why consider virtual LANs (VLAN) and emulated LANs (ELAN)? These need to be considered for two main reasons. First, the VLAN may be the campus feeder to the WAN, and there needs to be mappings of QoS or other signals from LAN protocols to WAN protocols. Second, ATM and new variants of "Ethernet over DWDM" have long range.

For either VLAN or ELAN technologies, the virtualization seen by the user organization is of a broadcast domain of MAC addresses. These actually map to shared LAN trunks or a LAN Emulation system (see Figure 5.7).

In a VLAN, the underlying transport marks frames with tags that identify the virtualized LAN. Another way to say this is that VLAN trunking identification is in-band.

The standard for marking is IEEE 802.1q, although Cisco's proprietary ISL is widely deployed. ISL is somewhat more feature-rich than the basic 802.1q, but the benefits of multivendor interoperability are quite

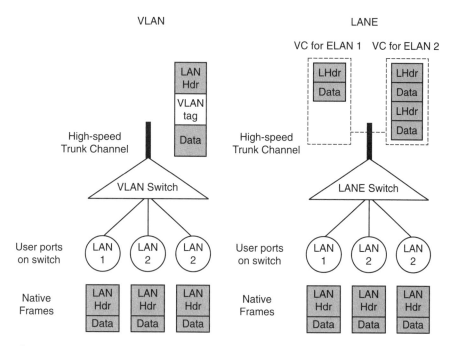

Figure 5.7 VLAN and ELAN trunking.

clearly sending the industry in a standards-based direction. Some Cisco devices only support 802.1q.

As frames are placed on ISL trunks, the ingress device prepends them with a header. ISL is much more clearly a tunneling approach than is 802.1q, which inserts a VLAN identifier field into the 802.3 or 802.5 headers.

In an ELAN, the frames themselves are not marked. Instead, the ELAN to which they belong is implied by the virtual circuits to which they are assigned.

LANEv1 provides essentially the same functionality as VLAN techniques, but runs over ATM media. For each emulated LAN, LANE creates virtual circuits among the LAN emulation clients (LECs), and passes unicast frames through these virtual calls. While the virtual circuit may go through more than one ATM switch hop, the switches are unaware that the cells going through them are associated with LANE. The interswitch topology is handled as any ATM call setup, either as permanent virtual circuits (PVC) in early implementations, or, in modern implementations as switched virtual circuits (SVC) set up using Q.2931.

Internally, LANE uses a client/server architecture to determine how paths should be set up for unicast frames. It uses other server functions to handle broadcast and multicast traffic.

Ethernet in the WAN

Ethernet in the WAN is not a typo. It is, however, a rather imprecise term. An amazing range of technologies fall under the general term Ethernet, and not all are the original set of LAN-oriented layer 1 and 2 technologies. There is a difference, for example, between using the IEEE 802.3 physical layer specification, and possibly the frame format, so that existing chipsets can be used for systems intended to be neither multiaccess or broadcast-capable. Calling a technology "Ethernet," in today's marketplace, does not necessarily mean the particular system supports bridging or VLANs. The technology may be intended only for point-to-point applications, such as Elastic Networks' EtherLoop, or it may connect to a router that does not run bridging protocols.

Even when bridging is supported, it is not necessarily a good idea. Enterprises have been seduced by the idea of "flattening" enterprise networks so they appear as one simple LAN, with extremely simple maintenance. In reality, flattened networks simply do not scale to appreciable size. Bandwidth is less likely to be a limit than broadcast loads on hosts. When everything is flattened into one LAN, it becomes difficult to isolate problems and to do capacity planning. Security is an obvious concern when everything goes everywhere.

Some of the newer broadband remote access technologies, such as data over cable TV and wireless, use the model of a bridged Ethernet. Such a model is perfectly reasonable for a shared medium, but access authentication and billing work far better with a point-to-point model. PPP over Ethernet (PPPoE) is a means of abstracting the point-to-point model of PPP over bridged media [RFC2516].

Just because you can do something, doesn't mean it's a good idea. Route and switch consistently to Ethernet interfaces? Of course. Flatten everything? Perhaps not.

In the WAN, the main areas of interest are Gigabit and 10 Gigabit Ethernet over an optical backbone using either SONET/SDH or *dense wavelength division multiplexing* (DWDM). 10GE actually maps onto

9.58 Gbps OC-192 channels, but Ethernets have never actually delivered data at the ostensible bit rate. No standard Ethernet has ever delivered 10 Mbps.

Look at Ethernet WANs less as a flattened network and more as a simple, cheap, high-bandwidth interface technique. At the customer site, the internal Ethernet (of any speed) links to a WAN Ethernet through a router or VLAN switch (see Figure 5.8). You want to have intelligence between the LAN and the WAN.

Internally, this quite new technology isn't necessarily a true end-to-end broadcast domain. Instead, the end users of the WAN service see an Ethernet or Fast Ethernet. Depending on the preferences of the carrier and its current network, the Ethernet frames may be carried over point-to-point fiber, SONET/SDH, ATM, or DWDM.

The carrier, such as Bell Nexxia (Canada), internally treats the customer LAN as a VLAN, and aggregates it into GE or 10GE. The carrier backbone does not use ATM, avoiding the "cell tax." Ethernet frames are either multiplexed onto point-to-point optical channels or run through MPLS tunnels.

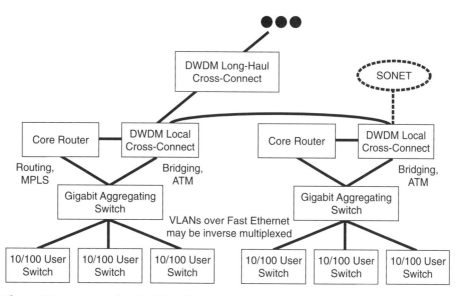

Figure 5.8   Aggregation in WAN Ethernet.

Inverse Multiplexed Service

From the user perspective, there is a single logical medium, which may be known to be a tunnel. The infrastructure to provide this view may include multilink PPP both in routers and external devices, virtual multilink PPP using L2TP, BGP TCP tunnels over multiple IP subnets, and inverse multiplexed ATM. The multiple links form a *bundle*.

Why inverse multiplex? The most obvious reason is to obtain more bandwidth than is available from a single physical medium. Inverse multiplexing also can make the logical medium more fault tolerant, since if one physical medium fails, traffic can move over the remaining physical links.

Why not inverse multiplex? It can take significant processor overhead in routers. Latency can increase. Depending on the load sharing, it can cause increased numbers of out-of-sequence packets, which increases the overhead for TCP (but not UDP) receivers.

Multilink PPP and LAP-B

One of the most basic methods of inverse multiplexing is to have multiple layer 2 streams interleaved. Both PPP and LAP-B support multiple links. Since LAP-B is more of a niche protocol, most work is with PPP.

As mentioned, managing multilink streams is processor intensive. Even for apparently straightforward bundling of several T1/E1 streams, many commercial routers have substantial configuration limitations, such as allowing only one high-speed bundle per physical chassis. One alternative comes from Tiara Networks, which has an interesting approach in which the MLPPP is offloaded from routers onto purpose-built aggregation devices (see Figure 5.9).

An even more complex issue in multilink PPP is creating a multiplexed stream from bit streams that connect to different physical chassis (see Figure 5.10). A common scenario for such applications comes when the remote device uses ISDN bandwidth on demand. Initially, it uses a single 64 Kbps B channel, but, with increasing load, the remote device decides to open a second B channel for increased bandwidth.

As shown in Figure 5.10, the PPP remote access server does not use individual BRI channels, but aggregates its ISDN access using PRI channels. In this example, the first B channel arrives at the second PRI

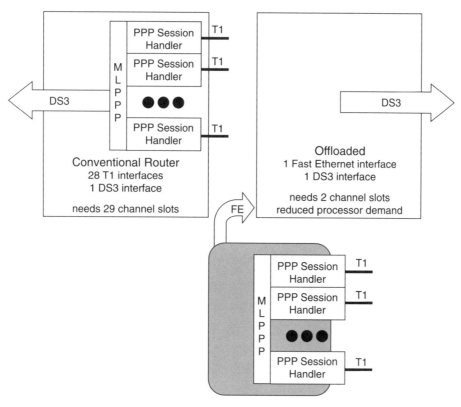

Figure 5.9 Multilink offload.

on Access Server 1. The second, however, arrives in the second PRI on Access Server 2.

BONDING, an acronym for Bandwidth on Demand Interoperability Group, is a different technique intended for videoconferencing applications. It interleaves at the bit, not frame, level, and is not appropriate for most data applications.

Multilink PPP over L2TP

L2TP is a tunneling mechanism that runs PPP over IP, which provides the ability for a dial-up user to call a local access point, be transported over a routed network, and appear at an enterprise as if it were a local dial-in there. The enterprise, not the carrier network, does the final authentication of the access request.

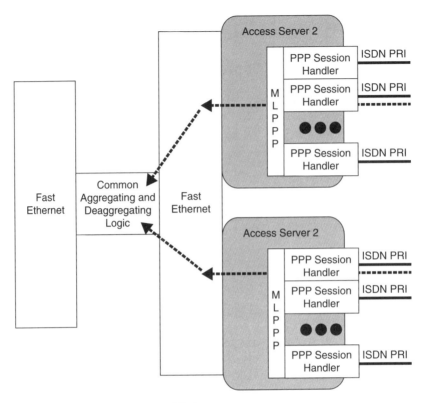

Figure 5.10 Multichassis multilink.

The PPP over L2TP has all the attributes of PPP over a physical medium, so more than one PPP stream can be multilinked into a bundle. Indeed, there can be multiple termination points for the L2TP stream, protecting against single points of failure in the enterprise (see Figure 5.11).

As does every other technique, L2TP has its costs. The major costs are significant processor loads for the reassembling host(s), overhead of additional tunneling between receivers, and potentially long latencies if the paths through the transport have significantly different delay. Service selection gateways discussed in Chapter 6, "Carrier Infrastructure and Optical Networking," can be optimized to terminate thousands of L2TP sessions. Such gateways come from firms including Nortel/Shasta and Redback.

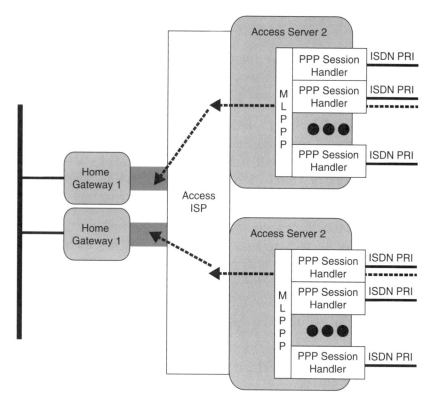

Figure 5.11 MLPPP over L2TP.

ATM Inverse Mux

The higher-speed ATM media may not be available at remote customer locations. T1, however, is reasonably ubiquitous, and the ATM Forum phy-0086 specification for inverse multiplexed ATM (IMA) provides a way to combine multiple T1/E1 streams into a single virtual circuit.

Widespread deployment of IMA probably dooms the SMDS service discussed in Chapter 4. SMDS was intended as a transitional service until B-ISDN customer interfaces were available, and connectivity to the ATM core needed to be done though T1 or T3 lines. It predated widespread customer use of ATM UNIs. SMDS hardware interfaces are expensive.

SONET Protection

SONET *alternate protection switching* (APS) gives the user the impression of a single SONET connection. The underlying reality is that of a primary SONET facility and an inactive backup facility (Figure 5.12).

Originally, SONET always used 1:1 redundancy, but 1:N schemes are going into service. See Chapter 6 for a discussion of 1:1, 1+1, and 1:N schemes. The entire idea of SONET APS is being challenged as gigabit and terabit routers, able to forward at full SONET speeds, become reality. 1:1 redundancy wastes a great deal of capacity.

The critical network described in the Chapter 4 section, "ATM and Integrated Services Today," relied on the underlying fault tolerance of SONET to avoid single points of failure. As shown in Figure 5.13, while the virtualization seen by the enterprise presented as ATM connections, redundant SONET rings were underneath the ATM service, preventing a single point of failure on the local and exchange carrier sides.

SONET proponents speak highly of the typical 50-millisecond time to switch to a backup ring. This number often is accepted as the Holy Grail of high availability, but the reason for this short a time deserves examination. Restoral times of hundreds of milliseconds or even seconds would cause only a slightly noticeable delay for most data applications. This goal is much more a voice objective. Two key factors

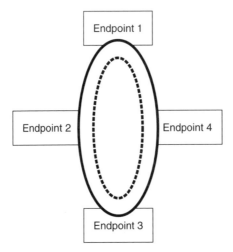

Figure 5.12   Basic SONET concept.

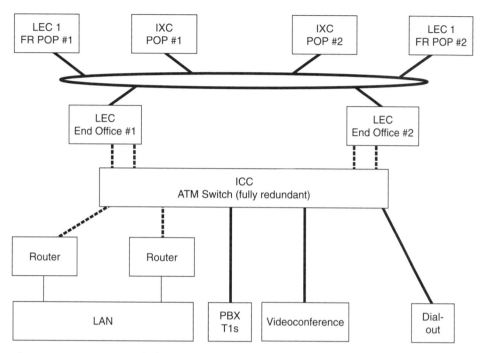

Figure 5.13 SONET underlying ATM.

apply to voice: the impact of loss on voice quality (e.g., Mean Opinion Score), and the time after which the voice switching system drops the connection. Dropped connections are much more serious from the perspective of telephone availability, because a large number of dropped connections means that a large number of calls will almost simultaneously be retried. Bursts of simultaneous calls can overload telephone switches and the Signaling System 7 network.

Multiprotocol Label Switching

A colleague recently called MPLS "ATM without cells." There is some truth to this. Both ATM and MPLS have link-specific identifiers, VPI/VCI for ATM and labels for MPLS. Both have specific paths.

MPLS, however, is an evolutionary technology that combines features of IP and of ATM. In a book such as this, there is a delicate line to draw between adequate descriptions of the technologies involved, and dropping into details of the protocol mechanisms.

The most important thing in understanding MPLS is to recognize it is a new way of looking at and combining older technologies. The second most important thing is recognizing that if you do not understand both how the paths are set up as well as how traffic is forwarded along the path, you do not understand MPLS in the particular application. Many presentations emphasize the forwarding part of MPLS, and, indeed, it looks very much like ATM when the focus is on that part. Often neglected, however, is the path determination part of MPLS, which builds on IP routing. It is not unfair to call MPLS an "overdrive" for IP forwarding, but MPLS is more than a simplified forwarding convention. It also provides a framework for traffic engineering, in which the assumptions of IP routing protocols can be overridden for good reasons.

The exact mechanism of labeling varies with the data link protocol over which MPLS runs. MPLS also has conventions for inserting label information into ATM and FR headers. With PPP and LAN protocols, MPLS inserts a "shim" header (or multiple headers) between the data link and network layer headers. The most general MPLS header is 32 bits long, with 20 bits devoted to the label itself.

MPLS architectural work and terminology is useful for other technologies. The issue of label retention, for example, provides terminology that is quite useful in discussing some NAT design issues.

MPLS has several benefits. It does improve forwarding performance, but not as dramatically as early advocates suggested, given that hardware-assisted IP routing continues to improve.

Probably the most important benefit of MPLS is that it provides a means, independent of the physical transport, of establishing constraint-controlled paths through a transmission system. Such *label-switched paths* (LSP) are the MPLS equivalent of IP or ATM routes, but are more flexible.

Many discussions of MPLS focus on the forwarding of tagged packets, but tend to simplify how the LSPs and label forwarding information base (LFIB) are set up. I would sum up some of the vendor presentations I've seen on the MPLS path determination process as "and here a miracle happens."

A better approach is to look at the problem this technology is trying to solve. The key realization of label switching, regardless of which vendor defined it, is the *forwarding equivalence class* (FEC).

Forwarding Equivalence Classes

Once I understood the idea of a FEC, I discovered that it is an extremely useful concept, applicable to design problems that do not even involve label switching. You can look at it as an extension of the Golden Rule: "Do unto others as you would have them do unto you."

In daily life, you really don't need to have different rules for doing unto most others; there are general ethical concepts that should apply everywhere. You probably have general sets of rules for dealing with the class of retail store clerks, the class of telemarketers (if, indeed, they have any class), and the class of armed robbers. You have special rules for dealing with people with whom you have special relationships.

Now, assume you have an enterprise that connects to the Internet through two ISPs, and you receive a full BGP feed from both. With the 70,000-plus routes of the global routing table, and tens of thousands of customer routes of a large ISP, your BGP routing table easily can approach 100,000 entries.

But from the standpoint of how you want to do unto the 100,000 destinations, how many classes of rules are there? The problem really will reduce to two classes of how you want to forward (see Figure 5.14):

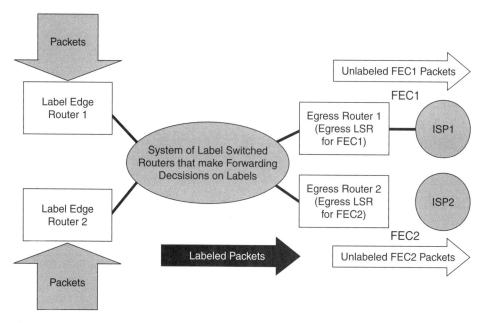

Figure 5.14 High-level view of MPLS.

those destinations to which you will forward via ISP1, and those to which you will forward to ISP2. Each class contains thousands of equivalent members, equivalent in the sense that they will be treated in the same way. That is not to say that different destinations will not be treated differently as they go to other autonomous systems in the Internet, but your routers have no direct control over external handling.

What if the ISPs provide VPNs with a choice of QoS? As long as these QoS values use the same interface, the number of FEC simply is the product of the number of ISP interfaces times the number of QoS categories.

In MPLS, packets are marked at an ingress *label edge router* (LER) as shown in Figure 5.15. This router adds a *label* to the packets. A label corresponds to a FEC, but is only significant between pairs of routers.

A *label-switched path* (LSP) is the end-to-end path taken from an ingress point for a given FEC. There is a link-local label value for each medium traversed along this path. When a labeled packet arrives at a label-switched router (LSR), the label tells the LSR the FEC to which the packet belongs. The LSR selects an outgoing interface, and changes the label to one that is meaningful to the next hop LSR (Figure 5.16).

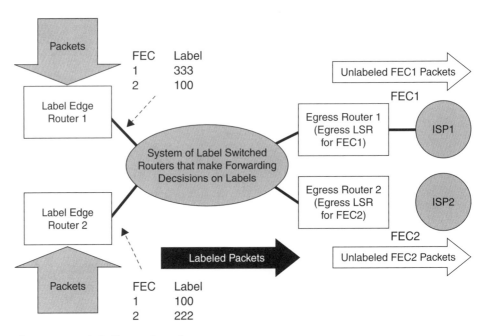

Figure 5.15 Labeling at the edge.

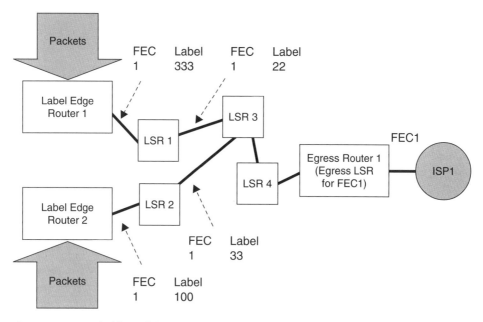

Figure 5.16   Label-based forwarding along an LSP.

FEC are global, while labels are local. FECs are not quite equivalent to ATM NSAP endpoint identifiers, but are a level of indirection between the endpoint identifier and the link-local connection identifier. In the MPLS architecture, an FEC is "a group of IP packets which are forwarded in the same manner (e.g., over the same Path, with the same forwarding treatment)" [Rosen 1999a]. Figure 5.17 shows the LSP for FEC 2.

ATM technologies, such as LAN emulation (LANE) and multiprotocol over ATM (MPOA), do not use the term FEC, but the idea is common to ATM and MPLS. Think of an ATM VC as equivalent to a MPLS FEC, but the FEC is associated with a sequence of VCs among ATM devices rather than a set of link-specific labels.

Operational Requirements

MPLS needs to obey the First Law of Plumbing: "If it don't leak, don't fix it." In other words, adding MPLS to an operational network should not break anything. Stated positively, MPLS must work with existing layer 3 routing, both unicast and multicast, both interior and exterior.

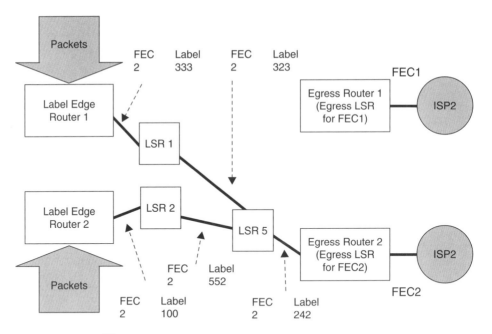

Figure 5.17 A different LSP.

While an admirable goal, this needs to comply at the level of functionality, not necessarily the level of protocol detail. **traceroute**, for example, breaks in an MPLS world in the sense that it cannot identify LSR hops. This behavior is due to the deliberate omission of the IP time-to-live loop prevention mechanism from MPLS. Modern routing protocols are loop-free, so a path derived from information supplied by routing protocols should be loop-free as well.

Operational MPLS systems, therefore, need an alternative function for checking connectivity. The IETF is examining ICMP interactions with MPLS, and extensions to deal with the **traceroute** problem have been proposed. Nevertheless, in the near term, there will probably need to be vendor-specific traceroute extensions that combine IP **traceroute** with knowledge of MPLS tunneling.

Traffic Engineering

Traffic engineering is a means of selecting the best path based on more information than conventional interior routing protocols provide. It addresses a variety of problems, which fall into two main classes, user services and network operations (see Table 5.3).

How does label switching help with traffic engineering? The question becomes, "where is the knowledge of traffic?" If the knowledge is in the minds of network planners, then they can use MPLS statically to define an explicit path. If evolving traffic-aware routing protocols are available, they can dynamically select paths that meet the constraint, beyond the routing metric, of having adequate capacity.

So What Are the Labels Being Switched?

Labels are not radically new ideas, and have equivalents in many protocols. They are similar to the connection identifiers introduced in Chapter 4. Examples in non-MPLS protocols include [Ashwood-Smith 1999a] those listed in Table 5.4.

In conventional routing, a packet is assigned to a FEC at each hop (i.e., L3 look-up); in MPLS, it is only done once at the network ingress.

LSP Setup

LSPs are set up manually, by a label distribution protocol, or by RSVP used as a setup protocol. One of the strengths of MPLS is that LSPs can be set up not simply with the basic approach of interior routing—find all possible paths, and use the "best"—but to find paths under constraints. Constraints go beyond traditional routing metrics.

There are both *ingress-driven* and *egress-driven* approaches to LSP setup. Ingress driven is closer to the traditional source routing model, in which a device enters the network and seeks a path to a destination. Ingress

Table 5.3 Traffic Engineering Problems

TRAFFIC-ORIENTED TE: OPTIMIZE USER SERVICES	RESOURCE-ORIENTED TE: OPTIMIZE PROVIDER ENVIRONMENT
Throughput	Congestion avoidance
Latency	Transient congestion
Availability	Congestion from inadequate resources (not enough bandwidth)
	Congestion from underutilized resources (bandwidth in the wrong place)

Table 5.4 Connection Identifiers In Non-MPLS Protocols

LAYER 1/2 LABELS	MPLS LABELS
ATM VPI/VCI	IP prefix
FR DLCI	Aggregated IP [3]
TDM timeslot	Source-destination pair [1]
X25 LCN	Aggregate of source-destination pairs[1,2,4]
Optical wavelength	Source-destination pair including higher layers [1]
	Aggregate of source-destination pairs including higher layers [1,2,4]
	Multicast tree

[1] Either end may be a wildcard.
[2] A traffic trunk in MPLS terminology.
[3] Prefix aggregation is also known as supernetting or summarization.
[4] Source-destination pairs frequently are called flows.

driven is a "pull" policy, where the user of the network pulls a route from the network. Egress driven setup is a "push" policy, where the exit points of the network advertise their existence and use protocol mechanisms to push, on a hop-by-hop basis, a path to them into routers along the path.

A common constraint would be bandwidth reservation. The setup mechanism is aware of the available bandwidth on each link, and how much has been allocated to other LSPs. MPLS setup is also aware of how much bandwidth is needed for a particular flow. Path setup will not select a path that has insufficient bandwidth for the desired flow.

In contrast to virtual circuits, MPLS does not necessarily lock up resources. It permits oversubscription at the discretion of the system designer.

Quality of service (QoS) is not the only possible constraint on paths. Other constraints can include administrative policy, security, billing arrangements, etc.

Label Distribution Protocol (LDP)

LDP uses both UDP and TCP, not reinventing reliable transfer as do OSPF and IS-IS. It uses UDP to send discovery messages similar to hellos in OSPF and IS-IS. Once neighbors are discovered, LDP uses TCP to establish adjacency with them.

LDP is the focus of most development activities, although work continues with RSVP. Basic LDP has two modes, *downstream unsolicited label distribution* and *downstream-on-demand label distribution*.

Consider two LSRs that share a common link. They are said to have a LDP adjacency. LSR2 is considered "downstream" from LSR1.

In DULD, LSR2, the downstream LSR, learns about a next hop for a new FEC destination. It generates a label for it and sends the binding of the label and FEC to LSR1, which inserts the information in its own table. LSR1 knows that any LSR2 next hop will understand the label.

DODLD, however, is triggered by a demand from the upstream router. During the setup process, LSR1, the upstream, determines that LSR2 is the next hop for a given FEC. LSR1 sends a request to LSR2, asking that LSR2 assign a label for the FEC, and, if so, to tell LSR1 what the label value should be.

Another aspect of LDP, which introduces terminology that is useful for a number of non-MPLS protocols, is that of label retention. In LDP, there are two label retention strategies: *conservative* and *liberal*.

In conservative label retention, labels received from other LSRs are kept only if they are known to be useful for routing. Usefulness means that they have been received from some LSR that appears as a next hop in the current LSR's routing table. Conservative label retention uses a minimum of memory, which is limited on devices such as ATM switches. The disadvantage of conservative label retention is that it will take longer to respond to changes in routing, because a new label has to be required if routing changes the next hop.

Liberal label retention responds faster to changes, but is more resource intensive. It can be useful in devices that normally have substantial memory, such as routers.

Assigning Packets to FECs

The ingress device needs to know how to assign packets to a particular FEC. This decision is made once, at the ingress.

Once the ingress device assigns a FEC, it prepends a label to the packet and forwards it. Intermediate LSRs do not make forwarding decisions on the packet header, but on the label. Each LSR looks up the label in a LFIB and determines the next hop (as in routing) and the link-local label to be associated with the outgoing packet. The process of receiving a packet with one label and sending it out with a new label is called *label swapping*. Label switching has also been called label swapping.

You can stack labels to form tunnels. LSRs always make forwarding decisions on the top label of the stack.

Trunks

MPLS trunks are at a logical level above LSPs. Trunks represent user requirements for traffic flow, and run over LSPs. As operational conditions change, trunks can move from one LSP to another. The term trunk is not quite the same as the simpler meaning used in multiplexing.

Trunks, like flows, are unidirectional (see Table 5.5). Real-world applications usually are bidirectional. It has been useful, therefore, to be able to define *bidirectional traffic trunks* (BTT). The *forward trunk* carries traffic from a source to a destination, and the *backward trunk* carries the responses from the destination back to the source. There is no requirement that the two trunks go symmetrically, on the same medium in each direction. The only requirement is when the two trunks are deleted, they are deleted on both media.

Table 5.5 Trunks

TRUNK DEFINITION INGRESS POINT	EGRESS POINT FEC CARRIED TRUNK ATTRIBUTES
Type	Examples.
Traffic parameter	As average rate, peak rate, token bucket size.
Generic Path selection and maintenance	Paths can be created manually or automatically. Basic automatic path selection uses a dynamic routing protocol, but more advanced selection involves considering constraints such as congestion avoidance.
Priority	When the network status changes and it is necessary to reroute trunks, in which order will they be selected for new paths?
Preemption	Closely related to priority, this attribute defines if this trunk preempts another trunk if resources are not available for both? Preemption can be associated with high priorities of differentiated service.

Table 5.5 (Continued)

TRUNK DEFINITION INGRESS POINT	EGRESS POINT FEC CARRIED TRUNK ATTRIBUTES
Resilience	In the event of a failure, should the trunk be rerouted? Even if this is a critical trunk, formal rerouting may not be needed if, for example, the trunk runs over an inverse multiplexed multilink medium. Basic resilience means the MPLS system is told to reroute on failure. Constrained resilience adds constraints on how the rerouting is done.
Policing	What should be done if the workload presented by a trunk exceeds the service contract of the trunk? Actions include rate limiting, buffering, dropping, tagging, or choosing to take no action.
Adaptivity	Can the path be rerouted if conditions changed, or is it "nailed" or "pinned" to a specific topology? The tradeoff in adaptivity is that reacting too fast threatens stability, but reacting too late leads to suboptimal resource use.
Re-optimization	Similar to, but different from, resilience. The ability to reoptimize implies resilience, but not necessarily the reverse.

CR-LDP

Constraint-based routing often is equated to QoS routing, but the MPLS group uses a broader definition. Given that traffic engineering has two goals, providing QoS-enabled services and optimizing network resource use, this broader definition makes perfect sense.

Perfection is the enemy of excellence. An absolutely perfect optimization is beyond reasonable computation. The practical alternative, however, involves two steps:

1. Go through the list of available routes and discard any that do not meet the constraint(s). For example, conventional routing protocols discard routes that do not satisfy the constraint of having a noninfinite metric. If the constraint is reserving bandwidth, links that have had all available bandwidth reserved do not meet the constraint. Constraints can reflect administrative policies, such as acceptable use.

Traffic engineering extensions for OSPF and IS-IS are under development.

2. Compute the shortest path available from the remaining links that meet the constraint.

No Miracles

Traffic engineering and constraint-based routing will not create capacity that does not exist. If the network is consistently congested, you may have to ask top management, "what part of 'we need more resources' do you fail to understand?"

Constraint-based LDP (CR-LDP) is an extension of basic LDP. It can coexist with conventional routing protocols, applying constraints to their output. It can also work with traffic engineering-enhanced routing protocols. RSVP with traffic engineering extensions (RSVP-TE), discussed later in the chapter, is an alternative to CR-LDP.

CR-LDP can produce an explicit route (ER), which may be *loose* or *strict*. ERs also can be configured manually, or through some nonreal-time process, and distributed through LDP.

Some of the non-QoS-related constraints understood by CR-LDP include whether or not the LSP can preempt existing LSPs. Different *setup priorities* and *holding priorities* can be set. The setup priority governs whether the new path can preempt existing paths. The holding priority ranks the established paths from least likely (i.e., high holding priority) to most likely to be preempted when preemption takes place.

RSVP-TE

RSVP, with traffic engineering extensions (RSVP-TE), is an alternative to CR-LDP. The two setup mechanisms have similar functions, and, indeed, RSVP is more the preferred mechanism of developers with a traditional Internet background, while CR-LDP is more preferred by developers with a telephony background. Emerging WANs, of course, do not strictly come from either culture.

RSVP-TE [Awduche 2000b] adds features to RSVP that include:

- Downstream-on-demand label distribution
- Creation of explicit label switched paths and allocation of network resources (e.g., bandwidth) to them

- Rerouting of established LSP-tunnels in a smooth fashion using the concept of make-before-break

- Tracking of the actual route traversed by an LSP-tunnel

- Diagnostics on LSP-tunnels

- The concept of nodal abstraction

- Preemption options that are administratively controllable

One of the keys to understanding RSVP-TE is to focus on the similarity and differences of traffic trunks and LSPs that carry traffic trunks. These are different levels of abstraction. A traffic trunk is more end-to-end oriented. Just as a bit stream offered to a user can actually be multiplexed or inverse multiplexed over physical facilities, traffic trunks can be inverse multiplexed over several LSPs or map to a single LSP. Alternatively, as long as there is a way to distinguish among different service classes, multiple traffic trunks can multiplex onto a single LSP.

Another way to think of end-to-end paths is as LSP tunnels. Such a tunnel might not be defined for QoS control, but for priority in restoral after network failures. A highly available tunnel could have multiple predefined failover LSPs. The use of RSVP-TE could very well have high-availability applications beyond the use of RSVP-TE in traffic optimizations.

If it has not yet become apparent, the first role of RSVP-TE is to establish and maintain tunnels, and then reserve resources for such tunnels. In contrast, the basic RSVP protocol is intended to reserve capacity for microflow sessions: single source host-destination host associations, usually considering source-destination transport ports as well as network addressing. In RSVP-TE, the basic session is " the set of packets that are assigned the same MPLS label value at the originating node of an LSP-tunnel."

Microflows will not scale to networks of large size. As a scaling response, RSVP-TE abstracts the idea of an RSVP flow to make it "of an arbitrary aggregation of traffic (based on local policies) between the originating node of an LSP-tunnel and the egress node of the tunnel."

So, a LSP-tunnel can very usefully be considered an aggregate of flows. As an aggregate, it is far more scalable than traditional RSVP.

There is another, subtle benefit of using RSVP-TE tunnels: traffic accounting for billing or for capacity planning. By definition, a traffic engineered path does not necessarily follow the path that traditional interior gateway protocols would dictate. Traffic engineered paths map to end-to-end paths, which, in turn, map to classes of service that have meaning to end users. By tracking the presence or absence of particular MPLS labels in given links, and by tracking the hop-by-hop performance associated with those labels, meaningful end-to-end traffic accounting becomes possible without using endpoint resources.

Virtual Address Space: Network Address Translation

Another virtualization is that of the IP address space. Originally, all IP addresses were globally unique and globally routable. As the public Internet grew, address space was no longer an unlimited resource, and it became necessary to justify the address space.

RFC1631 introduced NAT as an *address reuse* mechanism for reducing demands on the address space: "place network address translators (NAT) at the borders of *stub domains*. Each NAT box has a table consisting of pairs of local IP addresses and globally unique addresses. The IP addresses inside the stub domain are not globally unique. They are reused in other domains, thus solving the address depletion problem. The globally unique IP addresses are assigned according to current CIDR address allocation schemes. CIDR solves the scaling problem. The main advantage of NAT is that it can be installed without changes to routers or hosts." Since the publication of this RFC, more general views of NAT have emerged, which allow more complex configurations and services.

NAT provides translation between *address realms*, defined by RFC2263 as a network domain in which all addresses are unique, such that routing works normally inside the domain. Translation can work between realms with different address spaces, overlapping address spaces, or completely duplicated address space.

Within an address realm, hosts see a single IP address space. The user-visible address space, however, can map to other address spaces using a taxonomy of NAT functions, including 1:1 address translation, port/address translation, loadsharing NAT functions, and discontiguous address spaces linked by tunnels.

What is the particular role of NAT in respect to WANs? Above all, it offers the opportunity to decouple the enterprise's addressing from that of a provider. Such decoupling makes it far easier for a provider to offer logical level services, rather than the less flexible layer 2 services.

NAT also helps providers offer services, by reducing the size of the Internet routing table.

Some would-be network designers insist that NAT solves every problem, and others do not use it even when appropriate. Try to look at it realistically.

First, there is no single thing called NAT. There are a variety of related techniques, reviewed in Table 5.6. One very common variant of NAT is *network address and port translation* (NAPT), which translates transport layer port numbers as well as IP addresses.

Second, NAT, by any name, is not a panacea. Remember that it breaks the end-to-end model, and, as a consequence, it can break higher-layer protocols that expect end-to-end significance.

NAT, to many people, appears to be no more than a simple swap of inside and outside addresses. In reality, if it simply did that, it would not work. At a minimum, the IP header checksum has to be recomputed to reflect the new address values.

In practice, NAT cannot stop with the network layer. The checksums of TCP and UDP include parts of the IP header of the packets that carry them. If these transport checksums were not recalculated based on the new IP addresses after translation, the packets could be routed but would be unusable at their destination.

Table 5.6   Protocol Compatibility with NAT

NAT FUNCTIONS	PROTOCOLS
Checksum	X Windows, Activision games, TFTP, ICMP*, TLS, SSL, ssh
ALG for single session	RSVP, DNS, HTTP, RealAudio, HTML, telnet
ALG for multiple sessions	FTP, H.323
NAT irrelevant	Interior routing protocols
Likely to break	BGP, IPsec, HTML hard-coded IP, many multiplayer games, fragmented TCP, SNMP**

* Basic protocol will work, but there may be errors in the beginning of the header of the packet causing the error, which is captured by ICMP.

** Conceivably, an ALG could be built for SNMP, but it would need to have a huge amount of knowledge.

A NAT implementation that appropriately changes IP and TCP/UDP checksums can handle many application protocols. Problems remain, however, with application protocols that embed IP addresses in their data fields. NAT alone cannot cope with embedded addresses. The additional functionality of an *application layer gateway* (ALG), which is different for each protocol, is necessary to find and change embedded addresses.

Still, for some protocols, such as SNMP, the complexity that would be required of an ALG makes the function impractical. To remotely manage a system with SNMP, it is usually better to have some sort of tunneled access to a management address, rather than try to translate SNMP.

NAT and DNS

NAPT needs to consider both addresses and ports, but DNS only knows about addresses [RFC2694]. In principle, this would suggest that a single external address is a useful simplification. In practice, a single address may not have enough port space for a large number of NAT sessions.

Another issue is reverse DNS. When an outside host does a reverse DNS lookup, it will receive the name of the external interface of the NAT device, not that of the internal host.

Other DNS functions complicate life by using embedded IP addresses. For example, mail directed to a domain commonly is directed to the server defined in the DNS MX (mail exchanger) record, not the ultimate mail server.

NAT and the Transport Layer

NAT cannot ignore TCP and UDP, because their checksum calculations include fields in the IP header. Even when transport fields are corrected, there still may be incompatibilities that need to be solved at the application layer.

Some architectural limits on scaling need to be considered in large-scale NAT. There is a limit to the number of port translations that can be done by a single IP address, imposed by the 16-bit port fields of TCP and UDP. While in principle this field length would permit 64K ports, reserved port numbers make the space actually available 62K.

If this space limit is a concern, then the NAT function needs to be combined with DNS load sharing so the load is spread among multiple addresses.

NAT specifications distinguish between packet flows and *connection* or *session* flows. Session flows are bidirectional, and form the set of traffic that NAT manages as a quantum of translation. TCP and UDP sessions are identified by the source IP address and source TCP/UDP port, in combination with the destination IP address and destination TCP/UDP port.

From the perspective of a NAT device, the direction of a session is defined by the direction of the first packet of the exchange. If the first packet goes from the inside to the outside, the session is outgoing. Whatever the direction, it is at session establishment time that a binding is established between inside address/port and outside address/port. The state of this binding is internal to the NAT implementation. If there are multiple NAT devices, they need a common view of this state information. See "Multihomed NAT" later in the chapter.

Actually identifying the start and end of a session is straightforward for TCP, but much more difficult for UDP. TCP has a specific connection establishment phase, the start of which has a TCP packet with the SYN, but not ACK bits set. Since UDP has no connection establishment phase, the only real alternative at the transport layer is to use inactivity timers.

Murphy's Law applies to NAT as much as it does any other protocol. A given TCP session may fail, but not with a proper termination exchange. Inactivity timers can detect such a failure.

Adding to the complexity of sessions is the reality that an application layer protocol may use several transport layer sessions as a bundle. For example, FTP uses two connections, one for control and one for data transfer.

NAT and Application Protocols

The first types of NAT, discussed in the next section, would break a substantial number of higher-layer protocols that embedded IP addresses in their data fields. Real-world NAT products often have higher-layer protocol awareness, and really are not strict NAT but NATs with ALGs.

You should be aware, however, that incompatibilities still will occur. In the WAN marketplace, one of the chief areas of problems may come if you outsource your network management.

Types of NAT

There is no one type of NAT. No one NAT type only does inside-to-outside address translation and modifies no other protocol field. At a minimum, NAT will translate IP addresses and change IP and TCP/UDP checksums. It may also remap both IP addresses and TCP/UDP port numbers.

Keeping Track of the Ins and Outs

I sometimes have trouble, in dealing with NATs and proxies, keeping track of which is the inside and which is the outside. The usual convention is that if the Internet is involved, it is the outside.

Once upon a time, there was a single-parent of skunks: Mama Skunk, and her two sons, In and Out. Her children's habits made for chaos in the household, for the basic pattern was that when In was in, Out was out, and when Out was in, In was out. To have a relaxing family dinner, Mama Skunk had to go through significant effort to ensure that In was in at the same time that Out was in.

On one occasion, Out, being in at the time, sympathized with his mother's frustration as she called for In to come in, as she simultaneously ordered Out to stay in while In was out. Her repeated calls for In to come in were ignored as Out, who was in, watched her. Finally, Out volunteered to go out to get In to come in.

Mama gave him permission, and very shortly after, In came in with Out in tow, Out no longer being out but now in at the same time as In. Mama wondered, "How did you find him so quickly?"

"Easy, Mom," Out replied. "In stinked."

Clearly, Mama Skunk was the DMZ.

Figure 5.18 shows the location of three address spaces, Inside (I), DMZ (D), and Outside (O). The DMZ is not always present. The Outside space is further divided into Outside Local (O_L) and Outside Remote (O_R) for certain architectures.

O_L is the usual case, where the outside address space is under the control of the administrator of the local NAT device. This address space may or may not be registered and globally routable, but it is unique among the outsides of all NAT devices that use it. The special case is

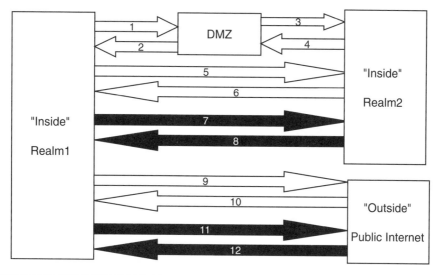

Rule	Owner	Source	Dest.	Rule	Owner	Source	Dest.
1	P1 or DMZ	P1	DMZ	7	P2	P1	P2
2	P1 or DMZ	DMZ	P1	8	P2	P2	P1
3	P2 or DMZ	DMZ	P2	9	P1	P1	Public
4	P2 or DMZ	P2 or DMZ	DMZ	10	P1	Public	P1
5	P1	P1	P2	11	ISP	P1	Public

Figure 5.18 NAT address spaces.

part of Realm Specific IP, where the local and remote NAT devices negotiate an address space to use.

An address mapping I->O means that an inside address $\underline{i}$ maps to an outside address $\underline{o}$. n(I) is the number of inside addresses, and n(O) is the number of outside addresses (see Table 5.7).

Traditional NAT (or) Outbound NAT

Traditional NAT virtualizes an "inside" user address space in a *stub domain*. A single NAT router, as shown in Figure 5.19, translates, for outgoing sessions, the "inside" address to an "outside" address.

Traditional NAT was first suggested as a means of registered address conservation, with the inside addresses being private enterprise address space and the outside addresses being globally routable, registered public Internet addresses. Many additional applications of NAT have emerged, as well as additional complexities.

Table 5.7   Mappings between Logical and Transmission Levels

NAT TYPE	TRANSLATIONS	INSIDE SENDS TO	OTHER
Basic NAT	I->O	Default gateway [1]	n(I) = n(O)
Basic NATP	I(p)->O(p)	Default gateway [1]	n(I) > n(O)
Bidirectional	I->O	Default gateway [1]	n(I) = (O)
Twice	I->O O->I	Default gateway [1]	n(I) = n(O) DNS ALG needed
Double	I->D D->O	Default gateway [1]	
Multihomed	Any	Default gateway [1]	Must retain state among all NAT devices, or use static translations
Realm-Specific	I-> OR if client	Default gateway [1]	
Load-Sharing	O->I	Inside sends to default route, preferably of virtual server	
Load-Sharing with Port translation	O(p)->I(p)	Inside sends to default route, preferably of virtual server	

[1] If hosts are routing-aware, they can send to a router with a more-specific route than the default.

Assume that you have a set of servers with assigned addresses that you do not wish to advertise to the outside. Let's say you have renumbered from PA to PI, and you have been bad and not used DNS. Static NAT can be useful here. It does not conserve address space.

Another application for static NAT is for extranets, when the address spaces do not overlap. With overlapping address spaces, double NAT is often needed.

Dynamic NAT without PAT has rather limited applicability. It may simplify configuration, but make troubleshooting more difficult.

Traditional NAT is outgoing only, and generally intended to let a private network connect to an external network, usually the public Internet but potentially a partner in an extranet. Sessions initiate only on the inside and go to servers on the outside. The inside and outside address spaces must not overlap.

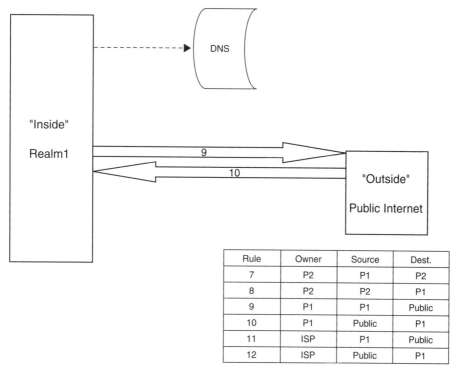

Figure 5.19 Traditional NAT.

In basic traditional NAT, there is one-to-one correspondence between inside and outside addresses. Since this method does not conserve addresses, it is more appropriate for extranet than Internet connectivity. Be warned that address overlap is quite common with extranets, so more advanced NAT mechanisms may be needed there.

Network address port translation (NAPT), the more common form of traditional NAT, maps many inside addresses to a lesser number of outside addresses. Session uniqueness is preserved by translation of port numbers as well as addresses.

Bidirectional NAT (or) Two-Way NAT

In traditional NAT and NAPT, sessions can be initiated only from the inside to the outside (see Figure 5.20). Bidirectional NAT allows sessions to be initiated in the other direction as well (Figure 5.20).

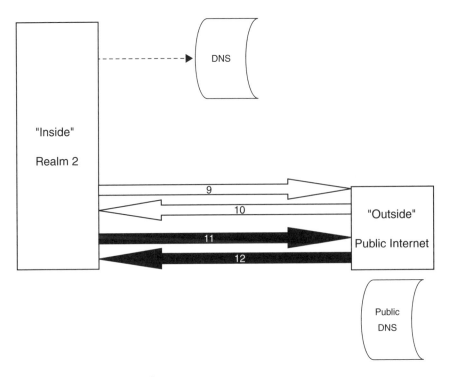

Figure 5.20 Bidirectional NAT.

When the "outside" is the public Internet, considerable care must be taken to avoid inappropriate access. Extranets between potential competitors also need substantial controls.

Security requirements may be more liberal when both the inside and outside are part of the same enterprise. Corporate mergers are a good example of such situations, assuming the two address spaces are nonoverlapping. Address overlap requires the "twice NAT" functionality.

This technique depends on basic NAT in each direction, coupled with a DNS application gateway. The name spaces in both the inside and outside must be unique. Outside hosts resolve the inside address using DNS.

Twice NAT and Double NAT

Twice NAT (Figure 5.21) is a form of NAT needed when there is address overlap between the "inside" and "outside" realms. When the

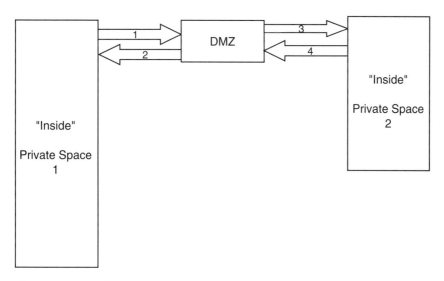

Figure 5.21   Twice NAT.

"outside" is the public Internet, the problem usually arose because an enterprise picked random addresses for internal use, and these addresses were registered to someone else. Such an enterprise, of course, is in a state of sin.

A less sinful requirement develops when a realm uses address space legitimately delegated by a provider, but changes providers. There is likely to be a transitional period where the external addressing changes, but not all internal hosts have been renumbered.

Another application of twice NAT occurs when two enterprises innocently use the private address space, and then need to intercommunicate in an extranet.

If basic NAT is a case of "I didn't really mean it," twice NAT is the case when "we both didn't mean it." Full twice NAT knows the logic needed to map between the two realms; it is aware of the addressing of both realms.

An alternative is double NAT, in which a NAT in each domain translates to a DMZ address (Figure 5.22). There is a translation from the inside space of one realm to the agreed shared space, and a second translation from the shared address space to the inside space of the

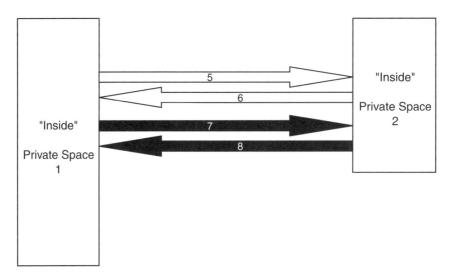

Figure 5.22 Double NAT.

second realm. This takes more hardware than twice NAT, but may be much easier to administer.

Multihomed NAT

NAT is straightforward when there is only a single point of connection from inside to outside. If there are multiple points, the challenge arises of how the multiple NATs are aware of the state of sessions.

Mechanisms for dynamic state exchange have not been generally accepted. Practical multihomed NAT tends to involve static translation definitions.

There are no generally accepted solutions to dynamic multihomed NAT, although it certainly can be engineered for specific situations.

Realm-Specific IP (RSIP)

Realm-specific IP is an evolving technique that may solve issues such as IPsec conflicts with NAT. It does appear to be intensive of both processing resources and administrations, and there are no large tests of its scalability.

I find it useful to picture RSIP as functionally similar to a dial-up PPP client that routinely calls different service providers. When it connects to each provider, it negotiates an IP address, in that provider's space, for each session (see Figure 5.23). RSIP negotiates in a similar manner, except that it is using routing, not PPP, for the setup. Once this address is assigned, it is not available for other uses until the session terminates.

RSIP defines clients that request addresses and servers that assign addresses. RSIP can operate at the level of addresses alone (RSA-IP), or of addresses and ports (RSAP-IP).

Once the external address enters a realm, how is it routed? This will depend on the routing and security policies of the realm. If the routing policies are permissive, a route to the remote realm can be installed. Access lists and firewalls may not accept the external address.

While RSIP does deal with application transparency and gatewaying, it may introduce problems with TCP [Hain 2000]. Indeed, ordinary dynamic NAPT may encounter the same problem as RSIP: conflict with the assumptions in TCP about preventing replay attacks against the source/destination pair of IP address and port number. The TCP protocol has a timer, TIME_WAIT, which expects that an address/port pair will not be reused for four minutes. This timer prevents both replays and the delivery of old data.

When a host or NAT tries to connect to a destination, that host or NAT is not aware that an address may have already been used by RSIP, and is still in the TIME_WAIT state.

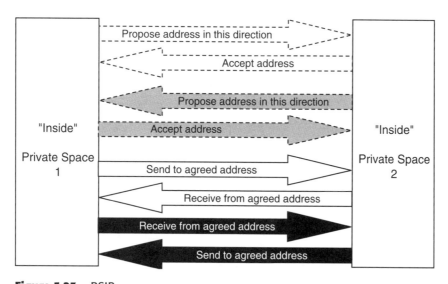

Figure 5.23 RSIP.

Load-Sharing NAT and NATP

NAT and NATP variants that load-share have been proposed. These techniques complement other methods at higher and lower layers. The logic of these variants is most appropriate for local load distribution, although they are extensible for distributed-load distribution.

Local load distribution inherently is susceptible to failures of WAN connectivity to the site, or failures of a single distribution device. Distributed load distribution helps protect against failures, but may introduce highly variable performance when some requests are serviced locally and some remotely.

LSNAT's virtualization presents a virtual server on the outside, which is passed to an address on an internal server (Figure 5.24). There is a connection from the LSNAT to each server for each session. LSNATs could not easily change server hosts during a session.

LS-NATP is more complex, but also allows more flexible topologies. LS-NATP virtualizes somewhat differently, in that it substitutes the virtual server address for the real client address, when translating in the inbound direction. By doing so, the real server can use any path inside the realm that has connectivity to the LS-NATP device. Indeed, the response could tunnel to another site.

In basic LS-NATP, there still will be only one LS-NATP router. Multi-homed extensions could work if they exchange state information.

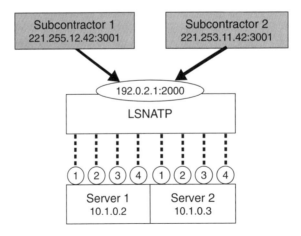

Figure 5.24 Load-sharing NAT with port translation.

The LS-NAPT router can translate to one of multiple internal servers, or redirect the transaction to an outside server. That sort of function will be seen frequently in Web caches.

The additional complexity of LS-NAPT does allow greater scalability, because new links can be dropped into the routing system without problem. As long as new client links can get to the virtual server address, the addition of these links is transparent to both servers and clients. In like manner, the internal servers can have multiple paths to the LS-NAPT device (Table 5.8).

LS-NAT, in contrast, requires either that the internal real servers send to the default route, or have routing awareness that tells them the best router for reaching the originating real client address.

Multihoming is still complex for both LS-NAT and LS-NAPT. The NAT device remains a single point of failure for individual sessions, as long as multiple NAT devices cannot share information on the state of their current sessions.

End-to-End Path (Routing Destination)

An increasing number of techniques work at what is more or less the transport layer. "More or less" means that these techniques simply do not fit the traditional OSI layering.

Some of these techniques are intimately associated with network address translation (NAT), discussed later in the chapter. This section deals with tunneling and redirection of end-to-end flows.

Tunnels

As mentioned in the introduction to this chapter, tunneling is an extension of basic protocol encapsulation. The basic model of tunneling is

Table 5.8   LSNAT and LSNAPT

SERVICE	SOURCE		DESTINATION	
	IP	PORT	IP	PORT
LSNAT	Real client	Real client	Real server	Real server
LSNAPT	Virtual server	Virtual server	Real server	Real server

that a protocol at one layer is encapsulated in a PDU not of the next lower layer, as is typical of general encapsulation, but in a protocol of the same layer (Figure 5.25).

The inner protocol is called the *payload protocol*. The protocol that actually carries the tunneled packet through the transport network is called the *delivery protocol*. In most cases, there is a small tunneling overhead protocol between the end of the delivery header and the start of the payload header. There is no absolutely standard name for this third protocol function, but the terms *glue protocol* or *shim protocol* often are used. Glue protocols are an instance of Schwarzenegger's Second Law.

If the payload and delivery model are of different protocol families, such as IBM SNA and IP, the simplification that both protocols are at the same layer tends to break down. The roles, however, of payload, delivery, and shim stay true.

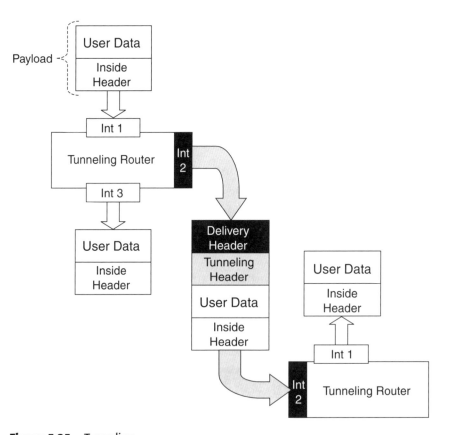

Figure 5.25 Tunneling.

Tunnels are usually invisible to the end host, which definitely can confuse troubleshooting.

Table 5.9 lists a variety of tunneling mechanisms in general use. Most, but not all, use IP as the delivery mechanism. Many discussions of tunneling assume IP, but I prefer to include proven layer 2 tunneling mechanisms. IP is the preferred delivery mechanism for most applications. You must be aware, however, that there are valid layer 2 solutions for which the superiority of IP delivery must be demonstrated before the old mechanism is replaced.

Also remember that the IP delivery mechanism need not be the general Internet, so that delivery addresses may or may not need to be private.

Table 5.9 also lists an assortment of tunneling mechanisms, some of which carry legacy protocols and will not be detailed further. It is assumed that the mechanisms that use IP as their delivery protocol are running over Internet facilities, which would require registered addresses. Obviously, if the underlying IP facilities are private, they simply need to be unique.

You will see that you cannot simply assume everything runs over IP. A legitimate, admittedly controversial, argument can be made that frame relay and ATM are tunneling mechanisms.

Troubleshooting with tunnels, to put it mildly, can be interesting. Consider what happens when you traceroute through a tunnel, as shown in Figure 5.26. The endpoints will show in the traceroute log, but none of the intermediate nodes will do so. Further complicating the situation is that you may not even know you are going through a tunnel, if part of your network is outsourced.

Generic Route Encapsulation (GRE)

From the perspective of virtualization, Generic Route Encapsulation gives its user the view of a dedicated line IP subnet, or the equivalent in other protocol families, such as an IPX network or an AppleTalk cable range. A particularly common practice is carrying IP over IP.

Originally developed by Cisco and described in information RFCs 1701 and 1702, the protocol has become widely supported. It became part of the IETF standards track when other working groups found it useful to specify GRE as the basis for other protocols. The basic protocol now has entered the standards track as RFC 2784. Applications include:

- Allowing discontiguous parts of OSPF areas
- Carrying non-IP traffic.
- Carrying unidirectional link routed traffic
- Handling bogus IP addresses and private IP addresses over a public core

Table 5.9 Tunneling Mechanisms

TUNNEL MECHANISM	PAYLOAD	TUNNEL ENDPOINT ADDRESSES	PAYLOAD ENDPOINT ADDRESSES	SECURITY
GRE	Any	Registered IP [1]	any	None
IPsec Transport	IP	Registered IP [1]	Registered IP	Integrity, confidentiality
IPsec Tunnel	IP	Registered IP [1]	Any IP	Integrity, confidentiality
L2TP, L2F, PPTP	Any PPP encapsulated	Registered IP [1]	Any	Access
MPLS	Any	IP	Any	None
RFC 1001	NetBIOS records	Registered IP [1]	NetBIOS name	None
RFC 1234	IPX packets	Registered IP [1]	IPX	None
RFC 1483 MPOA	Any	ATM	Any	None
RFC 1504 AURP	AppleTalk routing updates	Registered IP [1]	AppleTalk	None
RFC 1613 XOT	X.25 packets	Registered IP [1]	X.121	None
STUN	IBM SDLC	Layer 2 direct, TCP/IP	SDLC address	None
RSRB	IBM source route bridging	Layer 2 direct, IP only, TCP/IP	MAC address	None
PPP over Ethernet	PPP	MAC address	N/A	CHAP, IPCP
DLSw+	Any IBM or NetBIOS nonroutable	TCP/IP	MAC address	Session authentication
IP over IPX	IPv4	IPX	IP	None
RFC 2427	Any	Frame relay	Any	None

- Healing discontiguous networks
- Providing VPNs

Tunneling and NAT

NAT and tunneling can complement one another, and both can form VPNs and complement VPNs. An enterprise VPN, for example, is very useful to use private address space but be tunneled over a public network. If the VPN needs to connect to another enterprise that used private address space, the VPN can use NAT to establish extranet connectivity.

Individual sites of a VPN need not be tunneled internally, but need to be tunneled or translated to go across a public backbone. As you will see in Chapter 8, "VPNs, Security, and Roaming," there are two administrative models for VPN service. In an enterprise-oriented model, the enterprise creates tunnels that are not visible to the provider. In a provider model, the provider creates tunnels that are transparent to the enterprise.

IPsec

The IP security architecture (IPsec) provides a wide range of security services and defines some infrastructure services for them, although IPsec does not meet every security requirement. See Chapter 8 for the

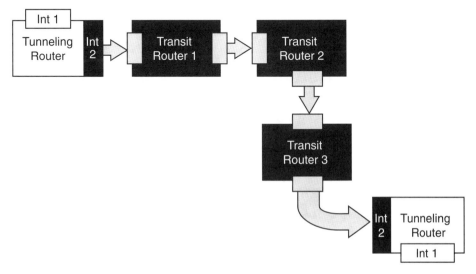

Figure 5.26 Tunneling and traceroute.

services provided. In the discussion here, the emphasis is on the virtualizations that IPsec creates.

One of its most basic is the *security association* (SA). I like to think of an SA as a one-way connection. Like a flow, an SA can be point-to-point or point-to-multipoint. SAs can be:

- End host to end host
- End host to security gateway
- Security gateway to security gateway

Another basic IPsec virtualization is the choice between *transport mode* and *tunnel mode*. In transport mode, only the end hosts are fully trusted. Encryption, whether for authentication or confidentiality, is done on the end hosts. If such hosts need to communicate across the public Internet, they must have registered addresses.

Tunnel mode allows the end hosts to have any address, which is quite useful when stub domains of private networks are being interconnected over public networks (see Table 5.10). The tunneling devices need to be trusted with encryption.

Transport Redirection

Application layer protocols have long had the ability to redirect a client to another server. Contrary to some glib opinions, this is not a recent contribution of HTML and HTTP, but goes back to the shining antiques of telnet and the *file transfer protocol* (FTP).

Virtual Private Networks (VPNs): Where Do They Fit?

Virtual private networks, whatever they are, are one of the most rapidly growing ways to let users see a single logical addressing struc-

Table 5.10 Transport and Tunnel Modes

SERVICE	SOURCE		DESTINATION	
	IP	PORT	IP	PORT
Transport	Real client	Real client	Real server	Real server
Tunnel	Security gateway of source	Security gateway of source	Security gateway of destination	Security gateway of destination

ture, or possibly a naming structure. The actual infrastructure is a mapping onto a WAN, the operation of which is normally outsourced. Details of VPNs are discussed in Chapter 7.

VPNs tend to fall into broad categories of access and transport. Another way to say this is that an access VPN links individual users to sites, and may very well be run by even a small enterprise as well as by a carrier. In contrast, transport VPNs link sites, and are most often operated by carriers. Table 5.11 compares some of the general characteristics.

Even within these user-oriented categories, a variety of technologies can be used to implement the VPN. Indeed, the IETF has not yet come up with a consensus definition of what constitutes a VPN. Traditional carriers make a not-unreasonable point that FR and ATM can qualify as VPNs, although the trend is to assume an IP or MPLS infrastructure.

RFC2547 defines a transport VPN architecture that runs over MPLS, and appears to be gaining market share.

Indirect Application Layer Virtualizations

Naming services, above all else, refer to hosts rather than routers or links. When the customer speaks of selecting specific hosts, rather than media or paths, be alert that at least part of the solution may come from naming services rather than lower-level routing. Naming services, as exemplified by DNS, are a common form of virtualization.

Table 5.11 Characteristics of Access and Transport VPNs

FUNCTION	ACCESS	TRANSPORT
Endpoint granularity	Individual user, small server site	Site, enterprise
Usual operator	Enterprise or carrier	Carrier
Security	Access authentication and encryption common	No
QoS	Infrequent	Frequent
Common technologies	IPSec, GRE, L2TP, PPTP	RFC2547 BGP/MPLS Virtual routers frame relay, ATM

Users see a name, which is virtualized by directory services. Basic directory services do name to address translation, which need not be one to one. The name server may be aware of server or routing load and return different addresses under different circumstances. Simpler returns by the server include round-robin rotations of a list of server addresses.

Host clients need to understand that multiple addresses may be returned, and how to use them. DNS TTL values need to be understood in the context of intelligent name service, both by caches and end hosts. Many DNS implementations will not accept a TTL less than five minutes, which dictates the time cycle over which load sharing can take place.

Certainly, basic DNS round-robin load sharing assumes all servers have equal capacity, and the network cost to reach each is the same. As discussed in the previous section "Load Sharing," this tends to be a simplistic assumption for the real world.

Intelligent load sharing devices such as the Nortel Accelar 700, Cisco DistributedDirector, F5 3DNS, etc., offer much more powerful load sharing algorithms.

Direct Application Layer Virtualizations

At the application layer, there are a variety of techniques that operate between the client and server. These can loosely be divided into *application layer gateways* (ALG) and caches. ALG accept an application protocol stream, manipulate it, and pass it on. ALGs are relays, just as routers are relays at the network layer, and bridges are relays at the data link layer.

A relay may be a true proxy, terminating the inside-to-relay connection and creating a new relay-to-outside connection. Alternatively, it can provide an "on-the-fly" inspection service, manipulating records or packets in a stream without actually terminating the connection.

Caches accept application requests and pass some to the ultimate destination, but replying to a significant proportion from local files. They are particularly important in the WAN context, because they can both improve responsiveness perceived by users, while simultaneously reducing bandwidth requirements. Users see the performance improvement because their requests are served from a LAN or at least a local device, while bandwidth requirements are reduced by the proportion of user requests that are serviced locally and do not need to cross the WAN to reach the master server.

Web caches virtualize the user's view of the ultimate server, in that the request may be serviced either from a local server or by the server actually requested. Other application caches also may either service requests locally or pass them on to the master server, but they differ from Web caches because they do not have additional administrative policies needed in the World Wide Web.

Web caches and intranet-oriented application caches are permissive, accepting any request and servicing it. The basic architecture of a cache can become more selective, implementing security policies as a firewall component. Indeed, a firewall may not have any local application caching, but it may use the same types of proxy logic that an application cache does. Alternatively, it may operate more at the transport than the application layer.

Web Caches

Think of a rather bureaucratic organization, concerned with image and the observance of declared business hours. Think of the employees of this organization, which, without attempting to correct any of its cultural problems, decides to Leap Into The New Millennium by Web-enabling its workforce.

In such an environment, I would wager that one of the first acts of said workforce, on any given day, is likely to be retrieving the Dilbert strip of the day.

Face reality. As much as each of us may wish that Scott Adams had Dilbert personalize a thought for us each day, there is only one Dilbert strip per day. The last employee to retrieve the strip of the day will receive the same information as the first to retrieve it.

In an enterprise with no caching, every employee will go through the Internet WAN to retrieve Dilbert, producing a bandwidth requirement of:

```
(DilbertStripSize * NumberOfUsers)/Time
```

Given the corporation's emphasis on punctuality, this load will hit over a small period of time. If, however, a cache scheme is used, the response of Dilbert's server to the first requester will be saved in the cache. The subsequent users will retrieve the information from the cache. Ideally, this will reduce the bandwidth requirement to:

```
(DilbertStripSize * 1)/Time
```

Dilbert is an ideal case. Web caches need to be intelligent about what they will provide from their disks and what requests they will make every time (see Figure 5.27). Caching makes no sense for real-time requests such as stock quotations or headline news. It makes no sense for interactive transactions.

Caching makes a copy of data, which may not be desirable under a security policy.

Another aspect that complicates caching is the advertiser-paid model of many Web sites. If the transaction is cached, the hit counts of the ultimate server do not increment, which ultimately results in a revenue loss to the server operator. This problem largely has been solved

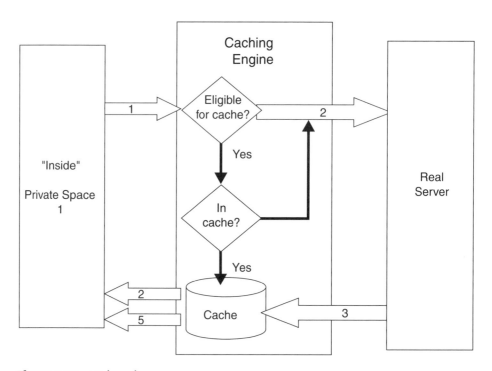

Figure 5.27 Web cache.

by an unusual collaboration of lawyers and technologists, which produced the Internet cache protocol (ICP).

Application-Specific Caches

In reality, they may retrieve the data (especially read-only) either from a synchronized cache (e.g., database or intelligent Web cache) or from a loosely synchronized cache as used in DNS or Lotus Notes.

Streaming multimedia does need high performance when being displayed, but, in many applications, the need for the information can be predicted. For example, Cisco's IP/TV products control both campus LAN distribution of video and retrieving and caching video files on campus servers.

Don't Forget that Networks Never Sleep

Application-specific caching can get quite creative. I had a medical application where an HMO was contracting with community cardiologists for consultations in a wide geographic area. These cardiologists often needed to consult historical ultrasound imagery, and the initial approach required budget-busting T1 lines from the central image store to each physician's office, if files were to be transferred in near real time. I asked my client how long in advance a patient scheduled a visit to a cardiologist, and was told the usual wait was three weeks.

As I suspected, the HMO had a centralized scheduling application for all specialists. I suggested that when an appointment was made, the ultrasound or other imagery should be retrieved, and sent at night and on weekends to caches at physician offices. In three weeks, it was quite possible to transfer the files over 128 Kbps ISDN.

Lotus Notes and many other database systems often do not require lock-step synchronization between a local cache and the master corporate database. It may be adequate to update the database every 10 minutes, or even every hour. Even time-sensitive information can be cached. Think of a stock quotation service that services a remote brokerage office. When a stock quotation arrives for a volatile stock, local brokers can depend on the cached entry being valid until the next quotation arrives.

Some databases, especially when they lock resources in tight synchronization, such as in travel reservations, do need to keep distributed databases tightly coupled. Rather than maintaining caches, these systems are likely to need commit protocols and fairly high-speed links between the database servers.

Firewalling

A basic application cache is permissive, in that it services every request. It can add functionality that lets it make decisions whether or not to let some traffic through and block other traffic, which takes it into the realm of the bastion host function of a firewall system. A bastion host, indeed, does not need to cache at all. The idea of how it manipulates protocol streams above the network layer, however, is a constant with application caches.

A *bastion host* is a device with two or more interfaces, flow between which is controlled by security mechanisms in this host. These mechanisms operate above the network layer. Some authors call the bastion host the firewall itself, and then identify routers that feed it, authentication servers that perform specialized services, etc. I prefer to think of a firewall as a multicomponent system, one component of which can be a bastion host. Indeed, a firewall can have different kinds of bastion hosts.

This is a functional similarity that may not be exact. But both NAT and bastion host devices can be considered specialized routers. A bastion host may not do address translation, but it does forward based on more specific criteria than a routing table.

Figure 5.28 shows three abstractions of a bastion host. The leftmost is a traditional bastion host that provides application or transport layer proxies.

Encrypted traffic is a special problem for bastion hosts: If they cannot read the traffic, they cannot proxy it. Some bastion hosts may be trusted to decrypt the data, perform proxy processing, and then reencrypt it for transmission to the ultimate destination.

The center bastion host does not break the transport or application connection, but inspects packets "on the fly."

Encrypted traffic challenges stateful packet screens in the same way it challenges proxy servers, only more so. It is more complex to change encryption "on the fly" than it is if the connections are terminated in a proxy.

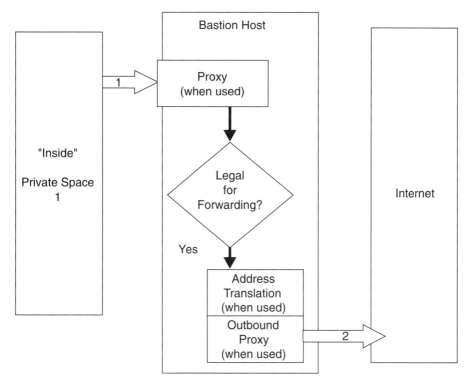

Figure 5.28 Bastion host.

The rightmost is a null function for a bastion host, but a perfectly meaningful one for the real world. Organizations often install a proxy server or stateful packet screen, and then poke holes in it to pass certain protocols that cannot be inspected by the bastion. Poking such holes is realistic if the traffic is encrypted in a way that prevents the bastion from examining the contents of packets. Poking holes is sinful when done simply to allow politically important services to pass, services that are let through in an uncontrolled manner because the bastions have no capabilities for examining them.

Circuit Proxy

A circuit proxy is not specifically aware of application protocols, but does require that clients implement a C-plane protocol to tell the proxy what destination server they are trying to reach. It provides transport layer security. This security always includes validating the requesting client's identity. It may involve determining if the destination server is approved for access, and also may involve encryption from the client to the proxy and from the proxy to the server (see Figure 5.29).

The reason there must be signaling between the client and proxy is that a TCP connection request only contains one destination address. The client needs to use that to establish a TCP connection to the proxy. Once there, the client needs to tell the proxy the destination address to which the proxy needs to establish an outgoing TCP session. An assortment of methods exists for the client to tell the proxy where it wants to go.

- The bastion host advertises the default route. In this case, clients do put the real destination address in their packets. Using this method, however, makes it much more difficult to use encryption. Does the bastion host act as a "man in the middle" that proxies the encryption?

- Alternatively, the user could manually log in to the bastion and issues commands to log in to the destination. This requires user training and inconvenience.

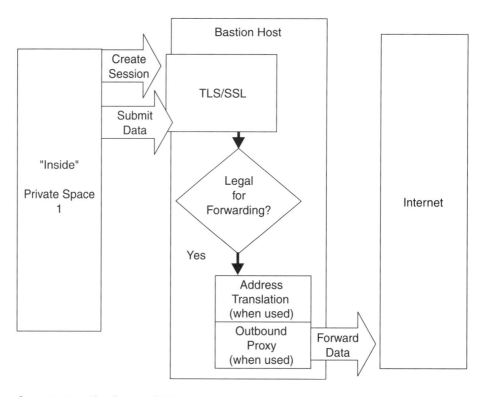

Figure 5.29 Circuit proxy/TLS.

- The most common approach is to have client software that is aware of the proxy. This software uses a protocol such as SOCKS or SSL to negotiate with the proxy to tell it where the user wishes to go, invisibly to the user.

First, the application client creates a TCP connection to the proxy, and then uses the C-plane protocol to tell the proxy the name or address of the application server the client wants to reach. The proxy then examines the request and decides whether or not to accept it.

This decision can be based on the source, the destination, or other criteria. To implement a policy on acceptable destinations, the proxy might be on the firewall of an elementary school, and has a list of approved, child-safe servers. Alternatively, the client may simply authenticate the client request.

Once the decision is made to accept it, the proxy will decide how to service the request. The usual case is to create a second TCP connection to the ultimate destination. This connection comes from a second IP address on the "outside" of the proxy.

Alternatives include redirecting the request to a local cache.

One enterprise redirects attempts to reach the . . .ummm. . . image repositories at www.playboy.com and similar sites to a very special streaming multimedia server. This server sends an image of the enterprise's CEO, a cigar in one corner of his mouth, snarling "get back to work!"

Circuit proxies can be used either from the trusted inside network to the untrusted outside network, or vice versa. Using SSL to access a public server, for example, may be much lower in cost and complexity than using the early deployments of IPsec. See Chapter 8 for a discussion of the security aspects here.

When using circuit proxies to access an internal server, it is critical that cryptographic authentication be used. In early 2000, it is often cheaper to deploy the digital certificates for circuit proxies than it is for IPsec. There is also more experience with SSL and SOCKS than there is with IPsec. As more experience is gained with IPsec, as IPsec products become cheaper and more reliable, IPsec will replace transport layer security in many applications. Transport layer security, as implemented in circuit proxies, and IPsec, however, are complementary techniques.

Stateful Packet Screening

Stateful packet screening firewalls often are higher performance than those that use proxies, but may not have the same level of intelligence. They can do network address translation.

At first glance, a stateful packet screen may appear to be a connection-less NAT function. At second glance, many apparently connectionless NAT functions actually must be aware of higher-layer sessions, as for port mapping.

Stateful packet screening imposes a session structure onto traffic that may or may not be connectionless. It then checks for security rules within this session context. The simplest possible example is a rule that for every packet sent to destination 2.2.2.2 by source 1.1.1.1, one packet from 2.2.2.2 to 1.1.1.1 is expected in response. When the initial packet leaves the inside for the outside, a timer is started. If the expected packet returns before the timer expires, the response packet is passed to the inside and the return rule is cancelled. The return acceptance rule also is cancelled if the timer expires.

Only the most trivial of higher-layer protocol sessions would usefully be handled by the logic of this example. In reality, the stateful packet screen has to have awareness of the upper layer protocol. Unlike circuit proxies, stateful packet screens are not transparent to the upper layer protocols.

One of the most basic things that would break an upper-layer-unaware stateful packet screen is the reality that a response might very well consist of multiple packets. How many response packets should be allowed in? While you could limit them with a timer or counter, the only accurate way to decide is to understand the application protocol, and make an application-protocol-specific decision when the response is complete.

Other reasons the stateful packet screen needs to be upper-layer aware is that a perfectly legitimate response may come from a host other than the one to which the original request was sent. The responding host could be different due to such things as HTTP or FTP redirection. A packet screen that understands HTTP or FTP will understand the application-level redirection.

Application Proxy

The good news about application proxies is that they understand specific application protocols and can be more intelligent in handling traffic than a circuit proxy. The bad news about application proxies is that a specific proxy program must be written for each application protocol (see Figure 5.30).

From the WAN standpoint, application proxies can redirect on a fine-grained level. Enhancements to basic application proxies, which give even more control, include *traffic-aware application proxies* and *content-aware application proxies*. Operating at the application layer, these proxies build on pure application proxies, maintaining traffic state.

It was said of George Allen, coach of the Washington Redskins in the 1970s, that he was able to exceed an unlimited budget. Unfortunately, this also tends to be true of bandwidth requirements.

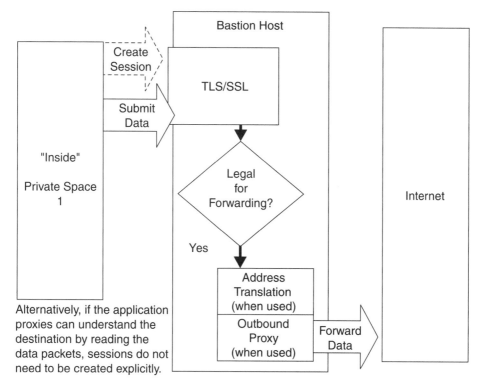

Figure 5.30 Application proxies.

A traffic-aware proxy has several ways of controlling demand. First, it can accept or reject destination addresses. Second, it can limit the amount or type of traffic carried during a session. Third, it can set QoS bits, the TCP window size or acknowledgment delay, and otherwise limit traffic.

Traffic-aware proxies consider the volume of the application data being transferred, but do not understand the meaning of the data, only of the protocol. Content-aware proxies go one step farther, examining the data itself.

Typical applications for content-aware proxies include virus scanning, blocking Web pages with inappropriate content, data types being downloaded, etc.

Looking Ahead

Virtualizations discussed in this chapter are primarily, although not exclusively, from the enterprise perspective. Chapter 6 goes more deeply into the carrier environment and the carrier side of WAN services.

Chapter 7 discusses multihoming and other fault-tolerance mechanisms, which can be used both in real networks and VPNs. The details of VPNs are the focus of Chapter 8. Chapter 8 also discusses the security services often, but not necessarily, needed by VPNs and roaming services.

6

Carrier Infrastructure and Optical Networking

Any sufficiently advanced technology is indistinguishable from magic.

ARTHUR C. CLARKE

Any sufficiently advanced technology is indistinguishable from a rigged demo.

OVERHEARD AT A TRADE SHOW

The Paris-Lille line, the first arm of the French State [optical semaphore] Telegraph, started operation in May 1794, and was first used to report the recapture of a town from the Austrians and the Prussians within an hour of the battle's end.

TOM STANDAGE

THE VICTORIAN INTERNET

In the previous chapter, we dealt with virtualized abstractions, crystalline concepts floating in a sea of imagination. Now, we will go down to the very real floor of the carrier systems that make the abstractions possible—and discover that some of the floor's supports may themselves be virtualized.

Boundaries between carrier and customer, between telephone companies and ISPs, are blurring. As the cartoon character Pogo says, "we have met the enemy and they are us."

Telephone competition began with alternative long distance providers, then with competitive local exchange carriers. Both IXCs and CLECs began as traditional telephone companies. Now, however, telephony is a service offered by providers that previously offered only IP services, cable television,

Much of this book focuses on WANs from the customer rather than the provider standpoint. The emphasis of this chapter, however, is on the provider, or provider-like organizations such as large hosting centers.

Just as *VPN* and *switch* tend to become overloaded terms, so does *carrier-classness*. The term *carrier-class* comes from the telephone industry, and it has some fairly consistent operational definitions associated with it. One of the challenges for ISPs, hosting centers, etc., is to use the shared parts of the carrier-class model, but not the parts that do not apply.

For example, one tradition in telephony operations is that if a configuration fails, the device it manages will roll back to the earlier configuration. Rollback could be catastrophic to the Internet routing system.

What's a Carrier These Days?

Originally, there were telcos and everyone else. Today, there is a broad spectrum of carriers and carrier-like organizations. Cultures are still evolving. At a minimum, there are cultures of telephone companies, major data center providers, and Internet service providers. They complement the enterprise culture.

Even within the traditional telecommunications space, there are complex issues of where equipment is placed. Traditionally, there was the end office. If the means of access to the customer premises is the original telco copper pairs, then the end office will be the termination point. With competitive LECs and xDSL service providers, however, there may be a minimum amount of equipment at the end office. There may be no more than a multiplexer at the end office, with a high-speed link to switching and other equipment either at a competitive carrier facility or at a shared *carrier hotel*.

From a business perspective, carrier grade organizations can be divided into *established*, *startup*, and *potential*. A potential organization is an enterprise that provides internal carrier-like services, and whose users have the same expectations they would of a more traditional carrier. Electrical and gas utilities, with their own rights of way, often provide internal carrier services. Utilities are one part of the critical national infrastructures, and financial networks are another.

Established carriers have the advantage of a continuing revenue stream provided by their installed base. Established carriers have the disadvantage that their installed base may include obsolescent components that are not fully amortized. They may be dinosaurs, but I would hate to have to be in hand-to-claw combat with a *Tyrannosaurus Rex*.

Critical Infrastructure

In the United States, President William Clinton signed Presidential Decision Directive 63 that established the concept of critical infrastructures, and an organization to help protect them. The directive defined *critical infrastructures* as are "those physical and cyber-based systems essential to the minimum operations of the economy and government. These systems are so vital, that their incapacity or destruction would have a debilitating impact on the defense or economic security of the United States."

Critical infrastructure missions include:

- **Information and communications.** Computing and telecommunications equipment, software, processes, and people that support: the processing, storage, and transmission of data and information, the processes and people that convert data into information and information into knowledge, and the data and information themselves.

- **Banking and finance.** Entities, such as retail and commercial organizations, investment institutions, exchange boards, trading houses, and reserve systems, and associated operational organizations, government operations, and support activities, that are involved in all manner of monetary transactions, including its storage for saving purposes, its investment for income purposes, its exchange for payment purposes, and its disbursement in the form of loan and other financial instruments.

- **Water supply.** "Source of water, reservoirs and holding facilities, aqueducts and other transport systems, the filtration, cleaning and treatment systems, the pipeline, the cooling systems and other delivery mechanisms that provide for domestic and industrial applications, including systems for dealing with water runoff, waste water, and firefighting."

- **Transportation.** "The physical distribution system critical to supporting the national security and economic well-being of this nation, including aviation; the national airspace system; airlines and aircraft; and airports; roads and highways, trucking and personal vehicles and intelligent transportation systems; waterborne commerce; ports and waterways and the vessels operating thereon; mass transit, both rail and bus; pipelines, including natural gas, petroleum, and other hazardous material; freight and long haul passenger rail; and delivery services."

- **Emergency services.** Medical, police, fire, and rescue systems and personnel that are called upon when an individual or community is responding to emergencies. These services are typically provided at the local level (county or metropolitan area). In addition, state and Federal response plans define emergency support functions to assist in response and recovery.

Continues

> ## Critical Infrastructure *(Continued)*
>
> - **Public health services.** Prevention Surveillance Laboratory Services Personal Health Services.
> - **Continuity of government services.** Sufficient capabilities at the Federal, state, and local levels of government are required to meet the needs for essential services to the public.
> - **Electrical power.** Generation stations, transmission and distribution networks that create and supply electricity to end users so that end users achieve and maintain nominal functionality, including the transportation and storage of fuel essential to that system.
> - **Oil and gas production and storage.** The production and holding facilities for natural gas and processing facilities for these fuels.

Startup carriers have the advantage of flexibility, like the fast little mammals that dodged the dinosaurs. Startup carriers have the disadvantage of being low in the food chain.

Of course, the grass is always greener on the other side, or, in the case of mammalian scavengers versus saurian predators, the other creature's kill is always tastier than your own. Startup carriers envy the revenue base of established carriers, and want to have their own solid stream. Established carriers spawn new business units to go aggressively after startup niches.

Carrier Motivations

I would be tempted simply to ask, "What part of money do you fail to understand?" but that is overly simplistic. Carriers are motivated by the bottom line of earnings, which has two cost and one revenue components:

- **Equipment cost.** Direct costs, one-time installation and training, facility preparation.
- **Operations cost.** Maintenance (internal or vendor), provisioning, customer installations, quality monitoring.
- **Service revenue.** Attracting new customers and keeping old ones. Service level delivery verification. Billing systems.

Carriers want to maximize revenue. Depending on the corporate financial model, a potential carrier inside an enterprise may also obtain revenue, but as an internal funds transfer. Alternatively, a potential carrier may focus on cost reduction.

See "EONS" later in the chapter for a discussion of how "carrier-grade" technical and operational attributes feed into these financial goals.

Types of Carriers

Changes in regulation and technology constantly spawn new types of carrier business. Several broad categories, however, are useful for discussion.

Internet Service Providers (ISP)

Most, but not all, ISPs are startup organizations. Unfortunately, many small startups have the early mortality rate of trendy restaurants. I remain unsure of whether an Internet cafe is the combination of the best or worst parts of the restaurant and ISP markets.

Internet service providers differ in focus. The most common offers public dial-up services to end users. Some larger ISPs specialize in business-to-business or business-to-Internet access, and deemphasize dial access. Other ISPs outsource their dial access to dial wholesalers.

The class of network service providers sells bandwidth to ISPs. They may also sell connectivity to enterprises, although their sales models often are geared to customers with significant bandwidth requirements.

Hosting Centers

Once upon a time, an enterprise was very proud of its information systems group, as they watched their last mainframe dinosaur leave to become a fossil, superceded by mammals...er...servers. And the servers grew and prospered, along with the enterprise. The servers multiplied until the old computer room was filled with them. The chief information officer could see that very soon, she would have no room for more servers, and went to the chief financial officer to request budget for computer room enlargement.

The CFO, however, had other ideas. Over one weekend, he decreed that large quantities of industrial shelving—the sort with bolt-together

The Trail of Tiers

ISPs and NSPs often are called Tier 1 through 5. Unfortunately, these categories have no universal meaning, although marketeers in the larger providers tend to define Tier 1 as whatever they are and their competitor is not.

General usage suggests that a Tier 1 provider has a national or international backbone with at least DS-3 or OC-3 rates. In addition, such a provider has a presence at several regional exchange points, and may have private peerings, usually more the better, with other providers high in the food chain.

Another way of describing Tier 1 providers, although an unfortunately circular one, is that Tier 1 providers primarily connect with other Tier 1 providers. Their connectivity is primarily mutual peering; they rarely buy transit.

Tier 2 providers also have their own broadband backbone, but are limited to a geographic region. They connect to at least one regional exchange point, and do buy transit.

Tiers increasingly become hazy from 3 downward. Tier 3 providers may be thought of as metropolitan area services, with uplinks of moderate bandwidth to at least two higher-level providers. Tier 4 providers are not multihomed.

gray metal frames—would appear in the computer room. He had work crews stack the servers on the gray shelves. Immense amounts of floor space became free, although the CFO neglected to tell the work crew to leave their ladders, making it a bit hard to reach the top servers.

Proudly, the CFO told the CIO, "Your problem is solved! Look at all the floor space!" Pointing to the gray shelving frame, he said, "We shall call this new innovation, which holds servers, the Main Frame." The more things change, the more they stay the same. In my youth, large facilities that provided time-shared services were mainframe-based organizations called service bureaus. To a large extent, a hosting center is a service bureau that uses many servers rather than a mainframe. Of course, things are further confused by the reality that modern servers, or even workstations, have significantly more computing power than 1970-vintage supercomputers.

Distributed servers have their place, but there are many incentives to move machines to large hosting centers. Such hosting centers are "carrier grade" in the sense of environmental hardening, security, 24/7/365 staffing, emergency power, etc.

Large hosting centers also can cost-justify being attached to redundant high-capacity WAN backbones, such as OC-48 or OC-192 SONET/SDH.

Another argument for hosting centers is routability of address space. The problem of having globally routable address space for small numbers of servers multihomed to different ISPs is not fully solved. It would seem reasonable that an enterprise with critical multihoming requirements would want provider independent addresses. Unfortunately, many enterprises with such requirements do not have enough Internet-reachable hosts to justify their own address space. Even if they did receive space, some large providers filter prefix advertisements longer (i.e., with a lesser number of hosts) than /19 or /20. Smaller enterprises simply do not qualify for this much address space, so even if they have registered space and advertise it, it may not be globally reachable. Hosting centers, however, often have large numbers of hosts and justify globally routable address space.

The term *hosting center* generally refers to a facility shared among enterprise servers. Carrier hotels are similar, except their customers are not enterprises but other carriers. A carrier hotel, for example, may be a point of presence for several ISPs in a locality, with shared high-speed uplinks. Carrier hotels also emphasize carrier-oriented infrastructure, such as –48 VDC power.

Yet another variant is the cooperative local exchange, where ISPs and enterprises may cooperate to avoid sending traffic destined across the street by way of a major carrier hub hundreds of miles away.

Traditional and Startup Telcos

Telephone companies are both entering data and multiservice provider markets themselves, and also providing colocation for competitive providers. After the AT&T divestiture, several classes emerged. In the established and, to some extent, startup category are:

- Long-distance carriers with national facilities
- Long-distance carriers with regional facilities (I-LEC) and local independent telephone companies (ITC)
- Value-added networks that lease facilities

Primarily in the startup category are:

- Competitive local exchange carriers (CLEC)
- Competitive long-distance providers (LDP)

These organizations primarily competed for voice services, but have extended their offerings into data. CLECs may lease copper from incumbent telcos, or could bypass the ILEC local loop with optical or wireless local loops of their own.

To confuse things even further, cable television providers are entering both the data and voice markets, while traditional data providers now support voice over IP. Figure 6.1 shows just a few of the potential competitive complexities that an enterprise might exploit, or by which an enterprise can be completely confused.

Remember that the new competitive environment sometimes, but not always, separates basic loop access from switching.

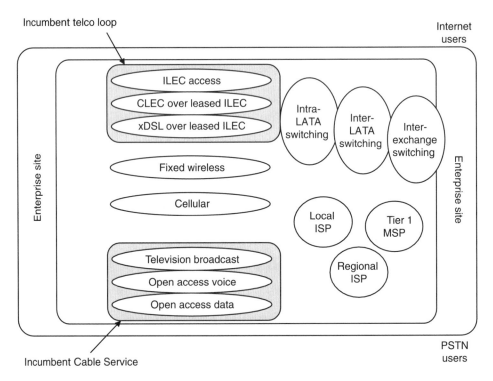

Figure 6.1   Competitive relationships.

Wholesalers/Virtual POPs

There is an increasing trend for modem pools to be wholesaled to ISPs. As new last-mile technologies enter the market, or as new data services are added to existing CATV or other providers, the general idea of a *service selection gateway* is gaining momentum.

According to the MS Forum, a *virtual switch* (VS) is a subset of resources on one or more physical access switches. A VS is the access service seen by ISP or enterprise customers of access service providers. These customers must be isolated from one another.

Besides access wholesalers, there are hosting centers with a wide range of operational support models. Some centers expect enterprise to give the center the software expected to run on a server, and the center installs, backs up, and otherwise operates the server. Other centers have models in which customers can build their own server, to be installed and operated by center staff. Yet another model gives a caged area to the enterprise, and simply deals with connectivity outside the cage.

Carrier Concepts

We dealt with some of the important historical background of communications carriers in Chapter 1, "What Is the Problem You Are Trying to Solve?" The concepts of user planes, control planes, and management planes still apply, but modern carriers extend their concepts.

Carriers have Operations, Administration, Maintenance and Provisioning functions. Provisioning is the function of selecting and installing the carrier circuits and switch resources that underlie a customer-ordered service.

Bearer versus Application Service

The classical bearer service is "dial tone," or plain old telephone service (POTS). It now extends to basic data services, both circuit- and packet-switched.

Carriers provide services to customers, who connect to the service providers via loops. A service is visible to the user, and something the user pays for. Since some carriers sell capacity to other carriers, what may be a service from one perspective is a networking capability from another.

Application services, in the telephony context, include such things as answering services and voicemail, directory assistance, conference bridging, credit card billing, etc. Enhanced telephony services such as call forwarding, three-way calling, and the dreaded call waiting also are applications. Another class of applications is *directory enabled services* ranging from toll-free number translation to personal number portability. Hybrid application services are developing and include voice-enabled Web applications, call centers, etc.

From the carrier perspective, VPNs for data and Centrex for voice are applications, as are IP services beyond routing, such as DNS and DHCP.

It is not unreasonable to suggest that broadcast channels over cable TV are its bearer service, while pay-per-view services are enhanced services.

Terminators are entry or exit points of flows. The *media gateway* (MG) is knowledgeable enough not to interconnect incompatible terminator types. Examples of terminators, or *bearer points*, are DS0s, ATM or frame relay virtual circuits, 4 Khz analog channels, etc.

Media resources include the *coder-decoders* (codecs) that convert voice to and from bit streams, modems, audio conference bridges, interactive voice response systems, etc.

The devices at terminators send edge signaling to the core. ISDN Q.931, ATM UNI, FR, and X.25 are all edge mechanisms A *signal gateway* will relay, convert, or terminate these signals in a manner compatible with the switching plane.

Trunking and Grooming

Carriers internally have *transports*, which run over trunks. The distinction between loop and trunk becomes blurred when a customer organization provides carrier-like services. For example, the line between a customer-owned PBX and the local end office is called a trunk. Trunks may be analog or digital, although analog trunks are becoming increasingly rare.

When not attached to elephants, trunks carry user information and may carry signaling information. Typically, trunks have a connotation of carrying aggregated user calls, and themselves are typically provisioned as trunk groups. The members of a trunk group provide the same transport function.

The process of provisioning trunks is not a static one, in which once the trunk or trunk group is established, it never changes. Carriers routinely perform *grooming* of their trunks in order to improve the efficiency with which trunk bandwidth is used. Trunk grooming is especially important to carriers that buy bandwidth from other carriers.

Grooming is a normal part of the operations of an efficient carrier. It has been called the bandwidth equivalent of defragmenting a disk, making sure that high-capacity channels are efficiently used. Grooming can, however, negatively impact special availability requirements.

Assume you have a main site in Virginia and connect to a critical server in Massachusetts. You carefully order two links from your service provider, LukeNet, specifying that you want route diversity. You have a less critical connection to New York.

LukeNet has some of its own fiber on the Boston–New York–Washington route, but almost all current capacity is committed. LukeNet does manage to obtain one of your channels through its own facilities. To meet the diversity requirement, LukeNet leases capacity from DarkSideNet. LukeNet also runs your New York traffic through DarkSideNet.

Some months after your service was activated, LukeNet adds *dense wavelength division multiplexing* (DWDM) to its existing SONET fiber, and gains a great deal of additional capacity. To maximize its return on investment in DWDM, LukeNet *grooms* its circuits to use internal bandwidth most efficiently.

Quite appropriately, LukeNet moves your New York circuit to its own facilities. Unfortunately, the provisioning engineer also sees your Massachusetts circuit routed via DarkSideNet, but does not notice that route diversity is part of the contract for this link. The engineer also does not notice that you already have one Virginia-Massachusetts link on the LukeNet fiber.

Your company is a manufacturer of manufacturing robots, and it has a new heavy-duty robot capable both of fine machining and heavy lifting. One of your competitive advantages is that the robot can be remotely controlled, although your firm does not recommend doing so other than over high availability networks, such as your diversely routed links to the robot controller in Massachusetts.

Proudly, your CEO shows the new robot to the press. She demonstrates that it can lift a 10-ton steel bar, yet delicately machine it. Once the robot has picked up the bar, she invites a photographer to join her and watch its magic machining, getting a great view by standing below the robot.

As the camera whirrs, a rogue backhoe (is there any other kind?) sinks its scoop into a toxic waste dump in New Jersey, not noticing the obscured sign "Buried Cable. Property of LukeNet."

The robot loses its control signal. Your CEO's last words, terminated by a crash and squish, are "watch the 50 millisecond recovery time!"

Murphy's Laws are as relevant to networking as is the speed of light. When contracting with providers for critical facilities, write into your contract a provision that lets you audit the *data circuit layout record* (DCLR) for the circuits you pay to have routed diversely. Most carriers do use the term DCLR, or slight variants of it.

Under normal circumstances, you may want to do this about every 60 days. Industry mergers also can cause combining of facilities you thought diversely routed; always audit your routing after any of your carriers merge or are acquired.

Control and Switching

A *network service instance* is the unit of providing service—a voice call, a data flow, etc. *Connections* are bidirectional or multidirectional sets of NSI, and may be considered an association of resources.

The decision on what path to take through the network is a *control plane* function. The carriage of bits of an NSI through the carrier network is a *switching plane* function. Control and switching functions do not have to reside in the same physical chassis, and it is quite common to share control elements over multiple switching elements, either LAN-connected inside a CO or remotely located. Figure 6.2 shows some options. Note that there is no single point of failure for communications.

Every instance has a near and far end address, a set of signaling requirements, and a path. When the generic service has options, such as QoS, the NSI identifies a particular set of options used for the particular unit of service.

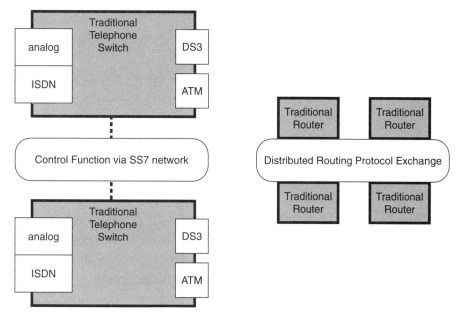

Figure 6.2 Central and distributed control and switching.

Carrier switching elements move bits for several reasons. One is *native services*, another is *service interworking*, and the next is *trunking*. Native services are of the same type at input and output; there are no protocol converters between the access to the service and the service proper. *Media gateways* convert between dissimilar networks, and are discussed further in the section "Evolution at the Edge."

Service interworking involves dissimilar types, perhaps one service at the customer access and another in the transport. Conversion is required, and may include one or more functions:

- Transport interworking, such as media encapsulation and conversion
- Control interworking, such as address mapping
- Application interworking, such as call screening

ISDN to ATM interworking, for example, uses Q.931 to access an ATM transport that uses UNI. frame relay to ATM, in a service that enforces QoS policy, uses all three types of interworking.

Trunking services are the function of the main transport. They carry bits between access points, interworking points, and internal network switches. Trunks carry signaling as well as user information, although the signaling and the user data may go by different systems within the provider network.

Classical telco trunks have been TDM or ATM. Classical data trunks have a wider range of transports. MPLS is likely to unify the data and voice worlds.

MPLS itself runs today over classical data transports, but these transports are themselves evolving with new optical technologies. Where ATM might be used today, there is increasing use of POS, and continued movement to new frame formats even more tailored to optical transports. PPP over SONET is more efficient than ATM, but even PPP can be improved for greater efficiency. Some of the fields in the PPP header really have no purpose, other than to maintain compatibility with some datalink layer chips developed for LAP-B.

Capacity

In the PSTN, there are separate capacity measures for the number of calls for which a switch can pass user traffic, and for the number of calls it can set up. Very high rates of calls can overwhelm the call setup of a switch that would actually have capacity to carry their traffic.

As provider networks grow more intelligent, there is a distinct separation between the switching and control functions. The idea of numbers of calls that can be set up applies to controllers, conventional circuit switches, and gateways that integrate control functions. Devices that interface to customers are sized in the number of ports they can handle, and the number of *busy hour call attempts* that can be processed.

Increasing capacity can call for adding different sorts of resources. They include the number of physical ports, the call setup capacity, and the user traffic through the switch. Capacity has to be considered on a network, not network element basis—what good is it to improve the port capacity of a switch so that it can accept 622 Mbps of bandwidth, but then give it only 155 Mbps to the next level of the switching hierarchy?

Physical Density Issues

Carriers have a constant problem of *footprint*, the amount of floor space taken by equipment. One way of stating their objective is optimizing the amount of equipment that can fit into a standard seven-foot rack.

The footprint problem is not only vertical and floor space footprint; *real estate* and *form factor* are other terms used to describe the next issue, which is the number and type of interface connectors that can physically fit onto a chassis.

As network speeds increase, the internal switching fabrics of high-performance routers and switches grow in power—and cost. Interface cards that plug into the fabric must have circuitry that is compatible with the fabric's speed.

If a card slot in a chassis is 7 inches high, there is a real limit to how many connectors it can have—8 to 16 seem to be the practical limit. Think of the waste in connecting T1 circuits to gigabit and terabit routers. A plausible T1 card could connect only approximately 25 Mbps of data. A SONET card, with connectors of similar size, could connect 10 Gbps.

One workable method of providing reasonable improvement in port density is to use not a *backplane* to which all cards connect, but a *midplane*, which has card connectors on both of its sides.

Hardware designers often separate the front and back of the midplane into different functions. On many current products, switching fabric and control cards are on the front, while line cards are on the back.

Midplane design also allows different card heights. On the Cisco 8850, for example, the front cards are full-height, while there are two half-height cards in most of the back slots. The half-height cards are used for line interfaces. One card deals with common logic at the media-independent part of the physical layer, and possibly the data link layer as well, while the other is specific to the physical optical or electronic interface used.

If the goal is to increase the number of ports, aggregation devices or shelves may be appropriate. Such devices can be local or remote to the physical switches.

Call Setup

If the goal is to increase the BHCA capability, it may be necessary to add processors to the device implementing the control function. In systems with high availability requirements, it is usually best to add additional processors rather than increase the speed of the existing main processor.

In a "carrier grade" implementation, it must be possible to add processors without interrupting service. Many older carrier devices, however, required system downtime when changing processors. These systems, however, would usually continue to handle preestablished calls.

Established Call Capacity

To increase the established call capacity, many switches allow switching fabric resources to be added. This is another motivation for midplane design, because it is rather difficult to replace a backplane without interrupting service, when all cards are connected to the backplane.

With the increasing separation of control and switching processing, it becomes practical to add the type of capacity that is needed. While there certainly are exceptions (e.g., switches serving rock concert reservation desks or talk radio), switching and port capacity tend to be limits before a system runs out of control capacity.

One of the reasons that control functions are quite efficient is the use of SS7 as the internal signaling architecture.

Signaling System 7 (SS7)

Demand for telecommunications service always has increased. In the original telephony model, the dialed digits went from the telephone to the switch, and from switch to switch until the destination was reached. A 4kHz analog circuit, or its DS0 digital equivalent, passed no user information while setup was in process.

As long as the signaling information passed through the same channels as user information, channels were inefficiently used. In common channel signaling, of which SS7 is one example, there are separate trunks for user traffic and for signaling.

Call setup is time consuming, and simply does not involve much data volume. Prior to common channel signaling, traffic trunks had to be committed from the initial off-hook to the network's decision about reachability of the destination. When the call setup took 10 seconds, that was 10 seconds when billable traffic could not be carried by that trunk. If user channels were committed only after SS7 had discovered that the called destination is not busy or otherwise unable to accept a call, utilization of the traffic trunks would become much more efficient.

Once the digital signaling information exists, a wide range of applications become possible. Toll-free numbers, for example, actually are aliases for real telephone numbers. Special billing rules apply to these numbers. When an end office receives a call request to a toll-free number, it sends a request over the SS7 network to a network control point, which returns the translation, routing and billing information. The end office then places the call to the real number.

Other specialized billing makes routine use of SS7. These include credit and prepaid calling cards, 900 services, and collect calls.

SS7 is capable of conveying short messages, such as caller ID or paging, using TCAP, an application protocol in the SS7 stack. It is not the intention of SS7 designers, however, that the main SS7 signaling network carry significant amounts of user data. As it has been said that war is too important to leave to the generals, SS7 trunks are far too important to network availability to leave them open to the possibility of congestion due to user traffic.

SS7 Stack

SS7 has its own architectural stack, shown in Figure 6.3.

In SS7 terminology, the upper layers are called *parts*. The ISDN user part carries information used for creating, maintaining, and terminating ISDN calls. The *transaction capabilities application part* (TCAP), as its

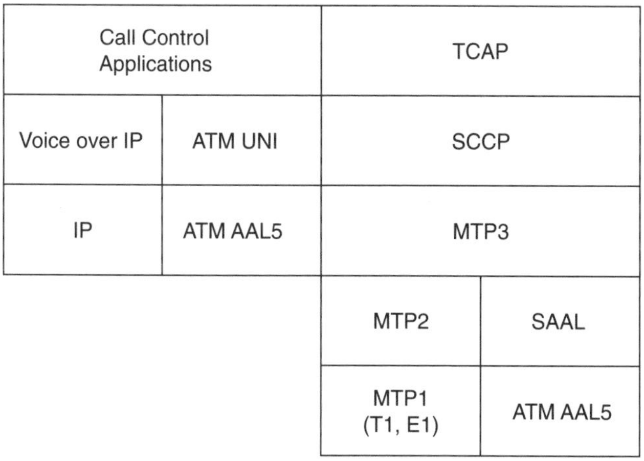

Call Control Applications		TCAP	
Voice over IP	ATM UNI	SCCP	
IP	ATM AAL5	MTP3	
		MTP2	SAAL
		MTP1 (T1, E1)	ATM AAL5

Figure 6.3 SS7 Protocol layers.

name suggests, carries transactions across SS7. Typical transaction databases include SCP directories, mobile access points, etc. *Message transfer part level 3* (MTP-3) manages routing, traffic, and links in digital transports.

The higher layer parts can be carried over various lower layers. Message transfer part level 2, or SSCOP, transports payloads across point-to-point links. In contrast, the ATM *signaling adaption layer* carries payloads across ATM transports. The *signaling connection control part* carries payloads across arbitrary connectionless and connection-oriented transports.

SS7 Points and Links

STPs are analogous to standalone path determination processors in routers and switches, or in multiservice selection gateways. In the PSTN, they tell the voice switches how to make connections. The generic term for the forwarding elements controlled by STPs is *signaling point. Access (A) links* connect the controlled devices to STP pairs.

Signaling points (SP), addressed in the SS7 network with *signaling point codes* (SPC), are the working parts of SS7, roughly corresponding to forwarding engines in IP. SPs also include directory functions such as 800 number translation at *service control point* (SCP) SPs. A general voice switch is a *service switching point* (SSP). *Mobile service centers* (MSC) provide connectivity to the PSTN for mobile telephone users (see Figure 6.4).

As critical components, individual STPs in the SS7 network are redundant. This redundancy does not mean that there are pairs of side-by-side STPs, vulnerable to the same fire, flood, or suddenly nonflying object. Instead, the STPs of a pair are geographically separated but with redundant communications links between them. The links between STPs in the pair are called *cross (C) links*. (see Figure 6.5)

Diagonal (D) *links* interconnect STPs at different hierarchical levels (see Figure 6.6), in contrast to *bridge* (B) *links*, which interconnect STPs with other STPs at the same hierarchical level of the SS7 network. Additional redundancy at the same level can be provided through *extended* (E) *links*, which are very similar to B links except that they go to additional STPs, farther away from the current STP pair.

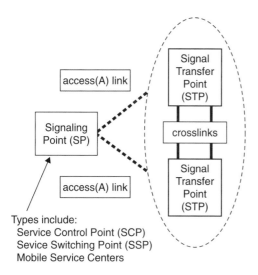

Figure 6.4 Basic SS7 functions.

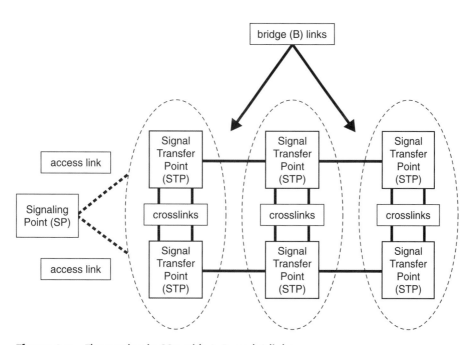

Figure 6.5 Flat routing in SS7 with A, B, and C links.

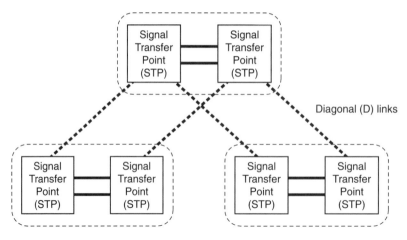

Figure 6.6 Hierarchical routing in SS7.

There may also be reasons to share information among only certain STPs, as in a software-defined enterprise network. This also might be done for traffic engineering. *Fully associated (F) links* are those that interconnect nodes that have some administrative association with one another.

SIGTRAN: SS7 over IP

Existing SS7 networks run at 64 Kbps. While this was a definite improvement over analog control networks, it is inadequate for the demands of modern networking. It would be possible simply to increase the speed of existing SS7 facilities, but that would not have the inherent fault tolerance of routed networks.

In any case, carriers are building significant IP networks for internal tasks, such as collecting accounting and billing information, software updates, monitoring SNMP-managed devices, etc. These networks are isolated from the public network and are built to "carrier-grade" standards of availability. Given that such internal networks will exist, it is logical for carriers to want to migrate their SS7 networks into them.

Telephone switch vendors had started to develop proprietary methods for carrying SS7 and Q.931 over IP. Because carriers inherently need multivendor interoperability to connect to other carriers, they are biased in favor of standards and against proprietary solutions. The IETF SIGTRAN working group was created to establish standards for carrying critical signaling information of the PSTN over IP networks with the same performance, security, and reliability as in existing SS7 networks.

Plausible uses for SS7 over IP include:

- Transport of signaling between a signaling gateway and media gateway or media gateway controller
- Transport of signaling ("backhoe") from a media gateway to a media gateway controller
- Transport of TCAP between a signaling gateway and other IP nodes

These uses do not necessarily involve the PSTN. When the services provided do require SS7 access, as, for example, to support ISDN, the IP network must carry the Q.931 or SS7 ISUP messages among the media gateways to which the ISDN users connect. The signaling gateway must send this signaling into the PSTN.

Carrier Classness

Carrier class and *carrier grade* have become popular marketing buzzwords. There really is no strict definition of the overall problem. It is reasonable to say that the best of traditional telephony availability is desirable for any service.

Sometimes, carrier grade is associated with a "five nines," or 99.999-percent availability. But what does this mean? Component availability? Probability of a call being dropped?

On other occasions, carrier grade is considered synonymous with the availability of SONET with alternate protection switching. Yet some of the recovery properties of SONET are needed for telephony but not necessarily data. SONET also wastes capacity in the backup ring.

From the enterprise perspective, a carrier cannot fix problems of availability caused by the enterprise. A central office may be nuclear-hardened, but if there is one local loop to it, and a backhoe cuts the loop, the enterprise is down. If the enterprise procures bandwidth independently from two long-haul carriers, without contracting to one carrier to be responsible for having physically diverse paths, the enterprise has no one but itself to blame if both carriers lease capacity from a third carrier, and a backhoe cuts the third carrier's medium.

Network Equipment Building Systems (NEBS)

NEBS, a set of documents issued by Telecordia (formerly Bellcore), defines a physical environment in which a component is expected to work, ranging from temperature and humidity, to heat dissipation, to electrostatic discharge. Telecordia specifications are widely used by carriers. There are three increasingly stringent levels of general NEBS requirements, and four levels of earthquake protection.

Meeting NEBS Level 1 does not so much speak to the reliability of the network element as much as it ensures the element does not interfere with other equipment in a carrier facility. Its focus is on safety and electromagnetic emissions. The FCC did order that complying with NEBS Level 1 qualifies a CLEC to colocate its equipment in an ILEC facility. NEBS Levels 2 and 3 actually deal with system reliability.

Be careful to understand the realities of NEBS, and the difference between compliance and certification. Compliance means that the vendor says that its product meets the NEBS requirements. Certification means that an independent third party has verified compliance.

Even the level of compliance means that the vendor has verified that the entire product, not just individual cards or shelves, meets the requirements in a practical configuration. It is less clear what certification means, because there are no formally approved testing laboratories such as those meeting the National Voluntary Laboratory Accreditation Program, or recognized organizations such as Underwriters Laboratories. A "certifying" organization, such as Telecordia, depends on its reputation.

Customers may find it acceptable to ask for the vendor's NEBS test results, and have them reviewed by an expert on their staff. This is not a trivial task, because the test results for a product of reasonable complexity can form a several-inches-thick pile of paper.

Alternatively, the customer may want independent NEBS testing. Depending on the complexity of the product, this can cost from hundreds of thousands to millions of dollars.

Once Up Always Up

Another aspect of carrier grade is called "once up always up" in telephony. This aspect includes the idea that cards, power supplies, and other electronics, including control processors, can be maintained or replaced without impacting the overall network element. At the level of circuit cards, rational layout of their cabling can be as operationally important as the card electronics. A hot-swappable card that cannot be swapped without disconnecting a cable to seven cards unrelated to the problem is *not* carrier grade.

There is a huge difference between failures that prevent new access to the network, and failures that interrupt existing service instances. Once up always up needs to be interpreted in that context.

Common components such as management processors and power supplies must be redundant and hot-swappable. In the real world, many network elements have some parts that cannot be replaced transparently, such as the backplane or midplane. Designers work hard to limit such parts to functions that are unlikely to need field maintenance, and try to remove the single points of failure. Even single points such as midplanes will be designed not to fail totally, but degrade during operation. Once up always up also refers to software. It must be possible to upgrade software on some processors without disturbing services.

Once up always up certainly pertains to availability, but it also means that the network must be able to grow. Scalability and maintainability mean that elements can be upgraded without interrupting current services.

Beyond the level of component failover inside a network element, carrier grade operations require failover mechanisms among network elements. Finding alternate paths, of course, has been one of the traditional strengths of IP networks, developed partially to find alternate paths around nuclear fireballs.

For data applications, the routing reconvergence time in well-designed networks may not be invisible to users, but reconvergence in seconds or low tens of seconds has minimal effect on transaction processing, Web browsing, etc., as long as data is not lost.

Telephony applications, however, have much more stringent requirements for reconvergence after failures. Outages of 200 milliseconds can begin to degrade voice quality, and two-second delays can cause calls to be completely disconnected. SONET alternate protection switching was developed because telephony needed reconvergence in the millisecond range.

An assortment of techniques are evolving to speed reconvergence in IP networks. These techniques may be pure IP, such as equal-cost load sharing or quasi-static routes, or may involve alternate MPLS paths.

Power, Power, I Want Power

Central offices routinely use –48-volt DC power, rather than 110- or 220-volt AC "household power." The DC voltage is protected by *large* banks of batteries, which are trickle-charged by utility power, but backed up with generators. Do not think of these battery systems as conventional computer room uninterruptible power systems (UPS). Think more, instead, of the last World War II submarine movie you may have seen, where a huge battery room provides all power to a submerged submarine.

There are likely to be small power distribution and circuit breaker units in each equipment rack, but one of the advantages of centralized DC power is reducing the amount of vertical space in racks taken up by AC power converters.

HINT

When putting more conventional data equipment into a central office environment, such as hubs or switches, you will need to provide an inverter that produces 110 VAC power from –48 VDC. Ironically, many small devices then need to convert the 110 VAC to various DC voltages that they use.

At the same time, be aware that unless the conventional data equipment meets at least NEBS Level 1, it may not be permitted in a central office. Hosting centers, carrier hotels, and exchange points may be more relaxed about non-NEBS equipment.

Power, no matter how well backed up, still can fail. If you are trying to provide a highly available service, you must consider the effects of a total power failure in a key facility. To put this in a proper perspective of Murphy's Law, a national ISP had a POP in a building that was supplied with utility power, entering the building on different sides, and flowing from two geographically separated utility substations. The facility also had a diesel generator.

All three electrical power sources met at an electromechanical transfer switch, which routed the active power source to redundant UPS. I can picture a power designer smirking, "nothing can go wrong."

In the wee hours of one morning, there was a loud BANG. Operators ran out of the network control center, to discover a large hole in the wall where the electromechanical power switch had been installed. Smoke was everywhere . . . and the operators discovered there were bits of . . . something . . . in the smoke. There was a gap of several feet in the thick copper that fed the UPS.

The mystery bits turned out to be ratburger, very well done. Analysis showed that a pair of rats had set up housekeeping inside the electro-mechanical transfer switch. Doing what rats do, they apparently rolled, in a deadly embrace, onto the main power lead. Perhaps the rats were Wagnerian heroes, cursed by the gods to end their lives in a bolt of lightning, but the bright side, if any, was that they ended their lives together. We shall never know.

We do know, however, that it was impossible to find an electrician to replace the UPS feeder at 3 A.M.. When the UPS batteries were drained, the POP shut down.

There is no way to protect against this sort of capacity other than being connected to multiple POPs. When connecting to multiple POPs, be sure they are not virtual POPs on the same physical switch!

EONS

Nortel Networks developed a concept to organize the concepts of carrier grade. While its EONS concept encompasses a wide range of network attributes, EONS does not pretend to suggest that there is a single definition of carrier grade for all carriers or carrier-like organization.

EONS stands for the four groups of attributes:

- Equipment reliability
- Operational reliability
- Networking reliability
- Supplier reliability

Attributes

It does identify 154 attributes that may be relevant to particular business models, and organizes them into groups.

Equipment

Equipment attributes affect the hardware and software implementation of network elements. They have one-time costs plus the continued cost of maintenance and training new staff. Representative attributes include:

- **Element-level availability.** Downtime expected from failures and maintenance.

- **Software reliability.** Software update frequency and process, debugging tools, problem reporting, and bug tracking.

- **Hardware reliability.** Fault isolation and circumvention, rate of component return to vendor.

- **Restart and recovery.**

- **Layer 1 protection.** Alternate media failover for switching devices.

- **Accounting performance._**Probabilities that an element will correctly and accurately collect data.

- **Physical and environmental characteristics.** Tolerance to environmental variations, effect on other equipment (i.e., electromagnetic compatibility), and on people (i.e., electrical safety).

- **Scalability.** Basic capacity of an element, modular upgrade capacity, number and types of interfaces, etc.

Operational

Operational attributes affect recurring costs involving element, network, and service management.

- **Security.** Access control, logging, log retention, and alarms.

- **Maintenance and troubleshooting.** Tools to simplify failure analysis and service impact.

- **Provisioning.** Tools to automate and assist repetitive tasks.

- **Statistics, billing, and SLA management.**

- **OAM signaling.** Ability to manage remote devices.

- **Scalability.** Growth capabilities of operational tools.

Network Attributes

"Network" is used here in the sense of the TMN concepts of service and network, as opposed to element management. Network attributes affect the end-to-end behavior of the network being managed.

From the financial standpoint, network attributes affect both revenues and costs. Customers are attracted to new network functions and cheaper alternatives for existing functions. They stay with a provider that meets service-level agreements.

- **End-to-end availability.** Layers 1, 2, 3, and higher as appropriate for the service. Downtime targets.
- **Optimization.** Grooming and other resource use tuning.
- **Fault isolation and recovery.** Capabilities.

Supplier Attributes

Enterprises often stress using a single vendor, to whom they can outsource operations, or at least have a single equipment vendor with whom to speak. Carriers have a somewhat more pessimistic tradition, where they prefer *not* to have a single vendor for any given critical function. Part of the philosophy of carrier grade is psychological, taking ultimate responsibility for availability.

The reality is that any vendor, no matter how competent, will have hardware or software bugs that only appear in operations. AT&T and MCI both have had national frame relay outages caused by bugs in Lucent/Ascend and Cisco switches. A bit of a disclaimer here: Even though I am a Nortel employee, I have stock in both Lucent and Cisco. I'm really not singling out these switch vendors, who make excellent products (although I like to think *we* do better, speaking from pride of ownership!).

Attributes include:

- **Outage metric collection.** Agreements on collecting, analyzing, and reporting outages to the supplier.
- **Technical support.** What support is expected? What is the vendor response time?
- **Professional services.** What are the business and technical services that the supplier can provide to the customer, improving the customer's effectiveness?

EONS Priorities for Carrier Types

Established carriers are most concerned with controlling their operating costs and the costs of adding capacity. Of the EONS attributes, their first priorities are operational and equipment attributes. Network attributes are next most important, since these contribute to keeping their customer base. Supplier attributes are their lowest priority, because they typically have well-understood supplier relationships in place.

Startup carriers want to maximize their service offerings under the constraints of deployment cost. To attract users to their new services, network attributes are most important. Operational attributes are next in importance, because ease of use is critical to rapid deployment. Supplier and equipment attributes are least important.

Potential carriers may not need some of the features that competitive features do, such as billing. Since their economic incentive is cost avoidance rather than revenue generation, their highest priority is operational attributes, minimizing the cost of ownership. They are next most concerned with supplier and network attributes, and least concerned with equipment attributes.

Evolution at the End Office

Digital end offices began with T1 channel banks. We have discussed T1/E1 channels as digital streams. These facilities were developed as digital carriers for voice. Formally, DS-1 is a signal format, and T1 is a specific transmission system that carries DS-1 signals over twisted copper pairs, but the terms are interchangeable in practice. In modern terms, you can think of the basic voice-data interface device, the *channel bank*, as a set of analog interfaces and codecs under a central multiplexing control. Each analog channel converts to a 64 Kbps DS0 signal (see Figure 6.7).

Algorithms used by the codecs differ in different parts of the world. Canada, the United States, and Japan use μ-*law*; Europe uses *A-law*; and there are a few other algorithms such as K-law used in Mexico. Mexico also uses E1 rather than T1 links. For end-to-end voice to work between different codecs, a gateway function will be needed.

Basic telephony multiplexing is fixed rather than statistical. North American channel banks combine 24 DS0 signals into a DS-1 signal. The

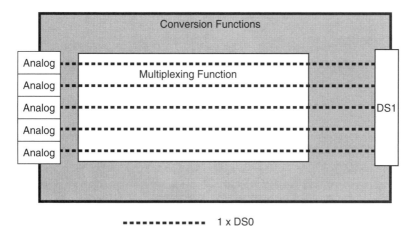

Figure 6.7 Channel banks convert analog to T1 or E1.

CCITT/ITU version, used in Europe, is the E-1 signal. It is worth noting that 64 Kbps is the basic rate at which a single voice call is digitized.

A T1 channel bank converts 24 analog channels to a single DS-1 stream. Twenty-four DS0 channels occupy 1.536 Mbps of bandwidth, and the remaining 8 Kbps of the DS-1 channel provides synchronization and diagnostics between the multiplexers, and thus is M-plane information. User-level information, such as dialing, is also carried within the digital streams, but the details of carrying it are beyond the scope of this discussion.

Channel Bank to DACS

DS-1 streams, at first, did not go outside the central office, or were physically patched to outgoing DS-1 spans. Fixed configuration multiplexers combined channels from one level of the PDH to another. M12 multiplexers combined DS-1 streams into DS2, and M23 multiplexers combined DS2 into DS-3. As DS-3 gained acceptance as a transmission technology, M13 multiplexers evolved, which combined multiple DS-1 into a DS-3. These multiplexers, however, did not allow the digital streams to be reconfigured.

Digital access crossconnect systems (DACS) are fundamental components of a carrier end office. They are physical layer devices that accept DS-x streams and combine them into DS-3 and faster trunks for interoffice communications. They can demultiplex a higher layer stream and send individual subchannels to different output ports (see Figure 6.8).

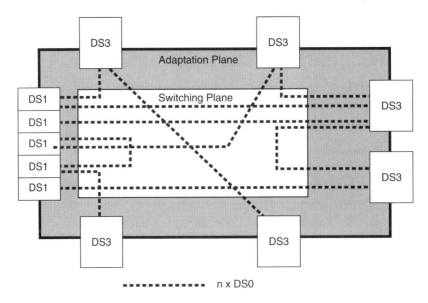

Figure 6.8 DACS.

DACS are the carrier building-block of fractional T1 and T3. The DACS can combine multiple DS0 channels into an aggregate stream sent to the customer over a physical T1 or T3.

DACS to DSL Access Multiplexer (DSLAM)

While DACS were specifically associated with DS-x technologies, a similar function arose for specific last-mile technologies. A *DSL access multiplexer* (DSLAM), for example, accepts customer streams, converts them to streams that are a multiple of DS-0, and puts them into appropriate time slots of outgoing trunks (see Figure 6.9).

As new last-mile technologies were introduced, they each had an equivalent to the DSLAM: a technology-specific termination of customer information, a switching function, and an outbound DS-x trunking function. To simplify the proliferation of different technology-specific DSLAM equivalents in the same CO, the idea of multiservice selection gateways evolved. These gateways are modular and can terminate different digital, and sometimes analog, services.

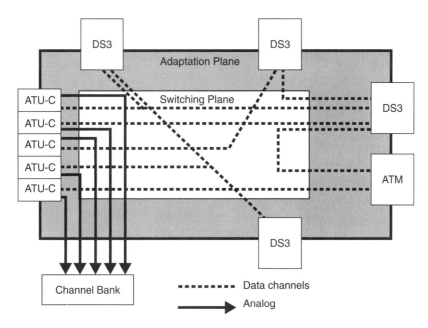

Figure 6.9 DACS and DSLAM.

Service Selection Gateways

Service gateways and *media gateways* are edge devices that terminate various edge technologies and convert them so that they interwork with the appropriate transports. These gateways may themselves provide some services, such as encryption and firewalling for data, or interactive voice response and conference bridging for voice.

The media gateway proper does adaptation and switching. One or more media gateways are under the control of a *media gateway controller*.

A virtual switch (VS) contains an assortment of adaption and switching functions under a single virtual controller. These elements can be remote from the switch controller, using single paths or redundant paths such as SONET/SDH with protection switching.

Service selection gateways (see Figure 6.10) are enabling devices for wholesale dial and for the newer connectivity methods such as cable and xDSL. The wholesaler partitions the gateway into multiple virtual switches, each servicing a retailer. Initially, these were established simply for analog dial, but now can include multiple local loop technologies.

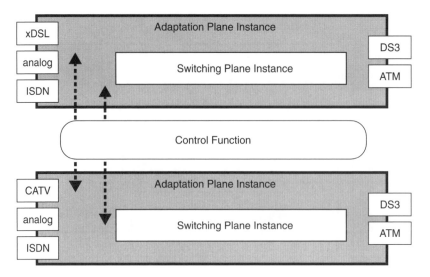

Figure 6.10 Service selection gateway.

The Multiservice Forum has been established to deal with implementation issues for distributed switching systems including backbones of ATM, Frame, and IP, and access technologies including analog, TDM, xDSL, wireless, and cable.

A *media gateway* is a network element that provides conversion between the information carried on telephone circuits and data packets carried over the Internet or over other IP networks.

Examples of media gateways include:

- **Trunking gateways** that interface between the telephone network and a Voice over IP network. In practice, these often are split into gateways for user streams and for signaling information.

- **Access gateways** that provide traditional analog or primary rate (PRI) line interfaces to a Voice over IP network.

- **Network access servers** that can attach a "modem" to a telephone circuit and provide data access to the Internet.

Adaptation Plane Description and Functions

Adaptation plane functions accept external interfaces. These interfaces may be user- or trunk-oriented. Adaptation plane resources are controlled by a logically independent controller. A controller can be dedicated to resources, a controller can be shared among multiple resources, or a set of controllers in fault-tolerant relationships can be shared by many resources.

Channel Banks: Sets of Adaptation Functions

Processing real-time services (such as voice and video) and nonreal-time services (such as file transfer) into bit patterns and protocol formats for the switching plane to process and transport between ports. ATM AAL and DTM adaptation are two examples of standards that may be used by the adaptation plane in order to format information for the switching plane to process.

Provides service-specific functions that do not directly affect the bit stream on the interface. For example, queue management and policing are best implemented in the adaptation plane.

Examples of dedicated resources include:
- Time slots on TDM or DTM ports
- VPI/VCI values on an ATM port
- DLCI values on a FR port

Examples of shared resources include:
- Conference bridges
- Tone receivers
- Buffers

Switching Plane Description and Functions

Where the adaptation plane is concerned with the "In and Out," the switching plane is responsible for the "Between." A service selection gateway often will need to be partitioned into several virtual switches, each serving a particular service provider, so the switching is more complex than a straightforward fabric.

In the MS architecture, ATM switches cells inside the switching plane. Its switch functions include:

- SAR and other adaptation
- Traffic management
- P-MP
- MPLS MP-P merging

Control Plane Description and Functions

In the MSF architecture, the control plane sets up traffic relationships among switching, application, and adaptation plane resources. This usage of "control" is broader than the control plane of B-ISDN, and includes aspects considered part of the management plane of B-ISDN.

The control plane has APIs used by the application plane, and controls the paths through the switching plane. It manages labels used for connections, including FR DLCIs, ATM VPI/VCI, and MPLS labels.

It controls the adaptation plane, terminating and originating the signaling information from media-specific (e.g., ATM) connections, and terminating and originating the user information on these connections, via the switching plane.

When there are two or more subnetworks that use different signaling, such as SS7 and H.323, the *signaling gateway function (SGF)* interfaces between them. It may translate or tunnel the protocols, or deny the call.

SS7 gateways can support large numbers of access switches, allowing data calls to be routed from the PSTN to the access switch technology. The media gateway control protocol (MGCP) is the lead contender for standard communications between gateways and the switches they control, but full consensus has not yet been reached. Proprietary protocols may be used.

Last-Mile Technologies

All of these technologies are still exploring the appropriate mode of operations for IP. Should they be "always on," or should they dynamically acquire an address when service is requested? The former mode conserves resources, much as the PSTN assumes that not all subscribers at a CO will be on the telephone simultaneously.

Many proposed Internet applications, however, will be sending content to users frequently. If television programming were delivered through a digital last-mile technology, there is no question that the percentage of customers using the system would be far higher than in the PSTN. Even simple applications still transmit and receive frequently. During the business day, I have my e-mail client check for mail every three minutes. Given my involvement in the worldwide Internet, the business day is 24 hours long.

With frequent transmissions to all nodes, the overhead and latency involved in setting up dynamic addresses may be unacceptable. There certainly may be compromises, such as the equivalent of DHCP with very long lease times.

When we speak of last-mile technologies as using existing telephone pairs, not all telephone pairs are usable for digital services. Each technology has a distance limitation, which, in the case of ISDN, is 18,000 feet. In addition, certain legacy components and installation methods interfere with these technologies.

Loading coils are components that improve the distance that analog signals can go, by reducing high-frequency signals that are outside the speech range but will interfere with long analog paths. Unfortunately, the high-speed last mile technologies use exactly those frequencies.

Loading coils may be on as many as 20 percent of U.S. lines. As lines are maintained, the telephone companies are removing them. Interestingly, the original 6,000-foot spacing of T1 repeaters was selected because the most common practice for loading coil placement, called H88, placed a loading coil every 6,000 feet. T1 repeaters were designed so that they could physically go into loading coil housings.

When telephone companies cite what seems to be a long time to provide a local loop for digital access, the limiting factor is often removing the loading coils. This may need to be underground or on telephone poles. Alternatively, telcos may route new loops through lines without loading coils, but that assumes that accurate records have been kept for decades—a loading coil might have been added to a link after its installation.

ISDN

The first technology that provided higher-than-modem bandwidth to end users connected by telephone lines, ISDN is a well-proven technology that is now available in many parts of the world. It has decent media range of up to 18,000 feet.

It also does not have the ability to grow as do other last-mile alternatives. There will be niches, however, where it can provide useful alternatives. Traditional ISDN is probably more tolerant of marginal physical facilities than are the newer xDSL services. It also has the advantage of being old enough to be a commodity, so ISDN equipment can be reliable and cheap. ISDN's fundamental problem—in the great information technology classification, "good, cheap, fast. Pick two"—it is slow.

When introduced, however, ISDN was fairly fast compared to available alternatives. Telephone companies, however, often did not do a good job of pricing and deploying it. In my local area, ISDN to my ISP would have cost approximately $250 per month, although in other areas, similar service was priced at approximately $20 per month. My current SDSL service, however, provides 768 Kbps at roughly the same cost as 128 Kbps of ISDN.

xDSL services, in particular, allow use of existing analog telephony equipment simultaneously with data use. Voice over IP even further lessens demand for ISDN channels.

Technology Alternatives

ISDN has more optional configurations and configuration parameters than other last-mile technologies. Part of the complexity is that the ISDN service directly connects to the PSTN, so it must have adequate signaling to do so.

Even though ISDN protocols have been nationally and internationally standardized, there are still variations in the implementation in CO switches, both by manufacturer and region/country.

National practice also varies as to whether the customer or the carrier controls the network termination.

Packaging

The ISDN architecture was introduced in Chapter 1. At sites with a basic rate interface (BRI), the first question concerns the NT. Is it carrier-owned or customer-owned?

When the NT is customer-owned, it can be integrated into end equipment or PBX. When used in this way, the external connection of the ISDN device can be the U reference point.

If there is a requirement for a subaddressing device on the same ISDN phone number, for conferencing ISDN telephones, or possibly for using intelligent signaling between end equipment and PBX, the S/T reference point defines the external interface.

On the local loop between the network termination at the customer location and the exchange termination at the end office, ISDN uses a modulation technique called 2B1Q (2 binary 1 quaternary). It is specified in ANSI T1.601. High bit rate DSL (HDSL) uses the same modulation.

Telephone end office switches may have native ISDN interfaces. A more scalable approach is to bring the ISDN local loop into a DACS and aggregate the ISDN channels into at least a DS-1 rate, which saves connector real estate on the end switch.

Bottlenecks

As a circuit-switched service, ISDN emulates a dedicated circuit once a connection is established. When ISDN bit streams are concentrated, they are put onto full capacity channels. If the call can be created, there will be capacity for it. ISDN is probably the most trustworthy of the last-mile technologies in providing guaranteed bandwidth.

Cable

The late 1940 technology introduced as *community antenna television (CATV)* had modest goals when it was introduced: in geographic areas where terrain masked the path from broadcast stations to the residential antenna, a tall antenna, which could reach over the blocking hills, connected to the head-end. The head-end then distributed television signals over coaxial cable.

CATV did not really become a substantial industry until satellites became widely used to distribute entertainment content. Cable began to offer far more diverse programming to homes. Cable operators also offered video-on-demand and pay-per-view services.

These entertainment networks were optimized for one-way transmission from the head-end to the subscribers, possibly with intermediate amplifiers.

Data was not an original CATV goal. Data applications on cable generally are a shared medium emulating an Ethernet, although it is possible to establish high-capacity dedicated line equivalents by giving them their own frequency. In the great information technology classification, "good, cheap, fast. Pick two," cable is less than good when it becomes heavily loaded. Good cable system designers have to plan very carefully to be sure the medium does not become overloaded.

Competitors to CATV include xDSL for data and potentially video-on-demand services, direct broadcast satellite (DBS) for entertainment access, and local wireless.

Technology Alternatives

As mentioned earlier, basic *single cable* systems were limited in the application they served. Their ability to carry bidirectional signals was limited. Bidirectional cable systems do exist, which separate the cable frequency band into upstream and downstream sets of channels.

The next generation is *hybrid fiber coax* (HFC), which continues to use coaxial cable to the end user, but uses optical fiber for the main distribution path from head-end to the *optical node* that converts photonic signals into electronic ones, onto the final coaxial *drop cable* into the residence.

Residential customers use increasingly complex *set-top boxes.*

Cable systems have amplifiers or digital repeaters between the customer premises and the head-end. The topology, however, is definitely a branched star. Connections to telephone end offices, ISP gateways, etc., will be made at the head-end.

Impacts of Digital and High-Definition Television

As digital TV and HDTV enters the marketplace, which consumes far more bandwidth than regular television, the lifetime of coaxial cable systems comes more and more into question. Digital encoding of conventional television actually requires less bandwidth than analog encoding, but HDTV requires much more bandwidth.

Bottlenecks

CATV service providers face both short- and long-term demands to upgrade the technology of their installed base. Two-way services are one immediate demand.

The real question is how and when cable operators will upgrade to optical technology, be it HFC, *fiber to the curb* (FTTC), or *fiber to the house* (FTTH).

Security is a real concern when a medium is shared, such as coaxial trunks. At the present, some cable data providers offer limited firewall and packet filtering services, the latter especially for protecting against broadcasts.

Evolved fiber systems will probably run an IPsec client in the set-top box or in end-user hosts, that link to a service selection gateway at or near the head-end. L2TP is another alternative for a cable provider with virtual switch access to multiple ISPs.

DSL

Digital subscriber loop (DSL) is a family of technologies for high-speed transmission primarily over existing copper pairs. This is a more recent technology than cable. It is a case-by-case decision whether cable or DSL is most appropriate in a given area. In my personal case, the cable carrier's inability to return phone calls and to support other than single-computer connectivity made the decision for me.

DSL is early in its deployment, and there are still lessons to learn about the physical plant needed to support it in the real world. There have been problems with electrical crosstalk, limiting the number of circuits that can be provisioned per cable bundle. The actual speed delivered can be quite dependent on medium quality.

Support can be complex. At the time of this writing in August 2000, I have 768 Kbps SDSL service that I ordered from an ISP. They subcontract layer 1 and 2 connectivity to a DSL service provider, which in turn leases local loops from the incumbent LEC. At times, it has taken my thirty-plus years of dealing with carriers to resolve fingerpointing and get problems fixed. Service is improving, but obtaining support could well be beyond the skill level of end users.

Technology Alternatives

A wide variety of technologies, shown in Table 6.1, fall under the general DSL framework. Fiber alternatives also can be used in CATV.

ADSL places a small *splitter* unit at the customer premises from which analog voice services run. Many installers prefer, however, to use a nonvoice pair when available. Using a separate pair eliminates the splitter cost, and really does simplify troubleshooting.

The equivalent splitter at the CO is a function called the *ADSL transmission unit-central office* (ATU-C). *DSL access multiplexers* (DSLAM) at

Table 6.1 Loop Technology Alternatives

ACRONYM	NAME	CHARACTERISTICS
ADSL	Asymmetric DSL	1.5–8 Mbps downstream, 64–800 Kbps upstream, simultaneous data and analog voice
FTTB	Fiber to the building	
FTTC	Fiber to the curb	
FTTH	Fiber to the home	
HDSL	High-density DSL	T1/E1 replacement, no analog capability
IDSL	ISDN DSL	
RADSL	Rate adaptive DSL	
SDSL	Symmetric DSL	Same bandwidth in both directions, 160 Kbps–1.168 Mbps
VDSL	Very high speed DSL	Multimegabit rates

the CO contain ATU-C functions for each customer loop, as well as DACS-like functions that transfer the customer data bits to trunks. The ATU-C also splits off the analog voice channels, which go to conventional channel banks in the CO.

VDSL has much less range than ADSL, HDSL, and ISDL. This technology assumes that copper pair will connect the actual subscriber to a nearby optical network unit (ONU), which connects to the CO via fiber. Total copper lengths should not exceed 300 meters. The ONU might be in an outside pedestal (fiber to the curb), inside a multiple-subscriber structure such as an office or apartment building (fiber to the building), or to the home (fiber to the home).

Lower-speed DSL services are pure stars, with individual copper pairs to the serving CO. As speeds increase, the medium's distance capability decreases, so remote terminals—repeaters and concentrators—will terminate end connections and concentrate them, creating a branched star.

Local loops are dedicated to individual users, and, even when concentrated at remote terminals, guarantee bandwidth to the central office. At the CO, however, there may be a bottleneck.

If there is no router colocated at the CO, xDSL user bit streams need to be put onto a link that will carry them to the service provider. The capacity of that link may not support simultaneous data flow from several users, or even full-rate bursts from individual users. I have seen ADSL rates in the hundreds of kilobits offered to multiple users, but with only a 384 Kbps virtual circuit from the CO to the first provider POP.

Economics

Most current systems require a CO port for each user, which is more expensive than connecting a cable to a head-end. Work is going into methods of oversubscribing the DSLAM ports, much as conventional analog switches cannot support calls from all subscribers. Going to an oversubscription model would lose the benefit of guaranteed bandwidth and connectivity, but that might be acceptable as a consumer service.

Another practical business issue for xDSL is the role of the traditional telephone company. Traditionally, telephone companies, especially when outside plant is concerned, have been slow to implement new technologies. Can you say ISDN? I knew you could! Telcos have become comfortable provisioning ISDN at the approximate time that ISDN became obsolete.

ISPs, however, do not have extensive experience with local distribution. An alternative may be arising with DSL wholesalers, such as Covad. In a manner similar to modem pool wholesalers, these companies handle the DSL access for multiple ISPs, and have the volume both to maintain an experience base and to gain economies of scale when installing equipment in COs. See Figure 6.11 for an example of how a wholesaler connects the ISPs.

Many xDSL providers differentiate between consumer and business use. Consumer services are cheaper, but may share bandwidth from the CO to the ISP. Consumer services also may implement the ATU-R as a card internal to a PC, lowering costs further.

SOHO business applications tend to have higher quality of service, and have an external box that may combine the ATU-R, an Ethernet hub, and a router. Such an implementation, using SDSL, is the primary way in which I connect externally from my home office, although I do have a more complex internal structure with additional routers and firewalls. My needs are more complex than most SOHO user requirements.

HDSL is an extremely attractive alternative to conventional T1 and E1, or at least to everyone except telcos with established T1 pricing. A

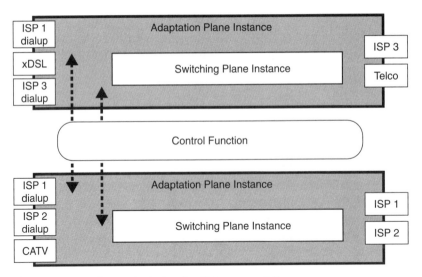

Figure 6.11   Telco and wholesaler DSL connectivity.

major advantage is that it does not need repeaters on most lines if it can use native HDSL 2B1Q modulation and rate adaption. Using these native modes does require that the CO equipment be able to accept this signal, which it may not because it only speaks a line encoding such as AMI.

T1 and E1 need repeaters to be installed every 4,000 to 6,000 feet. Current HDSL does use two pairs, as do T1 and E1. HDSL splits the T1 bandwidth into bidirectional 784 Kbps on each pair.

SDSL is a variant of HDSL, which provides lower speed over a single wire pair. SDSL has shorter range than HDSL.

ADSL can have higher speed in one direction than HDSL or SDSL. Asymmetrical bandwidth is perfectly reasonable for such applications as video on demand or Web browsing, where the majority of bytes are sent to the customer as responses to customer requests. Applications such as videoconferencing or voice over IP, however, need symmetrical bandwidth.

Fixed Wireless

Cellular radio is a blessing and curse of our time. Here in the Washington, DC, area, many restaurants are creating cell-free as well as smoke-free zones. Sidewalks containing both cellular callers oblivious to the

Trust Me, I'm from the Telco

When I first tried to order DSL service, I called the local telco and went through a strange dialogue, which is quoted here to the best of my recollection.

Howard: I'd like to order ADSL service.

Telco Representative #1: Whaaat?

H *(referring quickly to the marketing materials)*: Oh . . . Infospeed service.

We progressed, until the question was asked:

TR1: What kind of computer will you be using?

H: Why should you care? You're a bit pipe to me.

TR1: I need to know what kind of computer, sir.

H: I won't be plugging in a single computer, but a hub or router. I don't want to install an additional Ethernet port so I can still get to the printer.

TR1: Sir, if our installer sees a router, he will immediately leave.

H: What if I put a software router in a PC? How can the installer see it?

TR1: Ummm . . . sir, I need to escalate this call.

I reached TR2, who nattered on about needing to know the PC type. Eventually, I told her to stop referring to the PC type, because my main machine is a Mac.

TR2: I'm sorry, sir. We don't support Macs.

H: (deep sigh) Why?

TR2 *(and this really, really is a direct quote)*: Because Macs don't have MAC addresses.

H: Hey, if nothing else, the address of this Mac is 5012 South 25th Street. Are you referring to Medium Access Control?

TR2: Ummm...sir, I need to escalate this call.

Reaching TR3, I asked, What do you mean that Macs don't have MAC addresses? What do you think they use on an Ethernet?

TR3 *(somewhat technically)*: Ah, but the MAC address doesn't activate until the IP stack comes up. So we can't ping you if IP isn't up.

H: If IP wasn't up, how could you ping me with or without a MAC address?

TR3: Ummm...sir, I need to escalate this call.

TR4 apologized for the runaround, and was rather sympathetic.

TR4 explained: We note your MAC address during the installation. When you come out of the DSLAM, you go into an Ethernet switch that permits only known source MAC addresses.

H: OK. That makes some sense. Then I thought for a moment. I could deal with that. But what if your average Joe Sixpack PC user has a failed NIC changed, and his MAC address changes? What happens to his access?

TR4: Oh, easy. Joe Sixpack will note the new MAC address, call the operations center, give it to them over the phone, and they will reprogram the filter.

H *(in my best impression of Bill Cosby in his Noah skit):* R-i-g-g-g-h-t-t-t.

world, coexisting with crazed bicycle messengers, are frightening. Of course, crazed bicycle messengers using cell phones takes us into a new level of fear.

Fixed wireless, however, while it may use some of the transmission technologies of cellular telephony, is not intended to have moving endpoints. Cellular telephony has definitely lowered the cost of some previously unaffordable wireless technologies.

Applications of fixed wireless include serving geographically isolated customer sites and providing diverse local loops to enterprise in urban areas. Eastern Europe is experiencing explosive telecommunications growth, but, in cities like Budapest, founded in the Middle Ages, there are no underground cable ducts and few telephone poles. In such cities, it has been cost-effective to go directly to wireless local loops, skipping the entire generation of copper distribution.

Technology Alternatives

Fixed wireless transmission has several alternatives (see Table 6.2). Stepping outside the residential and normal business environment, there are microwave and optical systems that handle special requirements, such as pay telephones in remote areas.

Table 6.2 Wireless Alternatives

TECHNOLOGY	ADVANTAGES	DISADVANTAGES
Direct broadcast [geosynchronous] satellite	Established for TV	One-way orientation
Fixed cellular	Flexible topology in built-up areas	Low speed
Local multipoint distribution services (LMDS)	Extremely high speed	Line-of-sight with short range. Impacted by weather
Low earth orbit satellite	Lower latency than geosynchronous earth orbit satellites	Cost and complexity of telephones. Need for large numbers of satellites for complete coverage
Multichannel multipoint distribution services (MMDS)	Lower installation cost than cable TV. Bandwidth comparable to DBS	Line-of-sight with moderate range. One-way orientation

Fixed wireless usually connotes a terrestrial system, often line of sight but sometimes cellular. In some applications, satellites may be an alternative to terrestrial.

Well, Yes, There Is Competition . . .

Not to be forgotten, as any of these technologies go into wide deployment, is the clue level of real-world providers and installers. After two years of trying to convince Cable TV of Arlington that I really, truly, had paid my bill, I gave up.

The "not in my backyard" (NIMBY) syndrome may limit the places where antennas can be installed, if for no other reason than esthetics. Actually, backyards themselves can be a problem.

As an alternative, I tried to obtain DirectTV service to my home, from my local telephone company, Bell Atlantic. When the installer arrived, he took one look and said he couldn't install the antenna, because there were trees on the south side.

I sigh at provider ads that offer free professional installation of home antennas, for I was unable to get the installer to understand that putting the antenna on a mast would give him a line of sight *over* the trees.

Clearly, there is local competition. Unfortunately, it is a competition between accounting and installation incompetence.

Economics

Economics play a critical role in these capital-intensive services. Iridium, one of the early LEO players, has gone into liquidation, its satellites to burn up.

Evolution in the Transport

As they consume the fluid more essential for military aviation than jet fuel—beer—fighter pilots are apt to mutter the mantra, "I feel the need . . . for speed." The need for analog bandwidth, and then for digital speed, has been a constant in communications since Samuel Morse tapped out his first telegraph message.

Evolving from Time Division Multiplexed Networks

The telecommunications network originated with circuit switched and dedicated facilities, first analog and then digital. To obtain the most basic scalability, dedicated lines needed to be multiplexed onto high-capacity trunks in the carrier backbone. As discussed in Chapter 5, "Virtualizing in Modern Networks," *inverse multiplexing* is a complementary technique that allows high user data rates to be provisioned using multiple slower, but available, physical facilities.

Basic Digital Telephony Multiplexing

As DS0 feeds into DS-1, so do higher-speed DS-x signals feed into higher-speed multiplexers. The hierarchy of multiplexed rates in the United States, Canada, and Japan is called the *plesiochronous digital hierarchy*, mercifully referred to by the acronym PDH (see Table 6.3).

The rest of the world uses the European defined by Conference of European Postal and Telecommunications Administrations (CEPT) (see Table 6.4).

Refinements of Digital Telecommunications Multiplexing

Since a DACS is DS-0 aware, new services were developed to exploit this awareness. Originally, the DS-0 streams were simply routed among carrier trunks. The DACS function, however, began to extend to user services both multiplexed and inverse multiplexed.

In fractional T1 service, however, some multiple of DS-0 was provided to a customer over a T1 physical facility. This is a physical layer bit stream, not an interleaved service such as frame relay.

Table 6.3 U.S., Canadian, and Partial Japanese Digital Hierarchy

LEVEL	SPEED	VOICE CHANNELS
DS0	64 Kbps	1
DS-1	1.544 Mbps	24
DS-1C	3.152 Mbps	48
DS2	6.312 Mbps	96
DS-3*	44.736 Mbps	672
DS4*	274.176 Mbps	4,032

* In Europe and much of the world outside North America and Japan, a different hierarchy emerged, still based on multiples of 64 Kbps. Japan uses the DS-1 and DS2 rates, but has a different hierarchy above the DS2 level

Table 6.4   CEPT/Rest of World Hierarchy

LEVEL	SPEED	VOICE CHANNELS
E0	64 Kbps	1
E1	2.032 Mbps	32
E2	8.448 Mbps	120
E3	34.368 Mbps	480
E4	139.268 Mbps	1,920
E5	565.148 Mbps	7,680

Fractional services worked well, and have been extended to T3. They may be even more attractive there than with T1 services, since the crossover point where a T3 is more cost effective than multiple T1s may be as low as 6 or 7 T1s, while a T3 can carry 28 T1 equivalents. Installing the T3 local loop gives far more growth capacity.

T3 services are most commonly run over optical fiber. Originally, fiber was used as a simple range extender for a high-rate bit stream. Optical networking, however, has become far more than range.

Evolution to Optical Media

Optical transmission media came into use as alternatives to copper, often at the same speed but with longer range and lesser requirements for repeaters. Increased ranges that are possible with optical transmission, especially on the longer-reach systems that do not need repeaters, have major economic benefits on most carriers.

In many cases, optical networking has replaced satellite networks. There are still many applications for satellites, especially involving broadcasting or remote areas. Nowhere does the range of optical systems impact an application, however, as it does in transoceanic cables. Shall we say that it is not tremendously convenient to pay a service call on a malfunctioning repeater that is under several thousand feet of the stormy North Atlantic? Current systems have demonstrated unrepeated range of 4,000 kilometers.

Optical networking has moved beyond transmission alone. Now, intelligent gateways and cross-connects make some decisions at the true optical level, without the need to convert optical signals to electronic signals, manipulate them, and convert them back.

ATM was a major driver for optical networking. At speeds above 100 Mbps, ATM cells actually flow over synchronous optical network (SONET) or synchronous digital hierarchy (SDH) in Europe. SONET has a three-layered architecture:

- Paths interconnect optical service endpoints.
- Lines interconnect optical service multiplexers.
- Sections interconnect optical media and repeaters. In SONET-speak, repeaters are called regenerators.

You can see the SONET ancestry in ITU's new optical transport network (OTN) architecture [G.872]. As a whole, the OTN is a transport network bounded by optical channel access points (see Table 6.5).

SONET Architecture

Path terminating equipment (PTE) connects to the user of the SONET service, such as a router with a SONET interface, or a telephone circuit switch. *Line terminating equipment*, such as DACS and *add-and-drop multiplexers* (ADM) terminates a physical SONET transmission facility.

ADMs are not new concepts in telecommunications, having been used in DSx TDM. In SONET, however, they have additional capabilities.

ADMs can be configured in stars or rings. Basic SONET ADMs have synchronous in and out SONET connections, and a synchronous or asynchronous connection to their site. Only those subchannels relevant to the site are dropped to that site; the rest of the channel passes through unchanged. If the site link is asynchronous, it can rate adapt from a lower edge speed to a standard speed. Due to the synchronous nature of SONET, the ADM does not have to demultiplex the entire aggregate stream, but can simply extract the bandwidth of interest.

A variant on ADM is *drop and repeat*, essentially a multicast technology. With drop and repeat, a subchannel drops off to a site, but the ADM

Table 6.5 OTN versus SONET Terminology

OTN	SONET
Optical channel (OCh)	Path
Optical multiplex section (OMS)	Line
Optical transmission section (OTS)	Section

passes the same signal on to the next site. This is especially useful for video distribution or large audio conferences (see Figure 6.12).

Section terminating equipment is either the terminations of an optical link at PTE or LTE, or the connection a link to an optical regenerators. Optical regenerators are comparable to repeaters in data networks.

SONET Protection

Just because you are SONET-connected does *not* mean that you have automatic backup. You must explicitly have Automatic Protection Switching, SONET high-availability technology. In the original version, SONET LTE connects to a primary and backup SONET medium. The specific SONET terminology used is the working and protection ring.

In *automatic protection switching* (APS), only the working ring actually carries user traffic. A management protocol, however, runs over both rings. The APS Protect Group Protocol detects failures and triggers ring switchover.

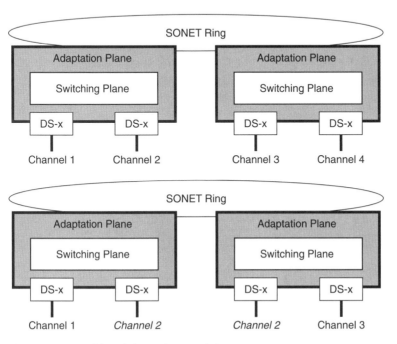

Figure 6.12 Add and drop, drop and repeat.

SONET, however, has been extremely reliable, and duplicating all rings is very expensive. In the 1:N variant shown on the right side of Figure 6.13, one protection ring covers four LTE. Current products can support up to 16 working rings with one protection ring. When a failure occurs, the protection ring is activated only between the endpoints affected by the actual failure.

Before the advent of SONET over DWDM, there were three basic variants of SONET protection:

- **Unidirectional path switched ring (UPSR).** All traffic homes to a centra l location. Really a star, in that bandwidth not in the direction of the core cannot be reused. Typically used for access networks that enter the ring through an ADM at the core.

- **Two fiber bidirectional ring (2F BLSR).** Separate transmit and receive fibers, but can be rehomed anywhere in the ring.

- **Four fiber bidirectional ring (4F BLSR).** Working and protection pairs that can be rehomed as needed.

Pressure to develop more cost-effective variants of protection switching comes from the perceived high capital cost of installing fiber and the even higher cost of installing regenerators along the fiber path. With experience, the industry realized that the economics of SONET in metropolitan areas, in comparison to long-distance paths, are different.

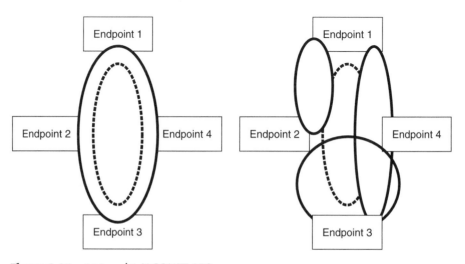

Figure 6.13 1+1 and 1:N SONET APS.

The extreme of cost in long-haul networks is that of underwater optical cables. Immense expense is incurred in repairing a cable under thousands of feet of water. The expense of regenerators designed to run in those conditions is also extremely high, and the trend has been to look for technologies that increase the spacing between regenerators.

As DWDM entered products for the carrier marketplace, an idea that had started in SONET products became far more apparent. Optical distribution in metropolitan areas is a quite different problem than long-haul distribution, and different products are appropriate for each problem. Metropolitan areas usually do not need expensive regenerators, so it can be reasonable to add more fibers and waste bandwidth in the interest of flexibility. Long-haul facilities do need to use their fiber bandwidth more efficiently, and the industry has responded. Long-haul systems that do not require regenerators for runs under 4,000 kilometers are commercially available.

A key development for the optical industry is that SONET does not need to run over its own physical fiber, but can run on a wavelength of DWDM. This allows links in multiple protection rings to run over the same fiber, with due regard not to put both links of the *same* ring over the same physical fiber.

This idea further generalizes to the idea that with sufficient wavelengths, it can be entirely cost-effective, in the metro area, simply to drop one user channel into each wavelength, even if the channel speed is far less than the fiber capacity. The cost of fibers, and, with DWDM, even more the bandwidth of fiber, is far less than the cost of multiplexers and regenerators needed to use that bandwidth most efficiently. SONET and DWDM, in the metro area, can have lower channel cost if they are willing not to optimize channel packing.

Some people think of ATM as providing rapid recovery from failures, but it is SONET, not ATM, that provides 50-millisecond restoral. If alternate paths are statically provisioned, ATM can use them as soon as it detects a failure, but IP routing is equally able to use alternate static routes without waiting for routing protocols to reconverge. Dynamic ATM call establishment is not instantaneous.

SONET Speed Hierarchy

Like the PDH and CEPT hierarchies, SONET has its own hierarchy of speeds. These speeds, shown in Table 6.6, include SONET overhead.

Table 6.6 SONET Hierarchy

OC LEVEL	SPEED
OC-1	51.84 Mbps
OC-3	155.52 Mbps
OC-9	466.56 Mbps
OC-12	622.08 Mbps
OC-18	933.12 Mbps
OC-24	1.244 Gbps
OC-36	1.866 Gbps
OC-48	2.488 Gbps
OC-96	4.976 Gbps
OC-192	9.953 Gbps (usually called 10 Gbps)
OC-768	39.813 Gbps (usually called 40 Gbps)

While SONET overhead is not as heavy as the ATM cell and AAL tax, the full SONET rate is not available to user traffic.

The 51.84 Mbps STS-1 rate is the basic building block of SONET. It is slightly faster than a DS-3, so it can encapsulate DS-3 or slower links into what are called *virtual tributaries*, shown in Table 6.7.

Packet over SONET

As introduced in the Chapter 4 section on ATM overhead, PPP over SONET has better bandwidth efficiency than ATM with any ATL type. If the optical link carries IP between two routers, the bandwidth between those routers is guaranteed—what else can use it? ATM's QoS capabilities are of no use in this situation.

Table 6.7 Multiplexing into an STS-1 Bit Stream

SERVICE	SPEED	CARRIES
VT 1.5	1.728 Mbps	DS-1
VT 2	2.304 Mbps	CEPT1/E1
VT 3	3.456 Mbps	DS-1C
VT 6	6.912 Mbps	DS2
VT 6.Nc	N X 6.912 Mbps	N X DS2
Async DS-3	44.736 Mbps	DS-3

If ATM is delivering end-to-end virtual circuits, it does have a role. But for intercarrier router links, it is hard to justify ATM in preference to POS.

SONET has become a transitional technology, just as ATM/SONET was an evolutionary step beyond TDM. Due to the large and effective SONET installed base, newer technologies must support SONET.

The Emerging Optical Network

The next generation is entering commercial service, although it certainly is in the early stages. Vendors regard it as an evolution rather than a revolution. Nortel's term, for example, is the *succession strategy for voice*.

As shown in Figure 6.14, the newer technologies fall into a model of long-haul backbones, metropolitan services, and local loops. Throughout the range of emerging optical technologies, including both switching and transmission, there are distinct requirements and products for metropolitan and long-haul environments. Major vendors are finding it appropriate to build different products for each environment. They are doing so even if there seems to be one function, such as cross-connection. In other words, you will see both long-haul and short-haul

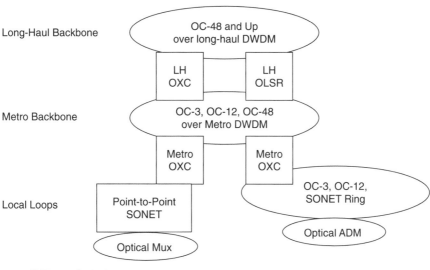

OXC: Optical cross-connect
OLSR: Optical label switched router
DWDM: Dense wavelength division multiplexing

Figure 6.14   Emerging optical hierarchy.

cross-connects, DWDM transmission systems, and optical routers in most vendors' product lines.

WDM

SONET/SDH is no longer the speed champion of optical networking, if speed is considered the aggregate of all bits on a fiber. Dense wavelength division multiplexing (DWDM) can carry multiple SONET/SDH channels over a single fiber. Deployed products offer up to 32 OC-192 channels per fiber, as R&D demonstrations show 240 or more channels. OC-768 channels have also been demonstrated, and the question here is more the nature of current requirements for multiple 40 Gbps channels rather than multiple 10 Gbps channels.

In DWDM, individual channels are carried in different wavelengths (i.e., frequencies) of light. DWDM advocates tend to call these wavelengths *lambdas*, after the Greek character λ, traditionally used in physics to represent wavelength.

DWDM has different market drivers for local exchange versus long-haul carriers. In the local market, there is a strong desire for transparency that can flow over a lambda dedicated to a user, or to competitive carriers. The user would have total control over the traffic mix on the lambda, even though that traffic might only be a few hundred megabits on a gigabit-capable lambda. In the local market, DWDM means bandwidth becomes almost free. DWDM has to be compared, however, to the cost of running additional fibers.

Local exchanges were not the original goal for DWDM, which was introduced to reduce the crunch on long-haul optical networks. Bandwidth is not free in transcontinental or intercontinental networks. In long-haul DWDM, the most important cost factor is regeneration. Long-haul providers will be reluctant to commit expensive regenerator capability to underused lambdas carrying transparent traffic.

Optical Gateways and Cross-Connects

Optical gateways, such as the Nortel Optera Packet Core or Alcatel OGX, provide a common meeting point for true optical transmission and electrically based systems such as ATM. Besides the obvious protocol conversion, optical gateways functionally are the bridge between broadband edge and core networks. They will aggregate data in multiple access wavelengths into higher-speed DWDM lambdas.

Optical gateways manage bandwidth in lambdas. Optical cross-connects (OXC) aggregate and groom it, and provide optical restoral using SONET protection switching. SONET restoral is faster than restoral using the OXC, but cannot handle as much capacity as the OXC.

An optical cross-connect (OXC) is an all-optical equivalent of a DACS. At the speeds in question, the OXC will usually have an optical switching fabric, as well as optical input and output ports. Where DACS often are manually programmed, however, management and control of OXCs will need to be done at high speed. Software-controlled OXC can provide rapid failover in point-to-point topologies as well as in rings.

One approach to achieving these speeds is to leverage existing (admittedly that have not existed for long) technologies being developed for MPLS.

Another related element is the *optical domain service interconnect* (ODSI), which allows on-demand creation of switched virtual circuits. It is analogous to an ATM UNI for DWDM. At the speeds of DWDM, of course, the user will, in many cases, be a carrier.

Optical Routing

While there are research projects that are examining optical elements for directly routing packets, the real interpretation of optical routing today is more a path routing problem, such as MPLS, ATM PNNI, etc. Dynamic optical routing still is on the bleeding edge of technology.

A great many products seem to be implemented with smoke and mirrors. On the active and frequently amusing Cisco certification mailing list hosted as www.groupstudy.com, one of the stock answers to an overly naive troubleshooting question is, "Did you do something to let out the magic smoke inside the router?"

Optical routing, however, really does deal with mirrors, as well as other components for manipulating wavelengths of light. Incoming lambdas are beamed at electronically tunable reflectors, which bounce them to an optical receiver for an appropriate output port. In other words, the switching function is optical, but the control function is electronic.

Other optical components can change lambdas between the input and input port, much as a DACS can move a DS0 channel from one DS-1 time slot to another. Optical splitters can create multiple copies of incoming lambdas, optically implementing multicasting.

A strong trend is to use MPLS setup protocols, such as LDP, for dynamically configuring the optical routing tables. The FEC in this class is the outgoing lambda. Label information distributed to optical switches along the path define the inbound and outbound labels at each switch. While this idea primarily has been proposed for optical systems, it can be extended to DACS and other layer 1 electronic multiplexing systems.

Looking Ahead

In this chapter, we concentrated on fault tolerance from the provider perspective. Services cannot have overall high availability unless enterprise-controlled features also are fault tolerant, or outsourced to carriers that will ensure their availability. Chapter 7 looks at fault tolerance from an overall standpoint, including enterprise, carrier, and enterprise-to-carrier techniques. Chapter 8, "VPNs, Security, and Roaming," then looks at tolerating faults caused by deliberate attacks rather than disasters or component failures.

Fault Tolerance

Communications are the nervous system of the entire Strategic Air Command (SAC) organization, and their protection is therefore, of the greatest importance. I like to say that without communications, all I control is my desk, and that is not a very lethal weapon.

GENERAL THOMAS S. POWER

What can go wrong, will.

MURPHY'S FIRST LAW

What has gone wrong, will get worse.

MURPHY'S SECOND LAW

Murphy was an optimist.

NETWORKING COROLLARY TO MURPHY'S LAWS

This chapter has been remarkably hard to name. It began as "Multihoming," but soon evolved to "High Availability." When I read the excellent server-oriented book by Evan Marcus and Hal Stern, *Blueprints for High Availability: Designing Resilient Distributed Systems*, I considered calling this the "resiliency" chapter.

But to me, resiliency has far too much sound of a stretched rubber band, a trampoline, or, in a shining phrase from a Mark Russell skit, "a ping-pong ball in a tile bathroom." Truly, I try to avoid designing networks that stretch too far, bounce up and down, or oscillate between normal and backup states. Eventually, I felt most comfortable with "fault tolerant."

Just What Is Fault Tolerance?

Fault-tolerant does not mean fault-free. It does not mean that a network is immune to any conceivable threat. In 1991, the KARI network, which ran the Iraqi air defense system, indeed tolerated many faults. A sufficient quantity of explosives, however, can overcome the tolerance of any network. Let's examine some real-world cases where the network needed to be quite tolerant to explosions, while asking the question, "Is this what my management *really* means when they say the network can't fail?"

Extremely Fault-Tolerant Networks

The U.S. Minimum Essential Emergency Communications Network (MEECN) originally was intended to operate for the key 20 minutes of a massive nuclear exchange, and has evolved into a "warfighting" system that can operate for a prolonged period. Even with extensive fault-tolerance features, continued operation of MEECN assumes multiple mobile command posts (the user sites) and hardened or hidden weapons sites. MEECN has multiple terrestrial, satellite, and radio networks, one of which is one of the systems used to communicate with ICBM silos. Does the following quote describe the environment under which your enterprise network is expected to operate?

> The below grade portion of the ICBM EHF system located in the Launch Control Center (LCC) and/or the Launch Control Equipment Building (LCEB) must survive and operate without damage/degradation or loss of Emergency Action Message (EAM) reception commensurate with the above grade portion of the EHF system including the Electromagnetic Pulse (EMP) portion of a nuclear event anticipated for the ICBM weapon system. The LCC and LCEB EMP environment is described in the Minuteman Weapon System Specification, S-133-128C, Appendix III. Nuclear survivability refers to the capability of the ICBM EHF system to accomplish its mission in the face of hostile nuclear environments resulting from an enemy attack.
>
> The ICBM EHF system must operate throughout the "Near Neighbor" nuclear environments and all induced High Altitude EMP (HEMP) environments without damage degradation or loss of system parameters, timing, keys, or ephemeris data. ICBM EHF system recovery shall be accomplished without operator assistance and shall be no greater than the loss of signal time specified for the Milstar system.

> **OPERATIONAL REQUIREMENTS DOCUMENT (ORD):**
> **AFSPC 005-95B-I/II FOR THE ICBM LAUNCH CONTROL CENTERS**

The hardest operational center acknowledged by the United States is the North American Air Defense Command (NORAD) headquarters inside Cheyenne Mountain, Colorado (see Figure 7.1). Its construction began in May 1961, and it went into operational service on February 6, 1966, at a cost of $142.2 million (in 1966 dollars).

Figure 7.1 Entrance and blast doors to Cheyenne Mountain operations center.

When this facility was built, nuclear-armed missiles were not nearly as accurate as they are today, and Cheyenne Mountain actually had a chance of surviving a limited nuclear attack. That is no longer the case.

Audits have shown, however, that 80 percent of the 1994 operating cost of Cheyenne Mountain, $152 million, is due to the mission, not the facility. In other words, while there may not be the nuclear threat that caused the facility to be built, there is no cost advantage to moving its responsibilities to a more conventional building. The cost of moving lines and antennas, however, would be high.

While your facility probably does not have the ruggedness of Cheyenne Mountain, the First Law of Plumbing applies to many commercial data centers: "If it don't leak, don't fix it." Build new facilities when there is a real reason to do so. Military lessons also apply to continuing to harden individual data centers. Just as the answer to increasing missile accuracy was not to superharden fixed command posts, but to go to mobile ones, there is a point of diminishing returns in making individual data centers resistant to disasters. Even if you make the data center totally resistant to earthquakes, tornadoes, floods, and rock concerts, the communications lines connecting the center to its users may not be as resistant. Facility diversity is often a far better idea than continuing to harden.

Broad Levels of Fault Tolerance

Infinitely reliable networks, unfortunately, have infinite cost. A balance needs to be struck between protection against specific threats, and more general business measures. Let me put this in personal terms: I drive an elderly Jeep Cherokee, which is more crash-resistant than a smaller car, and sufficiently dented and scratched that one more small insult will not matter. At the same time, I always wear my seat belt, and I have car insurance.

Assuming that I could get around petty restrictions on civilian ownership of weapons, I could drive a M1A2 main battle tank. Such a vehicle is far more crash resistant than my Jeep. An added advantage is that it parks wherever it wants, but the cost of ownership is a bit more than I can afford. I can deal with my Jeep's low miles per gallon, but I cannot deal with the gallons per mile of the Abrams tank.

So, the first step in fault-tolerant networking is to determine the budget and the threats to be protected against. Table 7.1 builds upon the broad server categories of Marcus and Stern.

As enterprise networks, be they intranets, extranets, or internets, become more mission-critical, enterprise managers demand more and more availability for their networks. Service providers who offer highly reliable services thus gain competitive advantages. As the Internet becomes more ubiquitous, more and more enterprises have no effective business if their connectivity fails. Other enterprises do not have mission-critical Internet applications, but become so dependent on routine e-mail, news, Web, and similar access that a loss of connectivity becomes a crisis.

Table 7.1 High Level Goals of Fault Tolerance

AVAILABILITY LEVEL	SERVER	NETWORK
1	"Do nothing special" Backups	Controlled physical access to network equipment
2	"Increased availability: Protect the Data" Full or partial disk mirroring, transaction logging	Dial/ISDN backup
3	"High availability: Protect the system" Clustered servers	Redundant routers No single-point-of-failure local loop
4	"Disaster recovery: protect the organization" Alternate server sites	No single-point-of-failure national backbone

Fault Tolerance

As you home in on the definition of fault tolerance relevant to your organization, there will be some key questions:

- Is fault tolerance redundancy?
- Is fault tolerance multihoming?
- Is it server based? Router based?
- Transmission system based?
- Is there some virtuous knight who will rescue the distressed damsel?

The answers to these questions are not always clear. A reasonable approximation is:

- Not completely
- Sometimes
- Sometimes
- Sometimes
- I'm not really sure what a damsel is. Knights, however, do demonstrate a form of redundancy if their strength is as the strength of 10 because their hearts are pure.

As enterprises depend more on networks, prudent management suggests there be no single point of failure that can break all connectivity. It is often useful to treat intranet and extranet networking as a somewhat different fault-tolerance problem than Internet connectivity.

Redundancy does not equate to fault tolerance. First, there is a class of systems, described by Radia Perlman, in which applying additional resources does not increase the protection against failures that disseminate control information that is in error. Routing protocols are an important member of this class that exhibits the *Byzantine Corruption Problem*.

Second, by Murphy's Law, if there is a single point of failure that is not backed up, that is the component that will fail. There are, however, diminishing returns in providing redundancy.

You May Not Even Know about a Potential Point of Failure

One of my clients had a large, highly reliable main router, which had redundant power supplies. The router was in a mainframe data center with a raised floor. Each power supply module was in the bottom of the router chassis, and had a separate power cord. In this data center, the two power cords came out of the chassis, were tie-wrapped to a strain relief bar, and dropped to two separate uninterruptible power connectors under the raised floor.

All of the router's data interface cards were above the power supplies. Their interface cables came straight out, made a reasonable bend over a strain relief bar, and down under the raised floor.

One fine day, power supply 1 failed. Not a bit of data was dropped as the second power supply took up the load. The router vendor shipped a replacement power supply.

When the replacement arrived, the horrible truth dawned. When the network administrator started to slide the failed power supply out of the chassis, he discovered that the rigid mass of data cables behind the router were too close—the power supply could not slide out completely as long as the data cables were in place.

The only way to replace the power supply was to disconnect the data cables. Of course, the entire motivation for having redundant power supplies was to prevent data outages. To my client, I could only quote that classic line from news coverage of the Vietnam war: "We had to destroy this village to save it."

A wide class of network protective measures is generically called multihoming. Unfortunately, multihoming is not well defined. It does usually mean that there is more than one path to a destination. There are marked similarities between load distribution mechanisms discussed in Chapter 5, "Virtualizing in Modern Networks," and multihoming, but there are also differences. Multihoming for reliability may not pay any attention to load; it may have a simple primary/backup logic.

While many people look at the multihoming problem as one of routing, the goal is often multihoming to endpoints. Finding an endpoint usually begins in DNS. Once an endpoint address is found, some application protocols, notably HTTP and FTP, may redirect the request to a different endpoint.

At the upper layers of the OSI model, from application to transport, multihoming is a technique to *find* a real or virtual server to process one's transaction. Multihoming solutions can be subtly different from *failover*, "the migration of services from one server to another." [Marcus].

Lower layer multihoming occurs at the OSI network through physical layers, and is about finding alternative paths *to* an endpoint.

These functions can overlap, but I find them useful when thinking about solutions, once the problem requirements are defined. Figure 7.2 shows the relationships among the functions.

Higher layer multihoming can involve selecting a site at which a cluster of servers is located, selecting a specific server within that cluster, or both. Failover mechanisms also include such non-network activities as disk mirroring. Manual activities also can be part of failover, such as restoring disks from a backup.

Multihoming most often refers to various means of enterprise-to-service provider connectivity that avoid a single point of failure. Such connectivity can be for enterprise access to the Internet, for general Internet access to designated enterprise servers, or for the enterprise's intranet or extranet VPNs. Multihoming also can describe connectivity between Internet service providers and "upstream" network service providers.

Chapter 5 needed to precede this one, because all multihoming mechanisms include some level of virtualization. Virtual private networks (VPN) may operate over transport infrastructures that have ordinary or high availability.

If we take the word *multihoming* in the broadest context, it implies there are multiple ways to reach a "home" destination. This "home"

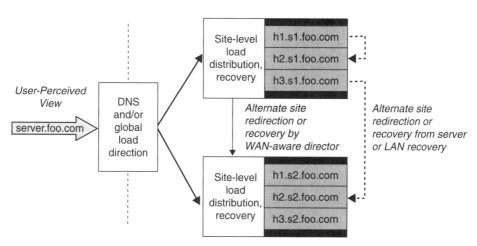

Figure 7.2   Fault-tolerance relationships.

may be identified by a name, an IP address, or a combination of IP address and TCP/UDP port.

Many discussions of multihoming focus on the details of implementation, using such techniques as the border gateway protocol (BGP), multiple DNS entries for a server, etc. Again, focus on the problem you are trying to solve, and look systematically at the requirements before selecting a means of resilient connectivity.

One implementation technique is not appropriate for all requirements. There are special issues in implementing solutions in the general Internet, because poor implementations can jeopardize the proper function of global routing or DNS. An incorrect BGP route advertisement injected into the global routing system is a problem whether it originates in an ISP or in an enterprise.

Goals

Requirements tend to be driven by one or more of several major goals for server availability and performance. Availability goals are realized with resiliency mechanisms, to avoid user-perceived failures from single failures in servers, routing systems, or media. Performance goals are realized by mechanisms that distribute the workload among multiple machines such that the load is distributed in a useful manner. Like multihoming, the terms *load-balancing* and *load-sharing* have many definitions.

In defining requirements, the servers themselves may either share or balance the load, there may be load-sharing or load-balancing routing paths to them, or the routed traffic may be carried over load-shared or load-balanced media.

Always remember to keep in mind, "what is the problem you are trying to solve?" If your goal is increasing availability, that doesn't necessarily equate to increasing redundancy. Uncontrolled increases in redundancy lead to uncontrolled increases in complexity, and may actually decrease availability.

There are major differences between defining a requirement for high availability of initial access, and making the connection stay up once access has been achieved. The latter tends to require transport layer awareness.

Security requirements can include various cryptographic schemes, as well as mechanisms to hinder denial-of-service attacks. The requirements analyst must determine whether cryptography is needed, and, if so, whether cryptographic trust must be between end hosts, or between end hosts and a trusted gateway. Such gateways can be routers or multiported application servers.

Access authentication and per-transaction security are relatively easy to make fault tolerant. Seamless failover of encrypted streams, whether for sequential integrity or for confidentiality, is extremely difficult.

Service-Specific Goals

These goals need to be agreed to by the people or organization responsible for the applications. Not to reach fairly formal agreement here can lead to problems of inappropriate expectations.

At the application layer, there will be expectations of connectivity. Not all applications will operate through classical NAT devices. Application designers should proceed on two fronts: following NAT-friendly application design principles [Senie 1999a] and being aware of potential application protocol interactions with NAT technologies [Holdredge 1999a].

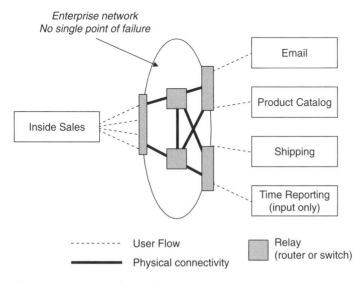

Figure 7.3 Fault-tolerant intranets.

Availability in the Enterprise Intranet

Begin looking at expectations inside the enterprise. At the level of defining application availability requirements, such as for the network in Figure 7.3, it is irrelevant if the underlying network is real or a VPN.

Once you have defined the overall service availability goal, you can then focus on server and network fault-tolerance requirements. You must consider them together. Total service availability is never greater than the availability of its least reliable component. When the enterprise uses a VPN, the fault-tolerant parts of the network are associated with high availability to the connectivity network that underlies the tunneling system.

Within an intranet, you have control of naming and addressing. When you connect to outside organizations, be they service providers or business partners, you will have to have mutually acceptable conventions for naming and addressing.

Availability in Extranets

Another category in which you deal with service availability involves strategic partners. As in the intranet, the connectivity to partners may be real or virtual.

In both intranets and extranets, endpoints do not magically appear. The configuration will be far more predictable than when general Internet connectivity is involved. A predictable environment will let you optimize for your specific situation (see Figure 7.4).

Administration, however, will be more complex than with intranets. Network address translation or other converters may be necessary.

Specific Server Availability to the Internet

Another requirement involves well-defined applications that run on specific servers visible to the Internet at large (see Figure 7.5). Such applications include e-commerce servers, mail gateways, and the like.

From an application standpoint, this is a many-to-one topology, many clients to one server, or a many-to-many topology when multiple servers are involved. It can be worthwhile to consider a many-to-few case, when the few are multiple instances of a server function, which

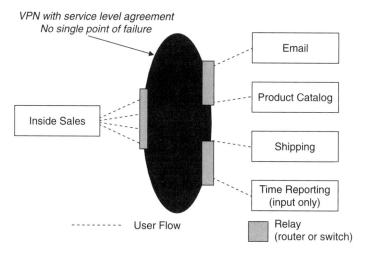

Figure 7.4 Highly available infrastructure for intranet VPNs.

may appear as a single server to the general Internet. The idea of many-to-few topology allows for a local optimization of inter-server communications, without affecting the global many-to-one model.

Addresses on interfaces that connect to the general Internet need to be unique in the global Internet routing system, although they may be translated, at the network address or port level, from public to internal space.

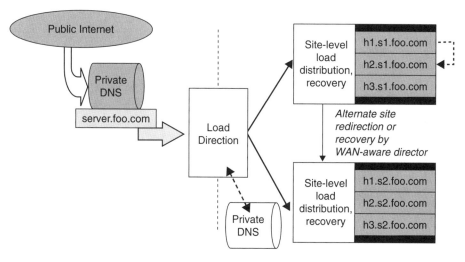

Figure 7.5 Highly available virtual server.

General Internet Connectivity from the Enterprise

Yet another problem is the requirement for high availability of general Internet connectivity for arbitrary enterprise users to the public Internet. (see Figure 7.6). Picture, for example, an engineering lab that must have mail and Web connectivity for day-to-day operations.

Addresses on interfaces that connect to the general Internet need to be unique in the global Internet routing system, although they may be translated, at the network address or port level, from internal private address to public space.

Planning and Budgeting

In each of these scenarios, organization managers need to assign some economic cost to outages. Typically, there will be an incident cost and an incremental cost based on the length or scope of the connectivity loss.

Ideally, this cost is then weighted by the probability of outage. In the 1980s, when I worked in the rapidly growing Tysons Corner, Virginia, area, the electrical power utility could not keep up with the demands of air conditioning. During the summer, brief outages took place at least weekly, and there would be a multihour outage every month or two. The probability of power outages was thus very high. Power outages

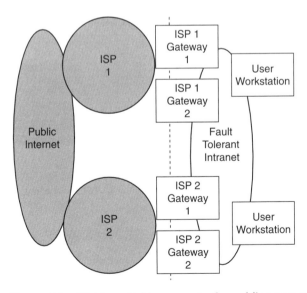

Figure 7.6   Highly available access to the public Internet.

would disrupt services until backup power was restored, but usually did not cause equipment damage. The shorter outages could be handled by uninterruptible power system batteries, and the longer ones by generators. When I worked for a network service provider, it was reasonable for them to have both large UPS and generators. When I worked for a consulting firm, a small UPS sufficed to let people save files.

While a terrorist bomb, to say nothing of a major nuclear attack, could have caused much more long-lasting disruptions, the likelihood of such an explosion was low during this period. It was reasonable not to turn our office buildings into Cheyenne Mountain clones.

TIP

Unless you think that initiation rituals help team building, please be sensitive to the effect of some fault-tolerance mechanisms on your staff. Soon after I started to work at a service provider in Tysons Corner, we had a power outage. At my desk, I saw the lights flicker and go out.

BOOOM! rrrRRROAR! Probably with some amusement, no one had told me that the instant-start, turbine-powered generators were directly under my window. Their startup was sufficiently loud that I dove to the floor, and then analyzed the sound.

A weighted exposure cost results when the outage cost is multiplied by the probability of the outage.

All components of an information system—servers, transmission media, routers and switches, clients, and personnel—are exposed to threats. One of the challenges for the information system architect is balancing the cost of protection against both the likelihood and the potential damage of each threat. If failure of a $50,000 server will cause total application outage for two days, that failure is far more devastating than a two-hour network connectivity failure that prevents transcriptionists from reaching the server. If it costs an additional $100,000 to make a more than 30-minute failure extremely unlikely, that $100,000 is not as well spent as well as another $50,000 for another server.

If the cost of a protective measure is equal to or less than the exposure, then using the protective measure makes good business sense. If the cost of protection is greater than the exposure, it makes more sense to self-insure or obtain business insurance against that risk.

Two common metrics are involved with computing availability, *mean time between failures (MTBF)* and *maximum time to repair (MTTR)*.

Failures in electronics often follow what is called the *bathtub curve*, shown in Figure 7.7 because of its resemblance to the cross-section of a bathtub. There are a high incidence of initial failures, as software bugs and incorrect components are uncovered. There is also a high incidence of failures late in the life cycle, as components wear out or fail under unexpected growth.

Overall availability comes from the interactions of MTBF and MTTR, according to the formula:

A = MTBF / (MTBF + MTTR)

Redundancy, be it component or the paths to components (i.e., multi-homing), improves MTTR. MTBF is primarily a matter of component design, although such things as well-regulated power and temperature help avoid failures.

You can look at MTBF as making things fireproof, and MTTR as the mechanisms that put fires out.

Different systems and technologies have different characteristics of MTBF and MTTR. An aircraft carrier, for example, by its very nature has to carry many things that burn (e.g., jet fuel) and/or go boom (e.g., bombs and rockets). Even with stringent safety measures, there will be accidents. Since World War II, the greatest loss of life on a U.S. carrier was caused by an accidental bomb explosion on the *USS Forrestal* on July 29, 1967.

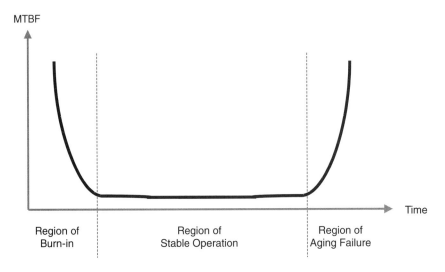

Figure 7.7 Bathtub reliability curve.

Table 7.2 Direct and Indirect Costs of Increased Availability

DIRECT	INDIRECT
Backup equipment	Design
Additional lines/bandwidth	Network Administrator time due to additional complexity; higher salaries for higher skills
Floor space, ventilation, and electrical power for additional resources	Performance drops due to fault-tolerance overhead

The U.S. Navy, however, has developed extreme skill in firefighting, and the *Forrestal* sailed again. One of the pilots on her deck during the fire was to become a senator and presidential candidate, John McCain. In the Navy's view, optimizing MTBF is important, but improving MTTR is what gets you home again.

Resiliency measures reduce the probability of sustained outages, but increase the cost of operation. As one auto repair commercial says, "you can pay me now or you can pay me later."

Assuming you choose to pay me now, and put in fault-tolerance mechanisms, what are the direct and indirect costs? When estimating the cost of a threat occurrence, be sure to consider all costs. Personnel costs for restoral are an obvious one, as are replacement parts and dial phone charges for temporary connectivity. Other factors to consider are loss of revenue, but also the potential of litigation by customers or investors, and the loss of competitive position (see Table 7.2).

If you choose to pay me later, and accept failures, what are some of the costs of failures when they occur (see Table 7.3)?

These costs refer only to failures that do not involve security breaches, so the data can be trusted. Chapter 8, "VPNs, Security, and Roaming," deals with additional costs of security problems.

Table 7.3 Direct and Indirect Costs of Accepting Failure Modes

DIRECT	INDIRECT
Revenue loss	Lost marketing opportunities
Overtime charges for repair	Shareholder suits
Salaries of idle production staff	Staff morale

Service Level Agreements

As I write these words, it is 12:30 A.M. on a Saturday morning. My DSL service provider is down with a router failure, and I have not yet used my dial backup. If I were working normal hours, would this be an outage?

When you define performance and availability goals, you need to specify the period over which they are expected. Requiring 24/7/365 service is not necessarily a good idea, because both server and network operators need some maintenance time. If you require continuous availability, it may cost heavily in backup resources for an application only used during normal business hours.

Enterprise networks, especially mainframe-based, are accustomed to building and enforcing service level agreements for application performance. A key to being able to do this is total control of the end-to-end communications path.

Symmetry

One of the reasons service level agreements are not enforceable in the general Internet is the reality that global routing cannot be guaranteed to be symmetrical. Symmetrical routing assumes the path to a destination is simply reversed to return a response from that destination. Both legs of a symmetrical path are assumed to have the same performance characteristics.

Global Internet routing is not necessarily optimized for best end-to-end routing, but for efficient handling in the autonomous systems (AS) along the path. Many service providers use "closest exit" routing, where they will go to the closest exit point from their perspective to get to the next-hop AS. The return path, however, is not necessarily of a mirror image of the path from the original source to the destination.

Closest exit routing is, in fact, a "feature" rather than a "bug" in some multihoming schemes [Peterson] [Friedman].

Especially when the enterprise network has multiple points of attachment to the Internet, either to a single ISP AS or to multiple ISPs, it becomes likely that the response to a given packet will not come back at the same entry point in which it left the enterprise.

This is probably not avoidable, and troubleshooting procedures and traffic engineering have to consider this characteristic of multi-exit routing.

In the current Internet, the enterprise(s) at one or both ends control their local environments, and have contractual control over connections to their direct service providers.

If service level control is a requirement, and both ends of the path are not under control (i.e., cases 1 and 2), the general Internet cannot now provide service level guarantees. The need for control should be reexamined, and, if it still exists, the underlying structure will need to be dedicated resources at the network layer or below. A network service provider may be able to engineer this so that some facilities are shared to reduce cost, but the sharing is planned and controlled.

Selecting Technologies

A basic way to tell which technology(ies) is applicable is to ask oneself whether the functional requirement is defined in terms of multihoming to specific hosts, or to specific networks/sites. If the former, some type of application or transport technology is needed, because only these technologies have awareness of specific hosts.

A given fault-tolerant implementation may draw on several of these technologies. For example, the Nortel Bay 790 switch, the Cisco Distributed Director, and F5 Networks' 3-DNS do DNS name-level redirection based in part on routing metrics. Servers may have limited routing awareness, so they can send their responses to the best exit.

Higher-Layer Technologies

Application-based technologies may involve referring a client request to different instances of the endpoint represented by a single name. Another aspect of application/name multihoming may work at the level of IP addressing, but specifically is constrained to endpoint (i.e., server) activities that redirect the client request to a different endpoint.

Application-level firewall proxy services can provide this functionality, although their application protocol modification emphasizes security, while a multihoming application service emphasizes availability and quality of service.

Security Interactions with Fault Tolerance

ISPs may be reluctant to let user routing advertisements or DNS zone information flow directly into their routing or naming systems. Users should understand that BGP is not intended to be a plug-and-play mechanism; manual configuration often is considered an important part of maintaining integrity. Supplemental mechanisms may be used for additional control, such as registering policies in a registry [RPS, RA documents], or egress/ingress filtering [RFC 2267].

Challenges may arise when client security mechanisms interact with fault-tolerance mechanisms associated with servers. For example, if a server address changes to that of a backup server, a stateful packet screening firewall might not accept a valid return. Similarly, unless servers back one another up in a full mirroring mode, if one end of a TCP-based application connection fails, the user will need to reconnect. As long as another server is ready to accept that connection, there may not be major user impact, and the goal of high availability is realized. High availability and user-transparent high availability are not synonymous.

A slight level of nontransparency can markedly simplify system design and cost. Nontransparency can mean that a given transaction in progress has to be restarted, or the user needs to go through a new login. These relatively painless acts mean that the service can reinitialize on a new session, and does not need to keep state on in-progress sessions on backup application or access servers.

Transport-based technologies are based on maintaining tunnels through an underlying network or transmission system. The tunnels may be true end to end, connecting a client host with a server host, or may interconnect between proxy servers or other gateways.

You need to consider the logic with which services are expected to fail over. The simplest failover configuration involves two servers, one that normally does all processing, and the other acting simply as a hot standby (see Table 7.4).

How many servers and sites do you need? One of my clients was a rapidly growing firm that supplied a specialized application to enterprise customers. Certain parts of the work on this application were outsourced to independent contractors who accessed through an Internet-based VPN. Individual servers within clusters could handle 50 enterprises and 75 contractors. We expected growth of 10 customers

Table 7.4 Threats and Countermeasures at Higher Layers

THREAT	ALTERNATIVE COUNTERMEASURES
1. At a single site, single server failure or out-of service for maintenance	Local clustering
2. Overload of the virtual server clusters at multiple sites	Intelligent load distribution with DNS
3. Loss of connectivity to a site	Intelligent directory
4. Server crash	Backup, checkpointing,

and 15 subcontractors per month. The plan assumed it would take one month to order and install each additional server.

Figure 7.8 shows a high-level view of this service. Customers accessed Application 1 primarily through a frame relay network, with VPN backup. Subcontractors used an Internet VPN to access Application 2, and the two applications communicated with each other, the backup server, and network management servers over a LAN.

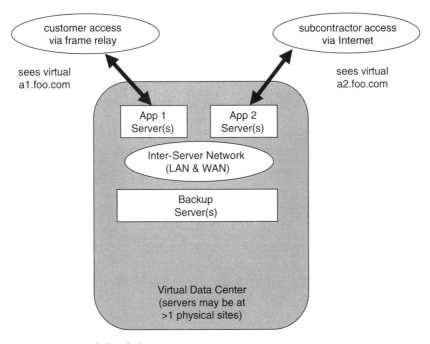

Figure 7.8 High-level view.

Static Load Distribution

Figure 7.9 showed an austere plan for this service. The austere service did not have explicit backup machines, but accepted that a certain number of users would be down if an application server failed. Each user was administratively assigned to a particular server.

Another way in which this plan was "austere" is that it did not allow for a server to be taken offline for maintenance. Since a failure either of the application 1 or application 2 server would disrupt the customer service, a wiser strategy was to start with two servers for each application.

NOTE
▬▬▬ The enterprise had a separate server for DNS, DHCP, and management. With growth, this server also was replicated.

With this firm's initial software, each application needed to run on its own server. A backup server could substitute for an application 1 or an application 2 server, but not both simultaneously. The austere plan, however, had no backup server. Table 7.5 shows a way to represent the deployment plan.

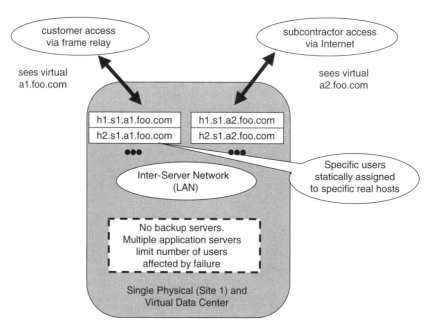

Figure 7.9 The austere environment.

Table 7.5 Austere

MONTH	ENTERPRISES	SUB-CONTRACTORS	SERVERS A1	A2	BACKUP	COMMENTS
1	10	15	1	1		
2	20	30	1	1		
3	30	45	1	1		
4	40	60	1	1		Order Application 1 server
5	50	75	2	1		Install Application 1 server 2, protecting against a single server failure
6	60	90	2	1		Order Application 2 server 2
7	70	115	2	2		Install Application 2 server 2. Slight exposure to degraded operation with one server only
8	80	130	2	2		
9	90	145	2	2		Order Application 1 server 3
10	100	160	3	2		Install Application 1 server 3
11	110	175	3	2		
12	120	190	3	2		Order Application 2 server 3

Backup Alternatives

While the austere plan was cheap, top management decided it offered too much exposure to failures. The next cheapest strategy was cold standby, in which one backup server could protect against a single server failure, but would have to be manually configured for the specific application (see Figure 7.10).

Relying on manual reconfiguration, however, required either having 24/7 coverage by database administrators, or accepting that the server could be reconfigured only during prime hours. Since the software

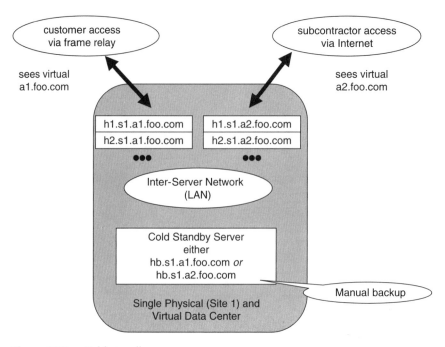

Figure 7.10 Cold standby.

still limited the server configurations, the next cheapest alternative was to provide a backup server for each application.

Asymmetric 1:1 Server Failover

Providing a dedicated backup server is an example of an asymmetric 1:1 failover scenario. This scenario is asymmetric in that a server either is running an application, or it is in a backup status to that application (see Figure 7.11).

Asymmetric 1:N Server Failover

Symmetric failover required a software rewrite that allowed both application 1 and application 2 to run on the same server. This still only protected against a single server failure. If an application server were taken offline for maintenance, there was no protection.

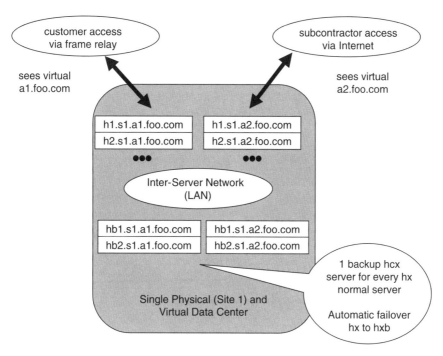

Figure 7.11 Asymmetric 1:1 server failover.

This scenario still did not offer enough operational flexibility. The next design involved 1:1 symmetric failover, in which there are no pure backup servers. Instead, the servers are paired (see Figure 7.12).

Symmetric 1:1 Failover

Remember that a server can handle 10 A1 enterprises and 16 A2 subcontractors. It was simplest to assume to halve those values, and divide the workload into pairs of servers, each of which processed half the load but could take over from its partner (see Figure 7.13).

While this solution was fairly easy to implement, given software that could run both applications, the solution used far more server boxes than other methods.

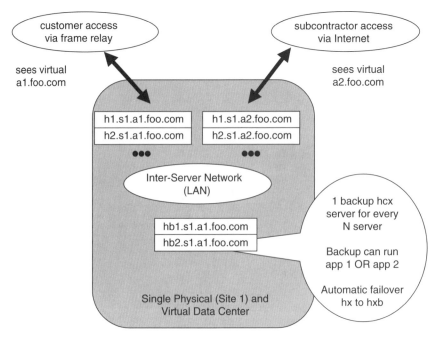

Figure 7.12 Asymmetric 1:N failure.

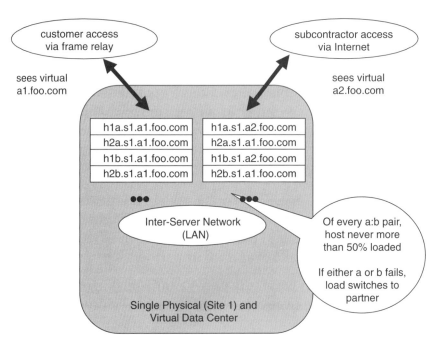

Figure 7.13 Symmetric 1:1 failover.

Symmetric N:1 Failover

A more complex, but more hardware-efficient, strategy is to provide a backup server for every **N** application servers (see Figure 7.14).

All of these solutions, however, still were vulnerable to a disaster affecting the data center itself. Before looking at the multiple data center solution, we need to examine fault tolerance in the network. In the specific enterprise, network reliability, specifically for subcontractor access from the Internet, became a perceived issue very early in the process. Top management demanded fault-tolerant Internet connectivity to the data center, even before there were multiple servers.

Figure 7.15 shows several considerations that had to be considered at the network layer: failure protection for customer sites, for the Internet cloud through which subcontractors accessed servers, and for backup and synchronizing among data centers.

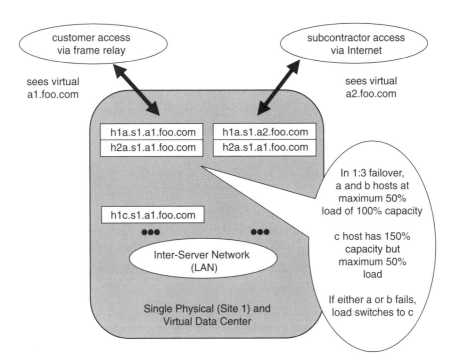

Figure 7.14 Symmetric 1:N failover.

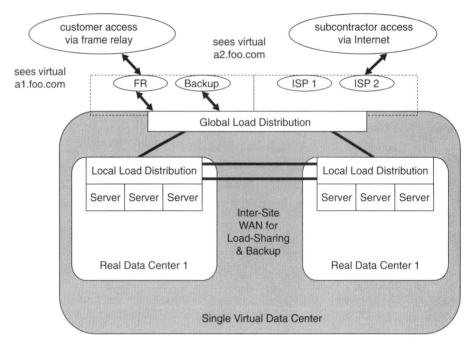

Figure 7.15 High-level view showing network requirements.

Lower-Layer Technologies

Network fault tolerance involves several OSI layers. *Network* layer approaches to multihoming are router-based. They involve having alternate next hops, or complete routes, to alternate destinations.

Data link layer methods may involve coordinated use of multiple physical paths, as in multilink PPP or X.25. If the underlying WAN service has a virtual circuit mechanism, as in frame relay or ATM, the service provider may have multihomed paths provided as part of the service. Such functions blur between data link and physical layers. Other data link methods may manipulate MAC addresses to provide virtual server functions.

Physical multihoming strategies can use diverse media, often of different types such as a wire backed up with a wireless data link. They also involve transmission media that have internal redundancy, such as SONET.

Simply to improve availability in Internet access, consider what threats concern you, and decide if the countermeasures in Table 7.6 are cost-effective.

Higher-Layer Multihoming and Failover

Since the focus of this book is on the WAN, failover mechanisms inside LAN-connected server clusters are outside its scope. They are covered extensively in [Marcus and Stern].

Higher-layer multihoming often occurs only when a client requests service, while failover is a decision made among servers. The basic idea here is that arbitrary clients will first request access to a resource by its DNS name, and certain DNS servers will resolve the same name to different addresses based on conditions of which DNS is aware, or using some statistical load-distribution mechanism.

There are some general DNS issues here. DNS was not really designed to do this. A key issue is that of DNS caching. Caching and frequent changes in name resolution are opposite goals. Traditional DNS schemes emphasize performance over resiliency.

Table 7.6 Threats and Countermeasures at Lower Layers

THREAT	ALTERNATIVE COUNTERMEASURES
1. Failure of a customer external gateway router on a LAN accessible to multiple customer routers and host.	Virtual router redundancy protocol (VRRP)/hot standby routing protocol (HSRP). If BGP is used, be sure peering is between loopback/circuitless interfaces.
2. Media failure of a single IP subnet to the ISP.	Inverse multiplexing with multilink PPP, fast/gigabit Etherchannel over optical transmission, SONET.
3. Failure of a single IP interface on a single customer or ISP router.	Run BGP over load-shared IP using multiple interfaces.
4. Failure of a single customer or ISP router.	Install multiple customer routers interconnected to each other with iBGP and to the ISP with eBGP.
5. Failure of the ISP's BGP routing system.	Connect to multiple ISPs with eBGP.
6. Failure of the ISP's BGP routing and failure of physical components.	Apply countermeasures 1 through 4 in combination.

DNS Caching

DNS standards do provide the capability for short cache lifetimes, which in principle support name-based multihoming. "The meaning of the TTL field is a time limit on how long an RR can be kept in a cache. This limit does not apply to authoritative data in zones; it is also timed out, but by the refreshing policies for the zone. The TTL is assigned by the administrator for the zone where the data originates. While short TTLs can be used to minimize caching, and a zero TTL prohibits caching, the realities of Internet performance suggest that these times should be on the order of days for the typical host. If a change can be anticipated, the TTL can be reduced prior to the change to minimize inconsistency during the change, and then increased back to its former value following the change. [RFC 1034] "

Several real-world factors limit the utility of simply shortening the cache time. Widely used BIND, the most widely used DNS implementation, does not accept cache lifetimes less than five minutes.

Dynamic DNS may be a long-term solution here. In the short term, setting very short TTL values may be help in some cases, but is not likely to help below a granularity of five minutes. Remember that the name normally is resolved when an application session first is established, and the decisions are made over a longer time base than per-packet routing decisions.

DNS Multiple Hosts and Round-Robin Response

The DNS protocol allows it to return multiple host addresses in response to a single query. At the first level of DNS-based multihoming, this can provide additional reliability. A DNS server knows three IP addresses for the server function identified by server.example.com, 10.0.1.1, 10.0.2.1, and 10.0.3.1. A simple response to a query for server.example.com returns all three addresses. Assume the response provides server addresses in the order 10.0.1.1, 10.0.2.1, and 10.0.3.1.

Whether this will provide multihoming now depends on the DNS client. Not all host client implementations will, if the first address returned (i.e., 10.0.1.1) does not respond, try the additional addresses. In this example, 10.0.2.1 might be operating perfectly.

A variant suggested by Kent England is to have the addresses returned in the DNS response come from the CIDR blocks of different

ISPs that provide connectivity to the server function [England]. This approach combines aspects of name and network multihoming. Again, this will work when intelligent clients try every IP address returned until a server responds.

Even more intelligent DNS functions, such as the Nortel/Bay Accelar 790, Cisco's DistributedDirector, F5 Networks 3-DNS, or the Alteon 180 products, involve communication between DNS servers and routers in the multihomed domain. When a DNS request is received by a DNS redirector, its server selects the IP address to be returned based on information on routing cost from the client entry point to closest server, on administrative weight, or other generally routing-associated factors.

Cache Servers and Application Multihoming

Web and other caches usually are thought of as solutions for reducing bandwidth requirements. They also, however, can have a benefit in fault tolerance.

In the first scenario where they help, the definitive server fails. The cache server can provide answers from its local storage. If this is a specific application server, it can even store updates that can subsequently be restored.

In the second server, the cache server fails. Since a cache is transparent, the traffic now goes to the definitive server. If each remote site has its own cache, the total additional load on the main server and the network to it are simply the incremental ones for the site with the failed cache.

Application Data Issues

There is a spectrum of relationships between the database instances in a multiple data center environment. There are really two sets of spectra, one dealing with the file/database level, and one dealing with individual transactions.

Local disk mirroring, using an appropriate RAID method, complements these techniques. Local mirroring protects against individual disk failures, and may eliminate the need for restoral (see Table 7.7).

While backing up to a local tape drive is straightforward, the disadvantage is that restoring from backups, which must take place before

Table 7.7   Data Integrity Alternatives

FILE/DATABASE-ORIENTED	TRANSACTION-ORIENTED
Backup	
Multiple Backup with Shipping	
	Reciprocal remote backup
Transaction log	
	Remote transaction log
Parallel database	
	Two-phase commit

failover, is slow when it involves large files or many tapes. Restoral can take many tapes either because the files inherently are large, or that the last full backup plus multiple incremental backups need to be applied.

Where are the backup tapes kept? Keeping them locally means that any disaster affecting the data center has a significant chance of disrupting the backups. A simple alternative is to create two sets of backup tapes, one of which is sent by an overnight delivery service to the other data center, or to a commercial data archive site. There is a story of a subtle variation of this, in which an organization took full backups every night, and then sent a copy of the backups to itself via two-day express. In this manner, the express company became responsible for security of the backup tapes.

A package of backup media, sent by overnight delivery, easily can have a bandwidth of a DS3. Sending backups in this manner, however, requires more human intervention than network-based mechanisms. It requires having delivery service pickup available at an appropriate time, having the staff to create the tapes and package them, etc.

A variant to shipping the tapes is to have one local backup drive (or multiple drives if parallelism improves backup time) and the other backup drive at the other data center. Obviously, this will require a reasonably fast line or lines between the data centers. There may be creative ways to use the bandwidth of links used only during the business day.

Backups also have the problem that they are snapshots at specific times. Transaction tapes complement backups. They have the effect of being continuously running incremental backups. You can restore from a full backup, then use incrementals if necessary, and then use the transaction log. Just as backup drives can be remoted, so can transaction logs.

At some point, the magnitude of restoral may make failover using backups and logs impractical. It may be both more flexible and more cost-effective to go to a parallel database at each data center. If the data centers were originally designed for mutual backup, the computers at those centers may already have most of the resources needed for parallel databases. You will, of course, incur additional cost for high-speed communications links among the centers.

How fast do these links need to be? By now, you should know the only proper answer to such a question is, "it depends." Obviously, the simple volume of application data will be a large part of the bandwidth.

A key issue, however, is how much, or little, synchronization is needed between the databases. Not all parallel databases need to be in absolute lock with one another. When I worked on the design of the U.S. government's Y2K Information Center, the overall service absolutely, positively, needed to be up. If one of our two identical public-access databases had a few updates that the other did not, however, the service was still useful. Oracle databases at the data centers and the operations centers were linked by 15 Mbps virtual circuits. As a center originated a transaction, it copied the transaction to a remote log at each of the other data centers. The remote centers mixed the log transactions with those that entered locally, and updated the database within seconds or short minutes.

A replicated database that deals with airline reservations or stock purchases must have all of its instances in exact synchronization, to avoid selling the same seat or the same block of shares more than once. Only transactions in process can differ among the instances. These requirements dictate the use of two-phase commitment protocols, with which a transaction can update a database only after confirmation that it is updating all databases.

Two-phase commit means that the time to complete a transaction cannot be less than the time it takes the slowest system to complete its instance of the transaction. This time includes both database processing and communications transfer time for protocol messages. You must consider, in planning bandwidth for such applications, both the absolute data volume and the latency imposed on the commitment protocol exchange.

Transport Multihoming

Transport layer functions are conceptually end to end. There are two broad classes of transport multihoming function, those maintained by the endpoints and those that involve intermediate translation devices.

A transport layer client may detect, or be told by higher layers, that a server is unreachable. It may then create a new tunnel without dropping the application session.

Basic point-to-point tunneling mechanisms include GRE, PPTP, L2TP and IPsec tunnel mode. Choices here will depend in part on the security policy and the administrative model by which multihoming is provided. GRE, for example, does not itself provide encryption. Microsoft's recent PPTP implementations do offer encryption for confidentiality. GRE and L2TP both can be encapsulated in IPsec, or IPsec can encapsulate GRE or L2TP.

"The differences between PPTP and L2TP are more of where one wishes the PPP session to terminate, and one of control. It really depends on who you are, and where you are, in the scheme of the control process. If your desire is to control where the PPP session terminates (as an ISP might wish to control), then L2TP might be the right approach. On the other hand, however, if you are a subscriber, and you wish to control where the PPP session terminates (to, say, a PPTP server somewhere across the cloud), then PPTP might be the right approach—and it would be transparent to the service provider). It really depends on what problem one is trying to solve, and if you are in the business of trying to create "services." [Ferguson-1998-2]

Application-aware transport proxies can have even more knowledge of application load. Load-sharing NAT with port translation (LSNATP) allows session-level redirection during a session, by changing the inside server address without breaking a TCP connection (see Figure 7.16). The outside client has a TCP connection to the outside of the LSNATP device. It does not see the changes in the sequence numbering and windows if the inside TCP session changes. LSNAT (i.e., with address but not port translation) could not make such transparent changes.

By replacing the real client address with the address of the virtual server as the address source seen by the inside, the real server can use multiple paths to return responses.

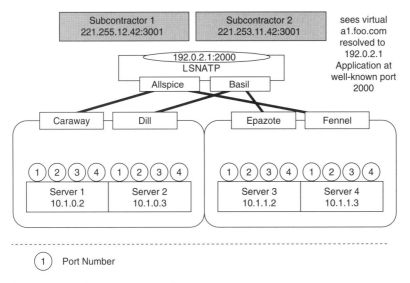

Figure 7.16 LSNATP WAN redirection.

There can be multiple paths to the LS-NAPT router. There remains the basic topological constraint that there will be only one LS-NAPT router, but there can more easily be multiple internal paths to it. This allows servers to be outside a stub domain. The LS-NAPT router can direct traffic to an internal server inside the private address space of a stub domain, or direct the traffic to a third-party server using registered addresses and WAN connectivity.

The additional complexity of LSNAPT does allow greater scalability, because new links can be dropped into the routing system without problem. As long as new client links can get to the virtual server address, the addition of these links is transparent to both servers and clients.

Fault-Tolerant Routing

A common concern of enterprise financial managers is that multihoming strategies involve expensive links to ISPs, but, in some of these scenarios, alternate links are used only as backups, idle much of the time. Detailed analysis may reveal that the cost of forcing these links to be used at all times, however, exceeds the potential savings.

Addressing issues need to be understood, especially when dealing with Internet connectivity, before the routing solution can be defined.

Addressing Issues

Addressing is definitely a part of the multihomed environment, and indeed may be crucial. One of the challenges of multihoming in the Internet is that carriers historically have filtered routes longer than some length, usually /19.

Now, consider a business selling on the Internet. It has no single point of failure, with two server farms at different locations. What needs to be at these locations?

- Two routers
- Two firewalls/server load distribution devices
- Two DNS servers

Six IP addresses only call for a /29, a prefix far longer than will pass through the length filters of many providers.

There is no simple answer. In discussions at ARIN, the address policy working group is considering the allocation of a specific address block for *microallocations*, which would be reserved for organizations that have been verified as routing to two or more ISPs. ISPs would be assumed to be willing to advertise addresses in this block.

In practice, microallocations are in limited use today. DNS root name servers and Internet exchange points are small addresses that every sensible provider allows through its prefix filters.

The policy is still emerging. At the April 2000 ARIN meeting, policy alternatives included [Jimmerson 00]:

1. Keep policy as is.
2. Lower minimum allocations size, when appropriate, and monitor routing tables.
3. Allocate to multihomed organizations from a reserved /8 (suggest that ISPs not filter [this] /8).
4. Keep policy as is, but include additional critical infrastructures.

ARIN alone cannot establish a worldwide policy. While ARIN closely cooperates with its regional equivalents, the RIPE NCC and APNIC, final global policy comes from ICANN. ICANN is thrashing with overall Internet governance and politics, and is much more concerned with naming than addressing policy.

Pending a microallocation policy, the prefix filtering issue often pushes content providers into the direction of colocating their equipment at large hosting centers. These hosting centers have their own allocations that are sufficiently large to pass the prefix length filters. An individual center may not itself have enough space for its own prefix, but a company that runs several centers usually justifies an allocation on its total volume. Allocations to the level of a national hosting provider, unfortunately, may result in suboptimal routing unless the individual centers have generally routable prefixes. See Figure 7.17, in which the traffic entering in New York will still go to San Jose to reach a data center in Philadelphia.

Local exchanges are an increasingly popular alternative that can be caused by backhaul. In a local exchange, local providers and significant enterprises share either a small switch or a distributed layer 2 subnet, and have a small router or route server that does peering on behalf of the local organizations. By using a local exchange, you can actually go across town rather than being backhauled across half a continent to go between major provides (see Figure 7.18).

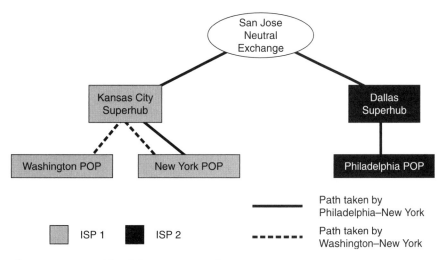

Figure 7.17 Backhaul due to aggregation.

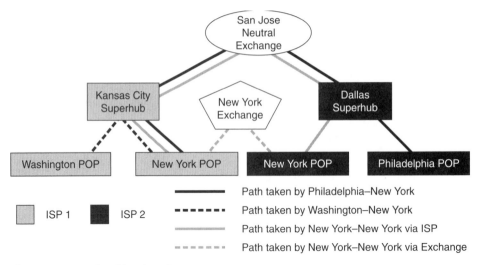

Figure 7.18 Role of local exchanges.

Some widely deployed protocols are not efficient in their use of address space. HTTP Version 1.0 makes the microallocation problem worse, because it needs a separate IP address for each domain, even when multiple domains are hosted on the same real server or server cluster. HTTP 1.1 allows these domains to share a single IP address. ARIN is discussing the question of whether organizations need to transition to HTTP 1.1 to be considered efficient users of address space, eligible for multihomed allocations.

There also may be administrative requirements for addressing, such as a service provider that contracts to run an extranet may require addresses to be registered, possibly from the provider's address space.

If the enterprise runs applications that embed network layer addresses in higher-level data fields, solutions that employ address translation, at the packet or virtual connection level, *may not* work. Use of such applications inherently is a requirement for the eventual multihoming solution.

Consideration also needs to be given to application caches in addition to those of DNS. Firewall proxy servers are a good example where multiple addresses associated with a given destination may not be supported.

Fault-Tolerant Routing in the Intranet

Inside an intranet, when the enterprise manages its own network, network load sharing and fault tolerance have definite value. If the enterprise uses virtual private line VPNs, the VPN service provider internally can manage fault tolerance.

In a real network, however, there are constant tradeoffs between optimal routing and network stability. Especially in an intranet where bandwidth costs are not extreme, stability is usually more important than optimizing end-to-end routes. Topology is more important than metrics.

You can impose topology using physical connectivity, address aggregation, or both.

Figure 7.19 shows a basic corporate network with a simple, highly reliable WAN core. The ring organization of the core is often better than a full mesh.

Collapsed backbones also can be very reasonable, especially when there is one main data center as shown in Figure 7.20.

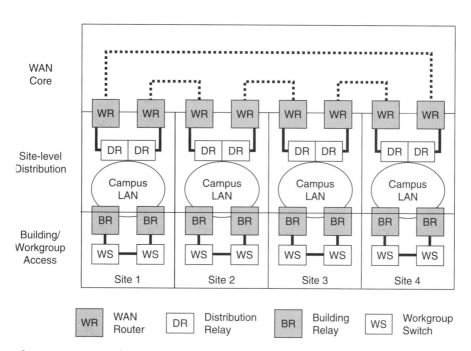

Figure 7.19   Basic hierarchical intranet.

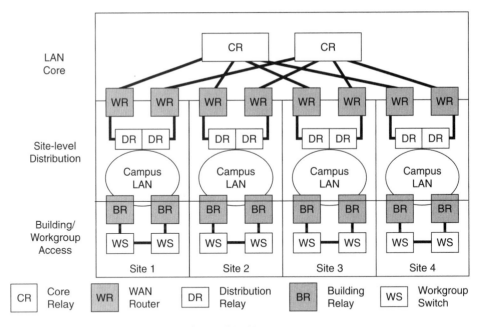

LAN
Core

Site-level
Distribution

Building/
Workgroup
Access

Site 1   Site 2   Site 3   Site 4

| CR | Core Relay | | WR | WAN Router | | DR | Distribution Relay | | BR | Building Relay | | WS | Workgroup Switch |

Figure 7.20 Collapsed backbone hierarchical intranet.

TIP

Even when there is a central data center, there is often sufficient traffic inside the data center to justify putting it into its own hierarchical area. Backbones should interconnect routers and switches, not application hosts.

Is This OSPF Thinking Heresy or Reformation?

Simply because you use OSPF, do not fall into the trap of assuming that you must have a single Area 0.0.0.0 for all of your network. When networks grow to sufficient size, it is quite reasonable to have several OSPF domains, each with its own Area 0.0.0.0, connected by a *backbone of backbones*.

Among many OSPF users, it is a matter of faith and morals that their entire enterprise appear as a single OSPF domain. As a consequence, I've seen designs with a single Area 0.0.0.0 spanning several continents, with each continent having significantly different line quality and speed, needs for demand backup circuits between parts of the area, etc.

Please don't do this. The ideal Area 0.0.0.0 is small, has links of the same cost, and has no single point of failure. There are no application servers in Area 0.0.0.0.

OSPF Techniques

A failure in Area 0.0.0.0 is critical. Methods to repair partitions in OSPF area 0.0.0.0 include appropriately redundant media (the preferred method, as in Figure 7.20) and virtual links.

Virtual links are tunnels to carry routing information through an area. At least one end of a virtual link must be in Area 0.0.0.0. Virtual links were originally developed for topologies in which some nonzero area could not have a physical connection to Area 0.0.0.0, as shown in Figure 7.21.

Figure 7.22 shows an Area 0.0.0.0 with a medium that presents a single point of failure. That area, however, has two interconnected Border Routers, BR1 and BR2. To avoid single router points of failure, there are two ABRs, each with three interfaces: Area 0.0.0.0, Area 0.0.0.1, and Area 0.0.0.2.

If the BR1-BR2 link fails, a virtual link can be defined between the Area 0.0.0.1 interface of ABR-1 and between the Area 0.0.0.1 interface of ABR-2. This reconstitutes backbone connectivity with a tunnel through Area 0.0.0.1.

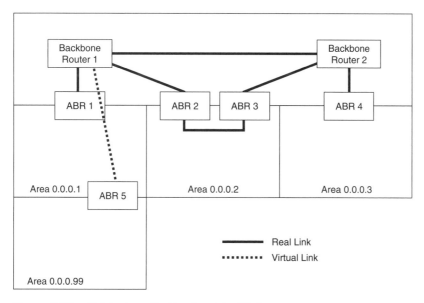

Figure 7.21 Original application for virtual links.

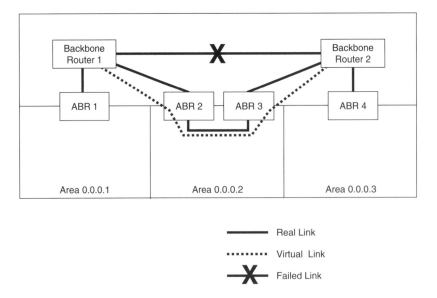

Real Link

Virtual Link

Failed Link

Figure 7.22 Area 0.0.0.0 restoral with virtual links.

Backbone of Backbone Methods

An alternative approach, especially useful if demand OSPF is not available, is to split Area 0.0.0.0 and create two OSPF domains. Each domain has a static route that points to the address range in the other domain. This route is advertised into the local domain as a Type 1 external.

True, OSPF's area structure has two levels, Area 0.0.0.0 and everything else. A routing architecture for an enterprise that uses OSPF, however, can be more than a simple hierarchy of backbone and nonbackbone areas. We can extend its notion of hierarchy both above Area 0.0.0.0 and below the nonzero areas. Even inside an area, there are some forms of hierarchy.

Such an architecture also lends itself to evolution to a high-performance layer 2 or multiprotocol label switching (MPLS) service in the core. It can also be reasonable to have interior routers that "concentrate" traffic, or act as collapsed backbones within an area.

It is also perfectly reasonable to have a broader OSPF routing environment, in which some routers do not speak OSPF but cooperate with those that do. At the "high" end, this involves redistribution of external routes into OSPF. At the "low" end, this involves static and default routes from stub routers to the lowest level of OSPF router inside a nonzero area. Let's talk about the lowest level first.

Edge Routing

The lowest level is a "stub" or "edge" router with a single outgoing path, such as a branch office router with several LAN links, perhaps a STUN serial interface for IBM support, and a single WAN link. There are no routers on any of the LANs.

Such a router really doesn't need to run any dynamic routing protocol. It should default to a higher-level router.

Assuming the higher-level router has multiple links going toward the backbone, that router does need to run OSPF. It doesn't need to connect directly to the backbone.

I Don't Want to Pay for Duplication!

A management imperative that often occurs after the merger of two enterprises is eliminating the "expense of duplicate backbones." At a slightly more technical level, this means an OSPF design that has a single Area 0.

Two companies, A and B, merge. Each has an existing OSPF system, with its own Area 0. These Area 0s are widely separated geographically, but they each have an Area 0.0.0.1 whose boundaries are in fairly close proximity. Each ABR has a single interface to Area 0.In designing solutions, engineers should consider not only pure OSPF mechanisms, but the use of non-OSPF tunneling mechanisms. OSPF virtual links are, of course, appropriate for some topologies. Also, consider having separate OSPF domains linked into a "backbone of backbones," using static or BGP routing among the domains. Let's say that the two companies merge, and want to put their Western Region into the same area because the geographic divisions will share a good deal of information that does not need to cross the backbone. Both areas, of course, could be connected separately to Area 0.0.0.0. There might not be sufficient backbone bandwidth to carry the combined Western Region traffic. If there were a management directive to merge these areas immediately, and dedicated WAN circuits between them were not immediately available, an alternative could be to tunnel between them. The next design issue would be deciding if the tunnels need to be secure. Tunneling, of course, will add overhead bytes to every routed packet, and will also impose additional processing workload on the routers at the endpoints of the tunnel. In spite of the overhead it produces, tunneling may still be a good interim step to achieving desired connectivity during network redesign.

The two companies perceive they want "a single backbone." They do not wish to renumber every network and router, but are willing to merge two nonzero areas if that were helpful. They are also unwilling, at the present time, to merge their two backbones, principally due to the geographic distance between them.

They merge their Area 0.0.0.1s, renumbering appropriately adding physical connectivity between the company A Area 0.0.0.1 and the company B Area 0.0.0.1. They now have a common Area 0.0.0.1, and then define a VL between the two ABRs.

There is now a "single backbone." Potentially, a large amount of inter-area traffic now flows through the combined Area 0.0.0.1. Neither Area 0.0.0.1 presumably was designed to support that flow, but that of the traffic of the community of routers for which it originally was built.

Single-Homed Routing

Single-homed routing is quite appropriate for enterprises without critical connectivity requirements (see Figure 7.23). Such enterprises con-

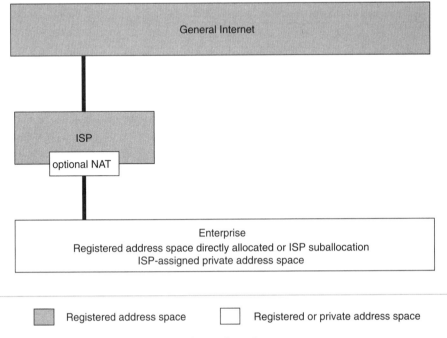

Figure 7.23 High-level view of single-homed routing.

tract to a single ISP for Internet access and Internet-based VPN services; they may run dial-based VPNs of their own.

Enterprises using single-homed routing minimize investment, and follow the often wise principle of keeping things as simple as possible. Single-homed routing generally should use static/default routes to the ISP, and it is acceptable that it will not always take the optimal end-to-end path. The customer is primarily concerned with protecting against link or router failures, rather than failures in the ISP routing system.

Single-Homed, Single-Link

There is a single active data link between the customer and provider. Variations could include switched backup over analog or ISDN services (see Figure 7.24).

In this configuration, multiple parallel data links exist from a single customer router to a provider router. There is protection against link failures.

The single customer router constraint allows this router to do round-robin packet-level load balancing across the multiple links, for resiliency and possibly additional bandwidth. The ability of a router to do such load balancing is implementation-specific, and may be a significant drain on the router's processor (see Figure 7.25).

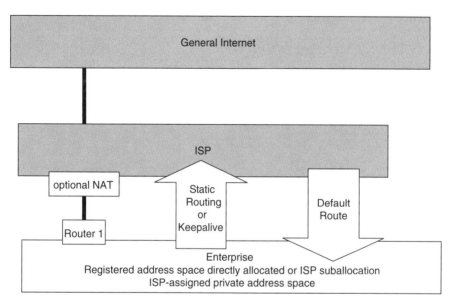

Figure 7.24 Single-homed routing with single active link.

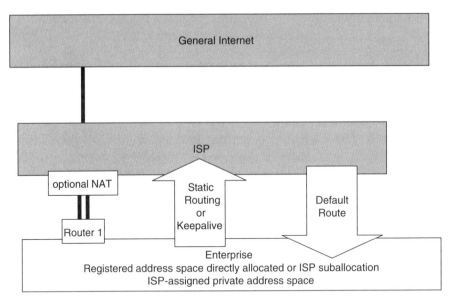

Figure 7.25 Single-homed balanced routing.

Different implementations load-share packets in several ways. They may cache on destination address, the default mode on Cisco routers. Destination-based load sharing works well when there are a large number of destination prefixes, but can lead to significantly unbalanced loads if there are a small number of destinations.

Alternatively, load sharing can be on pure packet round robin or on source-destination pairs. Round-robin load sharing is the most bandwidth efficient, but it often consumes significant resources on the processor. In general, it is practical only at T1 speeds and below.

Round-robin schemes also increase the probability that packets will be delivered out of order. Out-of-order delivery will flatly break some protocols, such as Cisco's Fast Sequenced Transport for IBM tunneling. When the applications are TCP-based, resequencing packets at the destination host will increase its processor load.

Whenever you use load sharing on multiple interfaces of the same router, make a point to monitor CPU utilization, both initially and to track the trend. The rule of thumb on newer Cisco routers is not to let the five-minute CPU utilization exceed 75 percent, and 50 percent is more reasonable on routers without a RISC. processor.

Source-destination pairs, long available on Bay/Nortel and recently introduced on Cisco, are a good compromise between the reduced processing load of destination caches and the bandwidth efficiency of round robin.

See the section on multilink paths later in the chapter for alternatives at the data link layer.

Multihomed, Single-Provider Routing

In multihomed single-provider routing, there is true layer 3 routing exchange between the enterprise and the provider. Such exchanges do not necessarily need to be dynamic; static routing will solve many problems.

Multiple Defaults

In the configuration of Figure 7.26, we have separate paths from multiple customer routers to multiple ISP routers at different POPs. Each provider POP router connected to the enterprise can listen to enterprise routing to find the best entry point to a given prefix. Default routes generated at each of the customer gateways are injected into the enterprise routing system, and the combination internal and external metrics are considered by internal routers in selecting the external gateway.

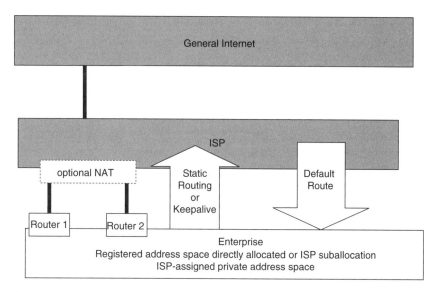

Figure 7.26 Multiple defaults.

This often is attractive for enterprises that want resiliency but wish to avoid the complexity of BGP. Providers tend not to like this because they are geared to operate with BGP, and coordinating customer routing can be labor-intensive.

Multihomed to Single Provider with Multiple POPs

An increasingly common case, is appropriate to enterprises that connect to the same service provider at multiple geographic POPs. This is a reasonable strategy if the enterprise has contracted with a national-level provider for facility diversity.

Quite decent arguments can be made for having BGP connectivity to multiple POPs of the same ISP. If, for example, a single ISP is responsible for upstream availability, it can be made responsible for ensuring that its upstream connectivity goes through diverse physical paths. Simply assuming that two arbitrarily chosen ISPs will use different upstream providers is a dangerous assumption.

The enterprise may want to receive full or partial Internet routes so it can pick the best exit to a particular destination, and so the provider has the best entrance to addresses in the enterprise domain. BGP is necessary to get this amount of routing information.

To run BGP with a service provider, an enterprise needs an AS number. Historically, AS numbers have been available, but, given they are a 16-bit value, they are not an infinite resource. There is, however, a range of private AS numbers (64512 to 65535) that is intended not to appear on the Internet, just as private address space is intended not to appear on the Internet.

The problem is that the enterprise needs an AS number to run BGP, but, since they only connect to a single provider, their routing policy is dictated by the provider. Under the criteria of RFC 1930, they do not qualify for an AS number.

There are, however, workarounds that do not waste a registered AS number. The first case, defined by RFC 1998, deals with the case where the multihomed enterprise uses address space assigned to it by its provider. The second case, defined by RFC 2270, deals with the case where the enterprise has provider-independent address space but is still multihomed to a single provider.

The enterprise wants the provider to know some details of its internal structure. Assume that the enterprise address space is delegated from the provider, so it makes little sense for the provider to announce the more-specific enterprise routes to the rest of the Internet. RFC 1998 describes the strategy to let the provider know the details: Have the enterprise use a private AS number to run BGP to the service provider, and mark the enterprise routes with the well-known NO-EXPORT community.

To load balance with redundancy, the enterprise in Figure 7.27 must advertise both the more-specific /23 route and the less-specific /22 route at each of its peering points. As long as both routers are up, traffic from the ISP will go via the router offering the appropriate /23 route. If either of those routers fail, the load will switch to the remaining router offering the /22 for the entire block.

There is a potential scalability problem on the provider side. RFC1930 reserves 1K of the AS number space for private applications. If more than 1024 customers of a given AS used the RFC 1998 technique, the registered AS would be out of private AS numbers. Even so, as long as the topology is carefully drawn to avoid ambiguity, private AS numbers can be duplicated in different parts of the provider.

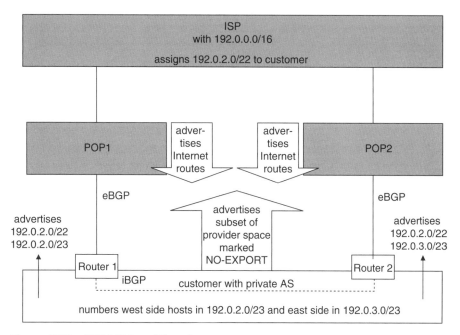

Figure 7.27 RFC 1998 multihoming.

Figure 7.28 shows a different case than RFC 1998. It involves enterprises that have existing provider-independent address space, typically addresses that they have had for years. To have their provider advertise their block, however, means that they either must advertise it with BGP to the provider, or the provider must define it statically and redistribute it.

RFC 2270 proposes a mechanism to allow multihoming to a single provider without wasting a registered AS number. The service provider assigns a private AS number to each enterprise it services. At the ingress routers to the provider, however, the private AS number is stripped, so the advertisement will appear to the Internet as being originated by the service provider. The feature that allows the private number to be stripped is called private AS path manipulation.

Proxy Communities

Another case involves significantly more administrative coordination than RFC 1998 multihoming. In this rare case, the enterprise uses dele-

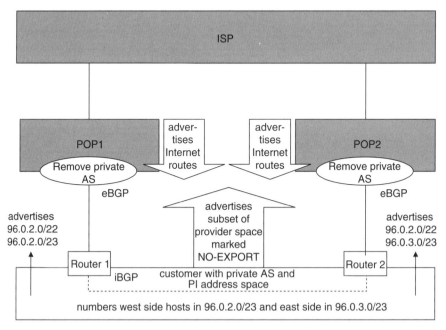

Figure 7.28 RFC 2270 multihoming.

gated address space, but has a routing policy that needs to be seen outside the enterprise. For example, the enterprise might be part of a joint industry-academic research program, so some of its routes need to be labeled with a BGP community that denotes them as meeting the Acceptable Use Policy for the research network.

It may be possible for the customer to avoid using BGP, if its provider will set a BGP community attribute, understood by the upstream, on the customer prefixesThis will involve more administrative coordination, but offers the advantage of leaving complex BGP routing to professionals.

Multihomed, Multiple-Provider Routing

The enterprise connects to more than one ISP, and desires to protect against problems in the ISP routing system. It will accept additional complexity and router requirements to get this. The enterprise may also have differing service agreements for Internet access for different divisions.

A generally accepted BGP technique has to be reconsidered in light of multihoming requirements. It has been a good general rule that only one AS should originate advertisements for prefixes. This rule assumes that any multihomed organization has its own address space and its own AS number.

Multihomed, Primary/Backup, Single Link

The enterprise connects to two or more ISPs from a single router, but has a strict policy that only one ISP at a time will be used for default. In an OSPF environment, this would be done by advertising defaults to both ISPs, but with different Type 2 external metrics. The primary ISP would have the lower metric (see Figure 7.29). BGP is not necessary in this case.

Standard IS-IS could not do this because it strictly follows closest-exit routing. Extensions to IS-IS, which allow externals to be injected into level areas, will allow this.

This easily can be extended to multilink (see Figure 7.30).

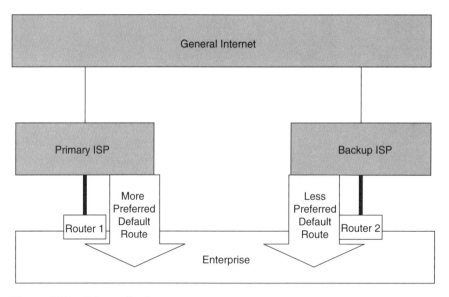

Figure 7.29   Primary/backup.

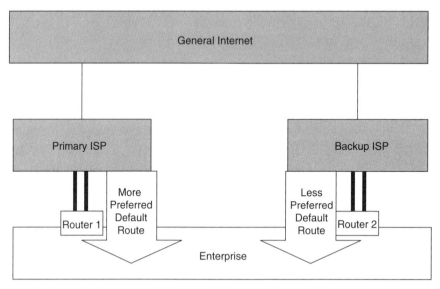

Figure 7.30   Primary/backup multilink.

Multihomed, Differing Internal Policies

I first encountered this problem when working with a large communications company that wished to consolidate its internal network. In most cases, this was a generally good idea, popular in part because it allowed shared use of DS-3 links to the Internet.

The research arm of this corporation, however, was among the pioneers of the Internet, and explained they would be more than happy to cooperate with the corporate network for reaching corporate destinations, but that their Internet access was not broken and they had no intention of "fixing" it. When offered a share in the high-speed access lines, they declined, commenting that they would continue to limp along on their OC-3 connectivity (see Figure 7.31).

In this example, assume OSPF interior routing, because OSPF can distinguish between type 1 and type 2 external metrics. The main default for the enterprise comes from one or more ASBRs in Area 0, all routing to the same ISP. One or more organizations brought into the corporate network have preexisting Internet access agreements with an ISP other

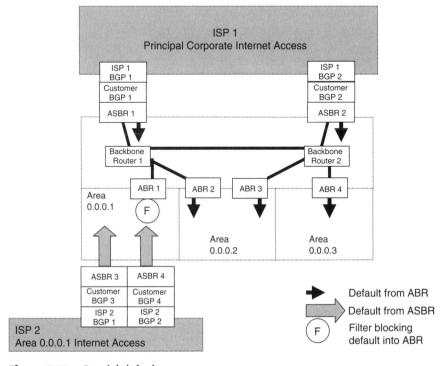

Figure 7.31   Special default.

than the corporate ISP, and wish to continue using this for their "divisional" Internet access.

In this situation, an additional ASBR(s) was placed in the OSPF areas associated with the special-case, and this ASBR advertises default. Filters at the Area Border Router block the divisional ASBR's default from being advertised into Area 0, and the corporate default from being advertised into the division. Note that these filters do not block OSPF LSAs, but instead block the local propagation of selected default and external routes into the Routing Information Base (i.e., main routing Table) of a specific router.

Multihomed, "Load Shared" with Primary/Backup

While there still is a primary/backup policy, there is an attempt to make active use of both the primary and backup providers. The enterprise runs BGP, but does not take full Internet routing. It takes partial routing from the backup provider, and prefers the backup provider path for destinations in the backup provider's AS, and perhaps directly connected to that AS. (Figure 7.32) For all other destinations, the primary provider is the preferred default. A less preferred default is defined to the second ISP, but this default is advertised generally only if connectivity is lost to the primary ISP.

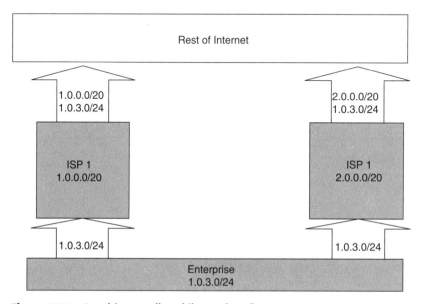

Figure 7.32 Reaching small multihomed prefixes.

Simply configuring this method does not guarantee global routability. Administrative coordination is even more complex than many basic situations where the enterprise has its own address space.

First, ISP1 needs to be willing to allow another AS to advertise a part of its address space. Second, ISP2 has to be willing to advertise it.

ISP1 also needs to advertise not just its aggregated block, but the more specific prefix that corresponds to the enterprise prefix. Otherwise, traffic destined for the enterprise will immediately go to ISP2, because ISP2 is advertising a more specific prefix than ISP1. ISP2, assuming its role is backup, also should prepend its AS number to the enterprise route advertisement.

Other ISPs may or may not propagate the enterprise route. If ISP3 had a policy of not propagating routes, other than the customers of ISP3, to its own neighbors, ISP4 would not learn about the route.

Finally, this may not appreciably reduce the amount of routing power needed in comparison with accepting full routes. I have accepted customer routes only from a tier 1 ISP, and still received 30,000+ routes.

Multihomed, Global Routing Aware

Multiple customer router receive a full routing table (Figure 7.33), and, using appropriate filtering and aggregation, advertise different

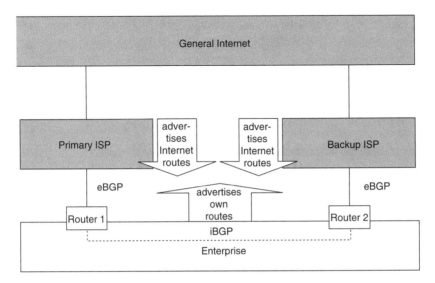

Figure 7.33 Full routing awareness.

destinations (i.e., not just default) internally. This requires BGP, and, unless dealing with a limited number of special cases, requires significantly more resources inside the enterprise if the enterprise runs its own BGP.

With one client of mine, who was connected to two tier 1 ISPs, there really was no benefit to considering one the primary and one the secondary.

Many providers will place a router at a customer site, and manage the ISP access router as a "black box." The enterprise uses an Ethernet connection to the access router, providing a clean demarcation point.

The provider may accept enterprise routes through redistribution, but that can be of limited value. If the provider, as it should, implements RFC 2827 ingress filtering, it will not accept route advertisements that are not expected from the enterprise. Since the provider needs administrative coordination before it knows that it should expect a certain prefix from the enterprise, the provider might as well use static routing.

Transit Multihoming

While we usually think of this in terms of ISPs, some enterprises may provide Internet connectivity to strategic partners. They do not offer Internet connectivity on a general basis.

Most plausible enterprises will have a relatively small, in ISP terms, number of eBGP speakers. Full mesh iBGP among the eBGP speakers is generally practical when there are no more than 20–30 eBGP speakers. Beyond that number, iBGP scalability methods are useful.

There are two methods for scaling iBGP, confederations and route reflectors. When ISPs deploy iBGP, they usually use route reflectors, which appear to scale better than confederations.

A large enterprise, however, may gain useful additional control by using confederations (see Figure 7.34). One of my consulting clients was an international transportation firm, with multiple sites in the US and regional data centers in Europe and Asia. There was significant traffic among all regions. This enterprise had complex routing policies in its backbone, and needed the controls of BGP.

If an Internet gateway failed, they wanted to prefer the U.S. gateways, even though there might be a closer path in Europe or Asia. Their ratio-

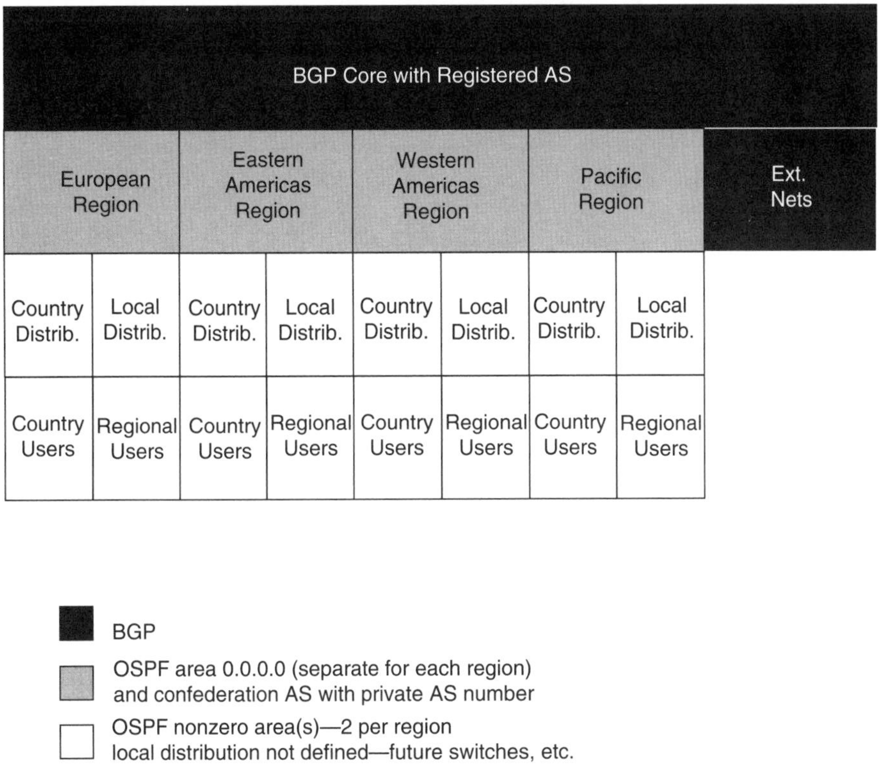

Figure 7.34 consists of a diagram showing the following labeled elements:

BGP Core with Registered AS								
European Region		Eastern Americas Region		Western Americas Region		Pacific Region		Ext. Nets
Country Distrib.	Local Distrib.	Country Distrib.	Local Distrib.	Country Distrib.	Local Distrib.	Country Distrib.	Local Distrib.	
Country Users	Regional Users	Country Users	Regional Users	Country Users	Regional Users	Country Users	Regional Users	

- ■ BGP
- ▣ OSPF area 0.0.0.0 (separate for each region) and confederation AS with private AS number
- □ OSPF nonzero area(s)—2 per region local distribution not defined—future switches, etc.

Figure 7.34   Intercontinental distribution using confederations.

nale was that Internet access bandwidth was cheaper in the United States, and they were already paying for transoceanic bandwidth.

Each continent had a single OSPF domain (i.e., with its own area 0.0.0.0). The OSPF domains each became a confederation-AS with a private AS number. BGP policies controlled inter-domain routing among the continents, as well as controlling access to the Internet.

BGP backbones, however, are not the solution for all problems. A different consulting client also had an intercontinental network, but traffic patterns different than the previous enterprise. Regions had substantial internal traffic, and communicated with the corporate headquarters. The limited traffic exchange among regions could reasonably be accomplished on the headquarters backbone.

The corporate data center and corporate site were treated as a separate domain that connected to the backbone, although they were at the same location. This was done to localize the substantial traffic inside the corporate site, and to simplify the backbone.

Alternate paths to corporate came from primary dedicated or frame relay links, with floating static routes for backup. This design will not be practical unless great care is taken to allocate addresses with a model based on regional aggregation (see Figure 7.35).

Data Link and Physical Layer Multihoming

Inverse multiplexing can go hand in hand with fault tolerance. The basic mechanism is multilink PPP, although LAP-B also supports multilinking.

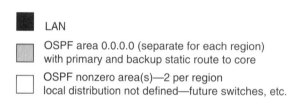

Headquarters Collapsed Backbone LAN				
European Region	Americas Region	Headquarters Region	Pacific Region	Ext. Nets
Country Distrib. / Local Distrib.	Country Distrib. / Local Distrib.	Local Distrib.	Country Distrib. / Local Distrib.	
Country Users / Regional Users	Country Users / Regional Users	HQ servers & users	Country Users / Regional Users	

■ LAN

▨ OSPF area 0.0.0.0 (separate for each region) with primary and backup static route to core

☐ OSPF nonzero area(s)—2 per region local distribution not defined—future switches, etc.

Figure 7.35   Intercontinental distribution using multiple static routes.

Multilink PPP and LAP-B

Multilink PPP (and LAP-B) do not only provide more bandwidth, but protect against media or interface failures. Assume you are combining two T1 lines to a service provider, for an aggregate of 3 Mbps. If one link failed, the aggregate speed would drop to 1.5 Mbps, but you would continue operating in a degraded mode.

Using multilink at the data link layer removes one problem of IP round-robin load balancing, out-of-order packet delivery. IP sees only a single link.

The separate media can go on different physical paths to avoid a single point of transmission failure. The downside of doing so is if the paths have significantly different latency, the longest delay path will impose its delay on each link. Frame reassembly will have to wait for the longest delay.

Multilink can impose a significant processing load on a router CPU, and it may be wise to offload this function into a coprocessor or external processor. Tiara Networks makes offload devices for the T1 to T3 speed range.

Transmission Considerations in Multihoming

"Multihoming" is not logically complete until all single points of failure are considered. With the current emphasis on routing and naming solutions, the lowly physical layer often is ignored, until a physical layer failure dooms a lovely and sophisticated routing system.

Physical layer diversity can involve significant cost and delay. Nevertheless, it should be considered for mission-critical connectivity.

Building Wiring

Never forget that problems in building wiring may prevent your traffic from ever reaching the WAN. From a typical server room, analog and digital signals physically flow to a wiring closet, where they join a riser cable. Depending on the specific building, the closet and riser may be the responsibility of the enterprise or ISP, the building management, or a telecommunications carrier.

Never Underestimate the Power of Human Stupidity

A good friend of mine was doing LAN upgrades at the Pentagon. In a particular set of Navy offices, she ran 10Base2 Ethernet in daisy chains of six offices. The segment began in the wiring closet, then to the first office, where there were two BNC connectors, IN and OUT. If no device were in the office, then these connectors were linked with a short loop cable. To support a device, we put in a T-connector between the IN and OUT ports.

At the end of the string in the last office, there was only one BNC connector. Again, if needed for a device in the office, we put in a T-connector, but we had to have a terminator either on the IN jack or the T-connector.

Unfortunately, the last office on one of the strings was occupied by a Navy commander. How shall I describe him? Dan Quayle without the intelligence is a first thought, but, independent of political views, Quayle is a nice guy. Rick Rockwell, perhaps.

Commander X was intensely concerned with being promoted to captain, and wanted to look good for his admiral boss. Somehow, he decided that the terminator on his wall jack didn't look "neat," and he kept removing it, bringing down the segment.

When the operations staff asked him about it, he refused to justify his actions. He simply said, "*I* am a commander! Do you know how important I am?" No one had the courage to answer properly—that in the Pentagon, a commander is important enough to get coffee for admirals.

Anyway, my friend asked me to come in and talk to the commander, in the guise of their Ultimate Consultant.

Meeting with His Commanderness, I started by saying, "I apologize for the team. They haven't been explaining this in a way that recognizes your intelligence." (I was REALLY saying they had been trying to explain they had been explaining things to him as if he were an intelligent human being, rather than a bureaucratic moron.)

"When the techs showed you the problem with the terminator, they drew a picture of the wiring from above" (Figure 7.36).

"That wasn't the right picture for you. You need to see it from the side (Figure 7.37).

"You see how the cable slopes downward to the jack? That's important. I know you want to look good to the Admiral. Did you know he's a reformed smoker? The kind that REALLY HATES smoking, which he's banned? You wouldn't want to irritate him by having him think you are smoking in your nonsmoking office, would you?" He agreed this would be most undesirable.

"Well," I explained, "the terminator is like a cork at the end of a bottle that's tilted down from the ceiling. If you take the terminator off the jack, the bits roll down the cable and out. *Continues*

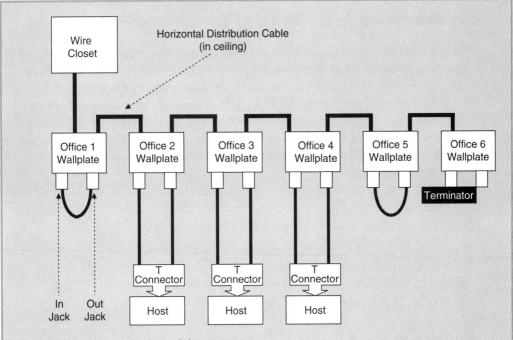

Figure 7.36 Top view of the Navy LAN.

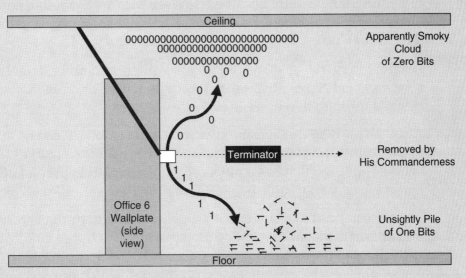

Figure 7.37 Side view of the Navy LAN.

Never Underestimate the Power of Human Stupidity *(Continued)*

"Now, there are two kinds of bits, zero bits and one bits. One bits aren't your problem. One bits are heavier than air, and fall to the floor. If the admiral sees a pile of one bits, he'll just blame the janitor for not sweeping properly.

"Zero bits, however, are lighter than air. They float upward and cling to the ceiling tiles. Once you have enough bits, which isn't hard at 10 million per second, the cloud of zero bits looks just like cigarette smoke. What would the admiral say?"

The commander thanked me profusely, and we never had another problem with the terminator.

The riser cable joins with other riser cables in a cable vault, from which a cable leaves the building and goes to the end switching office of the local telecommunications provider.

Local Loop

Most buildings have a single cable vault, possibly with multiple cables following a single physical route—the *local loop*—back to the end office. A single error by construction excavators can cut multiple cables on a single path. Local wireless services are becoming an increasingly cost-effective solution when there are no existing routes to the CO (or COs).

A failure in carrier systems can isolate a single end office. Highly robust systems have physical connectivity to two or more POPs reached through two or more end offices.

Alternatives here can become creative. On a campus, it can be feasible to use some type of existing ductwork to run additional cables to another building that has a physically diverse path to the end office. Direct burial, aerial cable between buildings, etc., are all possible.

In a noncampus environment, it is possible, in many urban areas, to find alternate means of running physical media to other buildings with alternate paths to end offices. Electrical power utilities may have empty ducts that they will lease, and through which privately owned fiber can be run.

Provider Core

To the North American Network Operators Group (NANOG), 1997 was known as "The Year of the Backhoe."

As demonstrated by a rash of fiber cuts in early 1997, carriers lease bandwidth from one another, so a cut to one carrier-owned facility may affect connectivity in several carriers. This reality makes some traditional diverse media strategies questionable. Chapter 6, "Carrier Infrastructure and Optical Networking," discusses current fault-tolerance methods used internally by carriers.

Many organizations consciously obtain WAN connectivity from multiple carriers, with the notion that a failure in one carrier will not affect another. This is not a valid assumption.

If the goal is to obtain diversity/resiliency among WAN circuits, it may be best to deal with a single service provider. The contract with this provider should require physical diversity among facilities, so the provider's engineering staff will be aware of requirements not to put multiple circuits into the same physical facility, owned by the carrier or leased from other carriers.

Looking Ahead

One of the major motivations for the VPN market is allowing enterprises, for which network operations are not their core competency, to outsource network operations. Chapter 8 deals with defining and using VPNs.

There's an old saying, "once is an accident, twice is coincidence, and thrice is enemy action." In this chapter, we dealt with tolerating faults due to accidents and disasters. Chapter 8 deals with defending against deliberate attacks. It also deals with the security aspects of VPNs, and with mobile network access.

8

VPNs, Security, and Roaming

What is to be done?

V.I. LENIN

On a boat, safety features include fire extinguishers and life jackets. While both are appropriate for their intended tasks, it would be unfortunate if one depended on a fire extinguisher for flotation, or used a plastic life jacket to snuff a gasoline fire. In like manner, different security features complement one another in networks.

HOWARD C. BERKOWITZ

The right of the people to be secure in their persons, houses, papers, and effects, against unreasonable searches and seizures, shall not be violated . . .

AMENDMENT IV TO THE CONSTITUTION OF THE UNITED STATES

Why does anyone want a VPN? I suggest that costs drive most requirements. For end users, there often will be savings in bandwidth and connection costs, but also there can be significant savings in personnel. Carriers offer VPN services to end users because there is a market for it, but also use VPNs to lower their internal operational costs.

But What Is a VPN?

Market and technical issues have combined to make the idea of a VPN apply to almost any technical concept. It is significant that the IETF was unable even to agree on a work scope sufficient to start a VPN working group. The IETF VPN BOF, in which I participated, terminated at the Orlando meeting in December 1998. A new BOF met in Pittsburgh in August 2000, and a network-oriented VPN working group may form.

Paul Ferguson and Geoff Huston wrote one of the first definitions of VPN: "A VPN is a private network constructed within a public network infrastructure, such as the global Internet." Informational RFC 2764 defines a VPN as "emulation of a private Wide Area Network

(WAN) facility using IP facilities (including the public Internet, or private IP backbones)."

There are many vendor-specific interpretations of VPN. It is not meant as a criticism that vendors tend to emphasize their core competence in their definition of VPNs. Those concerned with packet transport tend to emphasize the networking aspects:

- 3Com White Paper: "A VPN is a connection that has the appearance and many of the advantages of a dedicated link but occurs over a shared network."

- Ascend (now part of Lucent) describes VPNs as potentially meeting one of three architectures:

    - Virtual private remote networking (VPRN) with tunneling for remote LAN access.

    - Virtual private trunking (VPT) to establish the equivalent of leased lines among major facilities.

    - Virtual IP routing (VIPR) to internetwork branch offices or establish extranets with closed user groups.

- Cisco's VPN seminar in the Cisco University series calls it: Customer connectivity deployed on a shared infrastructure with the same policies as a private network.

- In contrast, vendors in the security business often emphasize the security features:

    - Infonetics. "VPNs use public networks to extend the reach of the enterprise network to remote sites, individual remote workers, and business partners."

    - V-One. "The security technology that will enable companies to leverage the Internet as private enterprise backbone infrastructure."

Personally, the only way I have been able to make sense of the chaos of VPNs is to separate the issues of requirements and implementation technology. User requirements include both a minimal set of core requirements, and an assortment of optional capabilities. VPNs with only the core requirements tend to be uninteresting and not extremely useful. Almost any VPN will need some of the optional capabilities, but the set needed by any arbitrary enterprise needs to be defined for that specific enterprise.

Table 8.1 Broad Classifications of VPN

ENDPOINT	OPERATOR	
	ENTERPRISE	**CARRIER**
Host	Virtual access service	Closed user group
Site	Virtual transport service	Virtual private line

The using organization has to define its expectations of the VPN. One fairly basic distinction is the planned operator: enterprises or carriers. Another basic expectation is the type of endpoints that will be interconnected (see Table 8.1).

An Introduction to VPNs

VPNs are an elusive concept. In many years in the industry, I've sadly learned that salespeople occasionally sell products that do not actually exist. But if VPNs existed, wouldn't they be real? Is a VPN the ultimate product for the sort of salesperson who answers technical questions with "let's do lunch?"

Before trying to reach any sort of general definition of a VPN, let's consider some attributes generally associated with them:

- They are WAN-oriented.
- They use some form of shared transport mechanism—the PSTN, the Internet, or bandwidth (as opposed to specific circuits) leased from a carrier.
- They may be more controllable than the public Internet, if some provider has responsibility for making them more controllable than the public Internet.
- There are multiple VPN technologies for different purposes. One size does not fit all.
- Specific technologies, however, increasingly are associated with particular classes of application.
- Many discussions of VPNs make the assumption that they are IP-oriented and carry packets. Frame and ATM services may challenge this assumption.

- Security is usually part of a VPN, most likely in those that have end-user hosts among their endpoints. Security can deal with access authentication, data integrity, and/or data confidentiality.

- VPNs can overlap; a host or site can belong to several VPNs.

- The justification for going to VPN service is almost always principally driven by a desire for cost reduction.

To meet a given set of user requirements, the designer needs to specify who belongs to the VPN, how the VPN is mapped on to the underlying transport, and the characteristics of the transport.

Core Requirements for This *Particular* VPN?

First, who are to be its members? In other words, what does it connect? Individual users to servers? Sites to sites? This is the *membership* problem.

Second, who has operational responsibility for the VPN? The enterprise? A service provider? Some mixture of the two?

Third, what is the economic justification for the VPN?

Membership

Before a member of a VPN can have traffic routed to it, it must be defined as part of the VPN. Such definition can be static configuration, or negotiated dynamically. The definition can be at the level of a user, an address, or a site.

Early in the process, list fixed servers and sites that will belong to the VPN. Estimate how many computers will attach to it. Provisioning a VPN that can have 10,000 dynamic members is different from provisioning a VPN with 100 dynamic members.

The first question of access is, "what is accessing the VPN?" The VPN may see the smallest unit of access as an individual user machine, a specific LAN, or as a site with routers and multiple media. An individual host or physical site can be a member of more than one VPN, and may also be able to access a real corporate intranet and the Internet. Access policies need to be determined very early in the process, and interact tightly with your security policy.

The second question of access is, "how does the VPN know an access attempt is valid?" When the VPN is aware of individual users, one approach to defining membership, without preconfiguration, is to assume that any user who can connect through security mechanisms at an access point is a legitimate member. For site-oriented VPNs that use encryption, if a new site or router can authenticate itself with a certificate, it can be assumed to be part of the membership.

Operational Policy

To ask the fundamental question of operational policy, think of the theme song from the movie *Ghostbusters*: "Who ya gonna call?" If you do not define clearly who has responsibility for adding hosts and sites to the VPN, troubleshooting the VPN and applications on it, and doing continuing capacity planning, your VPN will be haunted by evil spirits.

Operational responsibilities can be assigned to the enterprise, service provider(s), or consultants. The provider may place equipment under its control at the customer sites, or the VPN boundary may start at a provider POP. Those VPNs accessed through the PSTN use equipment in the PSTN, and at the POPs connected to the PSTN or that are linked to the VPN provider through roaming services.

When key operational functions are outsourced, it can become rather confusing to decide where to call for support. In a VPN, tunneling can make it impossible for one support center to do end-to-end troubleshooting.

Several operational issues apply in VPN deployment: whether the enterprise is responsible for any customer premises equipment (CPE) that intelligently interoperates with components of the shared provider infrastructure, whether a service provider is contracted to operate the WAN infrastructure, and how any VPN client software in user hosts is managed and operated. Some organizations consider a VPN using all dial facilities, or other public facilities operated by a service provider that is not aware of the VPN, to have a customer-operated shared infrastructure.

A service provider may place service-provider-operated equipment at a customer site, and present a LAN or serial interface to the customer. Anything beyond the provider device is contractually a provider responsibility, but it cannot be directly controlled by the customer.

Another aspect of the model is whether clients are aware of the VPN, and if provider access components are aware of it. In principle, a client could attach to a generic ISP, establish an encrypted tunnel to a destination host, and operate transparently to the ISP. The VPN provider may be the ISP. In such cases, the VPN provider responsibility is to provide logins and connectivity. The login might specify a class of service to be used in the provider network.

Trust/Security Policy

Never build networks without first deciding on a security policy. A security policy is *not* a technical document, but should be a one- to two-page document approved by top management. The security policy both reflects requirements and provides a framework for legal enforcement.

The fundamental elements of a security policy are:

- Who is authorized to use resources?
- If there are different classes of users—and there should be—who should be trusted to do what?
- What action will be taken if there is unauthorized use?

Very close to the policy are the domains of trust. Is the service provider trusted? The end user? Sites? Figure 8.1 shows the trust relationships used in IPsec.

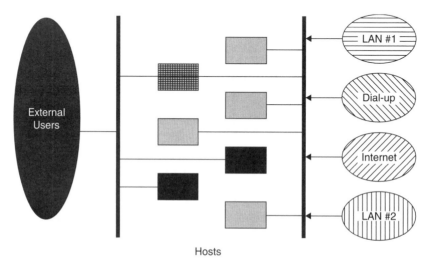

Hosts

Figure 8.1   Representative trust.

Things become even more complex when a VPN connects to other enterprises or the general Internet. I find it a useful technique to draw a matrix of user types and resources, and black out the cells where no access is permitted (see Table 8.2).

Later in the design process, I will assign specific security mechanisms to the cells where access is permitted.

Addressing, Weeds, and Naming

VPNs most commonly use private addressing. When Internet connectivity is needed, the firewall has both inside and outside addresses.

Addressing becomes more complex with extranets. It may be desirable to use registered addresses, perhaps with the restriction that they do not need global Internet routability. Address registries may be somewhat relaxed in their assignment rules when the requesting organization makes it clear that it does not expect global routability, and is willing to renumber if global routability becomes a need.

When pointy-haired bosses demand the instantaneous interconnection of several enterprises' intranets, crying, "Ready! Fire! Aim!" it is entirely common to find that the intranets all use the RFC1918 private address space and some of the addresses overlap. Routing with overlapping addresses, if I remember correctly, was in the Fifth or Sixth Circles of Dante's nine-ringed Hell.

See the discussion of "Double NAT and Twice NAT" in Chapter 5, "Virtualizing in Modern Networks," for methods of resolving

Table 8.2   Trust and Enforcement

RESOURCE TYPE	USER TYPE			
	ADMINISTRATOR	CLEARED STAFF	CONTRACTOR	PUBLIC
Infrastructure				
Data entry				
Research Files				
Public database				

overlapping address space. You do not need an intranet to have over-lapping addresses. Human error can cause it, and, mergers and acqui-sitions are the most fertile possible soil for the seeds of address confusion.

I enjoy my garden, in which I specialize in growing herbs and vegeta-bles. A few years ago, I planted Mexican marigolds. They have a fasci-nating citrusy flavor, but they also have some drawbacks. I could live with what I thought were small plants turning into six-foot bamboo-like stalks. I certainly had no problem with their small and fragrant flowers.

My problem is that Mexican marigolds are sex-mad plants, scattering their seeds everywhere. The general definition of a weed is a plant in the wrong place, rather than an inherently evil plant. Just as the right sort of "tough love" can straighten a wayward teenager, transplanting can turn a weed into a valued citizen.

Avoid cultivating fields of IP address weeds. Be extremely careful when interconnecting separate addressing domains. It may be quite useful, even when the two domains are fully trusted parts of the same enterprise, to initially link them with a firewall to help detect possible incompatibilities. When you understand the protocols, you may be able to get better, cheaper performance by replacing a full firewall with an address-translating router.

We will return to firewalls in more detail, but it is worth looking now at the idea of *split DNS*. As shown in Figure 8.3, a split DNS actually contains two primary servers, one for the "inside" address space and one for the "outside" space.

Optional Requirements for VPNs

VPNs of practical use will have one or more optional capabilities in addition to the core set. Not all VPNs will need every capability. Depending on the pundit to whom you are speaking, the Utterly Essen-tial Characteristics of VPNs fall into the matrix shown in Table 8.3.

Vendors defining products can prepare feature checklists against this section, with the perhaps idealistic hope that not all features are appropriate for every product, and that sheer number of features does not make one product better than another.

Table 8.3   Utterly Essential VPN Characteristics

PUNDIT IS SECURITY BIGOT	PUNDIT IS QOS BIGOT	
	YES	NO
Yes	VPN MUST have security and QoS.	VPN MUST have security.
No	VPN MUST have QoS.	VPNs can have anything they want.

Addressing and Naming

Having addresses is not optional. *Managing* and *assigning* addresses is an optional capability of a VPN service. The VPN may provide address assignment, presumably with DHCP or proxies used with IPCP or L2TP.

It also may provide network address translation (NAT), network address and port translation (NAPT), and load-shared network address translation (LSNAT). When providers support multiple VPNs, and/or the VPN must participate in end-to-end security, realm-specific IP (RSIP) may be a viable alternative to more traditional NAT. When defining VPN requirements, identify upper-layer protocols whose use is expected, and evaluate each to see if there is sensitivity to address manipulation mechanisms used in the VPN. Do not limit these evaluations to pure application protocols, but also consider tunnels internal to the VPN (e.g., for carrying non-IP protocols), security protocols, and special transports such as RTP.

In Chapter 5, we dealt with many means of address and name virtualization. Let's consider some applications with VPNs. Figure 8.2 shows a multisite corporate network where the real servers use private address space, but the virtual servers are on the public Internet.

This is a very real-world situation, although the terminology might get a little strange. If you think of the public Internet as "real" and the intranet as "virtual," then, in this example, the real servers are on the virtual network, and the virtual servers are on the real network.

DNS services may be associated with the VPN, and operated by the enterprise or the service provider. When the VPN provides dynamic addressing, the dynamic address server (DHCP, IPCP, etc.) should dynamically update the DNS zone seen by the members of the VPN.

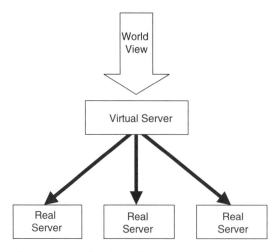

Figure 8.2 What is real?

When the VPN translates addresses or makes use of a firewall, it is likely to need split DNS. Split DNS requires two DNS servers, one on the "outside" and one on the "inside." The outside server contains the addresses of public servers on the "outside." It also contains the names of inside servers that can be accessed from the outside, but resolves these names to the outside interface of the gateway. The inside DNS has names and addresses of inside machines, but will resolve external names to the inside address of the gateway (see Figure 8.3).

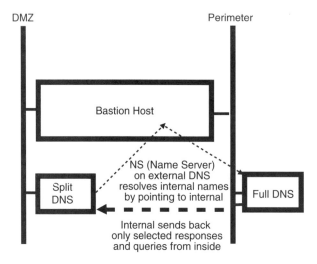

Figure 8.3 Split DNS for an environment with private and public address space.

While VPNs can appear as a single IP prefix (i.e., a single subnet), single prefixes will not scale to large size. The provider may set up multiple prefixes to serve user connectivity requirements. If there are multiple prefixes, it needs to be specified if routing among them is an enterprise or provider responsibility.

The IP VPN, as seen by end users, may support broadcast or multicast addressing. Multicast addresses should be assigned in conformity with the Multicast Allocation framework [Handley].

Tunnels Have Tolls

There may be requirements to deliver frames or packets in sequence. In addition, there may be a requirement to support, efficiently, larger MTUs that the provider might normally handle.

In particular, if IP fragmentation is to be avoided when the infrastructure has an MTU that is less than the length of a full payload packet plus tunnel and delivery header, manual MTU limitations on end hosts, or dynamic MTU path discovery, need to be used.

Security

Some VPN pundits say that VPNs are not useful unless they provide security services. Other VPN pundits say exactly the same thing about QoS. Reality is somewhat different. VPNs that go through the public Internet, and possibly those that are accessed through the PSTN, generally need security features for user traffic.

VPNs that are internal to carriers, and accessed only through dedicated physical facilities, do not have nearly as strong a need for user data security. It is not unreasonable to reassure people that they have not been demanding encryption for FR and ATM services, although these services do run through shared infrastructure inside the provider. Such VPNs do need to have security protections for their infrastructure. A reasonable clarification is that encryption is a service provided by access, not core VPNs.

User connectivity may be defined to include security using a variety of security mechanisms, including IPsec, L2TP, etc. These various mechanisms may provide other services, such as connectivity. L2TP can provide per-user authentication, or may have no security functions. Security may be requested on a discretionary basis by end-user hosts, or the VPN may enforce a mandatory security policy. Cryptographic protections may be under the control of the enterprise, using host-to-host or host-to-security gateway methods, or the infrastructure may be trusted to provide encryption. The responsibilities for user authentication, device authentication, encryption, logging, and audit must be specified as part of the design of any practical VPN.

Clear distinctions must be made for the responsibility and positioning of security mechanisms. Some security mechanisms, such as IPsec transport mode, are host-oriented and will normally be transparent to VPN providers. In particular situations, the maintenance of such mechanisms might be outsourced to the provider organization, but such maintenance will often require a different skill set (i.e., host and LAN operating system administration) than general VPN support. The user organization has final responsibility for the legal and management aspects of the security policy. In some cases, the policy may preclude outsourcing certain security functions, in that outside organizations are not trusted to manage these functions.

When the VPN provider is responsible for security functions, there still needs to be a distinction between edge and core requirements and functions. It will be quite common for providers to implement dial-up and other end-user access control mechanisms, and the provider might also furnish security services for sites and servers (e.g., IPsec tunnels among firewalls).

"Traditional" services such as frame relay, ATM, etc., rarely encrypt within the carrier's core network. Many security studies have suggested that the inherent difficulty of accessing and intruding into carrier layer 2 networks and private IP networks is a sufficient deterrent to casual intruders. The additional overhead of adding encryption to a physically protected optical network may overprice the service without a real improvement in security.

Availability and Quality of Service

When a network is down, its quality of service, by definition, is unacceptable. The enterprise may specify availability requirements for the infrastructure and for VPN gateway services. The implementer of the VPN needs to translate these user requirements into requirements for underlying fault-tolerance mechanisms.

The VPN may provide quality of service support. It either may accept QoS requests from end users signaled with RSVP, IP precedence bits, etc., or may internally assign quality of service requirements to be mapped to the transmission infrastructure. For quality of service to be effective, the infrastructure either must support explicit quality of service requests, or there must be a high level of confidence that the infrastructure consistently provides adequate QoS. Assumptions about QoS need to be stated as part of any VPN design.

I am agnostic about QoS requirements for VPNs. If there are QoS-critical applications, such as multimedia or voice, that will run over the VPN, specific QoS engineering is necessary. If the VPN handles important transaction traffic, provisioning adequate resources may be enough. Other VPNs simply need connectivity, possibly secure connectivity, but rigid QoS is simply not a strong requirement.

Requirements for QoS will restrict the transports that can be used for your VPN. VPNs based on the public Internet, and to some extent those based on the PSTN, inherit the unreliable QoS properties of their transports.

Ironically, I have found that many customers who are most emphatic about network performance and availability have no idea of the utilization and performance of their servers. A VPN is only part of an overall service, and the entire service needs to be considered.

Non-IP Protocol Support

While the emphasis of this taxonomy is on VPNs that support IP, the VPN may provide mechanisms for encapsulating non-IP protocols for transmission over an IP infrastructure. Techniques for doing so include NetBIOS over TCP [RFC1001/1002], IPX over IP [RFC1234], GRE [RFC1702], etc.

Security Requirements and Services

In Chapter 7, "Fault Tolerance," we discussed planning and budgeting for fault tolerance. I have found it quite useful to group together "faults" and "security incidents," because they both really deal with the same problem: ensuring that legitimate users can use the resources they need. Protecting against denial-of-service attacks, while usually considered a security measure, is just as much a fault-tolerance mechanism as a security mechanism. Fault-tolerant design and network management tools help protect against service failures due to errors and disasters. Additional security services deal with an additional problem: that unauthorized users do not have access to services or data.

- **Disclosure of information** *Confidentiality* mechanisms protect against this threat.

- **Unauthorized resource use** *Access authentication* and *access control* help here.

- **Alteration/replay/duplication of information** *Unitary integrity* protects against changes of single records, while *sequential integrity* protects against insertion or deletion of records in a sequence.

I find it useful to begin my security planning not so much with threats, but in a more positive manner, considering the characteristics of security success. Dennis Branstad created the excellent 5-S mnemonic for potential aspects of a secure communication. Not every application will require every aspect of the checklist:

- **Sealed** to protect against unauthorized modification. Unitary integrity mechanisms seal messages.

- **Sequenced** to protect against unauthorized loss or modification. *Sequential integrity* mechanisms ensure the sequencing of records is not altered.

- **Secret** so it cannot be disclosed without authorization. *Confidentiality* mechanisms protect the information from unauthorized eyes.

- **Signed** to assure the correct identity of its sender. *Authentication* and *digital signature* mechanisms verify the sender is who she or he claims to be, and that the sender attests to the authenticity of the information.

- **Stamped** to protect against delivery to an incorrect recipient. *Receiver authentication* mechanisms verify the receiver, and *nonrepudiation* mechanisms certify receipt.

Security Mechanisms

In an ultimately secure system, there is no privacy from the security administrator. Every user of a resource must be identifiable, and every activity of the users must be auditable.

In a practical system, auditability may not equate to tracking every event, but may be limited to significant actions or random samples. Privacy also is a consideration. It may be appropriate, for example, to know that a given user logged in, but not what information the user read or wrote.

Specific security mechanisms need to be applied to user/resource pairs. Selecting the mechanisms is always a delicate balance. A rule of thumb for security is that the more secure a resource, the more inconvenient it is to use (see Table 8.4).

Many security mechanisms are based on encryption, which can reliably authenticate hosts and users, and allow private communications hidden from unauthorized eyes. Encryption goes back into early human history, long before electronic communications.

Table 8.4 Security Mechanisms for User/Resource Pairs

| RESOURCE TYPE | USER TYPE | | | |
	ADMINISTRATOR	CLEARED STAFF	CONTRACTOR	PUBLIC
Infrastructure	Biometric ID RADIUS Internal access only			
Data entry	Biometric ID RADIUS 3DES	Password Internal access only		
Research Files	Biometric ID RADIUS 3DES	Password RADIUS 3DES	Password RADIUS 3DES	
Public database	Biometric ID RADIUS 3DES	Password RADIUS 3DES	Password RADIUS 3DES	Denial-of-service protection

Encryption Principles

An early example of encryption was described by the classic Greek historian, Herodotus. Histiaeus, a Greek revolutionary at the Persian court, wanted to send a secret message encouraging revolt to his son-in-law, Aristagoras. Histiaeus shaved the head of a slave, tattooed the message onto the slave's scalp, waited for the hair to regrow, and sent the slave to Aristagoras, carrying a message asking Aristagoras to shave his head.

In modern terms, the message that Histiaeus wanted to send is called *plaintext* or *cleartext*. Plaintext is mixed with a *key* by an *encryption algorithm* to produce *ciphertext*. In principle, ciphertext is unintelligible to any recipient not in possession of an appropriate *decryption algorithm* and *decryption key*. In this case, the slave's hair was the key. The *ciphertext* was the combination of hair, scalp, and message.

Hair, Steganography, and Covert Channels

Technically, Histiaeus' means of secret communication was not true encryption, but concealment of a message. Secret inks and microfilm dots are classic concealment methods, beloved of spy thriller authors. The proper term for concealment of a cleartext message is *steganography*.

Secret inks, of course, have little relevance to networks. There is a modern equivalent, the *covert channel*. Covert channels are quite advanced and not a serious threat to any other than the highest-security networks, but they are a way to secretly slip information out of protected systems.

Covert channels assign meaning to things that normally have no meaning. For example, the time between successive packets of a flow is normally fairly random. A covert channel that had access to the packet driver might delay packets by controlled amounts, with the delays corresponding to information units. One unit of delay could represent a "one," two units of delay could represent a "two," and so forth. Such a covert channel can only transfer very limited amounts of information.

A *cryptosystem* combines algorithm(s) for encryption and decryption, a set of keys, administrative mechanisms for distributing keys, and a device that applies the algorithm(s). There are two basic approaches to the combination of algorithms and keying: *symmetrical* and *asymmetrical*.

Encryption and Keys

In symmetrical cryptography, also called *shared secret*, the same key is used for both encryption and decryption. Asymmetrical cryptography uses different keys for encryption and decryption. Asymmetrical cryptography is often called *public key*.

Symmetrical Cryptography and Key Distribution

Symmetrical cryptography is much less computationally intensive than asymmetrical cryptography, so asymmetrical methods often are used to set up a shared-secret *session key* used for bulk data transfer. Symmetrical cryptography, however, is administratively more complex than asymmetrical cryptography, because all parties to a communication must receive a key before they can exchange information.

Cryptographic systems need keys. Since the security of a cryptosystem is, above all else, in its keys, not its algorithm, there must be a secure means of key distribution. Historically, key distribution has often been the most expensive part of managing a symmetric cryptosystem. For high-security systems, keys were distributed by armed couriers. Registered mail might serve for lower-security systems. In well-designed systems that used keys printed on paper, there are quite a number of guidelines for preventing disclosures [Smith].

Electronic key distribution offers obvious advantages, in scalability and speed, over physical key distribution. Electronic key distribution lessens the chance of losing physical keying material. If the electronic key distribution mechanism is compromised, however, the encryption system can be broken at the speed of light.

Key distribution centers (KDC) are the basis of electronic key distribution in symmetric cryptography. Each encryption device has a preshared *key exchange key* (KEK) used only to exchange session keys. Obviously, the KEK is the "family jewel," and needs maximum protection. There also needs to be a way to change the KEK if it is compromised.

The U.S. financial industry uses DES encryption with electronic key distribution according to the ANSI X9.17 standard.

Kerberos is a well-known means of authentication, access control, and key distribution, using symmetric cryptography. Microsoft NT 5 will use Kerberos as a major means of key distribution, so Kerberos will become even better known.

Asymmetrical Cryptography and Certificate Authorities

Asymmetrical cryptography actually has two kinds of keys, an *encryption key* and a *decryption key*. There is a mathematical relationship between the two keys, a relationship that is extremely difficult to reverse-engineer.

Depending on the application of asymmetrical cryptography, the encryption key may be *public* or *private*. When the encryption key is public, the decryption key is private, and vice versa.

WARNING

Never completely trust a source address received from the public Internet, unless the packet header is cryptographically authenticated, or at least some of the payload is cryptographically authenticated.

Never accept a source address associated with one of your internal networks, even if that network is registered, if you receive it from the public network.

Never buy a car from used car dealerships with "Honest" in their names.

Encryption can provide authentication and confidentiality. Authentication can deal with identifying the participants to a communication, as well as packet-level authentication that provides sequential integrity (see Table 8.5).

Digital signatures verify the sender's identity. They are most flexible with asymmetric cryptography, because the receiver does not need to prenegotiate information. The sender encrypts a well-known identifier (e.g., "Howard Berkowitz") with the sender's private key. If a receiver can retrieve the public information using the sender's public key, the sender's identity is validated.

Table 8.5 Algorithms and Services

	AUTHENTICATION	CONFIDENTIALITY
Symmetric	Well-known information encrypted and decrypted with shared secret	Private information encrypted and decrypted with shared secret
Asymmetric	Well-known information encrypted with private key and decrypted with public key	Private information encrypted with public key and decrypted with private key

Authenticating the Participants

At the start of any communications that are purported to be secure, the parties to the communications need to confirm their identities, and receive permissions based on their identity. Realistic authentication systems use *two-factor authentication*.

The two factors of authentication are:

- Who you purport to be—a user identifier
- Something verifiable you have

The verifiable "something" can be something you know, such as a password. It can be your physical location. It can be a handheld security device such as a smart card. It can be a *biometric* characteristic such as a fingerprint, the relative lengths of your fingers, your signature, etc.

Biometrics: No Longer Science Fiction

Biometric authentication techniques are becoming cost-effective. The specific technique, however, will depend on the application.

Fingerprint identifiers for individual workstations have dropped remarkably in cost and improved in reliability. To use them, one inserts one's finger in the scanner, which also has heat detectors to sense that it is a living finger rather than a rubber impression or something even more distasteful. I prefer not to go more deeply, however, into the symbolism of giving one's finger to one's computer.

Other techniques, such as hand geometry, are more appropriate for situations where many people need to be identified quickly. One U.S. intelligence agency tried to use fingerprint scanning to verify access through the main entrance, but lines backed up into the courtyard until they turned to hand geometry units.

Not all identification techniques prove practical. One early method, perhaps conceived under the influence of controlled substances, was based on the old fortune-telling technique of phrenology: seeking meaning in the bumps on one's head. Each workstation was equipped with a helmet something like a beauty-shop hair dryer, lined with rods that gently pressed on the head and sensed its contours.

Aside from complaints that the device destroyed hairdos, it might have worked . . . if it hadn't been improved. In an early example of intrusion detection and active response (see below), if the user did not enter the appropriate login after several attempts, a locking bar would snap out under the user's chin, restraining the user *in* the workstation.

Continues

Biometrics: No Longer Science Fiction *(Continued)*

Unfortunately, the first major trial of the device was in a data entry department, with approximately 200 operators. The users, following instructions, inserted their heads into their workstations.

By Murphy's First Law, the power chose to fail immediately after the mass insertion. By Murphy's Second Law, the designer of the locking bar had not designed it as fail-safe under power loss. The spring-loaded bar was held in the noncapture position as long as electrical power was applied to its solenoid.

Words may not exist to describe the reaction of the field service engineer who responded to 200 operators stuck in their security equipment. Remember this tale when implementing active countermeasures to intrusion.

Once the user is validated, either an address can be allocated with IPCP, or the process can go to a second stage of more precise validation with RADIUS or DHCP.

RADIUS and TACACS

Two major protocol families are used to communicate between the NAS and authentication servers: RADIUS and TACACS. RADIUS is an IETF standards track protocol, introduced by Livingston (now part of Lucent). TACACS begin with an informal protocol first documented by Cisco, which has evolved into the proprietary TACACS+ protocol. The original TACACS is obsolete.

Many RADIUS implementations have proprietary extensions, so do not automatically assume that two arbitrary RADIUS implementations will interoperate. They may or may not, and either you must get test results from the vendors or test interoperability yourself. Ironically, two TACACS+ implementations, running off the same licensed specification, may have a higher probability of interoperability.

RADIUS or TACACS+ servers typically can verify reusable passwords and passwords (e.g., S/Key), but need to use other server types to validate hardware-generated (e.g., password, such as Security Dynamics' ACE server for SecurID) or biometric passwords.

RADIUS and TACACS are not the only protocols involved in authentication and credentialing, only the protocols used for access authorization. They may be implemented on access servers, or on hosts such as the telnet port of a router.

There are other roles for authentication. A client may want to authenticate that it is connecting to a real server. Encryption devices need to verify their partner's identity.

RADIUS and TACACS+ can provide a superset of PPP address assignment. While IPCP can assign or confirm an IP address, it does not send such things as the subnet mask, MTU, compression, or filters. RADIUS and TACACS+ can.

PPP, IPCP, CHAP, and PAP

The IP control protocol (IPCP) negotiates IP addresses to be used for a given connection to a PPP *remote access server* (RAS). IPCP packets have a client address field into which the client either places an address it proposes, or the value 0.0.0.0 to indicate it wishes the RAS to assign an address for this particular connection.

As part of the PPP connection negotiation, the RAS can authenticate the requesting user's ID with one of two protocols, CHAP and PAP. PAP is obsolete. CHAP sends a random challenge string to the requesting client, which the client encrypts and sends back to the RAS, along with user identification information. If the RAS correctly decrypts the encrypted challenge, the connection is permitted. The RAS may act as a proxy to a RADIUS or TACACS server (see Figure 8.4).

Roaming and Mobility

Having read this far, you will know, by now, that my mantra is "What is the problem you are trying to solve?" The broad topic of *mobility* is still emerging, but offers opportunities for terminology confusion on a par with VPN and switch. Let's look at the spectrum of possibilities (see Figure 8.5).

If a mobile user is any that is not at a fixed location, then the simplest case of mobility is a user dialing into a network access server function. The ubiquity of the PSTN enables this sort of mobility. Even within this simple category, there are several modes of operation:

- Simple terminal applications such as credit card authorization, which do not have general IP capability.

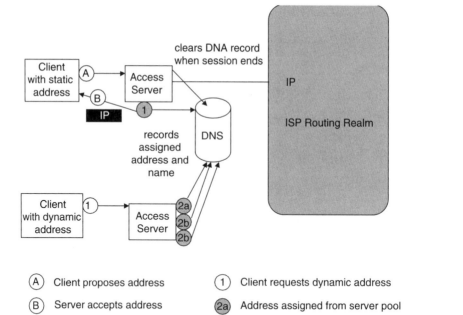

A — Client proposes address

B — Server accepts address

1 — Client requests dynamic address

2a — Address assigned from server pool

2b — Address assigned from AAA server

2b — Address assigned from AAA server proxying DHCP

Figure 8.4 How PPP clients get their address.

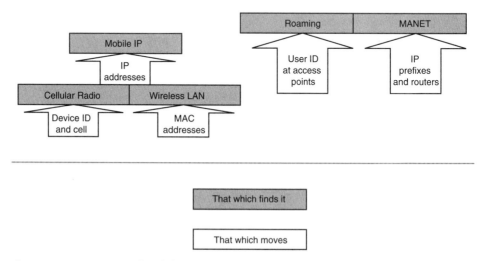

Figure 8.5 Spectrum of mobility.

- Remote access to workstations, as with PC/Anywhere or Timbuktu. The user appears at the IP address of the workstation.
- Entry into the full enterprise network as an IP host with a dynamically assigned address.

The key to this simple mobility is the user's ability to authenticate herself or himself as a valid user. The simple case assumes that the user is dialing into either the enterprise, or into an ISP with which the enterprise has a contract.

The IETF calls the next level of mobility *roaming*. Roaming deals with the movement of users, not hosts or subnets, among cooperating ISPs. The user may not have an account on a specific ISP, but, if that ISP has a cooperative relationship with the user's home ISP, the access ISP can act as an authentication proxy for the home ISP. Once the user is authenticated, his or her traffic is usually routed to the home ISP.

There is less a special protocol for roaming than there are a set of usage conventions for existing authentication protocols such as RADIUS. The foreign ISP needs to act as a proxy for the home ISP's authentication service.

A roaming service includes a *phone book* that contains the administrative information for dial-up. The latest version of this document comes from a *phone book server*.

Clients dial into NAS for a cooperating provider, which communicates with the home ISP, using authentication proxies and accounting proxies as required. The role of accounting cannot be overemphasized; roaming IP access services are not commercially viable unless the services can be billed and all participating providers compensated.

Yet another level of mobility is the scope of the Mobile IP working group. The IETF's IP mobility working group does not deal with wireless layer 2 networks, which is more the province of IEEE 802.11 efforts.

IP mobility, as defined by the IETF, includes "routing support to permit IP nodes (hosts and routers) using either IPv4 or IPv6 to seamlessly 'roam' among *IP subnetworks* and *media types* (emphasis added). The Mobile IP method supports transparency above the IP layer, including the maintenance of active TCP connections and UDP port bindings. Where this level of transparency is not required, solutions such as DHCP and dynamic DNS updates may be adequate and techniques such as Mobile IP not needed."

Yet another dimension recognized by the IETF is mobile ad-hoc networks, the focus of the MANET working group. It defines "mobile ad hoc network" (MANET) as an autonomous system of mobile routers (and associated hosts) connected by wireless links—the union of which form an arbitrary graph. The routers are free to move randomly and organize themselves arbitrarily; thus, the network's wireless topology may change rapidly and unpredictably. Such a network may operate in a standalone fashion, or may be connected to the larger Internet."

Firewalls

Think of a firewall not as a single "box," but as a set of security components. Common components include routers and bastion hosts. The classical definition of a firewall comes from Cheswick & Bellovin: "a hard crunchy shell around a soft chewy center [i.e., the protected network]."

Current practice is not to rely on a single crusty shell. A firewall, and the protective mechanisms in the protected network, should form a multilayered defense. Multilayered defense is important because not every protective mechanism gives optimal protection against every threat. The implementation of a protective measure may be flawed, and a multilayered defense means that an attacker will still need to breach multiple walls before reaching the target.

I prefer to think of the firewall system as an onion, with its many layers. Onions also have the property that the more they are cut, the more the cutter weeps—a fine metaphor for security alarms. (Figure 8.6)

If the user operates firewalls, VPN tunnels typically will terminate at the firewall. If the firewall is operated by the service provider, or if the user has stringent security requirements requiring end-to-end encryption, there may be compatibility issues of authenticated firewall traversal.

What is the role of firewalls in intranets and extranets? Wherever a firewall is used, it provides security enforcement based on more protocol knowledge than a stateless router can provide. In a pure intranet, without Internet or extranet connectivity, there may be no need for a firewall.

When that intranet, however, adds Internet access for its users, a firewall becomes necessary. When that intranet adds connectivity to busi-

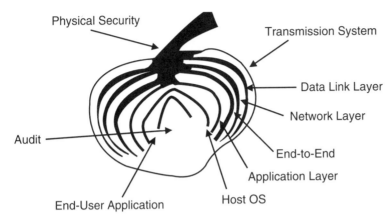

Figure 8.6 Security must be multilayered.

ness partners in an extranet, a firewall becomes necessary. These are basic "inside-and-outside" firewalls, as shown in Figure 8.7.

Firewall topologies, as shown in Figure 8.8, do not always require two physical routers.

When the enterprise adds public Internet servers, they can go onto the DMZ. Increasingly, however, the best practice is to add a third interface for public servers, as shown in Figure 8.9. It may even make sense to add an additional interface for extranet-only servers.

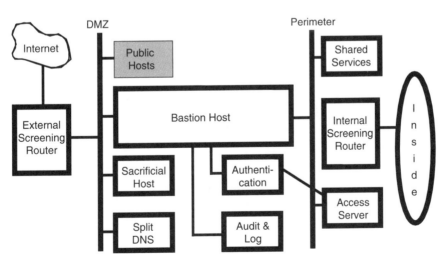

Figure 8.7 Two-interface firewall.

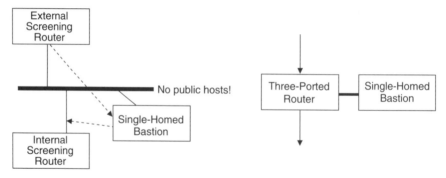

Figure 8.8 Alternative configurations.

Public servers are at the outer layers of the onion, but not on its skin. These servers need to be protected against alteration and denial of service, but should not contain the sensitive information that will be on servers deeper in the protected network.

Strenuously avoid any suggestions to save money by putting application server functions on firewalls. If there are no alternatives, only read-only applications should be on the firewall. If Web service must be supported, do not use forms, CGI, or Java.

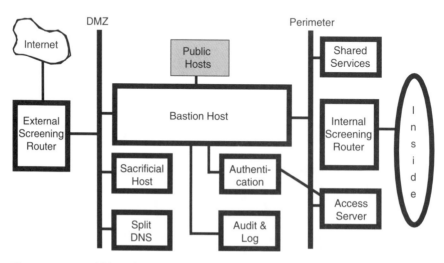

Figure 8.9 Multi-interface firewall.

Secure Data Transfer

Authenticated or encrypted transfer can be done with IPsec or TLS. The endpoints of these tunnels can be end hosts or *security gateways*. Security gateways serve multiple hosts, and may be implemented in LAN servers, in routers, or in firewalls.

IPsec

IPsec, introduced in Chapter 5, provides tunnels that provide authentication, confidentiality, or both. As a tunneling protocol, it allows the creation of VPNs over any IP transport.

IPsec security services are one-directional relationships called *security associations*. Think of a security association as a secure flow, which can be one to one or one to many. Each IPsec security association is explicitly identified by the combination of a destination address and a *security parameter index* (SPI). Destination addresses may be unicast or multicast IP addresses.

SPIs always contain the source of the secure information and the lifetime of both the SA and the key in use. They may contain additional information depending on whether IPsec is providing authentication, confidentiality, or both. Authentication services put an *authentication header* (AH) into each packet, while confidentiality services insert an *encapsulating security payload* (ESP) header and encrypted payload.

Layer 2 Tunneling

The layer 2 tunneling protocol (L2TP) is an IETF protocol that carries a virtual PPP connection over arbitrary IP networks. It is a fusion of the L2F proposal from Cisco and the PPTP proposal from Microsoft. L2TP is meant to run between access servers, while PPTP is oriented more to run between hosts.

Because the user payloads are carried in PPP, all PPP services are available, including dynamic address assignment with IPCP. Any protocol that can be carried in PPP can be carried in L2TP, allowing such non-IP services as AppleTalk Remote Access to run across the Internet.

To understand how L2TP works, think of a Presidential appearance. Before the VIPs enter, the Men in Black . . . er . . . Secret Service agents create a secure corridor. After the initial agents decide the area is secure, they notify the agents close to the President. The President then enters, greets the Duke of Grand Fenwick, and enters into a separate conversation, protected by the guards.

Before the Secret Service can inspect anything, they need to get physical access to the meeting place, which may have its own security guards, or be guarded by local police.

Think of an L2TP *network access server* (NAS) as the local police. Just as the Secret Service advance party needs to present its credentials, the *L2TP remote user* connects to an ISP and goes through whatever login identification is required by that ISP. L2TP users typically will reach the ISP through dial-up or ISDN, but they can use any medium that supports IP.

Just because you can get the White House switchboard to answer calls on its public number does not mean you can speak to the President. The remote ISP is in the role of the public switchboard; additional approvals are necessary before you can speak with a specific person.

Assuming the ISP NAS accepts the call, which will involve PPP-level user authentication with CHAP or PAP, and L2TP access is requested, the NAS will either create an L2TP tunnel to the *home gateway* (HG) at the enterprise, or add the user as a session to an existing L2TP tunnel to the HG. Depending on the manner in which the ISP and the enterprise contract, the user ID can automatically trigger an L2TP request, or the user may manually request it.

Manual requesting would allow a single user ID to be used either for enterprise or general Internet access. Allowing Internet access from the same ID as the privileged enterprise access is a potential security vulnerability. If the general users at the enterprise facility need to go through a firewall to reach the Internet, it probably makes sense that the dial-in user use the L2TP service provider only to reach the enterprise. That user would then use the enterprise firewall for external access.

At the enterprise, the HG accepts or rejects the connection. The HG may do a completely new CHAP exchange with the client, or it may make its decision based on CHAP information passed to it by the ISP.

When a connection is accepted, there now is a virtual PPP path between the client and the enterprise, over which any protocol can flow. Assuming the protocol is IP, the client then will do a new PPP

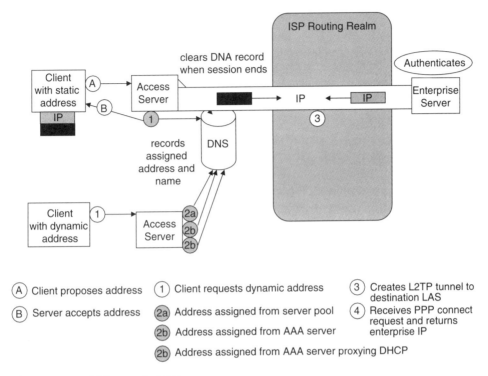

Figure 8.10 Addresses in L2TP.

IPCP negotiation, creating an IP address for the enterprise. Figure 8.10 shows that there are two pairs of IP addresses in an L2TP service, those from the client to the ISP and those from the client to the enterprise.

Remember that standard L2TP only provides access security, so one of the first steps may be to create IPsec connectivity between the client and enterprise (Figure 8.11).

ISPs, however, can extend their L2TP offerings and encapsulate their L2TP tunnels in IPsec, as shown in Figure 8.12.

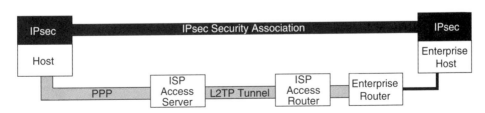

Figure 8.11 Host-centric IPsec with L2TP.

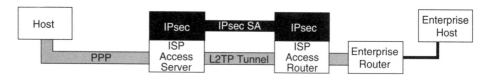

Figure 8.12 ISP-centric IPsec with L2TP.

Firewall Traversal

End-to-end, transport-mode IPsec cannot pass through firewalls. If the firewall is trusted, then it can act as a security gateway for IPsec, as shown in Figure 8.13. Alternatively, the security gateway can implement TLS, and use L2TP for connectivity.

Intrusion Detection and Response

Banks have vaults, but they also have alarms. While firewalls have always had mechanisms to detect violations, their major emphasis has been controlling traffic flow. As denial-of-service attacks become more commonplace, specialized monitors for detecting subtle attacks have evolved.

Basic intrusion detection devices are passive monitors placed on critical networks, such as a server farm LAN or Internet DMZ. They look for statistical patterns, such as the high rate of TCP SYN packets in a SYN flooding attack.

More advanced passive intrusion detectors recognize that attacks can be distributed, and may be detectable only by correlating information from multiple detection points. The IETF Intrusion Detection

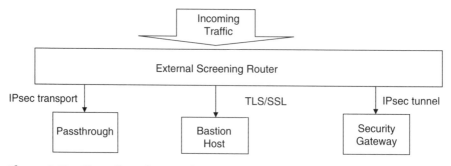

Figure 8.13 Firewalls and encryption.

Exchange Format working group is developing a vendor-independent means of communications among detectors.

Once an intrusion is detected, what should be done about it? In particular, what should be done, if anything, in real time? I've always been amused by customers who demand instantaneous notification of security events, yet are staffed only during normal business hours.

Generally, events should be logged and evaluated by a security specialist. If the event is interrupting service, or has corrupted data, more aggressive action is warranted.

A controversial area is that of active response, in which the intrusion detector independently takes action to mediate the threat. Fairly benign responses include generating packet filters against the apparent source of the attack, and automatically installing them in routers. This approach does require a secure channel between the intrusion monitor and the router(s) affected.

More aggressive measures could include interrupting suspected TCP connections. Launching automated counterattacks against the presumed source, however, is legally, technically, and ethically questionable in the civilian environment. Military information warfare may be necessary, but, like any military action, may not be "surgical."

Even in the military, a distinction is made between "soft" and "hard" countermeasures. Soft countermeasures for radar, for example, include jamming and spoofing methods that confuse the receiver.

I attended an Armed Forces Communications-Electronics Association (AFCEA) meeting not long after the Gulf War. There was a discussion of various Soviet-developed radars used by Iraq, and a senior officer was asked about the best countermeasures to them. He responded that a 500-pound laser-guided bomb down the antenna worked every time. Hard countermeasures are *not* appropriate for civilian use!

Appropriate to civilian use, however, may be the military's use of separate security and intelligence networks. A VPN service provider may need several internal networks in its infrastructure. One provides management of the routers and switches internal to the carrier. Another monitors for security problems. Yet another may be appropriate for managing customer equipment.

Technical Requirements for VPN Infrastructure

A VPN may be always on, or connectivity may be established on demand. Enterprise-managed VPNs tend to be initiated by end hosts or on per-site routers, while pure carrier VPNs tend to have permanent tunnels or circuits among points of presence.

Yet another model is traffic driven. Routers at customer sites sense when end user devices wish to send across the VPN, and either route them to predefined tunnels over dedicated infrastructure, or create appropriate dial calls to carry the traffic, encrypting if necessary.

Management is always a challenge. Some providers may simply manage their own access devices at customer sites or POPs. Other providers offer outsourced management for enterprise customers, sometimes including the enterprise LANs.

A carrier-managed router, for example, needs to have addresses in the customer address space if it is to be able to route. Carriers are hesitant to take responsibility when they do not have control of the network devices they manage. While a device may be in the customer address space, it may have management passwords or other access controls that, routinely, are known only by the service provider. It is wise for top management of the enterprise, when this is done, to have escrowed access to the controls.

It may also be useful for the carrier to establish a management network, which might, in the enterprise, be on VLANs to which user devices do not have access. Packet filters on the enterprise side of VPN access devices might prevent enterprise-initiated packets from reaching the management interface of the border router.

Mapping to Transport

Most, but not all, VPNs are tunnel-based. VPNs based on dial-up facilities are the significant exception. Virtual circuit based services such as ATM also may provide the transport. The major forms of tunneling in VPNs are listed in Table 8.6.

The specific means by which end-user views of the VPN are mapped onto the shared infrastructure generally involves tunneling, virtual circuit setup, or the establishment of a set of labels.

Table 8.6 VPN Tunneling

	ENDPOINTS	TRANSPORT	SECURITY	MAY BE COMBINED WITH
L2TP	1. Host 2. Access server	PPP to access server UDP/IP between access servers	Access proxy	IPSec
IPSec transport	Host	IP	Authentication and/or content encryption	
IPsec tunnel	Router	IP	Authentication and/or content encryption	
MPLS	Router	Any L2	No	
GRE	Router	IP	No	

When tunnels are used, they may provide no security (GRE), authentication (L2TP, L2F, and PPTP), or a wide range of security services (IPsec). Security services may also be provided by hosts, and a less secure tunnel mechanism used to carry host-encrypted data.

Alternatively, the mapping of IP connectivity may be to virtual circuits using frame relay or ATM, or to real circuits with ISDN or analog dial.

When the VPN seen by the user appears to be multicast-capable, but the infrastructure is connection-oriented, provisions need to be made for supporting multicast. Techniques here might involve point-to-multipoint circuits, or the use of multicast replication servers.

Tunnel technologies need to be coordinated between the enterprise(s) and the provider(s). There may be single tunnels between sites, or possibly multiple tunnels for load sharing and increased availability (e.g., with multilink PPP over IP).

Interprovider Connectivity

It may be necessary to provision the VPN infrastructure through multiple service providers. In such cases, the providers will need interprovider provisioning and VPN identification following conventions described in RFC 2547.

Much as a BGP confederation presents a single AS number to the outside but contains multiple internal ASNs, a multiprovider VPN identifier may map to a set of publicly visible ASNs. While BGP may be used to convey VPN reachability information among providers, the actual destinations may be prefixed with VPN IDs, and carried using the BGP-4 Multiprotocol Extensions. When VPN IDs are used in this manner, the routes carried need not be visible on the global Internet, but simply used to exchange information between ISPs with bilateral agreements.

Interactions with Customer Routing

Part of the confusion comes from glib statements of "we (or our customer) need/want to 'support' RIP, OSPF, etc." But what does such support mean?

It is a reasonable constraint, very consistent with current Internet address allocation policy, that most enterprises running intranets, even with Internet access through single provider, are expected to use private address space. RFC 2050 certainly is one starting justification for this assumption, as well as discussions at the ARIN meeting and with ARIN staff. Exceptions may be granted for multihoming, where specific protocols (especially IPsec) are incompatible with NAT, and other special cases.

Appropriate routing information about site reachability, should arrive in the appropriate VRFs. Many discussions seem to suggest far more intimate interaction between provider and customer routing than really is needed. Too much intimacy consumes resources, jeopardizes security, and may decrease availability.

Given that one of the major motivations to use VPNs, in the perceptions of many enterprises, is to outsource as much management as possible, it should not be a major constraint for the provider to assign CIDR blocks of private space on a site-by-site basis. There is no question that CIDR needs to be used if registered space is involved.

So, the provider knows the range of addresses at each site. Even if there were a huge routed enterprise network behind the customer router, there is only one intranet subnet for each VPN leaving the site. There may be an additional subnet for Internet access.

The larger routing system gains absolutely no useful information from knowing about details of routes behind the customer router. Let us focus on the real requirement:

- The provider routing system needs to know how to reach the CIDR blocks inside the VPN. When address space is reused, the duplicate addresses need to be disambiguated. RFC 2547 shows a way to do so by prefixing addresses with Routing Distinguishers.

- Each site with Internet access needs to know how to default to the ISP. That does not preclude having pure customer routes that do not go outside the provider, only that either the ISP is the default or explicitly is not the default. In general, it will be preferable to default to the ISP, and let any special cases be handled by more-specific routes inside the site.

- For management purposes, we should be aware when connectivity is lost to a site. If the layer 2 connectivity provides a keepalive, loss of reachability to the static route to the site may be sufficient. With Ethernet or other layer 2 mechanisms with no fault notification, we need at least a lightweight layer 3 hello protocol to keep the PE informed of reachability.

The most general solution to these problems is the use of lightweight routing between customer and provider routers. Lightweight routing really needs to advertise only one route in each direction.

- 0.0.0.0/0 from provider router to customer router
- The assigned CIDR block from customer router to provider router

What protocols support this requirement? RIPv1 does not support CIDR and is immediately excluded. RIPv2, if the specific implementation allows only a supernet to be advertised (i.e., suppressing more-specifics) will work. Since the amount of routing information exchanged is so small, the traffic load of RIP is trivial.

One consideration in dealing with RIP, however, is the relatively long failure detection times. RIP's update interval defaults to 30 seconds. A route is declared potentially unreachable after three updates are missed, meaning failure detection will take at least 90 seconds. Decreasing the time between updates could help. For failure detection, this timer should be in the range of 1 to 5 seconds.

OSPF is a definite alternative, given that it does have a hello subprotocol. OSPF's default hello interval is 10 seconds, which detects loss of layer 3 connectivity in approximately 30 seconds if there is no faster lower-layer failure detection.

BGP is a possibility, but its convergence behavior is not as fast as that of the IGPs. If BGP is used at the CE, there arise complexities of iBGP and eBGP relationships, and the possible limitation of assigning private AS numbers to sites or VPNs.

There are several ways in which errors in the configuration or implementation of customer routes might jeopardize the integrity of the transport routing system. These include an excessive number of routes being advertised, route flapping, or attacks in the customer routing system.

The first condition could be caused by improper deaggregation, or failure of a summarization mechanism. Limits of the number of prefixes accepted on a customer interface will help the provider integrity.

Route flap dampening is a specific BGP protection against flapping. If only one interface on a PE accepts traffic from a given VPN site, then standard eBGP route dampening should suffice for this service. MD5 authentication can help protect against attacks on the customer routing system.

Of course, when redistributed static routes describing CIDR blocks to customers are used, there is no dynamic routing to attack.

VPN Mappings to Specific Transmission Systems

When different kinds of infrastructure are proposed, the main requirement is for the infrastructure provider to take responsibility that all relevant user capabilities have matching capabilities in the infrastructure. The actual mappings are technology-specific and outside the scope of this document.

Specific VPNs may well be provisioned over one or more infrastructure types. In such cases, the designer needs to ensure that the user capabilities map into each of the infrastructures.

When the user or the enterprise can request explicit QoS, either the infrastructure must be able to understand the explicit requests, or it must consistently supply a QoS that meets the most stringent user requirement.

Providers can use registered or RFC1918 addresses internally in their networks. These may or may not be visible to the enterprise. When they are not, there should be a well-defined operational procedure that allows the user to request traceroutes through IP infrastructures.

When the provider uses VPN identifiers to distinguish between routing tables for different VPNs, the same addresses, especially from the private address space, may be reused. Provider engineers should take care to maintain appropriate separation. "Coloring" of duplicate address spaces may need multiple routing tables and/or MPLS [RFC 2547].

Dial

Until telephones disappear and there is a data access everywhere, modem access via the PSTN will remain a critical technology for low-speed, on-demand access to VPNs. Since the disappearance of telephones probably would cause a worldwide revolt of teenagers, this is unlikely to happen.

While V.90 modems probably have reached the limits of transmission speed over analog lines, there are an increasing number of products that provide greater speed by inverse multiplexing several modem links.

Frame Relay and ATM

Do not neglect layer 2 solutions. Frame relay is a perfectly reasonable means of connectivity for fixed sites.

ATM can be a relevant means of communication to fixed sites with high bandwidth requirements. On a worldwide basis, ATM is more available than some of the emerging last-mile technologies.

When there is existing ATM connectivity, it may be cheaper to add to it than to replace it. Applications that may already use ATM include voice switches, video production, and medical imaging.

New Local Transports

Several evolving services offer higher bandwidth than do modems on the PSTN, either with an on-demand or dedicated model. When used in a dedicated mode, these services are lower cost than traditional dedicated services such as frame relay, and offer high bandwidth to small and home offices.

Outside North America, parts of Western Europe, and Japan however, these emerging services may not readily be available. Americans often are surprised to learn that even dedicated access to frame relay, in much of the world, is prohibitively expensive. FR services worldwide often are accessed through ISDN.

"Dedicated" services of this sort may or may not be associated with a permanent IP address. Many providers of such services have different pricing structures based on the traffic expected to be associated with a user, and use dynamically assigned addresses, in part, to discourage using residential rates to provide public server access.

When enterprises connect telecommuters using such services, the enterprise cannot always assume a stable IP address.

ISDN

ISDN is "new" only with respect to the PSTN. It is more widely available worldwide than the newer last-mile services.

In areas where xDSL, CATV, or high-speed wireless services are available, ISDN will be hard to justify for pure data applications. Although not usually thought of as a VPN technology, ISDN may make good sense, however, when dealing with established integrated voice-data applications.

A good existing example of ISDN for a VPN is a travel reservation system where agents work from home. When an agent starts to work, one ISDN B-channel goes to the agency's voice automatic call distributor (ACD), and the other goes to the workstation.

ACDs are those automated devices I love to hate, which accept calls and connect them "to the next available agent." Many ACDs use interactive voice response (IVR), in which the user uses a telephone keypad to interact with the service:

"Welcome to 911. Press 1 if you are calling to report a murder . . . ."

"Press 1 if you are being murdered. Press 2 if you are murdering someone. Press 3 if you are watching a second party murdering a third party."

"If the murderer is using a handgun, press 1. Press 2 for a rifle. Press 3 for a shotgun. Press 4 for a machine gun. Press 5 for a pit bull. Press 6 for an elephant. Press 7 for a knife. Press 8 for a sword. Press 9 for other weapons . . . ."

In this example, the voice call first enters the ACD, and goes through the IVR interaction. Servers responding to the request are part of the static VPN. Only if a live agent is needed does the ACD transfer both the ISDN call and the associated terminal session to the agent.

CATV

Cable-based systems offer especially high bandwidth to the SOHO user. Cable is a shared medium, which raises concerns over security and congestion. Any serious business application running over shared cable should be encrypted.

Cable transmission can run over significant distances, and techniques to extend media distance are well known. Unfortunately, it is not a simple matter of adding data traffic to existing television broadcast systems, which are optimized, for one-way television broadcasting.

The electronic properties of existing coaxial cable are also not optimal for two-way data transmission. As discussed in Chapter 6, "Carrier Infrastructure and Optical Networking," CATV providers are migrating to optical fiber. One of the pressures to do so is the advent of high definition television, which, when in widespread use, will overwhelm the bandwidth of current residential coaxial cable systems.

Larger sites may justify dedicated cable channels. If the feeders to these all are encrypted, and the cable is physically protected from the cable POP to the site, it may not be necessary to encrypt this high-speed link since all communications on it are already encrypted.

xDSL

From the customer presences to the serving end office, xDSL services run, in principle, on dedicated media, as opposed to the shared media of CATV systems. You must verify that a particular xDSL service does or does not give guaranteed end-to-end bandwidth, because the link from the end office to the provider IP routers often are multiplexed. The carrier from which I obtain my SDSL service has two offerings, a consumer-oriented one that oversubscribes from the DSLAM to the ISP POP, and an enterprise-oriented one that provisions full bandwidth.

xDSL is approximately as secure as the PSTN. If wiretaps are a concern to the enterprise, then traffic over the xDSL facility should be encrypted.

First-generation ADSL can provide up to 6 Mbps of bandwidth, within a wire distance of 9000 feet from the central office. Longer-distance or higher-speed services need remote concentrating nodes to reduce the maximum wire distance. Depending on the market, the distance limitations of xDSL may make it less available than cable systems.

Wireless

Wireless data services are a new frontier in the local loop. These are not synonymous with cellular telephony, in that they are not intended for mobile operations.

Wireless LAN technologies are simpler and higher bandwidth than cellular services. Wireless systems, however, do face problems that wired or "fibered" systems do not. Commodore Ben Wyatt, an early naval aviator, explained that in the first days of flying, lost pilots often would drop to a few feet of altitude, find a railroad track, and follow it until they found civilization.

Unlucky lost pilots, however, found railroad tunnels before they found civilization. In like manner, wireless services can be far more limited by physical realities than are cabled systems. Many wireless technologies require unobstructed line-of-sight between transmitters and receivers. Their signals may be degraded by rain or snow.

From the security standpoint, the bad news is that free-space communications have no physical barriers to encryption; the good news is that the higher-bandwidth wireless services are not trivial to intercept.

Wireless services are especially attractive means to diversify local loops. They also offer advantages for point-to-multipoint distribution, as for financial information in a stock exchange.

MPLS/BGP Virtual Transport Service

L2TP is less attractive as a basic mechanism for interconnecting enterprise sites. It supports only a point-to-point topology. Another approach was first described in RFC 2547. From the IETF standpoint, this is an informational, not a standards-track RFC. It may evolve into a new standards-track document. Services based on RFC 2547 can support any topology. Because its bulk transfer mechanism inside the carrier network is MPLS, it has much less tunneling overhead than does L2TP.

Multiprovider VPNs are in their infancy. Nevertheless, the RFC 2547 approach seems the consensus solution. In non-MPLS networks, connectivity might be provisioned with virtual circuits.

MPLS/BGP VTN reduces the provisioning burden on carriers deploying VPN transport services. It offers the potential of multivendor interoperability.

VTN can be useful in an assortment of ISP business models, ranging from turnkey remotely managed enterprise networks, to VTN service with the demarcation point at the CE, to wholesale VTN service offerings to other ISPs.

Internet access is part of what the enterprise customer can see from a centrally managed service, although Internet access is not a function of the service core, but an alternate path taken at the edge. For Internet access, some globally routable addresses need to be associated with the customer sites, although NAT, address-translating firewalls, application layer gateways, etc., can help the enterprises minimize their public address space and maximize their use of private address space [RFC1918]. When connecting customers to the ISP, ISPs are strongly advised to implement RFC 2267 ingress filtering, which, when applied as routine in the global Internet, will help protect both enterprises and ISPs from denial-of-service attacks.

Extranet applications managed by the ISP are certainly possible and practical, with the major caveat being that the different enterprises that compose the extranet must have nonoverlapping address space. If any of the enterprises comprising the VPN have Internet connectivity, the security implications of such connectivity need to be evaluated on a case-by-case basis.

Enterprise customers access VPNs through customer edge (CE) devices at customer sites. The definition of "site" is flexible. From the 2547 standpoint, multiple physical sites linked by customer-operated facilities appear as one 2547 site. CE connect to one or more provider edge (PE) routers operated by the service provider (Figure 8.14).

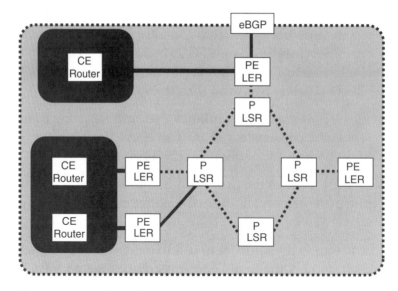

Figure 8.14 Major RFC 2547 components.

If the customer operates multiple VPNs at a physical site these appear to be multiple virtual sites.

CE may be managed by the enterprise or by the service provider. Most commonly, the CE is a non-BGP-speaking router that points the default route at one or more PE. According to RFC 2547, CEs do not have awareness of all routes in their VPN; that knowledge is on the set of PE that supports their VPM.

PE routers are aware of VPNs and map them to LSPs. A given PE has knowledge of only those VPNs that are connected to it. Cisco has a feature called "outbound filtering," which is rather like multi-cast join/leave: It allows a given PE to indicate it has no interest in a particular VPN.

On each PE is a virtual routing/forwarding instance (VRF), which is an expanded routing table consisting of an IP RIB, a set of interfaces, a set of import and export policies, and possibly an associated FIB. The VRF is conceptual and may be part of the main RIB of the physical PE router.

Why have a VRF? Its purpose is to have the necessary and sufficient number of routes to provide mutual reachability of sites in the same

VPN. These routes can belong to an intranet, an extranet, or in the general Internet.

Remember that a site or VPN having Internet access does not mean that it has to reach the Internet gateway via the VTS service. A vastly simplifying assumption is that CE will have multiple logical uplinks, one to the Internet and one to each VPN. The uplink to the Internet MUST use registered address space (Figure 8.15).

Each site needs to know how to default to the ISP. That does not preclude having pure customer routes that do not go outside the provider, only that either the ISP is the default or explicitly is not the default. In general, it will be preferable to default to the ISP, and let any special cases be handled by more-specific routes inside the site.

The relationship between sites and VRF is complex. A site can connect to only one VRF, even though a site may belong to more than one VPN. A VRF can contain information on multiple VPNs. More specifically, the VRF contains the information on all sites that are "owned" by the VRF. Membership in a VPN does not mean that members of a VPN can reach all of its other members; there may be closed user groups and partial mesh topologies.

PE connect to provider (P) backbone routers, which are interconnected with MPLS LSPs. P routers are unaware of the VPNs.

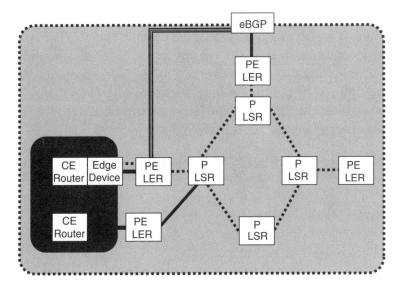

Figure 8.15 Simplifying Internet access in VTS.

The VTS allows there to be multiple VPNs that may reuse the same IPv4 address space. To avoid ambiguity, a VTS router sees IPv4 addresses as prefixed with a 12-byte route distinguisher (RD). Each RD is associated with a VPN.

The most common usage will assign an RD to each customer. Customers certainly can have multiple VPNs, and thus multiple RDs, if multiple VPN are a better fit to their administrative policies. With extranet VPNs, a given VPN may include several customers, but there must be clear "ownership" of a specific RD for the extranet.

RFC 2547 proposes a significant number of enhancements to basic BGP routing, such as closed user groups and VPN-specific routes (i.e., from one site) to the same destination. The key assumption that simplifies implementation is that the PEs are fully meshed with MPLS tunnels, and the VPN-specific information is needed only at the ingress PE.

Layer 2 Access

Layer 2 access connects the customer site to the POP. There are at least three refinements of layer 2 access: multiplexing/virtualizing, aggregation, and layer 2 multihoming.

The connection from the customer may or may not have multiple virtual layer 2 functions virtualized onto it, such as multiple 802.1Q VLANs or ATM VCs. Alternatively, just as Freud once suggested, "a cigar may be just a cigar," the layer 2 medium may simply map to a single subnet. Our abstraction should be to have each VPN instance coming from the site to have at least one layer 2 identifier associated with it, so that N layer 2 identifiers map to N layer 3 prefixes. While there is no defined immediate requirement for inverse multiplexing, protocols such as multilink PPP and inverse multiplexed ATM do exist, and would have N layer 2 identifiers map to M layer 3 prefixes, N>M.

Aggregation optimizes the use of high-speed interfaces on high-performance carrier routers. If, for example, the customer connectivity uses Fast Ethernet, an aggregation device aggregates Fast Ethernets into a Gigabit Ethernet compatible with the router. ATM services might be aggregated, in like manner, by a small access shelf or edge switchEdge switches and routers are asymmetrical, as they have a relatively large number of lower-speed interfaces and a relatively smaller number of high-speed interfaces. In contrast, most interfaces on core switches and routers are of the same speed.

Fault-tolerance requirements can be met at layer 2 or layer 3. At layer 2, they will depend on the particular layer 2 technology.

Routing in the Transport

VTS requires routing between the set of PE, and routing information for MPLS path setup among P and PE routers. At the core of this service is the ability to create iBGP-interconnected PEs that have VRFs for each VPN to which they are connected, and to create MPLS LSPs among P routers that interconnect the PEs.

Creation of a VRF on a specific PE is a matter of configuration. Populating this VRF may be static or dynamic. Once the VRF is populated, the contents of this VRF need to be propagated to other PE that support the same VPN.

Target VPNs

The idea of the target VPN, conveyed as an extended community (see below), was conceived as a scalability mechanism. In RFC2547, Rosen & Rekhter observed that BGP scales better with a lesser number of routes, each with multiple attributes, than a larger number of routes without as many attributes. They propose the latter alternative could be met with more RDs, but that such an approach would be less scalable.

Note that a route can only have one RD, but it can have multiple Target VPNs. In BGP, scalability is improved if one has a single route with multiple attributes, as opposed to multiple routes. One could eliminate the Target VPN attribute by creating more routes (i.e., using more RDs), but the scaling properties would be less favorable.

How does a PE determine which Target VPN attributes to associate with a given route? There are a number of different possible ways:

- Configure the PE to associate all routes that lead to a particular site with a particular Target VPN.

- The PE might be configured to associate certain routes leading to a particular site with one Target VPN, and certain with another.
- Have the CE router, when it distributes these routes to the PE, specify one or more Target VPNs for each route. The latter method shifts the control of the mechanisms used to implement the VPN policies from the SP to the customer. If this method is used, it may still be desirable to have the PE eliminate any Target VPNs that, according to its own configuration, are not allowed, and/or to add in some Target VPNs that according to its own configuration are mandatory.

Two kinds of extended community are defined, *route target community* and *route origin community*. The Route Target Community identifies one or more routers that may *receive* a set of routes (that carry this Community) carried by BGP. The Route Origin Community identifies one or more routers that *inject* a set of routes (that carry this Community) into BGP. The intersection of a Route Target Community and a Route Origin Community defines Target VPNs.

RFC2547 suggests the use of *extended communities*, which are longer than conventional 32-bit BGP communities. Longer length allows the communities to be structured, and effectively aggregated.

RFC 2547 and BGP

PE routers communicate routing information via iBGP. To support RFC 2547 requirements, BGP needs to be extended in several ways. Several BGP extensions, as well as extensions to the basic routing table structure, are needed to implement this product. Some of these extensions form the base product, while others are intended to improve scalability or to signal QoS.

RFC 2547 states that BGP scales better with a lesser number of routes, each with multiple attributes, than a larger number of routes without as many attributes. They propose the latter alternative could be met with more RDs, but that such an approach would be less scalable. The idea of the target VPN, conveyed as an extended community), was conceived as a scalability mechanism.

Connection establishment needs to use Capability Advertisement to agree with the potential peer that both support Multiprotocol Extensions to BGP. The basic extension mechanism is defined by Multiprotocol Extensions to BGP, which allows the extended addresses of this service to be treated as an address family separate from IPv4.

A potential scalability requirement for QoS comes from the limited number (1K) of private AS numbers.

VPN Examples

These examples explore alternative designs for VPNs, within the broad context of host-centric, site-centric, and carrier-centric solutions.

Host-Centric

In a basic example, assume you have a server site that is accessed by 100 telecommuters and mobile users. Users now communicate using dial-up to a remote access server connected to the LAN containing the application server. Many of these calls are long-distance (Figure 8.16).

This enterprise wants to keep security under its control. Since the enterprise will control only the endpoints, then authentication and confidentiality need to run between clients and either a trusted server or a trusted security gateway.

A basic cost analysis will trade off long-distance services versus a permanent connection from an ISP to the server site and a set of per-user logins. If there is any appreciable use of traffic-sensitive long-distance service, the VPN usually becomes attractive.

The internal networks of most carriers are physically hard to wiretap. It is also harder to wiretap dial and ISDN services than LANs. Dial services probably are most vulnerable in the office and wiring closet.

Enterprise-Operated Solution

At the very simplest, if the data are not sensitive and host passwords are acceptable protection, there are several options. Low technology may work: Sometimes a toll-free (i.e., 800) service can be inexpensive in an enterprise with a highly discounted telephone service contract. In such cases, you would install a NAS at the enterprise data center.

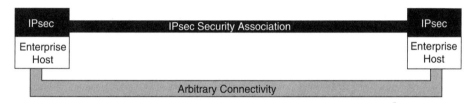

Figure 8.16   Host-oriented requirements.

The major alternative to toll-free service is to establish Internet access with dial-up accounts for the clients and a higher-speed connection for the server(s).

If toll-free dial is cost-effective for the particular traffic pattern, but security is a concern, host-to-host or host-to-RAS encryption can be used.

Your alternatives for security are IPsec and TLS. IPsec clients on personal computers are the standard approach, but have had limitations due to administrative complexity, overhead, and difficulty of installation.

Carrier-Oriented Solution

If the assumption is made that the carrier's network is adequately secure for normal communications, then specific access validation can come from a double-password scheme in which the user accesses the ISP with one authentication system run by the carrier, and another one run by the home enterprise. L2TP is used to carry the challenges and responses. After L2TP setup, there appears to be a PPP connection from the end user to the home site.

L2TP also can be carried inside IPsec, or IPsec can carry L2TP.

L2TP and MPLS VPNs solve different problems. L2TP is a method for providing carrier access to an enterprise network, where MPLS is more appropriate to virtualize the enterprise network.

Things become more complex, however, when you consider security. In principle, reusable passwords can be sniffed on the Internet, although there have not been a huge number of such events documented outside universities and other potentially insecure sites.

How are these passwords to be validated? In a pure customer-driven application, they will be validated at the server site. If you want this validation completely under enterprise control, PPTP and TLS become viable options. If it is acceptable for a carrier to convey authentication requests to the enterprise, L2TP becomes a viable alternative.

Yet another approach is to use IPsec clients, and a security service on a router or coprocessor at the main site. The cost of digital certificates will add to the total system cost.

Site-Oriented VPN

As opposed to the previous example, what if your goal is reducing the costs of the existing dedicated lines or frame relay virtual circuits that connect a set of fixed sites? One approach may be to tunnel securely across the Internet. You will still have the cost of access lines to an ISP, but your Internet access charges, combined with the costs of added security, may be less than the cost of end-to-end lines.

Each site has a router that can connect to all other sites. If Internet access is needed, you can consider that a virtual site. Mobile users can come from a trusted access point that also is considered a virtual site.

There will be obvious resource costs such as new equipment, training, and digital certificates. Less obvious costs include performance impact on routers and additional latency in the transmission path.

The VPN may not need to be responsible for security, because security is handled on an application level, or the transport is trusted. When security is needed in the VPN, each enterprise will have different tradeoffs in where to locate the security functions.

Site VPN with Security Requirement

Moving security features from hosts to common equipment certainly will reduce the administrative effort to update keys, and will expose keys in a smaller number of places. It will also reduce the number of software client licenses and digital certificates you will need.

What sort of common equipment should do the encryption? As always, it depends. Small sites often have small routers that do not have a great deal of extra processing capability, and encryption requires a great deal of processing. Low-volume encryption can work on a small router, but you soon will need a router either with a security coprocessor or a high-performance main processor.

An alternative to encrypting on the router is to encrypt on some type of server. When multiple secure sessions terminate at a server site, the processing load on a conventional server might be overwhelming. Server processor upgrades may be needed.

In general, CPU cycles are cheaper on general-purpose machines than in router main processors, although security coprocessors can be very cost-effective. Encryption coprocessors also are available for servers. Disadvantages of server-based security may include a lack of detailed networking knowledge on the part of the server administrator.

Yet another practical approach is to use a firewall product that supports secure VPNs. Many such products do, and even if you are not connecting externally, such products tend to have well-developed system administration tools.

If your sites do have Internet connectivity through the same provider that runs the VPN transport, combined firewalls and secure tunneling machines may make even more sense.

Site-Oriented VPN Not Required to Provide Security

The security requirement for some VPNs is that the VPN does not need to provide security, when host-based security is already in effect. GRE can be appropriate when the end systems (or enterprise gateways) provide all necessary security, and an existing provider IP network or the general Internet is adequate for connectivity.

Our example deals with a financial network that uses DES encryption and ANSI X9.17 key data distribution. Networks using this key distribution method have a trusted *key distribution center* (KDC). As shown in Figure 8.17, the sites in the network communicate with dedicated lines. Links between sites and from sites to the KDC are bulk encrypted. Some routers internally support DES, while others use inline encryption devices.

The financial organization is interested in reducing its communications costs by running a VPN over the Internet. Assume its security analysts agree that the DES encryption provides adequate security for the particular application.

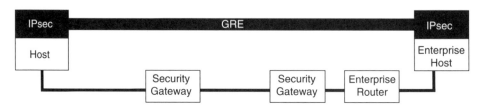

Figure 8.17 GRE with edge encryptors.

As the financial institution's requirements for availability and QoS grow, it realizes that it can still use a VPN, but it cannot accept the variability of the general Internet. It asks service providers for a potential solution, and the responding vendors offer an RFC 2547 BGP/MPLS solution.

Provider Core with MPLS

MPLS-based VPNs are new. One service provider. in the early deployment phase, provides data and voice services to its SOHO and enterprise customers, with the basic user interface being Ethernet or Fast Ethernet. 802.1Q VLANs are used to separate the different traffic classes from the customer site to the POP.

Figure 8.18 shows a representative customer site, which has a router that handles the data VPN, and acts as a firewall for Internet access. Also at the customer site is an intelligent edge device that accepts the individual Ethernets and concentrates them onto VLAN trunking to the POP. The edge device is does not participate in dynamic routing, but has sufficient awareness of layers 3 and 4 to do traffic policing and shaping. Typically, three Ethernets go into the switch, one for VPN data, one for Internet data, and one for voice over IP.

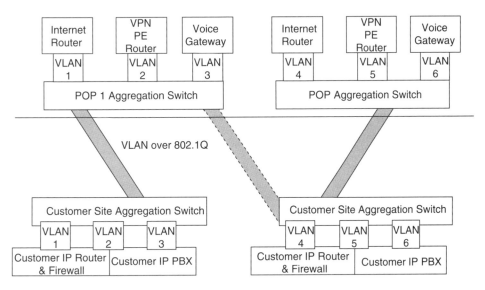

Figure 8.18 BGP/MPLS customer site.

There is no pure CE router in this application. Rather, the *edge device* at a user site has two hardware components: the router, which may be managed by the customer or the provider, and the switch, which is managed by the provider. This division of functions appears to be a common practical requirement. The CE routing function may be more maintainable and scalable if it is physically at the POP.

The edge device does not use MPLS for connecting to the POP, because there is only one path from the customer site to the POP. There would be no alternate paths that MPLS could set up. When there is a high availability requirement at a customer site, two edge devices are installed.

Fast Ethernet over fiber links are concentrated at the POP by an 10/100 to Gigabit Ethernet aggregation switch, which provides Gigabit Ethernet connectivity to the PE router at the POP.

From a POP, VPN traffic goes over MPLS to P routers, Internet traffic goes to the external BGP gateway routers, and voice traffic goes to the voice gateway. These devices interface with Gigabit Ethernet, but the GE runs over DWDM. In-place upgrades to 10-Gigabit Ethernet are planned as an upgrade.

Table 8.7 reviews the information you will need to build such a system.

Hybrid VPN

You may very well have a need for multiple VPN technologies for a specific enterprise. In Chapter 7, I introduced the fault tolerance requirements of one of my clients, which supplied a specialized application to enterprise customers. Certain portions of the work on this application were outsourced to independent contractors who accessed through an Internet-based VPN. The firm is in the healthcare industry, so all of its data was sensitive medical information.

From the enterprise-side perspective, the firm could be considered either an extranet or a specialized Internet service provider. An extranet model did not fit as well as a service provider model, because the customers never shared data.

The customers ranged from small professional offices to large institutions with extensive networks of their own. Some customers used private address space, while others had registered addresses. At the customer sites, we placed a router and specialized servers. Normally,

Table 8.7 Configuration Checklist for BGP/MPLS VPN

ELEMENT	INFORMATION NEEDED	SOURCE(S)
Customer router	1. Its IP address in the VPN 2. Default gateway address in the VPN 3. IP address for Internet access 4. Default gateway address for Internet access 5. Separate management address (when used)	Manual configuration Autoconfiguration from server
Edge device	1. Separate management address (when used) 2. Layer 2 identifier for each VLAN on an interface	
POP aggregation device	Separate management address (when used) Layer 2 identifier Mapping to PE router interface	
POP PE	VRF RD associated with VRF Route targets and import/export policy Route filtering CE interface feeding VRF	
POP P	MPLS connectivity to other P routers	

the router connected to our data center with frame relay, but ISDN and Internet backup were being introduced.

We needed to virtualize a consistent address space for our network. At each customer site, we configured NAT to translate the customer space into our registered provider space. While this worked for many applications, we did have problems with WINS and DNS, and had to obtain application-level gateway functions.

Under current U.S. healthcare regulations, defined by the Health Insurance Portability and Accountability Act (HIPAA), medical data must be encrypted when traveling over the Internet or dial facilities. While the frame relay circuits technically did not need to be encrypted, the customer backup links did. Since we would rather err in encrypting than not encrypting, we chose to use IPsec, with preshared keys, both for the dedicated and backup links (Figure 8.19).

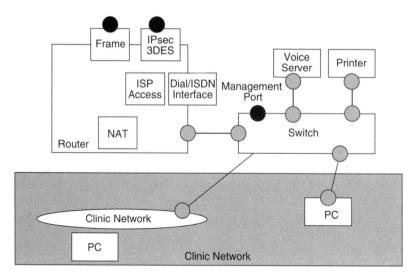

Figure 8.19 Access in a healthcare application.

Contractor access was a different problem. At the time of implementation, we did not have an affordable and reliable IPsec client for PCs, and the cost of digital certificates and the certificate authority was prohibitive. A realistic compromise was to use SSL for the contractors, terminating on a security gateway in the data center.

The operational network, therefore, used both IPsec and transport layer security.

References

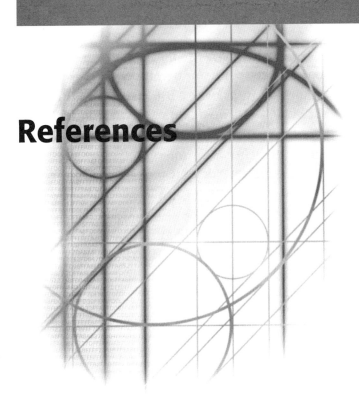

Ash, J., et al. 2000. "Applicability Statement for CR-LDP." Work in Progress, IETF MPLS Working Group.

Ashwood-Smith 1999a. "Introduction to MPLS." NANOG Montreal meeting. www.nanog.org/mtg-9910/ppt/peter.ppt

Awduche, D., et al. 2000. "RSVP-TE: Extensions to RSVP for LSP Tunnels." Work in Progress, IETF.

Awduche, D. 1999a. "Applicability Statement for Extensions to RSVPfor LSP-Tunnels." Work in Progress, IETF.

Berkowitz, H. 1998. *Designing Addressing Architectures for Routing and Switching*. Indianapolis: Macmillan.

Berkowitz, H. 1999. *Designing Routing and Switching Architectures for Enterprise Networks*. Indianapolis: Macmillan.

Berkowitz, H. October 1999. " Managing your Allocation." www.arin.net/minutes/tutorial/index.htm

Cisco. 2000. "QoS Features for Voice over IP." www.cisco.com/univercd/cc/td/doc/product/software/ios121/12 1cgcr/qos_c/qcprt7/qcdvoice.htm

Chapman, G., et al., ed. 1989. *The Complete Monty Python's Flying Circus: Just the Words*, vol. 1. New York: Pantheon Books.

Cottrell, L., W. Matthews, and C. Logg. 1999. "Tutorial on Internet Monitoring & PingER at SLAC." *Stanford Linear Accelerator Center* www.slac.stanford.edu/comp/net/wan-mon/tutorial.html

Durham, D., and R. Yavatkar. 1999. *Inside the Internet's Resource reServation Protocol*. New York: John Wiley & Sons, Inc.

Ferguson, P. 1998. "Re: Comments on 'What is a VPN?'" *Message to IETF VPN Mailing List* (March) 19:52:29

Ferguson, P., and G. Huston. 1998. *Quality of Service: Delivering QoS on the Internet and in Corporate Networks*. New York: John Wiley & Sons, Inc.

Friedman, A. 1999. "BGP 102: A Mid-Sized Network Configuration Case Study" Presentation at NANOG Denver meeting. www.nanog.org/mtg-9901/ppt/bgp102.ppt

ITU. 1999. "General Aspects of Quality of Service (QoS)." *No. DTR/TIPHON-05001 V1.2.5 (1998-99) Technical Report*. International Telecommunications Union.

Jamoussi, B., ed. 1999. "Constraint-Based LSP Setup using LDP." Work in Progress, IETF.

Jimmerson, R. October 1999. "How the Heck Do I Get Address Space from ARIN . . . and What's Up with Those Templates?" American Registry for Internet Numbers (ARIN) public policy meeting. www.arin.net/minutes/tutorial/index.htm.

Kaufman, E., and A. Newman. 1999. *Implementing IPsec: Making Security Work on VPNs, Intranets, and Extranets*. New York: John Wiley & Sons, Inc.

Kosiur, D. 1998. *Building and Managing Virtual Private Networks*. New York: John Wiley & Sons, Inc.

Marcus, E., and H. Stern. 2000. *Blueprints for High Availability: Designing Resilient Distributed Systems*. New York: John Wiley & Sons, Inc.

Maxwell, K. 1998. *Residential Broadband: The Battle for the Last Mile*. New York: John Wiley & Sons, Inc.

Packeteer. 1998. "Controlling TCP/IP Bandwidth." *TCP/IP Bandwidth Management Series No. White Paper 1*. Packeteer, Inc.

Peterson, A. 1997."Dynamic Selection of Geographically Distributed Servers." Presentation at NANOG (October). Meeting. notes at www.academ.com/nanog/october1997/dynamic-selection.html.

Shreedhar, M., G.Varghese 1995. "Efficient Fair Queueing Using Deficit Round Robin." *ACM SIGCOMM*. www.acm.org/sigcomm/sigcomm95/papers/shreedhar.html

Smith, R. 1997. *Internet Cryptography*. Reading, Mass.: Addison-Wesley.

Tiara. 2000a "Multimegabit Access: A White Paper." www.tiaranetworks.com/access.html.

US Air Force. 1999. Operational Requirements Document (ORD). AFSPC 005-95B-I/II for the ICBM Launch Control Centers.

Internet-Drafts

Internet-drafts are the working documents from which RFCs are finalized. The formal IETF internet-draft directory is at www.ietf.org/ID.html, but it is usually most convenient to go to the appropriate working group page at www.ietf.org/html.charters/wg-dir.html to determine the most recent version of the draft.

Ash, J., et al. 2000. "Applicability Statement for CR-LDP." Work in Progress, IETF MPLS Working Group.

Awduche, D., et al. 2000. "RSVP-TE: Extensions to RSVP for LSP Tunnels." Work in Progress, IETF.

Awduche, D. 1999a. "Applicability Statement for Extensions to RSVP for LSP-Tunnels." Work in Progress, IETF MPLS Working Group.

Duffield, P. et al. 1999. " A Performance Oriented Service Interface for Virtual Private Networks." Work in progress, Internet Engineering Task Force.

Hain, T. 2000. "Architectural Implications of NAT." Work in Progress, Internet Activities Board.

Handley, M., and S. Hanna. 1999. "Multicast Address Allocation Protocol (AAP)" Work in progress, IETF MALLOC Working Group.

Holdredge, M., and P. Srisuresh. 1999a. "Protocol Complications with the IP Network Address Translator (NAT)." Work in Progress, IETF NAT Working Group.

Lear, E. 2000. "NAT and Other Network 'Intelligence': Clearing Architectural Haze through the Use of Fog Lamps." Work in Progress, IETF.

Rosen, E., A.Viswanathan, and R. Callon. 1999. "Multiprotocol Label Switching Architecture." Work in Progress, IETF MPLS Working Group.

Senie, D. 1999a. "NAT Friendly Application Design Guidelines." Work in Progress, IETF NAT Working Group.

Srishuresh, P., and D. Gan. "Load Sharing Using IP Network Address Translation (LSNAT)." Work in Progress, IETF NAT Working Group.

Westerinen, A., et al. "Policy Terminology." Work in Progress, IETF Policy Framework Working Group.

Requests for Comments (RFCs)

RFC 1001. NetBIOS Working Group. 1987. "Protocol standard for a NetBIOS service on a TCP/UDP transport: Concepts and methods."

RFC 1002. NetBIOS Working Group. 1987. "Protocol standard for a NetBIOS service on a TCP/UDP transport: Detailed specifications."

RFC 1034. Mockapetris, P.V. 1987. "Domain Names—Concepts and Facilities."

RFC 1234. Provan, D. 1991. " Tunneling IPX traffic through IP networks."

RFC 1323. Jacobson, V., R. Braden, and D. Borman. 1992. "TCP Extensions for High Performance."

RFC 1631. Egevang, K., and P. Francis. 1994. "The IP Network Address Translator."

RFC 1702. Hanks, S., et al. 1994. "Generic Routing Encapsulation over IPv4 networks."

RFC 1775. Crocker, D. 1995. "To Be 'On' the Internet."

RFC 1812. Baker, F. 1995. "Requirements for IP Version 4 Routers."

RFC 1889 Schulzrinne, H., S. Casner, R. Frederick, and V. Jacobson. 1996. "RTP: A Transport Protocol for Real-Time Applications."

RFC 1900. Carpenter, B., and Y. Rekhter. 1996. "Renumbering Needs Work."

RFC 1918. Rekhter, Y., R. Moskowitz, D. Karrenberg, G-J. de Groot, and E. Lear. 1996. "Address Allocation for Private Internets."

RFC 1930. Hawkinson, J., and T. Bates. 1996. "Guidelines for Creation, Selection, and Registration of an Autonomous System (AS)."

RFC 1958. Carpenter, B. 1996. "Architectural Principles of the Internet."

RFC 1998. Chen, E, and T. Bates. 1996. "An Application of the BGP Community Attribute in Multi-Home Routing."

RFC 2022. Armitage, G. 1996. "Support for Multicast over UNI 3.0/3.1 based ATM Networks."

RFC 2050. Hubbard, K., M. Kosters, D. Conrad, D. Karrenberg, and J. Postel, 1996."INTERNET REGISTRY IP ALLOCATION GUIDELINES."

RFC 2071. Ferguson, P., and H. Berkowitz. 1997. "Network Renumbering Overview: Why Would I Want It and What Is It Anyway?"

RFC 2072. Berkowitz, H. 1997. "Router Renumbering Guide."

RFC 2208. Mankin, A. (ed.), F. Baker, B. Braden, S. Bradner, M. O'Dell, A. Romanow, A. Weinrib, L. Zhang. 1997. "Resource ReSerVation Protocol (RSVP)—Version 1 Applicability Statement: Some Guidelines on Deployment."

RFC 2211. Wroclawski, J. 1997. "Specification of the Controlled-Load Network Element Service."

RFC 2267. Ferguson, P., and D. Senie. "Network Ingress Filtering: Defeating Denial of Service Attacks which employ IP Source Address Spoofing." (Obsoleted by RFC2827.)

RFC 2280. Alaettinoglu, C., T. Bates, E. Gerich, D. Karrenberg, D. Meyer, M. Terpstra, and C. Villamizar. 1998. "Routing Policy Specification Language (RPSL)."

RFC 2390. T. Bradley, C. Brown, A. Malis. 1998. "Inverse Address Resolution Protocol."

RFC 2391. Srisuresh, P., and D. Gan. 1998. "Load Sharing Using IP Network Address Translation (LSNAT)."

RFC 2401. Kent, S., and R. Atkinson. 1998. "Security Architecture for the Internet Protocol."

RFC 2427. Brown, C. and A. Malis. 1998. "Multiprotocol Interconnect over Frame Relay."

RFC 2472. Haskin, D., and E. Allen. 1998. "IP Version 6 over PPP."

RFC 2516. Mamakos, L., et al. 1999. "Method for Transmitting PPP Over Ethernet (PPPoE)."

RFC 2547. Rosen, E., and, Y. Rekhter. 1999. "BGP/MPLS VPNs."

RFC 2581. Allman, M., V. Paxson, and W. Stevens. 1999. "TCP Congestion Control."

RFC 2663. Srisuresh, P., and M. Holdredge. 1999. "IP Network Address Translator (NAT) Terminology and Considerations."

RFC 2694. Srisuresh, P., et al. 1999."DNS extensions to Network Address Translators (DNS_ALG)"

RFC 2702. Awduche, D., et al. "Requirements for Traffic Engineering over MPLS."

Index